Catherine Madgwick.

3rd Edition

Introduction to
Psychological
Assessment

in the South African context

Cheryl Foxcroft • Gert Roodt

OXFORD
UNIVERSITY PRESS
SOUTHERN AFRICA

OXFORD
UNIVERSITY PRESS
SOUTHERN AFRICA

Oxford University Press Southern Africa (Pty) Ltd

Vasco Boulevard, Goodwood, Cape Town, Republic of South Africa
P O Box 12119, N1 City, 7463, Cape Town, Republic of South Africa

Oxford University Press Southern Africa (Pty) Ltd is a subsidiary of
Oxford University Press, Great Clarendon Street, Oxford OX2 6DP.

The Press, a department of the University of Oxford, furthers the University's objective of
excellence in research, scholarship, and education by publishing worldwide in

Oxford New York

Auckland Cape Town Dar es Salaam Hong Kong Karachi
Kuala Lumpur Madrid Melbourne Mexico City Nairobi
New Delhi Shanghai Taipei Toronto

With offices in

Argentina Austria Brazil Chile Czech Republic France Greece
Guatemala Hungary Italy Japan Poland Portugal Singapore South Korea
Switzerland Turkey Ukraine Vietnam

Oxford is a registered trade mark of Oxford University Press
in the UK and in certain other countries

Published in South Africa
by Oxford University Press Southern Africa (Pty) Ltd, Cape Town

Introduction to Psychological Assessment in the South African context 3rd Edition
ISBN 978 0 19 598836 9

© Oxford University Press Southern Africa (Pty) Ltd 2009

The moral rights of the author have been asserted
Database right Oxford University Press Southern Africa (Pty) Ltd (maker)

Third edition published 2009
Seventh impression 2012

Publishing manager: Alida Terblanche
Assistant commissioning editor: Marisa Montemarano
Managing editor: Lisa Andrews
Editor: Allison Lamb
Designer: Jade Minords
Cover design: Samantha Rowles
Indexer: Ethné Clarke
Cover image: The Bigger Picture

Printed and bound by ABC Press, Cape Town

118015

Acknowledgements
The authors and publisher gratefully acknowledge permission to reproduce copyright material
in this book. Every effort has been made to trace copyright holders, but if any copyright
infringements have been made, the publisher would be grateful for information that would
enable any omissions or errors to be corrected in subsequent impressions.

TABLE OF CONTENTS

LIST OF CONTRIBUTORS

- **Prof. Fatima Abrahams**, Department of Industrial Psychology, University of the Western Cape (UWC).
- **Dr Nicolene Barkhuizen**, Senior Lecturer in the Department of Human Resource Management, University of Pretoria (UP).
- **Caroline Davies**, Senior Manager: Access Assessment of the Centre for Access Assessment and Research, Nelson Mandela Metropolitan University (NMMU).
- **Prof. Marie de Beer**, Associate Professor in the Department of Industrial Psychology, University of South Africa (UNISA).
- **Prof. Gideon P de Bruin**, Professor in the Department of Industrial Psychology and People Management, University of Johannesburg (UJ).
- **Dr Karina de Bruin**, Senior Lecturer in the Department of Psychology, University of Johannesburg (UJ).
- **Dr Diane Elkonin**, Senior Lecturer in the Psychology Department, Nelson Mandela Metropolitan University (NMMU).
- **Prof. Cheryl Foxcroft**, Professor of Psychology and Senior Director of the Higher Education Access and Development Services (HEADS), Nelson Mandela Metropolitan University (NMMU).
- **Dr Carolina Henn**, Senior Lecturer in the Department of Industrial Psychology and People Management, University of Johannesburg (UJ).
- **Dr Loura Griessel**, Senior Lecturer in the Department of Industrial Psychology, University of the Free State (UFS).
- **Dr Kate Grieve**, Former Associate Professor in the Department of Psychology, University of South Africa (UNISA), and Clinical Psychologist (area of interest: Neuropsychology).
- **Dr Jenny Jansen**, Psychologist in the Education Department: Component Special Needs, Port Elizabeth.
- **Dr Anil Kanjee**, Executive Director, Research Programme: Assessment Technology and Education Evaluation (HSRC).
- **Prof. Gert Roodt**, Professor in the Department of Industrial Psychology and People Management, University of Johannesburg (UJ), and Head of the Centre for Work Performance.
- **Dr Louise Stroud**, Lecturer in the Psychology Department, Nelson Mandela Metropolitan University (NMMU).
- **Dr Nicola Taylor**, Consultant with Jopie van Rooyen and Partners, Randburg.
- **Nanette Tredoux**, CEO of Psytech South Africa, former Senior Research Specialist at the Human Sciences Research Council specializing in computerized assessments.
- **Dr Rene van Eeden**, Lecturer in the Department of Psychology, University of South Africa (UNISA).

INTRODUCTION

The start of an exciting journey

Hi there! You are about to embark on an interesting, challenging journey that will introduce you to the world of psychological assessment. Interesting? Challenging? 'That's not what I have heard about assessment,' you might say. Many people view courses and books on psychological assessment as dull, boring, and not relevant for students and professionals in people-oriented careers. Even if you have some doubts that you are going to enjoy learning about assessment, we beg you to give us a chance to share our enthusiasm about assessment with you and to show you why our enthusiasm is shared by countless others in South Africa and, indeed, all over the world. As you read this book, we hope that you will discover that assessment is an essential, integral part of psychology and other people-oriented professions. You will be exposed to the fact that assessment can be used in many different contexts, such as educational, counselling, clinical, psychodiagnostic, psycholegal/forensic, industrial (occupational), and research contexts. Furthermore, you will discover that assessment can be used for many different purposes (e.g. diagnosing learning problems, assessing whether a mass murderer is fit to stand trial, determining whether therapeutic intervention has been successful, and making job selection, placement, and training decisions). Does assessment still sound dull, boring, and irrelevant to you? No ways! Well then, let the journey begin.

Requirements for our journey

Whenever we set off on a journey, we need to make sure that we have a suitable mode of transport, a map, and other necessities such as fuel, refreshments, a first aid kit, a reliable spare tyre, and so on. For your journey into psychological assessment territory:

- your **vehicle** will be the contents of this book, which have been carefully put together by a number of prominent people in the assessment field in South Africa;
- you will be provided with a **map**, so that you have some idea of the places that we will visit and how those places can be grouped together;
- a set of **signposts** will be provided to help you to identify important landmarks along the way and to correlate the information that you obtain in the various chapters;
- you have to bring along an **enquiring, open mind** as you will find that we are going to challenge you to think about what you are reading and to develop personal insights;
- you will need to keep a **pen** and an examination pad or a **notebook** handy at all times so that you can record your responses to challenging questions, as well as document your growing understanding of psychological assessment.

The map for our journey

You will notice that the map has been divided into three zones which provide a logical grouping of the various stops (or chapters) that you will make along the way. This means that instead of thinking of this as a book (or journey) with eighteen chapters (or stops), you should rather visualize that there are three major focus points in your journey, as this makes it more manageable:

- In the **Foundation Zone**, which comprises Chapters 1 to 7, we will introduce you to the basic concepts and language of assessment as well as to how measures are developed and adapted so that they are culturally appropriate.
- In the **Assessment Practice Zone**, which comprises Chapters 8 to 9 and 15 to 18, we will tackle various issues concerning who may use measures, good assessment practices related to administration, scoring, interpretation and reporting, the contexts in which assessment is used, and the future of assessment.

- In the **Types-of-Measures Zone**, which comprises Chapters 10 to 14, we will focus on the different types of measures that are used to measure various aspects of human behaviour and functioning as well as on computer-based and Internet-delivered testing.

Please note that we indicated only key aspects of chapter titles on the map (e.g. 1 Assessment overview). An important aspect of your journey is the speed at which you travel. Take things at a pace that you find comfortable. Speeding could result in a failure to grasp some of the essential concepts. Do not be alarmed if you find that you sometimes need to retrace your steps, especially when you travel through the Foundation Zone. It is better to revisit any concepts that you find difficult to understand in the early part of the book, as the remainder of the book builds on the knowledge that you acquire in the Foundation Zone.

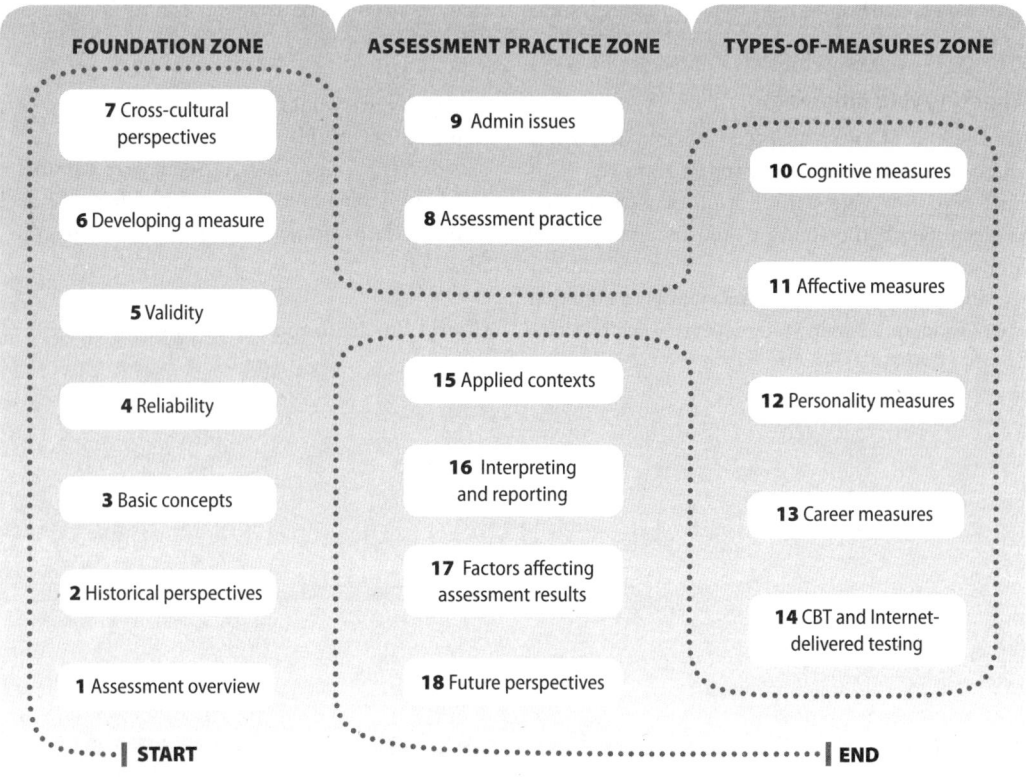

FOUNDATION ZONE

7 Cross-cultural perspectives

6 Developing a measure

5 Validity

4 Reliability

3 Basic concepts

2 Historical perspectives

1 Assessment overview

START

ASSESSMENT PRACTICE ZONE

9 Admin issues

8 Assessment practice

15 Applied contexts

16 Interpreting and reporting

17 Factors affecting assessment results

18 Future perspectives

TYPES-OF-MEASURES ZONE

10 Cognitive measures

11 Affective measures

12 Personality measures

13 Career measures

14 CBT and Internet-delivered testing

END

Signposts for our journey

As you travel through each chapter you will find a number of signposts.

Chapter outcomes

Before you are provided with any material, you will be given an overview of the outcomes of the chapter. This will enable you to work through the contents of the chapter in a focused way.

Concepts

To help you to identify the really important concepts in a chapter, they will always be presented in **boldface** or *italics*.

Critical thinking challenge

At an appropriate point in each chapter, you will find a case study, or something to get you thinking. The purpose of presenting you with this material is to encourage you to think critically about the material and to apply your new knowledge about assessment to real-life situations. We will provide you with some cues to help you with some of the critical thinking challenges.

Checking your progress

At the end of every chapter you will find a few questions that you should try and answer. This will give you a good indication of whether you understood all the concepts and issues explained in the chapter.

Something else that is important is to note that we have included many references to work published in South African journals. We would encourage you to access the relevant articles as they will expand on what has been included in this book. Furthermore, there are a number of web sites that could be accessed where you can get up to date knowledge and information about psychological assessment and testing. For example: http://en.wikipedia.org, www.psychtesting.org.uk, www.intestcom.org, www.intestcom.org/orta (the latter is a set of on-line readings in testing and assessment), http://www.apa.org/topics/topictesting06b.html www.psyssa.com, and www.siopsa.org.za.

We hope that you find your journey through this book as interesting as we found the conceptualization and preparation stages. We would also like to thank all those who contributed to making this book a reality, either by way of writing sections or on the editorial, typesetting, and production side. The contributors, in particular, need to be thanked for their time and effort in preparing their insightful, scholarly contributions.

Finally, we would like you to let us know your impressions of this book, and any suggestions you have for improving it. Send your comments to Cheryl at the following email address: **Cheryl. foxcroft@nmmu.ac.za** or to Gert at **groodt@ uj.ac.za.**

Cheryl Foxcroft and Gert Roodt

Foundation Zone

When you looked at the map that will guide your journey through this book, you probably did not realize that the first zone involves climbing up a rather steep hill. The reason why the hill is so steep is that you will be introduced to most of the important concepts in psychological assessment and measurement in this zone. These concepts are not always easy to understand, so we suggest that you drive slowly through this zone. Do not be afraid to turn back and retrace your steps if you need to.

Part

1

An overview of assessment: Definition and scope

CHERYL FOXCROFT AND GERT ROODT

CHAPTER OUTCOMES

By the end of this chapter you will be able to:
> distinguish between tests, assessment measures, testing, and psychological and competency-based assessment;
> name the characteristics of assessment measures; and
> explain assessment as a multidimensional process.

1.1 **About tests, testing, and assessment**

We constantly have to make decisions in our everyday lives: what to study, what career to pursue, who to choose as our life partner, which applicant to hire, how to put together an effective team to perform a specific task, and so on. This book will focus on the role of psychological assessment in providing information to guide individuals, groups, and organizations to understand and make informed and appropriate decisions. In the process you will discover that assessment can

serve many purposes. For example, assessment can help to identify strengths and weaknesses, map development or progress, make decisions regarding suitability for a job or a field of study, identify training and education needs, or it can assist in making a diagnosis. Assessment can also assist in identifying intervention and therapy needs, measuring the effectiveness of an intervention programme, and in gathering research data to increase psychology's knowledge base about human behaviour or to inform policy-making. As the South African society is multicultural and multilingual in nature, this book also aims to raise awareness about the impact of culture and language on assessment and to suggest ways of addressing them.

One of the first things that you will discover when you start journeying through the field of psychological assessment is that many confusing and overlapping terms are used. As you travel through the *Foundation Zone* of this book, you must try to understand the more important terms and think about how they are interlinked.

In essence, **tools** are available to make it possible for us to assess (measure) human behaviour. You will soon realise that various names are used to refer to these tools such as **tests, measures, assessment measures, instruments, scales, procedures, and techniques.** To ensure that the measurement is valid and reliable, a body of theory and research regarding the scientific measurement principles that are applied to the measurement of psychological characteristics has evolved over time. This sub-field of psychology is known as **Psychometrics**, and you will often come across the term **psychometric properties** of a measure and the term **psychometric measure. Psychometrics** refers to the systematic and scientific way in which psychological measures are developed and the technical measurement standards (e.g. validity and reliability) required of measures.

When we perform an assessment, we normally use assessment tools as well as other information that we obtain about a person (e.g. school performance, qualifications, life and work history, family background). **Psychological assessment** is a process-orientated activity aimed at gathering a wide array of information by using psychological assessment measures (tests) and information from many other sources (e.g. interviews, a person's history, collateral sources). We then evaluate and integrate all this information to reach a conclusion or make a decision. Seen from this perspective, **testing** (i.e. the use of tests, measures, etc.), which involves the measurement of behaviour, is one of the key elements of the much broader evaluative process known as psychological assessment.

Traditionally, psychology professionals have performed all aspects of the assessment process (test selection and administration, scoring, interpreting and reporting/providing feedback). Furthermore, as the outputs of psychological assessment are in the form of psychological traits/constructs (such as personality and ability), the expertise to perform psychological assessment is clearly embodied in an appropriately registered psychology professional. However, in the modern testing era, there has been a shift in the role of the psychology professional in the assessment process in the work and organisational context in particular (Bartram, 2003). This shift has been due to the advent of both **Internet-delivered computer-based tests** (which is covered in Chapter 14) and **competency-based assessment** (which focuses on assessing the skills, behaviours, attitudes/values required for effective performance in the work place or educational/training settings, the results of which are directly linked to the competency language of the work place or educational setting). These two factors have redefined who a test user is and the role of the psychology professional in assessment, given that computer-based tests require little, if any human intervention in terms of administration and scoring, and computer-generated test interpretation and reports are often available. This results in some test users in the work place only needing the skill to use and apply the competency-based outputs from a test, which does not require extensive psychological training. There is much controversy around the shifting role of the psychology professional and the role on non-professionals in assessment in some areas of psychology. This controversy will be debated further in Chapters 2, 8 and 14.

Having summarized the relationship between tests, testing, assessment, and drawn a distinction between psychological and competency-based assessment, let us now consider each aspect in more depth. However, you should be aware that it is almost impossible to define terms such as test, testing, assessment measure, and assessment.

> Any attempt to provide a precise definition of 'test' or of 'testing' as a process, is likely to fail as it will tend to exclude some procedures that should be included and include others that should be excluded (ITC Guidelines for International test-use, 1999, p. 8).

Instead of focusing on specific definitions, we will highlight the most important characteristics of assessment measures (tests) and assessment.

1.2 **Assessment measures (Tests)**

1.2.1 **Characteristics of assessment measures**

Although various names are used to refer to the tools of assessment, this book will mainly use **test** and **assessment measure**. Preference is given to the term **assessment measure** as it has a broader connotation than the term **test**, which mainly refers to an objective, standardized measure that is used to gather data for a specific purpose (e.g. to determine what a person's intellectual capacity is).

The main characteristics of assessment measures are as follows:

- Assessment measures include many different procedures that can be used in psychological, occupational, and educational assessment and can be administered to individuals, groups, and organizations.
- Specific **domains of functioning** (e.g. intellectual ability, personality, organizational climate) are sampled by assessment measures. From these samples, inferences can be made about both normal and abnormal (dysfunctional) behaviour or functioning.
- Assessment measures are administered under carefully controlled (**standardized**) conditions.
- **Systematic methods** are applied to score or evaluate assessment protocols.
- Guidelines are available to understand and interpret the results of an assessment measure. Such guidelines may make provision for the comparison of an individual's performance to that of an appropriate **norm group** or to a **criterion** (e.g. competency profile for a job), or may outline how to use test scores for more qualitative classification purposes (e.g. into personality types or diagnostic categories).
- Assessment measures should be **supported by evidence** that they are valid and reliable for

the intended purpose. This evidence is usually provided in the form of a technical test manual.

- Assessment measures are usually developed in a certain context (society or culture) for a specific purpose and the normative information used to interpret test performance is limited to the characteristics of the normative sample. Consequently, the appropriateness of an assessment measure for an individual, group, or organization from another context, culture, or society cannot be assumed without an investigation into possible test bias (i.e. whether a measure is differentially valid for different subgroups) and without strong consideration being given to adapting and re-norming the measure. In Chapter 7 you can read about cross-cultural test adaptation. Furthermore, in the historical overview of assessment provided in Chapter 2, you will see what a thorny issue the cross-cultural transportability of measures has become, especially in the South African context.
- Assessment measures vary in terms of:
  - how they are administered (e.g. group, individual, or on computer);
  - whether time limits are imposed. In a **speed measure** there is a large number of fairly easy items of a similar level of difficulty. These need to be completed within a certain time limit, with the result that almost no one completes all the items in the specified time. In **power measures** on the other hand, time limits are not imposed so that all test-takers may complete all the items. However, the items in a power measure get progressively more difficult;
  - how they are scored (e.g. objectively with scoring masks or more subjectively according to certain guidelines);
  - how they are normed (e.g. by using a comparison group or a criterion);
  - what their intended purpose is (e.g. screening versus diagnostic, competency-based testing);
  - the nature of their items (e.g. verbal items, performance tasks);
  - the response required from the test-taker

(e.g. verbally, via pencil-and-paper, by manipulating physical objects, by pressing certain keys on a computer keyboard); and
- the content areas that they tap (e.g. ability or personality-related).

All the characteristics of measures outlined above will be amplified throughout this book. Furthermore, various ways of classifying these measures are available. In Chapter 8 we discuss the classification system used in South Africa as well as the criteria used in deciding whether a measure should be classified as a psychological test or not. You will also notice that the different types of measures presented in Chapters 10 to 14, have largely been grouped according to content areas.

1.2.2 Important issues

There are two important aspects about assessment measures that you should always keep in mind. Firstly, *test results represent only one source of information in the assessment process.* Unfortunately, assessment measures, because they offer the promise of objective measurement, often take on magical proportions for assessment practitioners who begin to value them above their professional judgement or opinion. Lezak (1987) reminds us that psychological assessment measures:

> are simply a means of enhancing (refining, standardizing) our observations. They can be thought of as extensions of our organs of perception.... If we use them properly,.. they can enable us to accomplish much more with greater speed. When tests are misused as substitutes for rather than extensions of clinical observation, they can obscure our view of the patient. (Lezak, 1987, p. 46).

Secondly, *we need to recognize the approximate nature of assessment (test) results.* Why? The results obtained from assessment measures always need to be bracketed by a band of uncertainty caused by errors of measurement that creep in during administration, scoring, and interpretation. Furthermore, the social, economic, educational and cultural background of an individual can influence his/her performance on a measure to the extent that the

results present a distorted picture of the individual (see Chapter 17). Thorndike and Hagen (1977), however, point out that it is not just in the field of psychology where assessment information may be subject to error. The teacher's perception of how well a child reads, the medical doctor's appraisal of a person's health status, the social worker's description of a home environment, and so on, all represent approximate, informed, yet somewhat subjective, and thus potentially fallible (incorrect) opinions.

1.3 The assessment process

The assessment process is multidimensional in nature. It entails the gathering and synthesizing of information as a means of describing and understanding functioning. This can inform appropriate decision-making and intervention.

The information-gathering aspect of the assessment process will be briefly considered. 'Test performance in a controlled clinic situation with one person is not a representative sample of behavior!' (Bagnato and Neisworth, 1991, p. 59). Information-gathering itself must be multidimensional. Table 1.1 highlights the varied aspects across which information should be purposefully gathered.

By gathering a wide array of data in the assessment process, a richer and broader sampling of behaviour or functioning can be achieved. However, the assessment battery (i.e. the combination of measures used) must be tailored to an individual, group, or organization's needs (e.g. in terms of their age, level of ability and disability, capacity, job analysis) as well as to the purpose of the assessment. You can read more about the tailoring of assessment and the selection of tests for a battery in Chapter 9.

After gathering the information, *all* the information must be synthesized, clustered together, and weighed up to describe and understand the functioning of an individual, group or organization. Based on such descriptions, predictions can be made about future functioning, decisions can be made, interventions can be planned, and progress can be mapped, among other things.

It is particularly in the synthesis and integration of assessment information that much

Table 1.1 Multidimensional information-gathering

SOURCES OF INFORMATION	EXAMPLES
Multiple measures	Different types of assessment measures such as norm-based and criterion-referenced tests, interviews, behavioural observation, rating scales completed by teachers or supervisors, and ecologically-based measures that describe the social or occupational context of an individual should be used.
Multiple domains	The following could be assessed, for example: attention; motor, cognitive, language-related, non-verbal, and personality-related functioning; scholastic achievement; and job performance.
Multiple sources	Consult with other professionals, teachers, parents, extended family members, and employers.
Multiple settings	Assessment should take place in a variety of settings (e.g. home, school, work, consulting rooms) and social arrangements (e.g. one-to-one, with peers, with parents present) to get as broad a perspective as possible of a person's functioning and the factors that influence it.
Multiple occasions	For assessment to be relevant, valid, and accurate, patterns of functioning have to be identified over a period of time and not merely in a single assessment session.

skill and professional judgement is required to identify the underlying patterns of behaviour and to make appropriate deductions. This is why you need to draw on all your knowledge from all areas of psychology, and not just from the field of assessment, when you perform a psychological assessment.

However, *it is important to recognize the limits of human wisdom when reaching opinions based on assessment information.* Why? When assessment practitioners synthesize and integrate assessment information, they do so in as professional and responsible a way as possible, using all the wisdom at their disposal. At the end of this process, they formulate an informed professional opinion. Even though it is an *informed* opinion, it is nonetheless an opinion which may or may not be correct. The assessment practitioner may be fairly certain that the correct opinion has been arrived at, but absolute certainty is not possible. Nonetheless, increasing emphasis is being placed on the consequences of the outcomes of assessment for individuals and

organizations and the responsibility of the psychology professional in this regard (see Chapter 8). For example, if a wrong selection decision is made when hiring a senior level employee, possible negative outcomes for an organization could be added financial risk, lowering of effectiveness and efficiency, bad publicity and legal action (related to unfair labour practices if the employee is retrenched/fired).

As we conclude this section, another crucial aspect of the assessment process needs to be highlighted. Can you guess what it is? Various parties, often with competing motives and values, are involved in the assessment process. The person doing the assessment, the person being assessed, and external parties such as employers, education authorities, or parents, all have a stake in the outcome of the assessment. This is why it is important that the rights, roles, and responsibilities of all the stakeholders involved are recognized and respected. This aspect will be explored in more detail in Chapter 8.

>> **CRITICAL THINKING CHALLENGE 1.1**

In your own words, explain what the assessment process involves and where assessment measures fit into the picture.

CHECKING YOUR PROGRESS 1.1

1.1 Define the following terms:
- Psychometrics
- Psychological assessment
- Testing
- Competency-based assessment
- Assessment measure
- Assessment battery

Psychological assessment: A brief retrospective overview

CHERYL FOXCROFT, GERT ROODT, AND FATIMA ABRAHAMS

Chapter

2

CHAPTER OUTCOMES

By the end of this chapter you will be able to:
> understand how assessment has evolved since ancient times;
> appreciate the factors that have shaped psychological assessment in South Africa; and
> develop an argument about why assessment is still valued in modern society.

At the start of our journey into the field of psychological assessment, it is important to gain a perspective of its origins. Without some idea of the historical roots of the discipline of psychological assessment, the great progress made by modern assessment measures cannot be fully appreciated. You will also be introduced to some of the key concepts that we will be elaborating on in the *Foundation Zone* of this book.

As you journey through the past with us, you should be on the lookout for the following:
• how difficult it was in ancient times to find an objectively verifiable way of measuring human attributes; ask yourself the reasons for this;

• how the most obvious things in the lived world of ancient philosophers and scientists (such as the human hand, head, and body, as well as animals) were used in an attempt to describe personal attributes;
• the stepping stones that some of the ancient 'measures' provided for the development of modern psychological assessment;
• the factors both within and outside of the discipline of psychology that have shaped the development of modern psychological assessment; and
• the factors that shaped the development and use of psychological assessment in South Africa.

2.1 A brief overview of the early origins of psychological assessment

The use of assessment measures can be traced back to ancient times. One of the first recordings of the use of an assessment procedure for selection purposes can be found in the Bible in Judges Chapter 7 verses 1 to 8. Gideon observed how his soldiers drank water from a river so he could select those who remained on the alert. Historians credit the Chinese with having a relatively sophisticated testing programme for civil servants in place more than 4 000 years ago (Kaplan and Saccuzzo, 1997). Oral examinations were administered every third year and the results were used for work evaluations and for promotion purposes.

Over the years, many authors, philosophers, and scientists have explored various avenues in their attempts to assess human attributes. Let us look at a few of these.

2.1.1 Astrology

Most people are aware of the horoscopes that appear in daily newspapers and popular magazines. The positions of planets are used to formulate personal horoscopes that describe the personality characteristics of individuals and to predict what might happen in their lives. The origin of horoscopes can be traced back to ancient times, possibly as early as the fifth century BC (McReynolds, 1986). Davey (1989) concludes that scientists, on the whole, have been scathing in their rejection of astrology as a key to understanding and describing personality characteristics. Do you agree? State your reasons.

2.1.2 Physiognomy

McReynolds (1986) credits Pythagoras for being perhaps the earliest practitioner of physiognomy, in the sixth century BC. Later on, Aristotle also came out in support of physiognomy, which attempted to judge a person's character from the external features of the body and especially the face, in relation to the similarity that these features had to animals. Physiognomy was based on the assumption that people who shared physical

similarities with animals also shared some psychic properties with these animals. For example, a person who looked like a fox was sly, or somebody who looked like an owl was wise (Davey, 1989). What is your view on this?

2.1.3 Humorology

In the fifth century BC, Hippocrates, the father of medicine, developed the concept that there were four body humours or fluids (blood, yellow bile, black bile, and phlegm) (McReynolds, 1986). Galen, a physician in ancient Rome, took these ideas further by hypothesizing four types of temperament (sanguine, choleric, melancholic, and phlegmatic), corresponding to the four humours (Aiken, 1997). The problem with the humoral approach of classifying personality types into one of four categories was that it remained a hypothesis that was never objectively verified. Today the humoral theory mainly has historical significance.

However, based on the views of Hippocrates and Galen, Eysenck and Eysenck (1958) embedded the four temperaments within the introversion/extroversion and the emotionally stable/ emotionally unstable (neurotic) personality dimensions which they proposed. Of interest is the fact that Eysenck and Eysenck's (1958) two personality dimensions still form the basis for modern personality measures such as the Myers Briggs Type Indicator and the 16 Personality Factor Questionnaire. You can read more about these measures in Chapter 12.

2.1.4 **Phrenology**

Franz Gall was the founder of **phrenology**, the 'science' of 'reading people's heads' (McReynolds, 1986). Phrenologists believed that the brain consisted of a number of organs that corresponded with various personality characteristics (e.g. self-esteem, cautiousness, firmness) and cognitive faculties (e.g. language, memory, calculation). By feeling the topography of a person's skull, phrenologists argued that it was possible to locate 'bumps' over specific brain areas believed to be associated with certain personality attributes (Aiken, 1997). The fundamental assumptions underlying phrenology were later demonstrated to be invalid, and no one really places any value on phrenology today.

2.1.5 **Chirology – Palmistry**

Bayne asserted that palm creases (unlike fingerprints) can change and he found that certain changes appeared to be related to changes in personality. He also believed that all hand characteristics should be taken into consideration before any valid assessments could be made. However, to this day, no scientific evidence has been found that, for example, a firm handshake is a sign of honesty, or that long fingers suggest an artistic temperament (Davey, 1989).

2.1.6 **Graphology**

Graphology can be defined as the systematic study of handwriting. Handwriting provides graphologists with cues that are called 'crystallized gestures' that can be analysed in detail. As handwriting is a type of stylistic behaviour, there is some logic to the argument that it could be seen to be an expression of personality characteristics. Graphologists hypothesize that people who keep their handwriting small are likely to be introverted, modest, and humble, and shun publicity. Large handwriting on the other hand, shows a desire to 'think big' which, if supported by intelligence and drive, provides the ingredients for success. Upright writing is said to indicate self-reliance, poise, calm and self-composure, reserve, and a neutral attitude (Davey, 1989). Davey (1989) concluded that efforts of graphologists to establish validity of such claims have yielded no or very few positive results.

Although there are almost no studies in which it has been found that handwriting is a valid predictor of job performance, graphology is widely used in personnel selection to this day (Simner and Goffin, 2003). It is especially used in France, but also in other countries such as Belgium, Germany, Italy, Israel, Great Britain, and the United States of America. This has prompted Murphy and Davidshofer (2001) to ask why graphology remains popular. What reasons do you think did they unearth in attempting to answer this question?

Murphy and Davidshofer (2001) concluded that there were three main reasons that fuelled the popularity of handwriting analysis in personnel selection:

- It has high face validity, meaning that to the ordinary person in the street it seems reasonable that handwriting could provide indicators of personality characteristics, just as mannerisms and facial expressions do.
- Graphologists tend to make holistic descriptions of candidates such as 'honest', 'sincere', and 'shows insight', which, because of their vagueness, are difficult to prove or disprove.
- Some of the predictions of graphologists are valid. However, Murphy and Davidshofer (2001) cite research studies which revealed that the validity of the inferences drawn by the graphologists was related more to what they gleaned from the content of an applicant's biographical essay than the analysis of the handwriting!

Despite having found reasons why graphology continues to be used in personnel selection, Murphy and Davidshofer (2001) concluded that, all things considered, there is not sufficient evidence to support the use of graphology in employment testing and selection. Simner and Goffin (2003) concur with this and argue that the criterion-related validity of graphology is lower and more variable than that of more widely known and less expensive measures. For example, whereas the criterion-related validity of graphology varies between .09 and .16 (Simner and Goffin, 2003), the criterion-related validity of general mental testing and structured interviews in job selection has been found to be .51, and when used in combination, the validity coefficient increases to .63 (Schmidt and Hunter, 1998). Simner and Goffin (2003) thus caution that the continued use of graphology for personnel selection could prove to be costly and harmful to organizations.

2.1.7 Summary

All the avenues explored by the early philosophers, writers, and scientists did not provide verifiable ways of measuring human attributes. The common thread running through all these attempts (but probably not in the case of graphology), is the lack of proper scientific method and, ultimately, rigorous scientific measurement.

2.2 The development of modern psychological assessment: An international perspective

2.2.1 Early developments

Psychology has only started to prosper and grow as a science since the development of the scientific method. Underlying the scientific method is measurement. Guilford stated as long ago as 1936 that psychologists have adopted the motto of Thorndike that 'whatever exists at all, exists in some amount' and that they have also adopted the corollary that 'whatever exists in some amount, can be measured'. It was perhaps the development of objective measurement that made the greatest contribution to the development of Psychology as a science.

During the Italian Renaissance Huarte's book was translated into English as *The Tryal of Wits* (1698). This book was a milestone in the history of assessment, because for the first time someone proposed a discipline of assessment; gave it a task to do; and offered some suggestions on how it might proceed. Huarte pointed out that:

- people differ from one another with regard to certain talents;
- different vocations require different sets of talents; and that
- a system should be developed to determine specific patterns of abilities of different persons so that they can be guided into appropriate education programmes and occupations. This system would involve the appointment of a number of examiners (triers) who would carry out certain procedures (tryals) in order to determine a person's capacity (McReynolds, 1986).

A further milestone in the development of modern psychological assessment came from the work of Thomasius, a professor of philosophy in Germany. According to McReynolds (1986), Thomasius made two main contributions to the emerging field of assessment. He was the first person to develop behavioural rating scales, and furthermore, the ratings in his scales were primarily dependent on direct observations of the subject's behaviour.

Another milestone was the coining of the term **psychometrics** by Wolff. The term 'psychometrics' was used throughout the eighteenth and nineteenth centuries, but was mainly applied to psychophysical measurements (McReynolds, 1986). In the twentieth century, with the shift towards the measurement of individual differences, the term was applied to a wider variety of measuring instruments, such as cognitive (mental ability) and personality-related measures.

After the foundation had been laid by experimental psychologists such as Wundt, the latter half of the nineteenth century saw some promising developments in the field of assessment linked to the work of Francis Galton, James McKeen Cattell, and Alfred Binet. One of experimental psychology's major contributions to the field of psychological assessment was the notion that assessment should be viewed in the same light as an experiment, as it required the same rigorous control. As you will discover, one of the hallmarks of modern psychological assessment is that assessment measures are administered under highly standardized conditions.

2.2.2 The early twentieth century

The twentieth century witnessed genuine progress in psychological assessment. The progress has mainly been attributed to advances in:

- theories of human behaviour that could guide the development of assessment measures;

- statistical methods that aided the analysis of data obtained from measures to determine their relationship to job performance and achievement, for example, as well as to uncover the underlying dimensions being tapped by a measure; and
- the application of psychology in clinical, educational, military, and industrial settings.

Other than these advances, there was another important impetus that fuelled the development of modern psychological assessment measures in the twentieth century. Do you have any idea what this was?

During the nineteenth century and at the turn of the twentieth century in particular, a need arose to treat mentally disturbed and disabled people in a more humanitarian way. To achieve this, the mental disorders and deficiencies of patients had to be properly assessed and classified. Uniform procedures needed to be found to differentiate people who were mentally insane and those who suffered from emotional disorders, from those who were mentally disabled and suffered from an intellectual deficit. A need therefore arose for the development of psychological assessment measures.

According to Aiken (2002), an important breakthrough in the development of modern psychological assessment measures came at the start of the twentieth century. In 1904, the French Minister of Public Instruction appointed a commission to find ways to identify mentally disabled individuals so that they could be provided with appropriate educational opportunities. One member of the French commission was Binet. Together with Simon, a French physician, Binet developed the first measure that provided a fairly practical and reliable way of measuring intelligence. The 1905 Binet-Simon Scale became the benchmark for future psychological tests. The measure was given under standardized conditions (i.e. everyone was given the same test instructions and the format was the same for everyone). Furthermore, norms were developed, albeit using a small and unrepresentative sample. More important than adequacy of the normative sample, though, was Binet and Simon's notion that the availability of comparative scores could aid interpretation of test performance.

It is interesting to note that one of the earliest records of the misuse of intelligence testing involved the Binet-Simon Scale (Gregory, 2007). An influential American psychologist, Henry Goddard was concerned about what he believed to be the high rate of mental retardation among immigrants entering the United States. Consequently, Goddard's English translation of the Binet-Simon Scale was administered to immigrants through a translator, just after they arrived in the United States. 'Thus, a test devised in French, then translated to English was, in turn, retranslated back to Yiddish, Hungarian, Italian, or Russian; administered to bewildered laborers who had just endured an Atlantic crossing; and interpreted according to the original French norms' (Gregory, 2000, p. 17). It is thus not surprising that Goddard found that the average intelligence of immigrants was low!

The Binet-Simon Scale relied heavily on the verbal skills of the test-taker and, in its early years, was available in French and English only. Consequently, its appropriateness for use with non-French or non-English test-takers, illiterates, and with speech and hearing impaired test-takers was questioned (Gregory, 2007). This sparked the development of a number of non-verbal measures (e.g. Seguin form board, Knox's digit-symbol substitution test, the Kohs Block Design test, and the Porteus Maze Test).

World War I further fuelled the need for psychological assessment measures. Why? Large numbers of military recruits needed to be assessed, but at that stage only individually administered tests, such as the Binet-Simon scale, were available. So World War I highlighted the need for large-scale group testing. Furthermore, the scope of testing broadened at this time to include tests of achievement, aptitude, interest, and personality. Following World War I, with the emergence of group tests that largely used a multiple-choice format, there was widespread optimism regarding the usefulness of psychological tests (Kaplan and Saccuzzo, 1997). Samelson (1979, p. 154) points out that Cattell remarked that during the war period 'the army testing put psychology on the map of the United States'. Given that over a million people were tested on the Army Alpha and Army Beta tests in the USA, Cattell's observation has merit. Furthermore, the testing of pilots in Italy and France and the testing of truck drivers for the German army, for example, suggest that the world wars did not only put psychology on the map in the USA but elsewhere in the world as well.

2.2.3 Measurement challenges

Although the period between the two world wars was a boom period for the development of psychological measures, critics started pointing out the weaknesses and limitations of existing measures. Although this put test developers on the defensive, and dampened the enthusiasm of assessment practitioners, the knowledge gained from this critical look at testing inspired test developers to reach new heights. To illustrate this point, let us consider two examples, one from the field of intellectual assessment and the other from the field of personality assessment.

The criticism of intelligence scales up to this point, i.e. that they were too dependent on language and verbal skills, reduced their appropriateness for many individuals (e.g. for illiterates). To address this weakness, Wechsler included performance tests that did not require verbal responses when he published the first version of the Wechsler Intelligence Scales in 1937. Furthermore, whereas previous intelligence scales only yielded one score (namely, the intelligence quotient), the Wechsler Intelligence Scales yielded a variety of summative scores from which a more detailed analysis of an individual's pattern of performance could be made. These innovations revolutionized intelligence assessment.

The use of structured personality measures was severely criticized during the 1930s as many findings of personality tests could not be substantiated during scientific studies. However, the development of the Minnesota Multiphasic Personality Inventory (MMPI) by Butcher in 1943 began a new era for structured, objective personality measures. The MMPI placed an emphasis on using empirical data to determine the meaning of test results. According to Kaplan and Saccuzzo (1997), the MMPI and its revision, the MMPI-2, are the most widely used and referenced personality tests to this day.

World War II reaffirmed the value of psy-chological assessment. The 1940s witnessed the emergence of new test development technologies, such as the use of factor analysis to construct tests such as the 16 Personality Factor Questionnaire. During this period there was also much growth in the application of psychology and psychological testing. Psychological testing came to be seen as one of the major functions of psychologists working in applied settings. In 1954 the American Psychological Association (APA) pronounced that psychological testing was exclusively the domain of the clinical psychologist. However, the APA unfortunately also pronounced that psychologists were permitted to conduct psychotherapy only in collaboration with medical practitioners.

As you can imagine, many clinical psychologists became disillusioned by the fact that they could not practise psychotherapy independently, and, although they had an important testing role to fulfil, they began to feel that they were merely technicians who were playing a subservient role to medical practitioners. Consequently, when they looked around for something to blame for their poor position, the most obvious scapegoat was psychological testing (Lewandowski and Saccuzzo, 1976). At the same time, given the intrusive nature of tests and the potential to abuse testing, widespread mistrust and suspicion of tests and testing came to the fore. So, with both psychologists and the public becoming rapidly disillusioned with tests, many psychologists refused to use any tests, and countries such as the United States of America, Sweden, and Denmark banned the use of tests for selection purposes in industry. So it is not surprising that according to Kaplan and Saccuzzo (1997), the status of psychological assessment declined sharply from the late 1950s, and this decline persisted until the 1970s.

2.2.4 The influence of multiculturalism

In the latter part of the twentieth century and during the first decade of the twenty-first century, multiculturalism has become the norm in many countries. As a result, attempts were made to develop tests that were 'culture-free'. An example of such a measure is the Culture-free Intelligence Test (Anastasi and Urbina, 1997). However, it soon became clear that it was not possible to develop a test that is free of any cultural influences. Consequently, test developers focused more on 'culture-reduced' or 'culture-common' tests in which the aim was to remove as much cultural bias as possible from the test by including only behaviour that was common across cultures. For example, a number of non-verbal intelligence tests were developed (e.g., Test of Non-verbal Intelligence, Raven's Progressive Matrices) where the focus was on novel problem-solving tasks and in which language use, which is often a stumbling block in cross-cultural tests, was minimized.

Furthermore, given that most of the available measures have been developed in the United States of America or the United Kingdom, they tend to be more appropriate for westernized English-speaking people. In response to the rapid globalization of the world's population and the need for measures to be more culturally appropriate and available in the language in which the test-taker is proficient in, the focus of psychological testing in the 1980s and 1990s shifted to **cross-cultural test adaptation**. Under the leadership of Ron Hambleton from the United States of America, the International Test Commission (ITC) released their *Guidelines for Adapting Educational and Psychological Tests* (Hambleton, 1994, 2001). These guidelines have become the benchmark for cross-cultural test adaptation around the world. They have also assisted in advocating against assessment practices where test-takers are tested in languages that they are not proficient in, sometimes using a translator who translates the test 'on the run'. In addition, many methodologies and statistical techniques (e.g., Structural Equation Modeling) have been developed to assist in establishing whether different language versions of a test are equivalent (Hambleton, Merenda, & Spielberger, 2005). You can read more about how and why measures are adapted for use in different countries and cultures in Chapter 6.

A new trend that is emerging in the twenty-first century is to approach the development of tests that are used widely internationally (e.g., the Wechsler Intelligence Scales) from a multicultural perspective. For example, when it comes to the Wechsler Intelligence Scales for Children (WISC), the norm through the years has been to

first develop and standardize the measure for the United States of America and thereafter to adapt it for use outside of the United States of America. However, for the development of the Wechsler Intelligence Scale for Children – Fourth Edition (WISC IV), experts from various countries are providing input on the constructs to be tapped as well as the content of the items to minimize potential cultural bias during the initial re-design phase (Weiss, 2003). In the process, the development of the WISC IV is setting a new benchmark for development of internationally applicable tests.

A further recent trend in multicultural and multilingual test development is that of **simultaneous multilingual test development** (Solano-Flores, Turnbull and Nelson-Barber, 2002; Tanzer, 2005). This differs from the process outlined for the development of the WISC IV where people from different cultural and language groups provide input on the construct(s) to be tapped but the items are still developed in English before they are translated into other languages. Instead, in simultaneous multilingual test development, once the test specifications have been developed, items are written by a multilingual and multicultural panel or committee where each member has a background in psychology (in general and cross-cultural in particular), measurement and linguistics as well as with respect to the specific construct that the test will measure (e.g. personality, mathematics). Chapter 7 will provide more information on this approach.

Non-western countries are also rising to the challenge of not only adapting westernised measures for their contexts (e.g., Grazina Gintiliene and Sigita Girdzijauskiene, 2008, report that, among others, the WISC-III and the Raven's Colored Matrices have been adapted for use in Lithuania) but also to develop their own **indigenous measures,** which are more suited to their cultural contexts. For example, Cheung and her colleagues have developed the Chinese Personality Inventory (CPAI), which was revised in 2000 and is now known as the CPAI-2 (Cheung, Leung, Fan, Song, Zhang, and Zhang, 1996). This measure includes both indigenous (culturally relevant) and universal personality dimensions. Indigenous personality constructs were derived from classical literature, everyday descriptions of people, surveys and previous psychological research. Thereafter items and scales were developed according to the highest acceptable psychometric standards. You can get information on the CPAI and its development at http://www.psy.cuhk.edu.hk/~cpaiweb/public-document/PublicFiles.htm. The way in which the CPAI was developed is widely regarded as the benchmark to attain in the development of culturally relevant personality measures. How this approach is being successfully used in the South African context will be covered in Chapter 7.

Other than multiculturalism impacting on the nature of how tests are developed and adapted, due to rapid globalization which has led to increasing multiculturalism in most societies, the choice of which norm group to use to compare an individual's performance to has also become an issue. As will be outlined in Chapter 3, **norms** provide a basis for comparing an individual's performance on a measure with the performance of a well-defined reference group to aid in the interpretation of test performance. Norm or reference groups can be constituted in terms of various characteristics of people (e.g. age, gender, educational level, job level, language, clinical diagnosis). The key criterion when choosing an appropriate norm group to compare an individual's performance to is linked to the purpose of the comparison. For example, if the intention is to compare the performance with others in the same cultural group of a similar age, culturally and age appropriate norms must be used. However, what norms does a multinational organization use to make comparisons of its workforce across cultural and national boundaries? Bartram (2008a) argues that using locally developed national norms are not appropriate in this instance. Instead, he argues that **multi-national norms** should be developed and used provided that the mix of country samples is reasonable and the samples have similar demographics.

2.2.5 **Standards, training, computerized testing, and test users' roles**

In an attempt to address issues of fairness and bias in test use, the need arose to develop **standards for the professional practice of testing and assessment**. Under the leadership of Bartram from the United Kingdom, the ITC has developed a set of *International Guidelines for Test-use* (Version 2000). Many countries, including South Africa, have adopted these test user standards, which should ensure that, wherever testing and assessment is undertaken in the world, similar practice standards should be evident. You can read more about this in Chapter 8.

During the 1990s, competency-based training of assessment practitioners (test users) fell under the spotlight. The British Psychological Society (BPS) took the lead internationally in developing competency standards for different levels of test users in occupational testing in the United Kingdom. Based on these competencies, competency-based training programmes have been developed and all test users have to be assessed by BPS appointed assessors in order to ensure that a uniform standard is maintained. (You can obtain more information from the web site of the Psychological Testing Centre of the BPS at www.psychtesting.org.uk.) Building on the work done in the United Kingdom, Sweden, Norway, and the Netherlands, a task force on test user qualification of the European Federation of Psychology Associations is in the process of defining standards of competence related to test use for Europe as a whole. Their task also encompasses facilitating the recognition of qualifications that meet or can be developed to meet such standards. (Visit www.efpa.be for more information.)

With assessment being widely used in recruitment, selection, and training in work and organizational settings, 'a new standard is being developed by ISO (the International Organisation for Standardisation) to ensure that assessment procedures and methods are used properly and ethically' (Bartram, 2008b, p. 9) and that those performing the assessment are suitably qualified. Once published (in 2010), the **ISO standard** will be able to be used as a benchmark by providers of assessment services to demonstrate that they have the necessary skills and expertise to provide assessments that are 'fit for purpose'. In addition, the standard will be able to be used for certification purposes by individual organizations for internal quality assurance purposes, or for those contracting in assessment services to use as the minimum requirements that need to be met by the organization providing the services; or by professional bodies for credentialing purposes.

Advances in information technology and systems in the latter half of the twentieth century impacted significantly on psychological testing. Computerized adaptive testing became a reality as did the use of the Internet for testing people in one country for a job in another country, for example. Computerized testing and testing via the Internet have revolutionalised all aspects of assessment and have produced their own set of ethical and legal issues. These issues require the urgent attention of test developers and users during the early part of the twenty-first century. You can read more about computerized testing and its history in Chapter 14 and the future predictions regarding assessment and test development in Chapter 18.

Linked to, but not restricted to computer-based and Internet-delivered testing, a trend has emerged regarding who may use psychological measures and what their qualifications should be. Among the more important issues is confusion regarding the roles and responsibilities of people involved in the assessment process and what knowledge, qualifications, and expertise they require, which has been fuelled by the distinction that is drawn between competency-based and psychological assessment (Bartram, 2003). The block below presents a fairly simplistic description of these two types of assessment to illustrate the distinction between them.

Psychological assessment requires expertise in psychology and psychological theories to ensure that measures of cognitive, aptitude, personality, etc. functioning are used in an ethical and fair manner, right from the choice of which tests to use through to interpretation and feedback. Furthermore, the outputs of psychological assessment are in the form of psychological traits/constructs (such as personality and ability). The expertise to perform psychological assessment is clearly embodied in an appropriately registered psychology professional.

Competency-based assessment focuses on the skills, behaviours, knowledge, and attitudes/ values required for effective performance in the work place or in educational settings (e.g., communication, problem-solving, task orientation). The assessment measures used are as directly linked as possible to the required competencies. Indirect methods such as simulations and Assessment Centres are used to conduct competency-based assessment. As the outputs of such assessment are directly linked to the language of the work place or educational settings, the test user does not need expertise in psychological theories to be able to apply the results of competency-based assessments. What is required, however is that competency-based assessment needs to be performed by people with expertise in this area of assessment (e.g., skilled in job analysis and competency-based interviews).

Bartram (2003) argues that there is reasonable international consensus regarding the distinction between psychological and competency-based assessment. Consequently, some countries (e.g. Finland) have used this to legally distinguish between assessments that only psychologists can do (psychological assessment) and those that non-psychologists can do (competency-based assessment). The advent of computer-based and Internet-delivered assessment has further meant that the test user in terms of competency-based assessment is not involved in test selection, administration, scoring and interpretation. Instead, the test user receives the output of the assessment in a language congruent with the competencies required in the work place. In view of the changing nature of the definition of a test user, it is important that the roles, responsibilities and required training of all those involved in the assessment process is clarified to ensure that the test-taker is assessed fairly and appropriately.

To draw this brief international review of the history of psychological assessment to a close, one could ask what the status of psychological testing and assessment is a decade into the twenty-first century? Roe (2008) provided some insights at the closing of the sixth conference of the ITC that could provide some answers to this question. Roe (2008) asserts that the field of psychometrics and psychological testing is doing well as it continues to innovatively respond to issues (e.g. globalization and increased use of the Internet); develop new test development methodologies; and to be sensitive to the rights and reactions of test-takers. Among the challenges that Roe (2008) identifies are the fact that test scores are not easily understood by the public, that psychology professionals struggle to communicate with policy-makers, and that test security and cheating on tests are growing issues. He also argues that for testing to make a better contribution to society, psychology professionals need to conceptualise the fact that testing and assessment (from test selection to reporting) are part of the services that they offer to clients, and that the value add of tests should not be confused with the added value of test-based services.

2.3 The development of modern psychological assessment: A South African perspective

2.3.1 The early years

How did psychological assessment measures come to be used in South Africa? As South Africa was a British colony, the introduction of psychological testing here probably stems from our colonial heritage (Claassen, 1997).

The historical development of modern psychological measures in South Africa followed a similar pattern to that in the United States and Europe (see Section 2.2). However, what is different and important to note is the context in which this development took place. Psychological assessment in South Africa developed in an environment characterized by the unequal distribution of resources based on racial categories (black, coloured, Indian, and white). Almost inevitably, the development of psychological assessment reflected the racially segregated society in which it evolved. So it is not surprising that Claassen (1997) asserts that 'Testing in South Africa cannot be divorced from the country's political, economic and social history' (p. 297). Indeed, any account of the history of

psychological assessment in South Africa needs to point out the substantial impact that apartheid policies had on test development and use (Nzimande, 1995).

Even before the Nationalist Party came into power in 1948, the earliest psychological measures were standardized only for whites and were used by the Education Department to place white pupils in special education. The early measures were either adaptations of overseas measures such as the Standford-Binet, the South African revision of which became known as the Fick Scale, or they were developed specifically for use here, such as the South African Group Test (Wilcocks, 1931).

Not only were the early measures only standardized for whites, but, driven by political ideologies, measures of intellectual ability were used in research studies to draw distinctions between races in an attempt to show the superiority of one group over another. For example, during the 1930s and 1940s, when the government was grappling with the issue of establishing 'Bantu education', Fick (1929) administered individual measures of motor and reasoning abilities, which had only been standardized for white children, to a large sample of black, coloured, Indian, and white school children. He found that the mean score of black children was inferior to that of Indian and coloured children, with whites' mean scores superior to all groups. He remarked at the time that factors such as inferior schools and teaching methods, along with black children's unfamiliarity with the nature of the test tasks, could have disadvantaged their performance on the measures. However, when he extended his research in 1939, he attributed the inferior performance of black children in comparison to that of white children to innate differences, or, in his words, 'difference in original ability' (p. 53) between blacks and whites.

Fick's conclusions were strongly challenged and disputed. For example, Fick's work was severely criticized by Biesheuvel in his book *African Intelligence* (1943), in which an entire chapter was devoted to this issue. Biesheuvel queried the cultural appropriateness of Western-type intelligence tests for blacks and highlighted the influence of different cultural, environmental, and temperamental factors and the effects of malnutrition on intelligence. This led him to conclude that 'under present circumstances, and by means of the usual techniques, the difference between the intellectual capacity of Africans and Europeans cannot be scientifically determined' (Biesheuvel, 1943, p. 191).

In the early development and use of psychological measures in South Africa, some important trends can be identified which were set to continue into the next and subsequent eras of psychological assessment in South Africa. Any idea what these were? The trends are:

- the focus on standardizing measures for whites only;
- the misuse of measures by administering measures standardized for one group to another group without investigating whether or not the measures might be biased and inappropriate for the other group; and
- the misuse of test results to reach conclusions about differences between groups without considering the impact of *inter alia* cultural, socio-economic, environmental, and educational factors on test performance.

2.3.2 The early use of assessment measures in industry

The use of psychological measures in industry gained momentum after World War II and after 1948 when the Nationalist Government came into power. As was the case internationally, psychological measures were developed in response to a societal need. According to Claassen (1997), after World War II, there was an urgent need to identify the occupational suitability (especially for work on the mines) of large numbers of blacks who had received very little formal education. Among the better measures constructed was the General Adaptability Battery (GAB) (Biesheuvel, 1949, 1952), which included a practice session during which test-takers were familiarized with the concepts required to solve the test problems and were asked to complete some practice examples. The GAB was predominantly used for a preliterate black population, speaking a number of dialects and languages.

Because of job reservation under the apartheid regime and better formal education opportunities,

as education was segregated along racial lines, whites competed for different categories of work to blacks. The Otis Mental Ability Test, which was developed in the United States of America and only had American norms, was often used when assessing whites in industry (Claassen, 1997).

Among the important trends in this era that would continue into subsequent eras were:

- the development of measures in response to a need that existed within a certain political dispensation;
- the notion that people who are unfamiliar with the concepts in a measure should be familiarized with them before they are assessed; and
- the use of overseas measures and their norms without investigating whether they should be adapted/revised for use in South Africa.

2.3.3 The later development of psychological assessment (from the 1960s onwards)

According to Claassen (1997), a large number of psychological measures were developed in the period between 1960 and 1984. The National Institute for Personnel Research (NIPR) concentrated on developing measures for industry while the Institute for Psychological and Edumetric Research (IPER) developed measures for education and clinical practice. Both of these institutions were later incorporated into the Human Sciences Research Council (HSRC).

In the racially segregated South African society of the apartheid era, it was almost inevitable that psychological measures would be developed along cultural/racial lines as there 'was little specific need for common tests because the various groups did not compete with each other' (Owen, 1991, p. 112). Consequently, prior to the early 1980s, Western models were used to develop similar but separate measures for the various racial and language groups (Owen, 1991). Furthermore, although a reasonable number of measures were developed for whites, considerably fewer measures were developed for blacks, coloureds, and Indians.

During the 1980s and early 1990s, once the socio-political situation began to change and discriminatory laws were repealed, starting with the relaxation of 'petty apartheid', applicants from different racial groups began competing for the same jobs and the use of separate measures in such instances came under close scrutiny. A number of questions were raised, such as:

- How can you compare scores if different measures are used?
- How do you appoint people if different measures are used?

In an attempt to address this problem, two approaches were followed. In the first instance, measures were developed for more than one racial group, and/or norms were constructed for more than one racial group so that test performance could be interpreted in relation to an appropriate norm group. Examples of such measures are the General Scholastic Aptitude Test (GSAT), the Ability, Processing of Information, and Learning Battery (APIL-B), and the Paper and Pencil Games (PPG), which was the first measure to be available in all eleven official languages in South Africa. In the second instance, psychological measures developed and standardized on only white South Africans, as well as those imported from overseas, were used to assess other groups as well. In the absence of appropriate norms, the potentially bad habit arose of interpreting such test results 'with caution'. Why was this a bad habit? It eased assessment practitioners' consciences and lulled them into a sense that they were doing the best they could with the few tools at their disposal. You can read more about this issue in Chapter 8. The major problem with this approach was that, initially, little research was done to determine the suitability of these measures for a multicultural South African environment. Research studies that investigated the performance of different groups on these measures were needed to determine whether or not the measures were biased.

Despite the widespread use of psychological measures in South Africa, the first thorough study of bias took place only in 1986. This was when Owen (1986) investigated test and item bias using the Senior Aptitude Test, Mechanical Insight Test, and the Scholastic Proficiency test on black, white, coloured, and Indian subjects. He found major differences between the test scores of blacks

and whites and concluded that understanding and reducing the differential performance between black and white South Africans would be a major challenge. Research by Abrahams (1991), Owen (1989a, 1989b), Retief (1992), Taylor and Boeyens (1991), and Taylor and Radford (1986) showed that bias existed in other South African ability and personality measures as well. Other than empirical investigations into test bias, Taylor (1987) also published a report on the responsibilities of assessment practitioners and publishers with regard to bias and fairness of measures. Furthermore, Owen (1992a, 1992b) pointed out that comparable test performance could only be achieved between different groups in South Africa if environmentally disadvantaged test-takers were provided with sufficient training in taking a particular measure before they actually took it.

Given the widespread use (and misuse) of potentially culturally biased measures, coupled with a growing perception that measures were a means by which the Nationalist Government could exclude black South Africans from occupational and educational opportunities, what do you think happened? A negative perception regarding the usefulness of psychological measures developed and large sections of the South African population began to reject the use of psychological measures altogether (Claassen, 1997; Foxcroft, 1997b). Issues related to the usefulness of measures will be explored further in the last section of this chapter.

Remember that in the United States testing came to be seen as one of the most important functions of psychologists, and only psychologists. Well, during the 1970s important legislation was tabled in South Africa that restricted the use of psychological assessment measures to psychologists only. The Health Professions Act 56 of 1974 defines the use of psychological measures as constituting a psychological act, which can legally only be performed by psychologists, or certain other groups of professions under certain circumstances. The section of the Act dealing with assessment will be explored further in Chapter 8.

Among the important trends in this era were:
- the impact of the apartheid political dispensation on the development and fair use of measures;

- the need to empirically investigate test bias; and
- growing scepticism regarding the value of psychological measures, especially for black South Africans.

2.3.4 Psychological assessment in the democratic South Africa

2.3.4.1 Assessment in education

Since 1994 and the election of South Africa's first democratic government, the application, control, and development of assessment measures have become contested terrain. With a growing resistance to assessment measures and the ruling African National Congress (ANC) expressed purpose to focus on issues of equity to redress past imbalances, the use of tests in industry and education in particular has been placed under the spotlight.

School readiness testing, as well as the routine administration of group tests in schools, was banned in many provinces as such testing was seen as being exclusionary and perpetuating the discriminatory policies of the past. Furthermore, the usefulness of test results and assessment practices in educational settings has been strongly queried in the Education White Paper 6, *Special Needs Education: Building An Inclusive Education and Training System* (Department of Education, 2001), for example. Psychometric test results should contribute to the identification of learning problems and educational programme planning as well as informing the instruction of learners. Why is this not happening? Could it be that the measures used are not cross-culturally applicable or have not been adapted for our diverse population and thus do not provide valid and reliable results? Maybe it is because the measures used are not sufficiently aligned with the learning outcomes of Curriculum 21? Or could it be that psychological assessment reports are filled with jargon and recommendations which are not always translated into practical suggestions on what the educator can do in class to support and develop the learner?

Furthermore, within an inclusionary educational system, the role of the educational psychologist along with that of other professional support staff is rapidly changing. Multi-disciplinary pro-

fessional district-based support teams need to be created and have been established in some provinces already (e.g., the Western Cape) (Department of Education, 2005). Within these teams, the primary focus of the psychologists and other professionals is to provide indirect support ('consultancy') to learners through supporting educators and the school management (e.g. to identify learner needs and the teaching and learning strategies that can respond to these needs; and conduct research to map out needs (of learners and educators or to establish the efficacy of a programme). One way that psychologists can support educators in identifying barriers to learning in their learners is to train them in the use of educational and psychological screening measures (see Chapter 15 for a discussion on **screening** versus **diagnostic assessment**). The secondary focus of the professional support teams is to provide direct learning support to learners (e.g., diagnostic assessment to describe and understand a learner's specific learning difficulties and to develop an intervention plan). As is the case with the changing role of psychologists in assessment due to the advent of competency-based, computer-based and Internet-delivered testing, the policies on inclusive education and the strategies for its implementation in South Africa are set to change the role that educational psychologists play in terms of assessment and intervention in the school system. This can be viewed as a positive challenge as educational psychologists will have to develop new competencies (e.g. to train and mentor educators in screening assessment; applying measurement and evaluation principles in a variety of school contexts). In addition, psychologists will have to ensure that their specialist assessment role is not eroded. However, instead of the specialist assessment being too diagnostically focused, it also needs to be developmentally-focused so that assessment results can *inter alia* be linked to development opportunities that the educator can provide (see Chapter 15).

2.3.4.2 The Employment Equity Act

To date, the strongest stance against the improper use of assessment measures has come from industry. Historically, individuals were not legally protected against any form of discrimination. However, with the adoption of the new Constitution and the Labour Relations Act in 1996, worker unions and individuals now have the support of legislation that specifically forbids any discriminatory practices in the workplace and includes protection for applicants as they have all the rights of current employees in this regard. To ensure that discrimination is addressed within the testing arena, the Employment Equity Act No. 55 of 1998 (Section 8) refers to psychological tests and assessment specifically and states that:

> Psychological testing and other similar forms or assessments of an employee are prohibited unless the test or assessment being used:
> (a) has been scientifically shown to be valid and reliable;
> (b) can be applied fairly to all employees;
> (c) is not biased against any employee or group.

The Employment Equity Act has major implications for assessment practitioners in South Africa because many of the measures currently in use, whether imported from the United States and Europe or developed locally, have not been investigated for bias and have not been cross-culturally validated here (as was discussed in Section 2.3.3). The impact of this Act on the conceptualization and professional practice of assessment in South Africa in general is far-reaching as assessment practitioners and test publishers are increasingly being called upon to demonstrate, or prove in court, that a particular assessment measure does not discriminate against certain groups of people. It is thus not surprising that there has been a notable increase in the number of test bias studies since the promulgation of the Act in 1998 (e.g., Abrahams and Mauer, 1999a, 1999b; Lopes, Roodt and Mauer, 2001; Meiring, Van de Vijver, Rothmann and Barrick, 2005; Meiring, van de Vijver, Rothmann and Sackett, 2006; Schaap, 2003; Schaap and Basson, 2003; Taylor, 2000; Van Zyl and Visser, 1998).

A further consequence of the Employment Equity Act is that there is an emerging thought that it would be useful if test publishers and distributors could certify a measure as being 'Employment Equity Act Compliant' as this will aid assessment practitioners when selecting measures (Lopes, Roodt and Mauer, 2001). While this sounds like a very practical suggestion, such certification could be misleading. For example, just because a measure is certified as being compliant does not protect the results from being used in an unfair way when making selection decisions. Furthermore, given the variety of cultural and language groups in this country, bias investigations would have to be conducted for all the subgroups on whom the measure is to be used before it can be given the stamp of approval. Alternatively, it would have to be clearly indicated for what subgroups the measure has been found to be unbiased and that it is only for these groups that the measure complies with the Act.

The advent of the Employment Equity Act has also forced assessment practitioners to take stock of the available measures in terms of their quality, cross-cultural applicability, the appropriateness of their norms, and the availability of different language versions. To this end, the Human Sciences Research Council (HSRC) conducted a survey of test use patterns and needs of practitioners in South Africa (Foxcroft, Paterson, le Roux, and Herbst, 2004). Among other things, it was found that most of the tests being used frequently are in need of adapting for our multicultural context or require updating, and appropriate norms and various language versions should be provided. The report on the survey, which can be viewed at www.hsrc.ac.za, provides an agenda for how to tackle the improvement of the quality of measures and assessment practices in South Africa as well as providing a list of the most frequently used measures which should be earmarked for adaptation or revision first. You can read more about this agenda in Chapter 18.

Having an agenda is important, but having organizations and experts to develop and adapt tests is equally important. As was discussed in 2.3.3, the Human Sciences Research Council (HSRC), into which the NIPR and IPER were incorporated, developed a large number of tests during the 1960s through to the 1980s. For at least three decades the HSRC almost exclusively developed and distributed tests in South Africa. However, at the start of the 1990s the HSRC was restructured, became unsure about the role that it should play in psychological and educational test development, and many staff with test development expertise left the organization. Consequently, since the South African adaptation of the Wechsler Adult Intelligence Scales - III (WAIS-III) in the mid 1990s, the HSRC has not developed or adapted any other tests and its former tests that are still in circulation are distributed by Mindmuzik Media now. According to Foxcroft and Davies (2008), with the HSRC relinquishing its role as the major test developer and distributor in South Africa, other role players gradually emerged to fill the void in South African test development. Some international test development and distribution agencies such as SHL (www.shl.co.za) and Psytech (www.psytech. co.za) have agencies in South Africa. Furthermore, local test agencies such as Jopie van Rooyen & Partners SA (www.jvrafrica.co.za) and Mindmuzik Media (www.mindmuzik.com) have established themselves in the market place. Each of these agencies has a research and development section and much emphasis is being placed on adapting international measures for the South African context. However, there is still some way to go before all the tests listed on the web sites of the agencies that operate in South Africa have been adapted for use here and have South African norms.

The other encouraging trend is that there is a greater involvement of universities (e.g. Nelson Mandela Metropolitan University, North-West University, Rhodes University, Unisa, University of Johannesburg, and University of KwaZulu Natal) in researching and adapting tests, developing local norms and undertaking local psychometric studies, and even developing indigenous tests (e.g., Taylor and de Bruin, 2003). Furthermore, some organizations such as the South African Breweries and the South African Police Services (SAPS) that undertake large scale testing have undertaken numerous studies to provide psychometric information on the measures that they use, investigate bias, and adapt measures on the basis of their findings (e.g. Meiring, 2007).

South African assessment practitioners and test developers have thus not remained entirely passive in the wake of legislation impacting on test use. Although the future use of psychological assessment, particularly in industry and education, still hangs in the balance at this stage, there are encouraging signs that progress is being made to research and adapt more measures appropriate for our context and to use them in fair ways to the benefit of individuals and organizations. The way in which psychologists and test developers continue to respond to this challenge will largely shape the future destiny of psychological testing here. Consult Chapter 18 for future perspectives on this issue.

2.3.4.3 Professional practice guidelines

According to the Health Professions Act No. 56 of 1974, the Professional Board for Psychology of the Health Professions Council of South Africa (HPCSA), is mandated to protect the public and to guide the profession of psychology. In recent years, the Professional Board has become increasingly concerned about the misuse of assessment measures in this country, while recognizing the important role of psychological assessment in the professional practice of psychology as well as for research purposes. Whereas the Professional Board for Psychology had previously given the Test Commission of the Republic of South Africa (TCRSA) the authority to classify psychological tests and oversee the training and examination of certain categories of assessment practitioners, these powers were revoked by the Board in 1996. The reason for this was that the TCRSA did not have any statutory power and, being a section 21 company that operated largely in Gauteng, its membership base was not representative of psychologists throughout the country. Instead, the Professional Board for Psychology formed the Psychometrics Committee, which, as a formal committee of the Board, has provided the Board with a more direct way of controlling and regulating psychological test use in South Africa. The role of the Psychometrics Committee of the Professional Board and some of the initiatives that it has launched will be discussed more fully in Chapter 8.

The further introduction of regulations and the policing of assessment practitioners will not stamp out test abuse. Rather, individual assessment practitioners need to make the fair and ethical use of tests a norm for themselves. Consequently, the Psychometrics Committee has actively participated in the development of internationally acceptable standards for test use in conjunction with the International Test Commission's (ITC) test use project (see Section 2.2 and Chapter 8) and has developed certain competency-based training guidelines (see www.hpcsa.co.za). Furthermore, the various categories of psychology professionals who use tests have to write a national examination under the auspices of the Professional Board before they are allowed to practise professionally. Such a national examination helps to ensure that professionals enter the field with at least the same minimum discernible competencies. In Chapter 8, the different categories of assessment practitioners in South Africa will be discussed, as will their scope of practice and the nature of their training.

There is also a growing recognition amongst South African psychologists that many of the measures used in industry and the educational sector do not fall under the label of 'psychological tests'. Consequently, as the general public does not differentiate between whether or not a test is a psychological test, there is a need to set general standards for testing and test use in this country. This, together with the employment equity and labour relations legislation in industry, has led to repeated calls to define uniform test user standards across all types of tests and assessment settings and for a central body to enforce them (Foxcroft, Paterson, le Roux and Herbst, 2004). To date, such calls have fallen on deaf ears.

As you look back over this section, you should become aware that psychological assessment in South Africa has been and is currently being shaped by:
- legislation and the political dispensation of the day;
- the need for appropriate measures to be developed that can be used in a fair and unbiased way for people from all cultural groups in South Africa;
- the role that a new range of test development and distribution agencies and universities are playing to research, adapt and develop measures that are appropriate for our multicultural context;
- the need for assessment practitioners to take

personal responsibility for ethical test use; and
- training and professional practice guidelines provided by statutory (e.g. the Professional Board for Psychology) and other bodies (e.g. PsySSA, SIOPSA).

>> **CRITICAL THINKING CHALLENGE 2.2**

Spend some time finding the common threads or themes that run through the historical perspective of assessment from ancient to modern times, internationally and in the South African context.

2.4 Can assessment measures and the process of assessment still fulfil a useful function in modern society?

One thing that you have probably realized from reading through the historical account of the origins of psychological testing and assessment is that its popularity has waxed and waned over the years. However, despite the attacks on testing and the criticism levelled at it, psychological testing has survived, and new measures and test development technologies continue to be developed each year. Why do you think that this is so? Especially in the South African context do you think that, with all the negative criticisms against it, psychological testing and assessment can still play a valuable role? Think about this for a while before you read some of the answers to these questions that Foxcroft (1997b), Foxcroft, Paterson, le Roux, and Herbst (2004) and others have come up with for the South African context.

Ten academics involved in teaching psychological assessment at universities were asked whether there is a need for psychological tests in present day South Africa and they all answered 'Yes' (Plug, 1996). One academic went so far as to suggest that 'the need for tests in our multicultural country is greater than elsewhere because valid assessment is a necessary condition for equity and the efficient management of personal development' (Plug, 1996, p. 3). In a more recent survey by Foxcroft,

Paterson, le Roux, and Herbst (2004), the assessment practitioners surveyed suggested that the use of tests was central to the work of psychologists and that psychological testing was generally being perceived in a more positive light at present. Among the reasons offered for these perceptions was the fact that tests are objective in nature and more useful than alternative methods such as interviews. Further reasons offered were that tests provide structure in sessions with clients and are useful in providing baseline information, which can be used to evaluate the impact of training, rehabilitation or psychotherapeutic interventions. Nonetheless, despite psychological testing and assessment being perceived more positively, the practitioners pointed out that testing and assessment 'only added value if tests are culturally appropriate and psychometrically sound, and are used in a fair and an ethical manner by well-trained assessment practitioners' (Foxcroft, Paterson, le Roux and Herbst, 2004, p. 135).

Psychological testing probably continues to survive and to be of value because of the fact that assessment has become an integral part of modern society. Foxcroft (1997b) points out that, in his realistic reaction to the anti-test lobby, Nell (1994) argued that:

> psychological assessment is so deeply rooted in the global education and personnel selection systems, and in the administration of civil and criminal justice, that South African parents, teachers, employers, work seekers, and lawyers will continue to demand detailed psychological assessments (p. 105).

Furthermore, despite its obvious flaws and weaknesses, psychological assessment continues to aid decision-making, provided that it is used in a fair and ethical manner by responsible practitioners (Foxcroft, Paterson, le Roux and Herbst, 2004). Plug (1996) has responded in an interesting way to the criticisms leveled at testing. He contends that 'the question is not whether testing is perfect (which it obviously is not), but rather how it compares to alternative techniques of assessment for selection, placement or guidance, and whether, when used in combination with other processes, it leads to a more

reliable, valid, fair and cost effective result' (Plug, 1996, p. 5). Is there such evidence?

In the field of higher education for example, Huysamen (1996b) and Koch, Foxcroft, and Watson (2001) have shown that biographical information, matriculation results, and psychological test results predict performance at university and show promise in assisting in the development of fair and unbiased admission procedures at higher education institutions. In industry, 90 per cent of the human resource practitioners surveyed in a study conducted by England and Zietsman (1995) indicated that they used tests combined with interviews for job selection purposes and about 50 per cent used tests for employee development. This finding was confirmed by Foxcroft, Paterson, le Roux and Herbst (2004) when, as part of the HSRC's test use survey, it was found that 85 per cent of the industrial psychologists surveyed used psychological tests in work settings. In clinical practice, Shuttleworth-Jordan (1996) found that even if tests that had not been standardized for black children were used, a syndrome-based neuropsychological analysis model made it possible to make appropriate clinical judgements which 'reflect a convincing level of conceptual validity' (p. 99). Shuttleworth-Jordan (1996) argued that by focusing on common patterns of neuropsychological dysfunction rather than using a normative-based approach which relies solely on test scores, some of the problems related to the lack of appropriate normative information could be circumvented. Huysamen (2002), however, cautions that when practitioners need to rely more on professional judgement than objective, norm-based scores, they need to be aware that the conclusions and opinions 'based on so-called intuitions have been shown to be less accurate than those based on the formulaic treatment of data' (p. 31).

Foxcroft (1997b) contends that the examples cited above suggest that there is South African research evidence to support the value of psychological test information when it is used along with other pertinent information and clinical judgement to make decisions. Furthermore, Foxcroft (1997b) asserts that in the process of grappling with whether assessment can serve a useful purpose in South Africa:

attention has shifted away from a unitary testing approach to multi-method assessment. There was a tendency in the past to erroneously equate testing and assessment. In the process, clinicians forgot that test results were only one source of relevant data that could be obtained. However, there now appears to be a growing awareness of the fact that test results gain in meaning and relevance when they are integrated with information obtained from other sources and when they are reflected against the total past and present context of the testee (Claassen, 1995; Foxcroft, 1997b, p. 231).

To conclude this section, it could probably be argued that the anti-test lobby has impacted positively on the practice of psychological assessment in South Africa. On the one hand, psychology practitioners have taken a critical look at why and in what instances they use assessment measures as well as how to use tests in the fairest possible way in our multicultural society. On the other hand, it has forced researchers to provide empirical information regarding the usefulness of assessment measures.

>> **CRITICAL THINKING CHALLENGE 2.3**

You have been asked to appear on a TV talk show in which you need to convince the South African public that psychological assessment has an important role to play in post-apartheid South Africa. Write down what you plan to say on the talk show.

CHECKING YOUR PROGRESS 2.1

2.1 Define the following terms:
  • Phrenology
  • Graphology
  • Psychometrics
  • Standardized
2.2 Describe how the following has impacted on psychological test use and development in South Africa:
  • Apartheid
  • The Employment Equity Act

So far we are about one quarter of the way in our journey through the *Foundation Zone* on our map. Have you picked up some of the fundamental assessment concepts already? You should be developing an understanding that:
• psychological assessment is a complex process; and
• psychological measures/tests represent a scientific approach to enquiring into human behaviour; consequently they need to be applied in a standardized way and have to conform to rigorous scientific criteria (i.e. it must be empirically proved that they are reliable and valid and, especially in multicultural contexts, that they are not biased).

Let's move on to the next chapter where you can explore some of the foundational assessment concepts further.

Basic measurement and scaling concepts

GERT ROODT

Chapter

3

CHAPTER OUTCOMES

The next three chapters are the next stops in the Foundation Zone and they introduce you to the basic concepts needed for understanding the properties of psychological measures and how test results are interpreted. The topics covered in these three chapters include basic measurement and scaling concepts; reliability and validity. In the first chapter the following themes, namely, levels of measurement, measurement errors, measurement scales, basic statistical concepts, and test norms are introduced.

Once you have studied this chapter you will be able to:

> describe the three distinguishing properties of measurement levels;
> describe and give an example of the four different measurement levels;
> describe and give an example for each of the different measurement scales;
> explain for each of the different scaling methods what type of data (measurement level) it will generate;
> define and describe the three basic categories of statistical measures of location, variability and association; and
> name and describe the different types of test norms.

In order to understand and work with basic psychometric principles, you need to have a good understanding of some fundamental principles of statistics. If you have not completed a course in statistics, we suggest that you invest in an introductory text to statistics. Such a book should explain the basic statistical concepts and procedures which will be highlighted in this chapter.

3.1 **Levels of measurement**

Guilford (1936) referred to the great philosopher Kant who once asserted that the *sine qua non* of a science is measurement and the mathematical treatment of its data. He (Kant) therefore concluded that psychology could never rise to the dignity of a natural science because it is not possible to apply quantitative methods to its data. Guilford concluded that if Kant were to browse through one of the contemporary journals of psychology, he would at least be forced to conclude that psychologists as a group are expending a large amount of energy in maintaining the pretense that their work is science. Following this, Guilford then posed the question: What would be the motive of modern day scientists for spending this arduous amount of energy to express their findings in terms of statistical probability and significance coefficients? He then concluded it is all in our '…struggle for objectivity. Objectivity is after all the touchstone of science…' (p. 1) (own emphasis). This objectivity can be achieved through effective measurement. Measurement can be defined as (Runyon and Haber, 1980, p. 21):

> Measurement is the assignment of numbers to objects or events according to sets of predetermined (or arbitrary) rules, or to frame it more precisely in psychometric terms, the transformation of psychological attributes into numbers.

In psychometrics there are numerous systems by which we can assign numbers. These systems may generate data that have different properties. Let us have a closer look at these properties now.

3.1.1 **Properties of measurement scales/levels**

There are three properties that enable us to distinguish between different scales of measurement, namely magnitude, equal intervals, and absolute zero (De Beer, Botha, Bekwa and Wolfaardt, 1999).

3.1.1.1 **Magnitude**

Magnitude is the property of 'moreness'. A scale has the property of magnitude if we can say that one attribute is more than, less than or equal to another attribute. Let us take a tape measure, for example. We can say that one person is taller or shorter than another, or something is longer or shorter then something else, once we have measured their/its height/length. A measure of height/length therefore possesses the property of magnitude.

3.1.1.2 **Equal intervals**

A scale assumes the property of **equal intervals** if the difference between all points on that scale is uniform. If we take the example of length, this would mean that the difference between 6 and 8 centimetres on a ruler is the same as the difference between 10 and 12 centimetres. In both instances the difference is exactly 2 centimetres. In Example A on p. 29, an example of an equal interval response rating scale is provided. This response rating scale represents equal intervals and it would typically generate **continuous** data. In all instances the interval between scores is exactly one.

In the case of the scale in Example B, numbers are assigned to different categories. In this case, the distances between categories are not equal and this scale would typically generate **categorical** data.

Although the scale numbers in Example A possess equal intervals, one should however note that there is evidence that psychological measurements rarely have the property of equal intervals. For example, although the *numerical* difference between IQ scores of 50 and 55 is the same as the difference between 105 and 110, the *qualitative* difference of 5 points at the lower level does not mean the same in terms of intelligence as the difference of 5 points at the higher level.

3.1.1.3 **Absolute zero**

Absolute zero (0) is obtained when there is absolutely nothing present of the attribute being measured. If we take the example of length again, zero centimetres means that there is no distance. Length therefore possesses the property of absolute zero. By the same token, if you were measuring wind velocity and got a zero reading, you would say that there is no wind blowing at all.

With many human attributes it is extremely difficult, if not impossible, to define an absolute zero point. For example, if we measure verbal ability on a scale of zero to 10, we can hardly say that

Table 3.1 Equal interval scales

EXAMPLE A						
Totally disagree	1	2	3	4	5	Totally agree

EXAMPLE B				
Totally dis-agree	Disagree somewhat	Unsure	Agree some-what	Totally agree
1	2	3	4	5

a zero score means that the person has no verbal ability at all. There might be a level of ability that the particular scale does not measure; there can be no such thing as zero ability.

3.1.2 Categories of measurement levels

Some aspects of human behaviour can be measured more precisely than others. In part, this is determined by the nature of the attribute (characteristic) being measured. In part, this is also determined by the level of measurement of the scale used.

Measurement level is an important, but often overlooked, aspect in the construction of assessment measures because it remains an important consideration when data sets are analyzed. Measurement serves different functions, such as sorting, ordering, rating and comparisons. As a consequence numbers are used in different ways, namely to name (i.e. group according to a label - nominal numbers); to represent a position in a series (i.e. to order - ordinal numbers); and to represent quantity (i.e. rating or comparing - cardinal numbers).

Each of these measurement approaches results in different types of measurement data. Two broad groups of measurement data are found; namely **categorical data** and **continuous data**. **Categorical data** is in the form of discrete or distinct categories (e.g. males and females). Only a specific set of statistical procedures can be used for data analysis on categorical (discrete) data sets. Categorical measurement data, in turn, can be divided into nominal and ordinal measurement levels:

- **Nominal**: With a nominal scale, numbers are assigned to an attribute to describe or name it, such as telephone numbers or postal box numbers. For example, a nominal measurement scale

is used if the eleven official languages of South Africa are coded from 1 to 11 in a data set or if the 15 positions of a rugby team rank players from 1 to 15. Languages or rugby players can then be sorted according to these numbers.

- **Ordinal**: An ordinal scale is a bit more refined than a nominal scale in that numbers are assigned to objects that reflect some sequential ordering or amounts of an attribute. For example, people are ranked according to the order in which they finished a race or in terms of the results of their class test.

Continuous data represents data that have been measured on a continuum which can be broken down into smaller units (e.g. height or weight). Furthermore, continuous data can be divided into two subdivisions, namely, interval and ratio measurement levels:

- **Interval**: In an interval scale, equal numerical differences can be interpreted as corresponding to equal differences in the characteristic being measured. An example would be employees' rating of their company's market image on a ten-point scale (where 1 is poor and 10 is excellent). IQ test scores are usually considered to be an interval scale. Why? A difference between two individuals' IQ scores can be numerically determined (e.g. the difference between IQ scores of 100 and 150 is 50, or between 100 and 50 is also 50). However, as was pointed out in Section 3.1.1.2, the meaning of a difference between two IQ scores would be very different if the difference was between 150 and 100 rather than between 50 and 100. Example A can be classified as an interval scale.

- **Ratio**: This is the most refined level of

measurement. Not only can equal difference be interpreted as reflecting equal differences in the characteristic being measured, but there is a true (absolute) zero which indicates complete absence of what is being measured. The inclusion of a true zero allows for the meaningful interpretation of numerical ratios. For example, length is measured on a ratio scale. If a table is 6 metres away from you while a chair is 3 metres away from you, it would be correct to state that the table is twice as far away from you as the chair. Can you think of an example related to a psychological characteristic? No. The scores on psychological measures, depending on the response scales used, either represent ordinal or, at the most, interval data rather than ratio measurement, since they do not have a true zero point.

Continuous data, if normally distributed, are ideally suited for a wide range of parametric statistical analysis procedures. Selecting a particular measuring instrument that will generate data suitable to your needs is no safeguard against measurement errors. Psychometricians and researchers should therefore always be aware of possible measurement errors.

3.2 Measurement errors

In most measurement settings two broad types of errors may occur. They are random sampling errors and systematic errors. The scores generated by measuring instruments can potentially be negatively affected by either sampling or measurement errors (or both these errors). Stated differently, this means that causes of measurement errors can be attributed to sampling, the measure itself or the combination between these two factors. These errors will be briefly introduced here and discussed in more detail in the next chapters.

3.2.1 Random sampling errors

Random sampling error can be defined as (Zikmund, 2003, p. 176):

> Random sampling error occurs if a random sample from a population and a census from that same population differ only because of chance factors present in the sample.

The effects of these chance factors, referred to as random sampling error, are normally countered by increasing the sample size. In practical terms this means that larger sample sizes (e.g. >500) yield more accurate data than smaller sample sizes (e.g. <100) for the standardization or validation of measuring instruments, since they can estimate the population parameters more accurately (less measurement error). This has important implications for sampling norm groups that are representative of particular populations. Sampling errors may therefore produce erroneous and skewed data.

3.2.2 Systematic error

Systematic errors or non-sampling errors are defined as (Zikmund, 2003, p. 177):

> Systematic errors or non-sampling errors are attributable to some systematic error in the execution of the research design (or in the application of the measure).

Systematic error or measurement bias is present where the results show a persistent tendency to deviate in a particular direction from the population parameter. This type of error can be ascribed to possible measurement error or bias. Measurement errors may therefore also negatively affect the scores obtained from norm groups.

The way in which measurement scales are constructed can help psychometrists and researchers to counter the effects of measurement errors, specifically those of response bias and non-response errors. Non-response error is the real difference between the actual respondents in a survey and those who have decided not to participate (if they could be objectively surveyed). Response bias on the other hand is a tendency that occurs if respondents choose to respond to questions in a set manner. Both these errors can be minimized if the principles of sound scale construction are adhered to.

3.3 **Measurement scales**

In psychological measurement (psychometrics), we are mostly dealing with the measurement of abstract (intangible) constructs. Although these constructs are not visible or tangible, it does not mean that they do not exist. We can still measure their existence in the different ways that they manifest themselves. For instance we can measure intelligence by assessing people's ability to solve complex problems; or by assessing their mental reasoning ability, or sometimes even by the way people drive.

3.3.1 **Different scaling options**

In deciding on possible measurement formats of these abstract constructs we have a choice of using different measuring scales. The choices we make in this regard can potentially lead to generating data on different measurement levels. (For a more comprehensive discussion on scaling methods refer to Schnetler, 1989). Lets us consider some of the most frequently used scales:

3.3.1.1 **Category scales**

Category scales are, as the name suggests, scales where the response categories are categorized or defined. According to both Torgerson (1958) and Schepers (1992) a scale loses its equal interval properties if more than two points on the response scale are anchored. Usually several response categories exist in category scales and they are ordered in some ascending dimension; in the case below – the frequency of use. This type of scale would generate categorical data; more specifically ordinal data.

How frequently do you make use of public transport?

Never	Rarely	Sometimes	Often	All the time
(1)	(2)	(3)	(4)	(5)

Figure 3.1 Category scale

3.3.1.2 **Likert-type scales**

The Likert scale or summated rating method was developed by Rensis Likert (1932). Likert-type scales are frequently used in applied psychological research. Respondents have to indicate to what extent they agree or disagree with a carefully phrased statement or question. These types of items will generate categorical data. Below are two examples of such response scales:

My supervisor can be described as an approachable person.

Strongly disagree	Disagree	Uncertain	Agree	Strongly agree
(1)	(2)	(3)	(4)	(5)

Or

Strongly disagree	Disagree	Neutral	Agree	Strongly agree
(-2)	(-1)	(0)	(+1)	(+2)

Figure 3.2 Likert-type scale

The supervisor can be rated on different dimensions that then provide a profile of the supervisor according to the different rated dimensions. The combined scores on several of these items would provide a composite (summated) score of the supervisor in terms of how favourable or unfavourable he was rated overall. In the case of the second response scale example above, a zero is used to indicate a neutral or uncertain response. Any idea on what problem will occur if scores on such response scales in the latter example are added? Respondents may therefore opt for the zero if they find the choice difficult, resulting in an abnormally peaked (leptokurtic) response distribution.

3.3.1.3 **Semantic differential scales**

Semantic differential scales provide a series of semantic differentials or opposites. The respondent is then requested to rate a particular person, attribute or subject in terms of these bipolar descriptions of the person or object. Only the extreme poles are in this instance described or anchored. An example of such a scale is the following:

How would you best describe your supervisor?

Emotional	1	2	3	4	5	6	7	Intellectual
Conventional	1	2	3	4	5	6	7	Modern
Lazy	1	2	3	4	5	6	7	Active
Traditional	1	2	3	4	5	6	7	Progressive

Figure 3.3 Semantic differential scale

The scores obtained on the different dimensions would provide an overall profile of the supervisor. This format is often referred to as a numerical scale or an intensity scale and equal intervals are assumed in this case.

3.3.1.4 **Intensity scales**

Intensity scales are very similar to the response scales described in paragraph 3.3.1.3. In this case several questions are posed and the extreme poles of the response scales are anchored and there are no descriptors of categories between these two anchors. Examples of two items and their respective response scales (five and seven point) are listed below:

How approachable is your supervisor?

Not approach-able at all	1	2	3	4	5	6	7	Highly ap-proachable

How frequently are you in disagreement with your supervisor?

Never	1	2	3	4	5	6	7	Always

Figure 3.4 Intensity scale

The number of response categories (e.g. five or seven) may be decided on, depending on the sophistication level of the respondent group. It is generally accepted that more sophisticated groups can deal more effectively with a wider range of response options. In this instance, the assessor will assume equal interval properties of the scale, which makes it an interval scale.

3.3.1.5 **Constant-sum scales**

In the constant-sum method (Torgerson, 1958) the respondent is requested to allocate a fixed percentage or proportion of marks between different available options, thereby indicating the relative value or weight of each option. The following is an example of such an ipsative scale:

Divide 100 points among the following characteristics of customer service you have received from company A:

Delivery on time	30
Quality products	50
Affordable price	20
	100 points

Figure 3.5 Constant-sum scale

By framing several similar questions the attributes are compared to different characteristics, thereby determining their relative weight.

3.3.1.6 **Paired comparison scales**

Paired comparison scales (one of Torgerson's (1958) fractioning techniques) function on the same principle as described above, except that they only compare two characteristics or attributes at a time. Respondents are in this instance requested to divide 100 marks between or allocate 100 points to two attributes. This procedure is then repeated where the same attribute is also systematically compared with all other attributes (compare Claassen, Schepers and Roodt, 2004). The following example illustrates this ipsative scale:

Divide 100 points between the two opposing values

Professionalism	20	80	Integrity
Integrity	60	40	Transparency
Competence	55	45	Professionalism

Figure 3.6 Paired comparison scale

This procedure allows one to determine an overall comparative weighting or ranking for each value.

3.3.1.7 **Graphic rating scales**

In the case of graphic rating scales the response scale is presented in the form of a visual display. The respondent would then indicate which option best represents his/her choice or attitude. The smiling faces scale and ladder scale are frequently used variations in this case. An example of the smiling faces scale is displayed below:

How happy do you feel today?

Very unhappy    Very happy

Figure 3.7 Graphic rating scale

A word of caution needs to be mentioned here. Smiling faces may mean different things to different cultures. If this response format is therefore used in a multi-cultural context, it should be kept in mind that the obtained ratings may be culturally biased.

3.3.1.8 **Forced choice scales**

In some cases where intra individual differences have to be assessed, one can also make use of forced choice scales. The individual would in this instance choose the option that describes him or her best. Provided below is an example of this ipsative scale that would generate nominal data:

How do you typically respond in a conflict situation? (tick the box that describes you best)

☐ I dislike conflict. I avoid it whenever I can

☐ I thrive on conflict. I search for conflict situations

☐ I feel pretty neutral about conflict. I do not search or avoid it

☐ I am unsure how to respond to this question

Figure 3.8 Forced choice scale generating nominal data

The following item example will generate ordinal data:

How do you typically respond in a conflict situation? (tick the box that describes you best)

☐ I dislike conflict. I avoid it whenever I can

☐ I feel neutral about conflict. I do not search or avoid it.

☐ I thrive on conflict. I will search for conflict situations

Figure 3.9 Forced choice scale generating ordinal data

A last type of scale is the following:

3.3.1.9 **Guttman scales**

Guttman scales are normally used in social psychology or in attitude and prejudice research. This method was initially developed to test the single dimensionality of a set of items. Stated differently, it is to test whether items belong to the same attitude dimension. A total attitude is defined and a set of sample items is developed that represent this universe of possible items of the total attitude. A respondent is then requested to respond to each item of such a scale. The number of items the respondent answered in the affirmative would reflect his/her score on this attitude. An example of such a scale is presented below:

My attitude about crime is based on my experience of an incident that happened in -

	Yes	No
The vicinity of the neighbourhood I live in	1	0
The neighbourhood I live in	1	0
The street I live in	1	0
The house of a next-door neighbour	1	0
My own home	1	0

Figure 3.10 Guttman scale

This example would for instance assess the degree of exposure a person had to crime.

Several considerations have to be kept in mind when designing items and response scales.

3.3.2 **Considerations in deciding on a scale format**

If you were to design a measurement scale, you will have to keep several considerations in mind in order to affect the properties of the data that you will generate with this measure.

3.3.2.1 **A single dimensional versus a composite scale**

Is your scale multi-dimensional or does it measure only a single dimensional construct? This consideration is determined by the underlying theoretical definition of the construct. If the theoretical definition suggests a single dimension, the scale should then be operationalised in a similar manner. In the case of multi-dimensional theoretical definitions the scale should then also be multi-dimensional; that is, measuring multiple facets.

3.3.2.2 Question versus statement item formats

A consideration that test or questionnaire designers often have to face is whether they should make use of question or statement item formats. Research by Hanekom and Visser (1998) experimentally tested whether items formulated in question or statement formats would yield different response distributions. Their research did not find any significant differences. Some researchers (e.g. Schepers, 1992; Swart, Roodt and Schepers, 1999) however suggest that statement items generate extreme responses resulting in response distributions that are approximately bi-modally shaped as opposed to question items that result in more normally distributed (mesokurtic) response distributions.

3.3.2.3 Type of response labels versus unlabelled response categories

If assessors need to determine which type of response categories they are going to use, they may decide to use category descriptors and assign numbers to each category (measurement on a nominal level). Alternatively, assessors can decide to get rid of all category descriptors, except for the extreme ends, as in the cases of semantic differential scales or intensity scales (measurement on an interval level). These two approaches will lead to distinctively different levels of measurement and data characteristics.

3.3.2.4 A single attribute versus comparative rating formats

Assessors may decide to assess only one particular construct (e.g. job satisfaction) with an assessment instrument. All items of this instrument will thus tap into this construct. Or alternatively, they can decide to comparatively assess different constructs (e.g. price, quality or service delivery of a product) in order to determine their relative importance or weight as perceived by the respondents.

3.3.2.5 Even-numbered versus odd-numbered rating options

A question assessors are frequently confronted with is: How many response categories should be included for each item? Should it be five or seven? Or should it be four or six? Or should there be an even or an odd-number of response options? There is no easy answer – it all depends on who the targeted respondents are. It is known that less sophisticated respondents find it conceptually difficult to deal with many response options. For instance, if your respondents only have primary school education (e.g. grade 7) a three or four point response scale may be most appropriate.

It is a known fact that lesser response categories (3 or 4) have a truncation effect (restriction of range) as opposed to more response categories (6 or 7) that result in a wider range of scores. In the latter case such measures have higher reliability coefficients. An uneven number of response categories may also result in respondents to opt for the neutral middle position as opposed to even-numbered response categories.

3.3.2.6 Ipsative scales versus normative scale options

Forced choice scales lead to ipsative measurements which only have restricted intra-individual application value, because there can be no normative comparison base. Normative scales on the other hand have the advantage that assessors can establish a normative comparison base for a scale which gives the scale a far wider application potential.

3.4 Basic statistical concepts

Psychological assessment measures or survey instruments often produce data in the form of numbers. We need to be able to make sense of these numbers. Basic statistical concepts can help us here, as well as when it comes to establishing and interpreting norm scores. Statistical concepts and techniques can also help us to understand and establish basic psychometric properties of measures such as validity and reliability.

It is recommended that you study sections 3.4.1 to 3.4.4 below while working through the relevant topics in an introductory statistical textbook.

3.4.1 Displaying data

We cannot interpret a set of data consisting of rows and columns (a matrix) of figures sensibly.

One meaningful way to make sense of the data is to plot it, that is, to display it graphically by constructing either a histogram or a line graph. From this graphic representation you can get an idea whether the characteristic being measured is normally distributed or whether the distribution is skewed in any way, in which case it could tell you something about how difficult or easy a test is. In an easy test, many people would answer the questions correctly and the distribution would be negatively skewed. In a difficult test, few people would answer the questions correctly and the distribution would thus be positively skewed (see Figure 3.11).

3.4.2 **Measures of central tendency (location)**

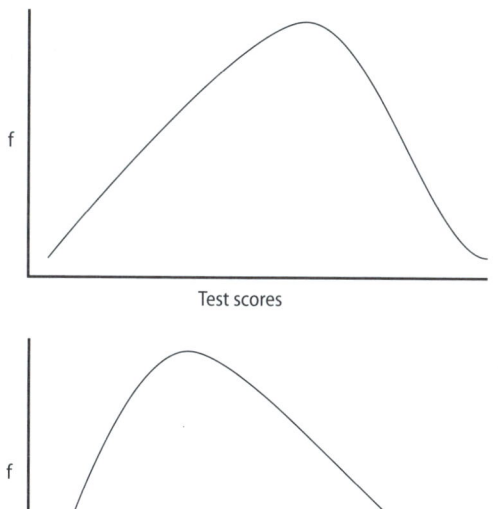

Figure 3.11 Negatively and positively skewed distributions

Measures of central tendency are numerical values that best reflect the centre of a distribution of scores. There are three measures of central tendency – the **mean** (denoted by $\overline{X}$ which is the arithmetic average), the **median** (denoted by M_e which is the middle point of the distribution), and the **mode**

(denoted by M_o which is the most frequently occurring score). No formula exists for calculating the mode, except for counting the most frequently recorded score.

The formula for calculating the arithmetic mean (denoted as $\overline{X}$) is as follows (Howell, 1995):

$$\overline{X} = \frac{\Sigma X}{N}$$

formula 3.1

The mean ($\overline{X}$) is thus calculated by the sum (Σ) of all scores divided by the number (N) of the scores.

The formula for calculating the median (M_e) is as follows (Howell, 1995):

$$M_e = \frac{N+1}{2}$$

formula 3.2

The median position thus presents the score where 50% of the distribution is below that point and the other 50% is above that point.

In Table 3.2 (on p. 36) we have a fictitious data set of 10 machine operators. The shaded column on the extreme left presents the individual machine operators (A–J), the second and third column their aptitude scores (lighter shaded columns for odd and even-numbered items) as well as their combined (total) scores in the fifth column, and the job performance scores in the sixth column. We will use this example to do some very basic calculations to illustrate the different concepts that we want to introduce.

Now see if you can determine the following values.

SELF-ASSESSMENT EXERCISE **3.1**

Calculate the means for the test scores provided in Table 3.2 using the formulae provided above (please note that upper and lower case descriptors are used):
(a)   What is the mean score for column x?
(b)   What is the mode for scores in column y?
(c)   What is the median position for scores in column X?
You can find the answers at the end of the chapter.

Table 3.2 Aptitude and job performance scores of machine operators

OPERATOR	APTITUDE TEST X SCORES				JOB PER-FORMANCE SCORES (Y)	PRODUCT OF XY
	Score for Odd items (x)	Score for Even items (y)	Product of xy	Total score (X)		
A	5	6	30	11	7	77
B	8	10	80	18	8	144
C	7	7	49	14	10	140
D	8	9	72	17	8	136
E	7	6	42	13	6	78
F	6	8	48	14	9	126
G	5	4	20	9	6	54
H	8	7	56	15	9	135
I	6	5	30	11	8	88
J	2	3	6	5	6	30
	$\Sigma x = 62$	$\Sigma y = 65$	$\Sigma xy = 433$	$\Sigma X = 127$	$\Sigma Y = 77$	$\Sigma XY = 1008$
		$\Sigma x \Sigma y = 4030$			$\Sigma X \Sigma Y = 9779$	

3.4.3 Measures of variability

A measure of variability is a statistic that indicates the degree to which individual scores are distributed around the mean. The **range** (i.e. the difference between the largest and smallest score) is the simplest measure of variability to compute.

The **variance** gives an indication of how scores vary about the mean or how they deviate from the mean $(\overline{X} - X)$. You will find that half of these scores will have positive values while the other half has negative values, with the result that the sum of these deviations will always equal zero. By squaring the deviations one can overcome the problem of the zero sum (squared minuses become a plus) and the outcome will therefore always have a positive value. The variance (denoted as S^2) can now be calculated as the sum of the squared deviations about the mean, divided by $N - 1$. According to Runyon and Haber (1980) the formula for the variance is as follows:

$$S^2 = \Sigma \frac{(\overline{X} - X)^2}{N-1} = \frac{N\Sigma X^2 - (\Sigma X)^2}{N-1}$$

formula 3.3

SELF-ASSESSMENT EXERCISE 3.2

Can you determine the following ranges of the different sets of scores in Table 3.2?
(a) for the scores in column X?
(b) for the scores in column Y?

You can find the answers at the end of the chapter.

SELF-ASSESSMENT EXERCISE 3.3

(a) Can you calculate the variance for the scores in column x of Table 3.2?

The **standard deviation (SD)** represents the most common form of variability that can be computed. It is simply the **square root of the variance** and is also referred to as **sigma** (Runyon and Haber, 1980):

$$S = \sqrt{S^2} = \sqrt{\frac{N\Sigma X^2 - (\Sigma X)^2}{N-1}}$$

formula 3.4

SELF-ASSESSMENT EXERCISE 3.4

(a) What is the standard deviation of the obtained variance in column y of Table 3.2?

3.4.4 **Measures of association**

Looking at the psychometric data in Table 3.2, you might wonder: Do the machine operators who score high on the aptitude test also have high job performance scores? When you ask whether one variable (X) is related to another variable (Y), the statistic you have to compute is the **correlation coefficient** (also denoted as r). The correlation coefficient is calculated as the **covariance of XY divided by the product of the variances** of the two moments (X and Y) and can be portrayed as (Howell, 1995):

$$r = \frac{COV_{xy}}{S_x S_y}$$

formula 3.5

Runyon and Haber (1980) propose that this formula can be simplified further by replacing the variances and covariances with their computational formulae and by resolving the equation. This formula is also known as the **Pearson product-moment correlation**:

$$r = \frac{N\Sigma XY - \Sigma X\Sigma Y}{\sqrt{[N\,\Sigma X^2 - (\Sigma X)^2] \cdot [N\Sigma Y^2 - (\Sigma Y)^2]}}$$

formula 3.6

SELF-ASSESSMENT EXERCISE 3.5

(a) Now see if you can calculate the Pearson correlation between columns x and y from the values in Table 3.2.

Having determined that a relationship exists between two variables, for instance the aptitude scores of the machine operators and their job performance, you can compute a simple **regression equation** so that job performance can be predicted from the aptitude test scores (**one predictor and one criterion**). We can use this information to build a prediction model. The greater the magnitude (size) of the correlation between the two measures (X and Y), the more accurate the prediction will be (of $\hat{Y}$ from X). However, we need to know the values of the slope (b) and the intercept (a) first, before we can resolve the **simple regression equation** (Howell, 1995):

$$Y = bX + a$$

formula 3.7

The value of the slope (b) and the intercept (a) can be calculated, once we know the value of r (Howell, 1995).

$$b = \frac{COV_{xy}}{S_x^2} = r\left(\frac{S_y}{S_x}\right) = \frac{N\Sigma XY - \Sigma X\Sigma Y}{N\Sigma X^2 - (\Sigma X)^2}$$

formula 3.8

Since we know the value of b, we can now proceed by calculating the value of a by using the following formula (Howell, 1995):

$$a = \overline{Y} - b\overline{X} = \frac{\Sigma Y - b\Sigma X}{N}$$

formula 3.9

SELF-ASSESSMENT EXERCISE 3.6

(a) Can you calculate the values of a and b from your calculated values of ΣX and ΣY in Table 3.2?

(b) With the values of a and b known now, what would the predicted values of $\hat{Y}$ be, if we have an X value of 15?

In the case of multiple predictors (X and C), the equation slightly changes to become a **multiple regression equation**:

$$\hat{Y} = b_1 X + b_1 C + a$$
formula 3.10

In the case of the multiple regression equation the b_1 denotes the different regression weights of the predictor variables X and C with a as the value of the intercept.

3.5 **Norms**

We have alluded earlier in the book to the fact that some measures may be norm-referenced while others are criterion-referenced. We pointed out that with norm-referenced measures each test-taker's performance is interpreted with reference to a relevant standardization sample or norm group. Criterion-referenced measures on the other hand compare the test-taker's performance to the attainment of a defined skill or content. The last of the basic concepts in testing that you need to understand before studying the rest of the book is **norms**. We will discuss definitions and types of norms in this section.

Other aspects concerning the use of norms and interpretation of test scores are covered in Chapters 5 and 16.

3.5.1 **The standard normal distribution**

Many human characteristics measured in psychology are assumed to be normally distributed in the population. The normal distribution, which is constantly referred to in psychometrics, is the standard normal (bell-shaped) distribution, which has a mean of zero and a standard deviation of 1.

Raw scores obtained by test-takers on psychological measures have little or no meaning. In order to make the interpretation more meaningful, these raw scores are converted to normal (standardized) scores through statistical transformation. A norm can therefore be defined as:

A norm is a measurement against which an individual's raw score is evaluated so that the individual's position relative to that of the normative sample can be determined.

The procedure for establishing such normative samples or norm groups is of crucial importance in any selection procedure. Let us briefly have a look at norm groups.

3.5.2 **Establishing norm groups**

Norm groups consist of two sub-groups, namely the applicant pool and the incumbent population. The choice of such a norm group has to be representative of both the applicant pool and the incumbent population as well as appropriate for the position the assessment is conducted for. The similarities between the norm group on the one hand and applicant and the incumbent groups on the other hand are established by means of comparative aspects such as ethnicity, gender, age and educational background (Society for Industrial and Organisational Psychology of South Africa (SIOPSA), 2006b).

This can explained in more practical terms as follows: Say for instance we want to establish a norm group as the comparative base for our pilot selection test battery. The norm group should then be selected from both the pool of applicants for pilot training (the applicant group – not yet competent) and the population of licensed pilots (the incumbent group – already competent). The norm group should thus be representative of these two groups as is reflected by similar proportions of the biographic data of these two groups.

The entire test battery is then completed by the norm group. Standardized or normal scores (any one of the types of scores explained below) are calculated for each of the tests in the battery. New applicants' test scores can now be compared to these newly established standardized (normal) scores.

3.5.3 **Co-norming of measures**

It often happens that an assessment practitioner wants to compare scores obtained on different, but related measures, in order to test for possible learning or memory effects. This is where the practice of co-norming comes into play.

> Co-norming entails the process where two or more related, but different measures are administered and standardized as a unit on the same norm group.

This practice can address a range of potential issues such as test-order effects (between such measures); learning and memory effects; gender, age and education effects; and variations of scaling format effects.

A recent study that has used co-norming in an attempt to test for gender, age and education effects was the study by Kern, Nuechterlein, Green et al. (2008) where the consensus cognitive battery was used developed by the National Institute of Mental Health's (NIMH) Measurement and Treatment Research to Improve Cognition in Schizophrenia (MATRICS) initiative. This battery includes 10 independently developed tests that are recommended as the standard battery for clinical trials of cognition-enhancing interventions for schizophrenia. In this case age, education and gender effects were detected.

Another, but more dated study is that of Zhu and Tulsky (2000) where the WAIS-III and the WMS-III scores were evaluated using the same WMS-III standardization sample. In this instance the study detected significant test-order effects, but only with small effect sizes.

Co-norming may yield several practical benefits where the same norm group is used for comparable, but different measures. A range of different effects can tested for such as test-order, learning and memory effects. These issues cannot be addressed if different norm groups are used. The problem where obtained effects are merely ascribed to sample differences can now be overcome by using a common sample group.

3.5.4 **Types of test norms**

We will discuss the most commonly used norm scores. The description of the norm scales is based on Anastasi and Urbina (1997) and Smit (1996). You are referred to these references for a detailed discussion of the topic.

3.5.4.1 **Developmental scales**

The rationale of developmental scales is that certain human characteristics increase progressively with increases in age and experience.

- **Mental age scales:** A so-called basal age is computed, that is, the highest age at and below which a measure was passed. A child's mental age on a measure is the sum of the basal age plus additional months of credit earned at higher age levels. The development of a child with a mental age of ten years corresponds to the mental development of the average ten-year-old child, no matter what his/her chronological age is.

- **Grade equivalents**: Scores on educational achievement measures are often interpreted in terms of grade equivalents. Used in a school setting, a pupil's grade value, for example, is described as equivalent to seventh-grade performance in arithmetic, eighth-grade in spelling, and fifth-grade in reading. It is used especially for expressing performance on standardized scholastic measures. Drawbacks of this scale are that scale units are not necessarily equal and that they represent the median performance with overlapping from one grade to another.

3.5.4.2 **Percentiles**

A percentile score is the percentage of people in a normative standardization sample who fall below a given raw score. If an individual obtains a percentile score of 70, it means that 70 per cent of the normative population obtained a raw score lower than the individual. Percentiles are frequently used for individual test performance. The 50th percentile corresponds to the median. The 25th and 75th percentiles are known as the first (Q1) and third (Q3) quartiles respectively as they cut off the lowest and highest quarters of the normal distribution.

Percentiles should not be confused with percentages. The latter are raw scores expressed in terms of percentage correct answers, while percentiles are derived scores, expressed in terms of percentage of persons surpassing a specific raw score.

The disadvantage of percentiles is the inequality of their scale units, especially at the extreme ends of the distribution. In addition, percentile ranks are ordinal level measures, and cannot be used for normal arithmetic calculations. Percentile ranks calculated for various variables and on various populations are not directly comparable.

3.5.4.3 Standard scores

Standard scores can be classified as z-scores, linearly transformed z-scores, and normalized standard scores.

- **Z-scores**. A z-score expresses an individual's distance from the mean in terms of standard deviation units. A raw score equal to the mean is equal to a z-score of zero. Positive z-scores indicate above average performance and negative z-scores below average performance.
- Advantages of z-scores are that they represent interval level measurements and may thus be statistically manipulated. The frequency distribution of z-scores has the same form as the raw scores on which they are based. Disadvantages are that half of the z-scores in a distribution have negative values and the range of the distribution of the scores is limited (from −3.0 to +3.0).
- **Linearly transformed standard scores**. To eliminate the disadvantages of z-scores the following linear transformation can be done:

  - multiply Z by a constant (A) (to compensate for the limited range of scores); and
  - add a constant (B) (to eliminate negative scores).

In formula form this would appear as follows:

$Z_{LT} = AZ + B$
formula 3.11

It is recommended that A = 10 and B = 50 be used.

The disadvantages are that these scores are less evident than ordinary z-scores and they are statistically more complex and less useful.

- **Normalized standard score**. Normalized standard scores are standard scores that have been transformed to fit a normal distribution. This is done if there is a reason to assume that the particular human attribute (e.g. intelligence) is normally distributed in the population. If the original distribution of raw scores was skew, z-values based on the table for normal distribution curves are allocated to different raw scores than they would have been if the distribution of test scores had been normal. The advantage is that the distribution of test scores corresponds to the normal distribution. The disadvantages are the same as for z-scores as well as the fact that normalized standard scores change the form of the original distribution of raw scores.

Three frequently used normalized standard scores are McCall's T-score, stanine scores, and sten scores.

McCall's T-score. To eliminate negative values, a transformation to a more convenient standard scale is done using McCall's T-score, where the mean is equal to 50 and the standard deviation to 10. Normalized standard scores, Z_N, are transformed as follows:

$T = Z_N 10 + 50$
formula 3.12

Stanine scale. Another well-known and frequently used transformed scale is the stanine (a contraction of 'standard nine'), with a range from 1 (low) to 9 (high), a mean of 5, and a standard deviation of 1.96. The normal distribution curve percentages which fall into each of the nine categories are given in Table 3.2.

Some advantages of the stanine scale are the following:

- scale units are equal;
- it reflects the person's position in relation to the normative sample;
- performance in rank order is evident;
- they are comparable across groups; and
- they allow statistical manipulation.

The disadvantage is that it is an approximate scale because it has only 9 scale units.

Sten scale. The rationale for the sten scale (a contraction of 'standard ten') is the same as for the stanine scale except that it consists of 10 scale units. The mean is 5.5 and the standard

Table 3.3 Normal curve percentages for the stanine scale

STANINE	1	2	3	4	5	6	7	8	9
PERCENTAGE	4	7	12	17	20	17	12	7	4

Table 3.4 Normal curve percentages for the sten scale

STEN	1	2	3	4	5	6	7	8	9	10
PERCENTAGE	2	5	9	15	19	19	15	9	5	2

deviation 2. The normal distribution curve percentages which fall into each of the 10 categories are given in Table 3.4.

The sten scale has the same advantages and disadvantages as the stanine scale.

3.5.4.4 Deviation IQ scale

This scale, which is used by well-known individual intelligence measures (see Chapter 10), is a normalized standard score with a mean of 100 and a standard deviation of 15. Some of the advantages are that this scale is easily comprehensible and interpretable and that it is suitable for age levels above 18. The disadvantage is that it is not directly comparable with transformed standard scores, because the standard deviations differ. If measure ABC has a mean of 100 and a standard deviation of 10, a score of 130 is three standard deviation units above the mean. If measure PQR also has a mean of 100 but a standard deviation of 15, a score of 130 is only two standard deviation units above the mean.

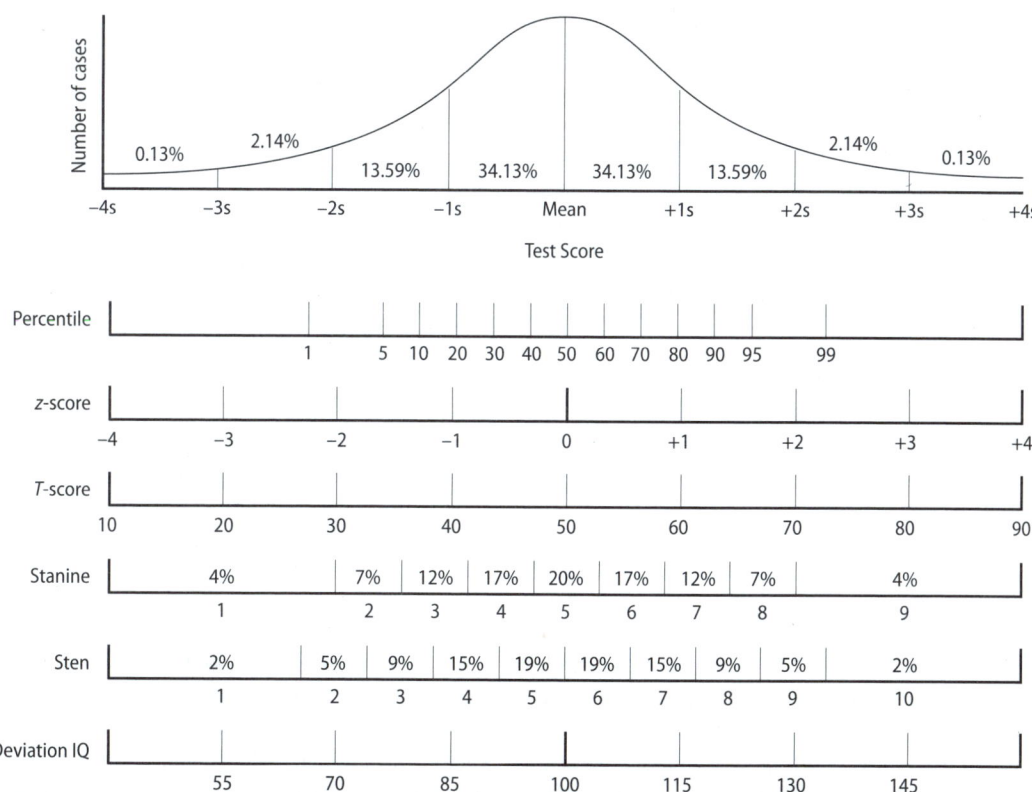

Figure 3.12 Interrelationship between various types of test norm scores

3.5.5 **Interrelationships of norm scores**

The choice of a norm score for a newly developed measure depends mainly on personal preference. Standard scores and the deviation IQ have generally replaced other types of norm scores such as percentiles due to the advantages they offer (as mentioned in Section 3.5.2) with regard to the statistical treatment of test data. Provided they meet certain statistical requirements, each of these scores can be converted to any of the others.

An inspection of Figure 3.12 will show you how the various types of norm scores are interrelated. Note the relative position of the mean and standard deviation of the standard normal distribution with reference to the various types of norm scores.

3.5.6 **Setting standards and cut-off scores**

As you have seen in Section 3.5 so far, the use of norms to interpret test scores usually involves comparing an individual to a group of people. That is, a norm score tells you an individual's standing in relation to the norm group. There is another way in which test scores can be interpreted. Instead of finding out how an individual has performed in relation to others, you can compare performance to an external criterion (standard). For example, in the psychometrics examination that is set by the Professional Board for Psychology, the passing standard has been set at 70 per cent. Someone who obtains a mark of 60 per cent may have performed better than a classmate who obtained 50 per cent (norm-referenced comparison), but would fail the examination nonetheless, as his/her percentage is below that of the 70 per cent standard (cut-off) that has been set.

Particularly in settings where large numbers of people are assessed, it is necessary to set cut-off scores to determine who passes or fails the measure, for accepting or rejecting job applicants, or for deciding who does or does not receive treatment or further assessment. The process by which cut-off scores are determined in relation to a criterion for a measure involves a 'complex set of legal, professional, and psychometric issues' (Murphy and Davidshofer, 1998, p. 105). One way of

setting cut-off scores, is to draw up an **expectancy table** that tabulates performance on the predictor measure against the criterion variable. If we take the example of the machine operators that we have used throughout this chapter, Table 3.5 represents an expectancy table that shows the relationship between scores on the aptitude measure and job performance ratings, which have been classified as successful or unsuccessful.

From an expectancy table you can determine the probability that a person who obtains a certain aptitude score will be a successful machine operator, for example. A person who obtains an aptitude score of 5 has only a 10 per cent probability of being successful, while a person who obtains a score of 18 has a 90 per cent probability. An expectancy table can also be represented graphically by plotting the relation between performance on the predictor and success on the criterion.

The main advantage of **cut-off scores** and expectancy tables is that they provide an easily understandable way of interpreting the relationship between test scores and probable levels of success on a criterion (Murphy and Davidshofer, 1998). There are, however, pitfalls associated with using cut-off scores and expectancy tables. In the first instance, correlation data can be unstable from sample to sample, so large sample sizes need to be used when establishing cut-off scores to avoid this. A second important consideration is related to the magnitude of the correlation between the predictor and criterion variables. The higher the relationship, the more faith we will have in the accuracy of our predictions. Thirdly, a criterion changes over time (e.g. as job requirements change); this will influence the relationship between the test scores (predictor) and the criterion and will impact on the accuracy of decisions made based on these scores. Fourthly, throughout this book, assessment practitioners are encouraged to base a decision on more than one test score. Thus, even when cut-off scores are used, attempts should be made to have a band of cut-off scores, rather than a single cut-off score. Furthermore, other assessment information should be considered alongside the predictive information obtained from cut-off scores and expectancy tables before any decision is reached.

Table 3.5 Expectancy table

APTITUDE SCORE	NUMBER OF PEOPLE	JOB RATING: SATISFACTORY (PERCENTAGE)	JOB RATING: UNSATISFACTORY (PERCENTAGE)
16–20	10	90	10
11–15	8	80	20
6–10	15	30	70
Below 5	10	10	90

A final word of caution regarding the use of cut-off scores to predict performance on a criterion. A measure may have differential predictive validity in relation to a criterion for various subgroups (e.g. gender, culture). In such an instance, if a cut-off score is determined for the whole group, one or other subgroup could be discriminated against. Various models have been proposed to decrease selection bias and increase the fairness of selection decisions that are made, especially for minority groups. There is no easy solution to eliminating bias, however, as statistics can only go so far and cannot correct social inequalities. The real issue is to try to balance conflicting goals such as providing equal employment opportunities, maximizing success rates and productivity, and redressing past imbalances by obtaining a better demographic spread of people in the work force through providing preferential opportunities for those who have been historically disadvantaged. Open discussion and successive approximations are required to achieve this (Anastasi and Urbina, 1997).

3.6 **Review**

This chapter introduced you to the basic concepts in psychological measurement. You learned about the four types (levels) of measurement and different methods of measurement scaling. You were also introduced to the basic statistical concepts of displaying data; i.e. measures of central tendency, variability, and association. The chapter ended with a discussion of the different types of norm scores and procedures for applying norms in assessment settings.

ANSWERS TO SELF-ASSESSMENT EXERCISES **3.1–3.6**

3.1 (a) mean score in column $X = 6.2$
   (b) modes for column y $= 6$ and 7
   (c) median position $= 5.5$ and median value $= 13.5$

3.2 (a) range for column $X = 5 - 18$
   (b) range for column $Y = 6 - 10$

3.3 (a) variance for scores in column
   $x = \frac{31.6}{9} = 3.511$

3.4 (a) standard deviation of the obtained variance in column y
   $y = \sqrt{\frac{42.5}{9}} = \sqrt{4.722} = 2.173$

3.5 (a) Pearson correlation between scores of columns x and y
   $y = \frac{300}{366,46964} = 0,819$

3.6 (a) values of a and b respectively 4.8552 and 0.224 for $\sum X$ and $\sum Y$
   (b) the value of $\hat{Y} = 8.2152$

Reliability: Basic concepts and measures

GERT ROODT

CHAPTER OUTCOMES

Once you have studied this chapter you will be able to:
> define 'reliability';
> name and describe the different types of reliability;
> interpret a reliability coefficient; and
> explain which factors may affect reliability coefficients.

4.1 Introduction

The Employment Equity Act (Act 55 of 1998) specifies amongst other things that psychological measures or other similar assessments need to meet two technical criteria, namely those of **reliability** (own emphasis) and validity. Users of such instruments therefore need to know what reliability is precisely and also understand how to determine the reliability of their assessment instruments.

In Table 4.1 (on p. 46) we have a fictitious data set of 10 machine operators. The shaded column on the extreme left presents the individual machine operators (A–J), the second and third column their aptitude scores for odd and even-numbered items, as well as their combined (total) scores for times one and two in the fifth and sixth column respectively. We will use this example to do some very basic calculations to illustrate the different concepts that we want to introduce.

As a psychologist at a packaging organization you wish to use an aptitude measure consisting of 20 items to assist you in the selection of machine operators. You decide to assess ten current operators to determine the reliability of the measures. On both the aptitude test and the performance evaluation, higher scores indicate more favourable results.

Table 4.1 Aptitude and job performance scores of machine operators

OPERATOR	APTITUDE TEST SCORES					
	Score for Odd items (x)	Score for Even items (y)	Product of (xy)	Total score (X_1) T_1	Total score (X_2) T_2	Product of $(X_1 X_2)$
A	5	6	30	11	12	132
B	8	10	80	18	16	288
C	7	7	49	14	15	210
D	8	9	72	17	17	289
E	7	6	42	13	14	182
F	6	8	48	14	13	182
G	5	4	20	9	9	81
H	8	7	56	15	14	210
I	6	5	30	11	13	143
J	2	3	6	5	6	30
	$\sum x = 62$	$\sum y = 65$	$\sum xy = 433$	$\sum X_1 = 127$	$\sum X_2 = 129$	$\sum X_1 x_2 = 1747$
	$\sum x^2 = 1747$	$\sum y^2 = 1761$	$\sum x \sum y = 4030$		$\sum X_1 \sum X_2 = 16383$	

One of the best ways to get to grips with the topics discussed in this chapter is to try out some of the calculations. In order to gain a better understanding of the concepts that we introduce in this and the following chapter you can use the data provided in Table 4.1 to do the calculations yourself.

4.2 Reliability

In the previous chapter we defined measurement as the process of assigning numbers to objects according to clearly specified rules. If for example, we obtain repeated measures of the same object; these measures should provide us with a fairly consistent result. This measurement process entails that we should have a clear conception of at least three aspects, namely:

• what the entity is (e.g. weight or height) that we want to measure;
• what exactly the nature of the measure is (e.g. the scale or ruler) that we want to use; and
• finally, the application of the rules on how

to measure the object (e.g. with or without clothes, shoes, etc.)

In order to obtain reliable measures of these objects we therefore have to apply or consider these three aspects in a consistent manner. Let us have a closer look now at what reliability is precisely.

4.2.1 Definition

Consider the following scenario: one day you travel along a national highway between two cities and the speedometer of your car indicates 120 km/h. If you travelled on the same highway again and wanted to complete your journey in the same time, you would drive at 120 km/h again. You would not be pleased if the car's speedometer indicated 120 km/h when, in actual fact, you were only travelling at 100 km/h. This is what reliability is about: a measured speed of 120 km/h must always be ± 120 km/h (within a certain error margin), not 100 km/h one day and 130 km/h the next.

From the above discussion we can deduce that reliability is linked to **consistency** of measurement.

Thus:

> The reliability of a measure refers to the consistency with which it measures whatever it measures.

However, as indicated in the previous example, consistency always implies a certain amount of error in measurement (random error and systematic error were introduced in the previous chapter). A person's performance in one administration of a measure does not reflect with complete accuracy the 'true' amount of the trait that the individual possesses. There may be other systematic or chance factors present, such as the person's emotional state of mind, fatigue, noise outside the test room, etc. which may affect his/her score on the measure.

We can capture the true and error measurement in equation form as follows:

$$X = T + E$$
formula 4.1

where:

X = observed score (the total score),
T = proportion true score (reliability of the measure), and
E = proportion error score (unexplained variance).

If we obtained the test scores of the target population, the variance of the observed test scores (X) would be expressed as follows in terms of true (T) and error (E) variance:

$$S_X^2 = S_T^2 + S_E^2$$
formula 4.2

Reliability (R) can be defined as the ratio of true score variance to observed score variance:

$$R = \frac{S_T^2}{S_X^2} = \frac{S_X^2 - S_E^2}{S_X^2}$$
formula 4.3

Assume that, for a measure, the:

true score variance = 17;
error score variance = 3; and
observed score variance = 20 (i.e. 17 + 3).

If this information were substituted into Formula 4.3, the reliability of the measure would be computed as being $\frac{17}{20} = 0.85$.

You might well ask now: How do we compute the reliability of a measure? **True score** is a theoretical concept. Do we ever know a person's true score? The answer is *no*. We use observed data to compute the reliability of tests. The numerical expression for reliability is a reliability coefficient, which is nothing more than a correlation coefficient.

4.2.2 **Types of reliability**

We will now consider the five types of reliability coefficients. These are test-retest, alternate-form, split-half, inter-item (Kuder-Richardson and Coefficient Alpha), as well as inter- and intra-scorer reliability (Anastasi and Urbina, 1997; Huysamen, 1996a; Smit, 1996).

4.2.2.1 **Test-retest reliability**

An obvious method for determining the reliability of a measure is to administer it twice to the same group of test-takers. The reliability coefficient in this case is simply the correlation between the scores obtained on the first (T_1) and second (T_2) application of the measure. This coefficient is also called a **coefficient of stability**. Although straightforward, the test-retest technique has a number of drawbacks. The testing circumstances may be different for both the test-taker (emotional factors, illness, fatigue, worry, etc.) and the physical environment (different venue, weather, noise, etc.) which may contribute to systematic error variance. Transfer effects, such as practice and memory, might play a role on the second testing occasion. For most types of measures, this technique is not appropriate for computing reliability.

SELF-ASSESSMENT EXERCISE 4.1

In Table 4.1 you will find two sets of measures for the aptitude total scores (at time 1 and at time 2).
(a) Calculate the test-retest reliability (coefficient of stability) for the aptitude measure.
(b) Is this coefficient acceptable?

4.2.2.2 **Alternate-form reliability**

In this method two equivalent forms of the same measure are administered to the same group on two different occasions. The correlation obtained between the two sets of scores represents the reliability coefficient (also called a **coefficient of equivalence**). It must be noted that the two measures should be truly equivalent, that is, they should have the same number of items; the scoring procedure should be exactly the same; they must be uniform in respect of content, representativeness, and item difficulty level (see Chapter 6); and the test mean and variances should be more or less the same. Because the construction of equivalent tests is expensive and time-consuming, this technique is not generally recommended.

4.2.2.3 **Split-half reliability**

This type of reliability coefficient is obtained by splitting the measure into two equivalent halves (after a single administration of the test) and computing the correlation coefficient between these two sets of scores. This coefficient is also called a **coefficient of internal consistency**.

How do you split a measure? It is not advisable to take the first and second halves of the measure, since items tend to be more difficult towards the end, especially with ability tests. The most common approach is to separate scores on the odd and even item numbers of the measure.

The correlation between the odd and even item scores is, however, an underestimation of the reliability coefficient because it is based on only half the test. The corrected reliability coefficient (r_{tt}) is calculated by means of the Spearman-Brown formula:

$$r_{tt} = \frac{2r_{hh}}{1 + r_{hh}}$$
formula 4.4

in which:

r_{hh} = the correlation coefficient of the half-tests.

SELF-ASSESSMENT EXERCISE 4.2

In Table 4.1.you will find the scores for the odd-numbered (x) and the even-numbered items (y). These two sets of scores represent two equivalent halves of the aptitude test.
(a) Calculate the split-half reliability (coefficient of internal consistency) of the aptitude measure.
(b) Use the Spearman-Brown formula above for correcting your internal consistency coefficient.
(c) Is this coefficient acceptable?

4.2.2.4 **Inter-item consistency**

Another coefficient of internal consistency, which is based on the consistency of responses to all items in the measure (or **inter-item consistency**), is obtained using the Kuder-Richardson method. The formula for calculating the reliability of a test in which the items are dichotomous, that is scored either a 1 or a 0 (for right or wrong responses), is known as the Kuder-Richardson 20 (KR 20) formula:

$$r_{tt} = \left(\frac{n}{n-1}\right) \cdot \left(\frac{S_t^2 - \Sigma p_i q_i}{S_t^2}\right)$$
formula 4.5

where:

r_{tt} = reliability coefficient
n = number of items in test
S_t^2 = variance of total test score
p_i = proportion of testees who answered item i correctly
q_i = proportion of testees who answered item i incorrectly.

SELF-ASSESSMENT EXERCISE 4.3

You have the following data on a fictitious measure called Cognitive Functioning under Stress (De Beer et al., 1999):

$$n = 10$$
$$\Sigma pq = 1.8$$
$$S_t^2 = 12$$

(a) Compute the reliability of this test using the Kuder-Richardson 20 formula.
(b) Could this measure be included in a selection assessment battery? Give reasons for your answer.

Some psychological measures, such as personality and attitude scales, have no dichotomous responses (i.e. no yes/no responses). They usually have multiple response categories. Cronbach developed the Coefficient Alpha (a), which is a formula for estimating the reliability of such measures. The formula is as follows (also see Huysamen, 2006 for an in-depth discussion of the Cronbach Alpha):

$$\alpha = \left(\frac{n}{n-1}\right) \cdot \left(\frac{S_t^2 - \Sigma S_i^2}{S_t^2}\right)$$

formula 4.6

where:

α = reliability coefficient
n = number of items in test
S_t^2 = variance of total test score
ΣS_i^2 = sum of individual item variances.

SELF-ASSESSMENT EXERCISE **4.4**

You have the following data on a fictitious questionnaire called Interpersonal Skills Scale (De Beer et al., 1999).

$$n = 12$$
$$\Sigma S_i^2 = 4.2$$
$$S_t^2 = 14$$

(a) Compute the reliability for this questionnaire using the Coefficient Alpha formula.
(b) Could this questionnaire be included in a selection assessment battery? Give reasons for your answer.

4.2.2.5 **Inter-scorer (rater) reliability**

The reliability coefficients discussed so far apply especially to measures with highly standardized procedures for administration and scoring. Where this is not the case (e.g. in individual intelligence tests, projective techniques, or in the case of assessment centre ratings and finally answers to open-ended questions as encountered in class tests), examiner variance is a possible source of error variance. Inter-scorer (or inter-rater) reliability can be determined by having all the test-takers' test protocols scored by two assessment practitioners. The correlation coefficient between these two sets of scores reflects the **inter-scorer reliability coefficient**. Inter-scorer reliability thus refers to the

consistency of ratings between raters which can also be expressed in the form of a slightly adapted version of the Cronbach Alpha:

$$\alpha = \left(\frac{n}{n-1}\right) \cdot \left(\frac{S_t^2 - \Sigma S_i^2}{S_t^2}\right)$$

formula 4.7

where:

α = inter-rater reliability coefficient
n = number of items or rating dimensions in a test
S_t^2 = variance on all the raters' summative ratings (total scores)
ΣS_i^2 = the sum of the raters' variances across different rating dimensions (sub-scores).

4.2.2.6 **Intra-scorer (rater) reliability**

Whereas the inter-scorer reliability refers to the consistency of ratings between raters, the **intra-scorer reliability coefficient** refers to the consistency of ratings for a single rater. Repeated ratings or scores by the same rater would give an indication of the degree of error variance between such ratings for that particular rater. The same Cronbach Alpha formula as above is then slightly adapted in the following manner:

$$\alpha = \left(\frac{n}{n-1}\right) \cdot \left(\frac{S_t^2 - \Sigma S_i^2}{S_t^2}\right)$$

formula 4.8

where:

α = intra-rater reliability coefficient
n = number of items or rating dimensions in a test
S_t^2 = variance of a rater's scores on different individual's summative ratings (total scores)
ΣS_i^2 = the sum of the raters' variances on each rating dimension (sub-scores) for different individuals being assessed.

4.2.3 **Factors affecting reliability**

We have briefly referred to random sampling error and systematic or non-sampling error in our discussion on measurement in the previous chapter where we indicated that both these factors may affect reliability. Systematic error or non-sampling error basically originates from two broad sources, namely testee or respondent error as well as administrative error. Let us have a closer look at each of these sources:

4.2.3.1 Respondent error

In this section four categories of systematic respondent (or testee) errors can be identified (compare Zikmund, 2003):

- **Non-response errors / self-selection bias**
  Non-response errors occur when respondents do not fully complete their tests or assessments. This is not a large problem when psychological tests are administered under standard classroom conditions, because the test administrator can check if the scales are fully completed. But for researchers who are working with volunteers this can be a major source of systematic bias. Research is in most instances conducted amongst volunteers. Voluntary respondents therefore have a choice to participate or refuse to participate in the research. Why do some participants choose to participate while others merely refuse or decide not to respond? Self-selection bias provides an answer to this question. This occurs when some respondents feel positive about the research subject while the non-respondents feel negative or indifferent about the topic and decide on these grounds not to participate.

- **Response bias**
  A response bias occurs when respondents decide to systematically respond in a set or fixed manner to the item or the question, thereby purposively presenting a skewed picture. Different forms of response bias exist that may systematically skew the obtained scores (also compare Smith, 2002; Smith and Roodt, 2003):
  - **Extremity bias** is a type of bias that occurs when a respondent responds either very positively or very negatively to a particular question. Opposed to extremity bias is centrality or neutrality bias where a person constantly opts for the neutral or the central response options. Considering the use of questions versus statements; it seems that the use of statements with Likert type response scales may amplify extreme respons-

es as opposed to the use of questions (see Swart, Roodt and Schepers, 1999).
  - **Stringency or leniency bias** is a type of bias frequently encountered when raters or assessors are used to generate scores. These raters can then either be very strict or lenient in their ratings or assessments of an object.
  - **Acquiescence bias** occurs when a respondent is in agreement with all statements or questions he/she is asked about. No clear preferences or dislikes are therefore registered.
  - **Halo effect** occurs where respondents are systematically influenced by favourable or unfavourable attributes of the object that they rate or assess. It is argued for instance that raters would rate the subjects that they like more positively.
  - **Social Desirability bias** refers to a very similar response bias where the respondent reacts in a manner which is socially desirable or acceptable. The respondent thereby wishes to create a favourable impression or wishes to present a positive image of him or herself.

- **Purposive falsification**
  Falsification occurs when respondents or testees purposefully misrepresent facts or deliberately provide factually incorrect responses. Persons may do this to prevent embarrassment; or to conceal personal information; or even to protect their privacy. Persons may also do this purely out of boredom when they for instance decide to tick only the second option or merely randomly respond on all the questions.

- **Unconscious misrepresentation**
  Unlike falsification, misrepresentation is not done on purpose. People may not have factually correct information; or can not recall the correct information or may even not understand questions in the way they were intended. The recorded responses may therefore be unintentionally incorrect.

More specifically, some intra-individual factors that affect reliability coefficients according to Anastasi and Urbina (1997) are as follows:

- **Whether a measure is speeded**. The difference between speed and power measures was pointed out in Chapter 1. Test-retest and equivalent-form reliability are appropriate for speeded measures. Split-half techniques may be used if the split is according to time rather than items (i.e. half-scores must be based on separately timed parts of the test).
- **Variability in individual scores**. Any correlation is affected by the range of individual differences in the group. Figure 4.2 indicates a moderate to strong positive correlation for the total group, while the correlation for the smaller subgroup in the block is close to zero. This phenomenon is known as **range restriction**. A reliability coefficient should be computed for the group for which the measure is intended.

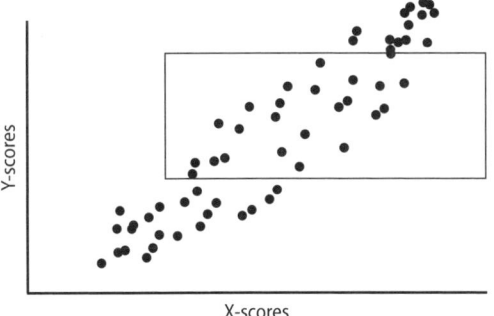

Figure 4.2 Illustration of range restriction of scores

- **Ability level**. The variability and ability level of samples should also be considered. It is desirable to compute reliability coefficients separately for homogeneous subgroups, such as gender, age, and occupation, instead of for the total heterogeneous sample. If mean scores are significantly different for these subgroups one can conclude that there may be some form of systematic error variance.

The second source of variability in systematic error variance is administrative error:

4.2.3.2 **Administrative error**

Variations in administrative procedures normally occur when non-standardized assessment practices

are followed. Containing these sources of error variance is of the utmost importance if assessments are conducted in standard classroom conditions, which is also the case with assessment centres. A host of different causes may exist that can be grouped under the following headings (compare Schlebusch and Roodt, 2008):

- **Variations in instructions**
  It may happen that instructions to respondents or test-takers are inconsistent or not provided in a standardized manner. Test manuals or instruction booklets are important aids in assisting the test administrator or researcher in providing standardized instructions.
- **Variations in assessment conditions**
  Test administrators should also ensure that tests are conducted under standardized conditions. Typically, reference is made to 'standard classroom conditions.' Any deviation from these 'standard conditions' would therefore compromise the consistency of conditions and the assessment context.
- **Variations in the interpretation of instructions**
  The variation in the interpretation of instructions of the test or assessment in general or with reference to specific sections of a questionnaire or tests, may result in variable assessment outcomes. Care should therefore be taken that testees or respondents understand all oral or written instructions in exactly the same way.
- **Variations in the scoring or ratings**
  Most test or assessment instruments have clear instructions on how responses on the instrument should be scored or rated. If computer scoring is used, care should be taken that the data is correctly edited, coded and processed. Any deviation from these scoring or rating instructions will also result in variations in assessment outcomes.

  Utmost care should therefore be taken in the standardization of assessment conditions, administration procedures and the clarity of instructions that will avoid any ambiguity. You will learn more about measurement error in Section 5.3.4.2.

4.2.4 **Interpretation of reliability**

Now that you have learned about reliability and the various methods for determining reliability, it is time to consider some practical aspects of the assessment of reliability of measures. You must be able to answer questions such as:

- When is a reliability coefficient acceptable in practice?
- How are reliability coefficients interpreted?
- What is meant by standard error of measurement?

4.2.4.1 **The magnitude of the reliability coefficient**

When is a reliability coefficient acceptable in practice? The answer depends on what the measure is to be used for. Anastasi and Urbina (1997) state that standardized measures should have reliabilities in the 0.80s and 0.90s. Huysamen (1996a) suggests that the reliability coefficient should be 0.85 or higher if measures are used to make decisions about individuals, while it may be 0.65 or higher for decisions about groups. According to Smit (1996), standardized personality and interest questionnaires should have a reliability of 0.80 to 0.85, while that of aptitude measures should be 0.90 or higher.

4.2.4.2 **Standard error of measurement**

How are reliability coefficients interpreted? Another way of expressing reliability is through the standard error of measurement (*SEM*). *SEM* can be used to interpret individual test scores in terms of the reasonable limits within which they are likely to vary as a function of measurement error. It is independent of the variability of the group on which it was computed. The *SEM* can be computed from the reliability coefficient of a test, using the following formula:

$$SEM = S_t \sqrt{1 - r_{tt}}$$

formula 4.9

Where:

S_t = SD of the test score
r_{tt} = reliability of the test

Like any standard deviation, *SEM* can be interpreted in terms of the normal distribution frequencies (see Section 3.5). If, for example, *SEM* = 4, the chances are 68 per cent that a person's true score on the test will be 4 points on either side of his/her measured score (e.g. between 26 and 34 if the measured score is 30).

SELF-ASSESSMENT EXERCISE 4.5

If a measure has a standard deviation of 9 and a reliability coefficient of 0.88:
(a) What would the *SEM* be?
(b) What does this mean in practical terms?

4.2.4.3 **Reliability and mastery (competency) assessment**

In mastery testing or criterion-referenced assessment, there is little variability of scores among testees. Mastery measures try to differentiate between people who have mastered certain skills and knowledge for a specific job or training programme and those who have not. The usual correlation procedures for determining reliability are therefore inappropriate. References to different techniques used in this regard may be found in Anastasi and Urbina (1997).

ANSWERS TO SELF-ASSESSMENT EXERCISES 4.1–4.5

4.1 (a) The test - re-test reliability is: $\frac{1087}{1139.925}$ = 0.954
  (b) Assuming that internal and external conditions remain equal and that no transfer effects occur, there is a high test - re-test reliability.

4.2 (a) The split-half reliability (coefficient of internal consistency) is: $\frac{300}{366.46964}$ = 0.819
  (b) Using the Spearman-Brown formula, the corrected internal consistency coefficient is: $\frac{1.638}{1.819}$ = 0.901
  (c) Yes this coefficient is highly acceptable

4.3 (a) The KR 20 is: $(1.111)\left(\frac{10.2}{12}\right)$ = 0.9444
  (b) Yes, it can be used because there is little error variance (high reliability).

4.4 (a) The coefficient Alpha is:
$(1.091)(0.7) = 0.764$

(b) Yes, the questionnaire is moderately-high reliable (considering the amount of error variance in the questionnaire).

4.5 (a) The SEM is: $9\sqrt{0.12} = 3.12$

(b) A person's true score will vary +/- 3.12 about the obtained score

Validity: Basic concepts and measures

GERT ROODT

Chapter

5

CHAPTER OUTCOMES

Once you have studied this chapter you will be able to:
> define 'validity';
> name and describe the different types of validity;
> provide examples of indices of validity as well as their interpretation; and
> explain which factors may affect validity coefficients

5.1 Introduction

In the previous chapter we mentioned that the Employment Equity Act (No 55 of 1998) specifies that psychological measures and other assessments should be reliable and **valid**. Reliability and validity are two important criteria that all measuring instruments have to meet. Now let us return to our practical example that we introduced in the previous two chapters.

In Table 5.1 below we have a fictitious data set of 10 machine operators. The shaded column on the extreme left presents the individual machine operators (A–J), the second and fourth column their mechanical aptitude scores for Test X and B respectively, and their job performance scores (Y) in the sixth column. We will use this example to do some very basic calculations to illustrate the different concepts that we want to introduce.

As a psychologist at a packaging organization you wish to use an aptitude measure consisting of 20 items to assist you in the selection of machine operators. You decide to assess ten current operators to determine the validity of the measures. On both the aptitude test and the performance evaluation, higher scores indicate more favourable results.

Table 5.1 Aptitude and job performance scores of machine operators

OPERATOR	MECHANICAL APTITUDE TEST SCORES				JOB PERFORMANCE SCORES (Y)	
	Total score Test (X)	X^2	Total Score on Test B	B^2		Y^2
A	11	121	15	225	7	49
B	18	324	27	729	8	64
C	14	196	15	225	10	100
D	17	289	10	100	8	64
E	13	169	17	289	6	36
F	14	196	13	169	9	81
G	9	81	8	64	6	36
H	15	225	11	121	9	81
I	11	121	7	49	8	64
J	5	25	7	49	6	36
	$\sum X = 127$	$\sum X^2 = 1747$	$\sum B = 130$	$\sum B^2 = 1783$	$\sum Y = 77$	$\sum Y^2 = 611$
		$\sum X \sum Y = 9779$		$\sum B \sum Y = 10010$		

In order to get to grips with the topics that we introduce in this chapter, you can try out some of the calculations yourself by using the data provided in Table 5.1 above.

5.2 **Validity**

At this point you should already know what reliability is. The other requirement of any measure is that it must be **valid**. In this section we will focus on the concept of **validity**.

5.2.1 **Definition**

Let us return to the example of the aptitude test outlined above. From the reliability calculations that you have conducted in Chapter 4 you can accept the fact that Test X measures consistently (i.e. it is reliable). Now consider this: What does this instrument really measure – a person's mechanical aptitude? Ideally, this is what you would want – you would **not** want the instrument to indicate a

person's comprehension ability or his/her language proficiency. This is what validity is all about. Validity can therefore be defined as:

> The validity of a measure concerns what the test measures and how well it does so.

Validity is **not** a specific property of a measure – a psychological measure is valid for a specific purpose (i.e. it has a high or low validity for that specific purpose). Therefore, validity is always the interaction of both the purpose of the instrument and the sample. An instrument may yield valid scores for a sample from the norm group, but may yield invalid scores from a different sample and population (compare Schepers, 1992).

In the previous chapter we also mentioned that the measurement process entails that we should have a clear conception of at least three aspects, namely:
- What the **entity** is (e.g. a person's weight or height) that we want to measure – in other

words, the exact purpose of the test or construct that we want to measure;

- What the exact **nature** of the measure is (e.g. the scale or measuring tape) that we want to use – i.e., how well it would measure the construct; and
- Finally, the application of the **rules** on how to measure the object (e.g. with or without clothes, shoes, etc.)

Different types of validity inform us about these three questions.

5.2.2 **Types of validity**

There are three types of validity or validation procedures, namely content-description, construct-identification, and criterion-prediction procedures (Anastasi and Urbina, 1997). Other authors call them aspects of validity (Smit, 1996) or types of validity (Huysamen, 1996a). These types of validity follow in a particular logical sequence to establish a larger 'validity picture' of a measure. We will now consider these types of validity.

5.2.2.1 **Content-description procedures**

There are two important aspects when considering the content validity of a measure:

- **Face validity**
  Face validity is a type of validity in non-psychometric or non-statistical terms. It does not refer to what the test measures, but rather to what it appears to measure. It has to do with whether the measure 'looks valid' to test-takers who have to undergo testing for a specific purpose. In this sense, face validity is a desirable characteristic for a measure. Sometimes the aim of the measure may be achieved by using phrasing that appears to be appropriate for the purpose. For example, an arithmetic reasoning test for administrative clerks should contain words like 'stationery' and 'stock' rather than 'apples' and 'pears'.
  Testees or a panel of subject experts are normally used to assess the face validity that is, the 'look and feel' of the measuring instrument. Once a test developer is satisfied with this content validity facet, he/she can proceed with the content validation procedure.
- **Content validity**

Content validity can be defined in the following way:

> Content validity involves determining whether the content of the measure covers a representative sample of the behaviour domain/aspect to be measured.

It is a non-statistical type of validity and rather refers to a specific procedure in constructing a psychological measure. (The different phases of this procedure will be discussed in more detail in Chapter 6). A frequently used procedure to ensure high content validity is the use of a panel of subject experts to evaluate the items during the test construction phase.

Content validity is especially relevant for evaluating achievement, educational, and occupational measures (also see Schepers, 1992). Content validity is a basic requirement for domain-referenced/criterion-referenced and job sample measures. Performance on these measures is interpreted in terms of mastery of knowledge and skills for a specific job which are important for employee selection and classification.

Content validity is usually not the most appropriate aspect of validity to establish for aptitude (as in our above example) and personality measures. Although the content of these types of measures must be relevant and representative of a specific domain, the validation of aptitude and personality measures usually requires validation through criterion-prediction procedures (see Section 5.2.2.3).

Only when an instrument is content valid, can it be elevated to the next level of validity assessment, namely construct validation.

5.2.2.2 **Construct-identification procedures**

- **Construct validity**
  Construct validity involves a quantitative, statistical analysis procedure that can be defined as:

> The construct validity of a measure is the extent to which it measures the theoretical construct or trait it is supposed to measure.

Here are just a few examples of such theoretical (intangible) constructs or traits: intelligence, verbal ability, numerical ability, neuroticism, anxiety, spatial perception, eye-hand coordination, introversion-extroversion. The measures to be discussed in subsequent chapters concern many possible theoretical constructs in psychology.

There are a number of different statistical methods to ascertain whether the measure actually measures what it is supposed to be measuring. They are the following:

- **Correlation with other tests**
  A high correlation between a new measure and a similar earlier measure of the same construct indicates that the new measure assesses approximately the same construct or area of behaviour. The correlation should be only moderately high, otherwise the measure is just a duplication of the old one.

SELF-ASSESSMENT EXERCISE 5.1

In our example in Table 5.1 you can calculate the correlation between the total score of the aptitude test X and the scores obtained on the second aptitude test B.
(a) What correlation coefficient did you get?
(b) Is this aptitude test construct valid?

- **Factorial validity**
  Factor analysis is a statistical technique for analyzing the interrelationships of variables. The aim is to determine the underlying structure or dimensions of a set of variables because, by identifying the common variance between them, it is possible to reduce a large number of variables to a relatively small number of factors or dimensions. The factors describe the factorial composition of the measure and assist in determining subscales. The factorial validity (Allen and Yen, 1979) of a measure thus refers to the underlying dimensions (factors) tapped by the measure, as determined by the process of factor analysis. This procedure is normally used when a new measure is developed or when an existing measure is applied in a different context where the original one was validated.
- **Convergent and discriminant validity**
  A measure demonstrates construct validity when it correlates highly with other variables

with which it should theoretically correlate and correlates minimally with variables from which it should differ. Campbell and Fiske (1959) describe the former as convergent validity (sometimes referred to as mono-trait, hetero-method) and the latter as discriminant validity (also referred to as hetero-trait, mono-method). This method is normally used to determine whether a new construct is sufficiently 'isolated' from other dissimilar instruments or constructs.

- **Incremental validity**
  Sechrest (1978) suggests another validity construct, namely incremental validity, which should be presented in addition to other validity information such as convergent and discriminant validity. Sechrest argues that if a new test is reducible to an intelligence or a social desirability measure, its *raison d'être* will most probably disappear. A measure therefore displays incremental validity when it explains numerically additional variance compared to a set of other measures when predicting a dependent variable. For instance, a measure of emotional intelligence would possess incremental validity if it explains additional variance compared to a set of the 'big five' personality measures in the prediction of job performance. Do you think this is indeed the case?

SELF-ASSESSMENT EXERCISE 5.2

If we use both the aptitude tests' scores in the prediction of the job performance scores;
(a) Would aptitude test X explain more variance than aptitude test B?
(b) What do the results suggest?

- **Differential validity**
  A measure possesses differential validity if it succeeds in differentiating or distinguishing between characteristics of individuals, groups or organizations. These entities are grouped based on *a priori* differences and then compared against the selected measure. For instance, a measure of self-efficacy would exhibit differential validity if it can distinguish between

different individuals' levels of self-efficacy. Or, a personality measure should be able to generate different personality profiles for two unique individuals. This validity requirement is often overlooked in the development of measures to assess group or organizational processes (also see Du Toit and Roodt, 2003; Petkoon and Roodt, 2004; Potgieter and Roodt, 2004).

If we return to our practical example above, we can form two contrasting groups based on their job performance scores (low and high). If the aptitude test scores for these two groups are statistical significantly different, then we can conclude that the aptitude test has differential validity.

It would be nearly futile to try and predict some criterion (or construct) with measures that are not construct valid. Therefore, only if a construct has met the requirements of construct validity, can it effectively enter into the third validation level.

5.2.2.3 Criterion-prediction procedures

*   **Criterion-prediction validity**
    Criterion-prediction validation, or criterion-related validation as it is also known, is a quantitative (statistical) procedure. It can be defined in the following way:

    Criterion-related validity involves the calculation of a correlation coefficient between a predictor, or more than one predictor, and a criterion.

Two different types of criterion-related validity can be identified, namely concurrent and predictive validity. The distinction between these two types of criterion-related validity is based on the purpose for which the measure is used. The two types of criterion-related validity can be defined as follows (Huysamen, 1996a; Smit, 1996):

*   **Concurrent validity**
    Concurrent validity involves the accuracy with which a measure can identify or diagnose the current behaviour or status regarding specific skills or characteristics of an individual.

This definition clearly implies the correlation of two (or more) concurrent sets of behaviours or constructs. Let us briefly consider the following example:

> **SELF-ASSESSMENT EXERCISE 5.3**
>
> If we assume for a moment that aptitude test X and the job performance measures were taken at the same point in time, then we can calculate the concurrent validity of the aptitude test:
> (a) What is the concurrent validity in this case?
> (b) Is this acceptable or not?

*   **Predictive validity**
    Predictive validity refers to the accuracy with which a measure can predict the future behaviour or category status of an individual.

The fact that psychological measures can be used for decision-making is implicit in the concept of predictive validity. Let us have a brief look at the following exercise:

> **SELF-ASSESSMENT EXERCISE 5.4**
>
> Now let us assume in our above example that the job performance scores were taken at a different point in time.
> (a) What is the validity coefficient now?
> (b) Will it be different from exercise 5.3?
> (c) Do you think that the job performance scores are good (reliable and valid) criterion scores?
> (d) Why do you say this?

Any psychological measure described in this book can be a possible **predictor**. A **criterion,** as the name suggests, is a benchmark variable against which scores on a psychological measure are compared or evaluated (which can be another psychological measure). Apart from the correlation coefficient, the predictive validity of a measure used to select or classify people is also determined by its ability to predict their performance on the criterion (e.g. job performance).

- **Possible criterion measures**

  A few possible measures for a criterion are mentioned below. However, before various criterion measures are discussed, you must take note of the concept of **criterion contamination**. This is the effect of any factor or variable on a criterion such that the criterion is no longer a valid measure. For example, a rating scale (e.g. performance ratings) is often used to operationalize the criterion variable. Among the shortcomings of ratings are rating biases where the rater may err on being too lenient or may make judgments on a 'general impression' of a person or on a very prominent aspect only. These response errors or biases (referred to in Chapter 4) also have a negative effect on the criterion validity. In such an instance, we would say the criterion is 'contaminated'. The criterion must thus be free from any form of bias. From your statistical knowledge you should realize that this will influence the correlation coefficient with a predictor. Obviously, a criterion should also be reliable.

  The most commonly used criterion measures are mentioned briefly below. You are referred to other sources, such as Anastasi and Urbina (1997), for a more complete discussion.

- **Academic achievement**

  Academic achievement is one of the most frequently used criteria for the validation of intelligence, multiple aptitude, and personality measures. The specific indices include school, college or university grades, achievement test scores, and special awards.

- **Performance in specialized training**

  A criterion frequently used for specific aptitude measures is **performance in specialized training**. Think about achievement performance related to training outcomes for typists, mechanics, music and art courses, degree courses in medicine, engineering and law, and many others.

- **Job performance**

  The most appropriate criterion measure for the validity of intelligence, special aptitude, and personality measures is actual job performance. Any job in industry, business, the professions, government, and the armed services

is suitable. Test manuals reporting this kind of validity should describe the duties performed and how they were measured. When validating personality measures, contrasted groups are sometimes used. For example, social traits may be more relevant and important for occupations involving more interpersonal contact, such as executives or marketing personnel, than occupations not requiring social skills (e.g. office clerks).

- **Psychiatric diagnoses**

  Psychiatric diagnoses based on prolonged observation and case history may be used as evidence of test validity for personality measures.

- **Ratings**

  Ratings by teachers or lecturers, training instructors, job supervisors, military officers, co-workers, etc. are commonly used as criteria. A wide variety of characteristics may be rated, such as competency, honesty, leadership, job performance, and many more. Ratings are suitable for virtually every type of measure. Although subjective, ratings are a valuable source of criteria data for test validation – in many cases they are the only source available. Keep in mind that raters may be trained to avoid the common errors made during rating (discussed in Chapter 4) such as ambiguity, halo error, errors of extremity or central tendency (giving most people average ratings), and stringency or leniency errors.

- **Other valid tests**

  Finally, an obvious way to validate a new measure is to correlate it with another available valid test measuring the same ability or trait.

  Two approaches that have become popular over the last few decades are validity generalization and meta-analysis (Anastasi and Urbina, 1997). We will only briefly introduce these here as a detailed discussion is beyond the scope of this chapter.

5.2.3 **Validity generalization**

Many criterion validity studies are carried out in an organization in which the validity for a specific job is to be assessed. Generally, the samples are too small to yield a stable estimate of the correlation between the predictor and criterion. Anastasi and

Urbina (1997) mention research done by Schmidt, Hunter, and their co-workers, who determined that the validity of tests measuring verbal, numeric, and reasoning aptitudes can be generalized widely across occupations. Apparently the successful performance of a variety of occupational tasks is attributable to cognitive skills which are common to many occupations.

Validation studies can be conducted in an incremental way where the focus ranges from validating a measure in a single organization to validation of traits across national and cultural boundaries. These studies can therefore be:

- firstly, conducted in a specific organization,
- secondly, conducted for a specific industry,
- thirdly, conducted across industries in a specific country, and
- fourthly, conducted across different countries and cultures.

The above categories suggest that validation studies may have different foci and different levels of generalization.

Meta-analysis. Meta-analysis is a method of reviewing research literature. It is a statistical integration and analysis of previous research studies' data on a specific topic. Correlational meta-analysis is quite commonly used in the industrial psychological field for assessing test validity.

To conclude this section on criterion-prediction procedures, we point out another concept, namely **cross-validation.** No measure is ever 'perfect' after one administration to a group or one sample of the target population for the measure. It is essential to administer a second, refined version of the measure, compiled after an item analysis (see Chapter 6), to another representative normative sample. Validity coefficients should then be recalculated for this (second) sample. During cross-validation, shrinkage or a lowering of the original validity coefficient might take place due to the size of the original item pool and the size of the sample. Spuriously high validity coefficients may have been obtained the first time due to chance differences and sampling errors.

5.2.4 'Unitary' validity

Against the above background, validity is viewed as a multi-dimensional construct – that is, it consists of different validity facets (content-descriptive, construct validity and criterion-predictive validity) as we explained above. Several authors (Anastasi, 1986; Nunnally, 1978) introduced the idea that validity is also not a singular event, rather, a process that evolves over a period of time. A 'body of evidence' on validation information regarding validity facets is developed over a period of time by means of multiple validation events, conducted on diverse groups. **Unitary validity** therefore considers the whole 'body of evidence' and includes all the facets of validity mentioned above. It is clear from this viewpoint that validation is never completed, or that a single validation study in a specific setting that addresses predictive validity, for instance, cannot fully inform one on the unitary validity of an instrument.

Efforts to validate a particular instrument should therefore address all facets of validity so that it can inform the unitary validity of the instrument. Test developers and distributors should systematically compile validation data on their different instruments so that all validity facets are included.

5.2.5 **Indices and interpretation of validity**

We will now discuss the various indices of the validity coefficient.

5.2.5.1 **Validity coefficient**

We stated earlier that the predictive validity coefficient is a correlation coefficient between one or more predictor variables and a criterion variable. If differential performance leads to the necessity of determining different validity coefficients for different demographic groups, such as gender, language or race, it is said that the measure exhibits differential validity (compare paragraph 5.2.2.2).

- **Magnitude of the validity coefficient**
  How high should a validity coefficient be? Anastasi and Urbina (1997) and Smit (1996) state that it should be high enough to be statistically significant at the 0.05 and 0.01 levels. Huysamen (1996a) states that it depends on the use of the test. Values of 0.30 or even 0.20 are acceptable if the test is used for selection purposes.

5.2.5.2 Factors affecting the validity coefficient

The following factors may impact the validity of a measure:

- **Reliability**
  The validity of a measure is directly *proportional to its reliability*, that is, the reliability of a measure has a limiting influence (imposes a ceiling) on its validity (also see Schepers, 1992). According to Schepers (1992) the validity of a test can never exceed the square root of its reliability. Therefore, there is no point in trying to validate an unreliable measure. Also, remember that reliability does not imply validity. Thus, reliability is a necessary but not sufficient precondition for validity.

- **Differential impact of subgroups**
  The nature of the group under investigation is also important. The validity coefficient must be consistent for subgroups that differ in age, gender, educational level, occupation, or any other characteristic. If this is not the case these subgroups (according to biographic factors) may have a *differential impact* on the validity coefficient.

- **Sample homogeneity**
  Sample homogeneity is also relevant. If scores are very similar, because group members are very similar (for instance a group of post-graduate students), we may have a restriction of range case. Therefore, the wider the range of scores (sample heterogeneity), the higher the validity coefficient (refer to range restriction in Section 3.3.3).

- **Linear relationship between the predictor and criterion**
  The *relationship* between predictor and criterion must be linear because the Pearson product-moment correlation coefficient is used.

- **Criterion contamination**
  If the criterion is *contaminated* it will affect the magnitude of the validity coefficient. However, if contaminated influences are known and measured, their influence can be corrected statistically by means of the partial correlation technique.

- **Moderator variables**
  Variables such as gender, age, personality traits, and socio-economic status may affect the validity coefficient if the differences between such groups are significant. These variables are known as *moderator variables* and need to be kept in mind, as a specific measure may be a better predictor of criterion performance for, say, men than for women, thus discriminating against or adversely impacting the latter. You will learn more about adverse impact or test bias in Chapter 7.

5.2.5.3 Coefficient of determination

The **coefficient of determination** (r^2) is the square of the validity coefficient. It indicates the proportion of variance in the criterion variable which is accounted for by variance in the predictor (test) score, or the amount of variance shared by both variables (Huysamen, 1996a; Smit, 1996).

Look at the following example:
Validity coefficient: $(r) = 0.35$
Coefficient of determination:
$(r^2) = 0.352^2 = 0.1225$
r^2 can be expressed as percentage of common variance: $0.1225 \times 100 = 12.25\%$
This can be depicted graphically as in Figure 5.3.

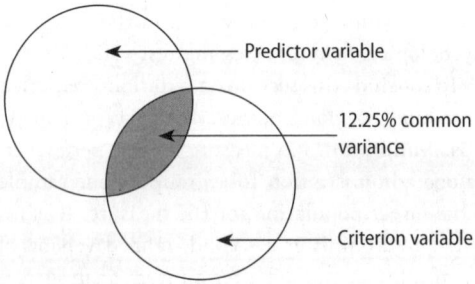

Figure 5.3 Common variances between predictor and criterion variables

SELF-ASSESSMENT EXERCISE 5.5

With reference to our example above;
(a) What would the coefficient of determination be for the aptitude test X and the aptitude test B?
(b) Is this an acceptable coefficient?
(c) What is the shared common variance between X, B and Y?
(d) Why do you say this?

5.2.5.4 **Standard error of estimation**

When it is necessary to predict an individual's exact criterion score, the validity coefficient must be interpreted in terms of the standard error of estimation. The formula is as follows:

$$SE_{est} = S_y \sqrt{1 - r^2_{XY}}$$
formula 5.1

Where:

S_y = SD for scale Y
r^2_{XY} = coefficient of determination for scales X and Y

The standard error of estimation is interpreted in the same way as a standard deviation. If, for example, $r_{XY} = 0.60$ and $SE_{est} = 0.80$, where $S_y = 1$, it can be accepted with 95 per cent certainty that the true criterion score will not deviate (plus or minus) more than $(1.96 \times 0.8) = 1.57$ from the predicted criterion score.

SELF-ASSESSMENT EXERCISE 5.6

With reference to our example (exercise 5.3) aptitude test scores (x) were used to predict performance scores within a 95 per cent confidence interval:
(a) Compute the standard error of estimation of the job performance criterion where $r_{XY} = 0.61$, $S_y = 1.42$.
(b) How much would these scores vary about an obtained score of 30?

5.2.5.5 **Predicting the criterion: regression analysis**

Essentially, regression has to do with prediction. If there is a high positive correlation between a measure and a criterion, the test score can be used to predict the criterion score. These predictions are obtained from the regression line, which is the best fitting straight (linear) line through the data points in a scatter diagram.

Regression analysis always involves one criterion variable. Simple regression implies that we have only one predictor variable, while we talk of multiple regression when we have two or more predictor variables.

The regression equation (formula for the regression line) for simple regression is as follows:

$$\hat{Y} = bX + a$$
formula 5.2

The symbol $\hat{Y}$ represents the predicted Y-score (the criterion). The regression coefficient is designated by b. This is the **slope** of the regression line, that is, how much change in Y is expected each time the X-score (the predictor) increases by one unit. The **intercept a** is the value of $\hat{Y}$ when X is zero. An interesting fact is that the means of the two variables will always fall on the regression line.

The regression equation for a multiple regression with three predictors is:

$$\hat{Y} = b_1X_1 + b_2X_2 + b_3X_3 + b_0$$
formula 5.3

where:

X_1, X_2, X_3 = predictors 1, 2, 3
b_1, b_2, b_3 = weights of the predictors
b_0 = intercept (i.e. the a in simple regression).

We provided a brief overview of validity in this chapter. Readers are referred to a comprehensive set of guidelines for the validation and use of assessment procedures compiled by the Society for Industrial and Organisational Psychology of South Africa (SIOPSA) (2006b). The intention of these guidelines is to assist psychologists in industry, managers or any assessment practitioner to adhere to the requirements laid down in the Employment Equity Act (1998) to ensure that assessment practices are reliable and valid as well as unbiased and fair.

SELF-ASSESSMENT EXERCISE 5.7

You have conducted the correlation and regression between the aptitude scores (X) and the job performance scores (Y) in exercise 5.3. If b = 0.22 and a = 4.91:
(a) What would the predicted values of $\hat{Y}$ be for values X = 16?

ANSWERS TO SELF-ASSESSMENT EXERCISES 5.1–5.7

5.1 (a) $1320/2103.6397 = 0.628$

   (b) Yes, because it is correlated with another similar construct.

5.2 (a) Yes, X correlates 0.611 ($r^2 = 0.373$) with Y and B correlates 0.341 ($r^2 = 0.116$) with Y.

   (b) Test X thus shares more variance with Y.

5.3 (a) Concurrent validity is: 0.611

   (b) Yes, it is acceptable.

5.4 (a) The predictive validity would remain the same, namely: 0.611

   (b) No, the numbers are the same.

   (c) It seems as if they are valid and reliable.

   (d) Unreliable measures would not yield significant correlations.

5.5 (a) Coefficient of determination for X ($r^2 = 0.373$) and for B ($r^2 = 0.116$)

   (b) It seems that X is acceptable, but B not.

   (c) The percentage shared variance is 37.3% for X and 11.6% for B.

   (d) Based on the obtained coefficients of determination in (c).

5.6 (a) The $SE_{est} = 1.42 \sqrt{1 - 0.373} = 1.124$

   (b) The true score will (with 95% certainty) not deviate more than 2.2 from the predicted score of 30, that is vary between 27.8 to 32.2 ($1.96 \times 1.124 = 2.20$)

5.7 (a) Predicted value of Y where X = 16 is: 8.43

Developing a psychological measure

CHERYL FOXCROFT

Chapter

6

CHAPTER OUTCOMES

The development of a psychological measure is a time-consuming and people-intensive process. At a minimum, it takes three to five years to develop a measure from the point at which the idea is conceived to the moment when the measure is published and becomes available to the consumer. In-depth, advanced psychometric knowledge and test development expertise is required by those who initiate and guide the development process. It is beyond the scope of this book to provide detailed information regarding the development of a measure. Instead, this chapter will give you a brief glimpse of the steps involved in developing a measure. The main purpose of this is to enable you to evaluate the technical quality of a measure and the information found in a test manual.

By the end of this chapter you will be able to:

> list the steps involved in developing a measure;
> explain the essential psychometric properties and item characteristics that need to be investigated when developing a measure;
> explain what a test manual should contain; and
> explain how to evaluate a measure.

6.1 Steps in developing a measure

Have you ever had the opportunity to develop a test of any sort? Maybe it was a short test that you compiled for you and your friends to work out when you were studying for your Grade 12 exams? Or maybe it was one that you developed for your younger brother or sister when you were helping them prepare for a test at school? What was the first thing that you needed to know? That's right! The subject the test had to cover. Next, you had to consider the number and type of questions you wanted to include. Then you had to write the questions down, making sure that the wording was as clear and as understandable as possible. You then probably gave the test to your brother, sister, or friends. Once they had completed the test, you had to mark it. To do this, you would have needed to develop a memorandum in which you wrote down the correct answer to each question. You would have found the memorandum very useful if your brother, sister, or friends complained about your marking afterwards!

The process of developing a psychological measure is similar to that of the informal test described above, only it is a little more complex. Briefly, a psychological measure needs to be planned carefully, items need to be written, and the initial version of the measure needs to be administered so that the effectiveness of the items can be determined. After this, the final items are chosen and the measure is administered to a representative group of people so that the measure's validity, reliability and norms can be established. Finally, the test manual is compiled.

Now that you have the 'big picture', let's add a little more detail. The phases and steps involved in the development of a psychological measure are set out in Table 6.1.

Table 6.1 The development of a psychological measure

PHASE	SPECIFIC STEPS
Planning	• Specifying the aim of the measure. • Defining the content of the measure. • Developing the test plan.
Item writing	• Writing the items. • Reviewing the items.
Assembling and pre-testing the experimental version of the measure	• Arranging the items. • Finalizing length. • Answer protocols. • Developing administration instructions. • Pre-testing the experimental version of the measure.
Item analysis	• Determining item difficulty values. • Determining item discrimination values. • Investigating item bias.
Revising and standardizing the final version of the measure	• Revising test and item content. • Selecting the items for the standardization version. • Revising and standardizing administration and scoring procedures. • Compiling the final version. • Administering the final version to a representative sample of the target population.
Technical evaluation and establishing norms	• Establishing validity and reliability. • Devising norm tables, setting performance standards or cut-points.
Publishing and ongoing refinement	• Compiling the test manual. • Submitting the measure for classification. • Publishing and marketing the measure. • Ongoing refinement and updating.

This probably looks quite an intimidating process. So, let's take each of the phases and steps listed above and amplify them. You should also be aware that although there are different phases in developing a measure, the process is dynamic. Sometimes a previous phase is revisited based on a decision made during a subsequent phase (Foxcroft, 2004c; Wilson, 2004).

6.1.1 **Planning phase**

We need a blueprint or a plan for a measure that will guide its development. Foxcroft (2004c) argues that the planning phase is not always given sufficient emphasis and that when a measure is developed for use in a multicultural and multilingual context, a considerable amount of time needs to be spent planning it. This section will give you insight into the key elements of a test plan.

6.1.1.1 **Specifying the aim of the measure**

The test developer needs to clearly state the following:
- the purpose of the measure;
- what attribute, characteristic, or construct it will measure;
- whether the measure is to be used for screening purposes or for in-depth diagnostic assessment, or for competency-based selection and training purposes;
- what types of decisions could be made on the basis of the test scores;
- for which population (group of people) the measure is intended (e.g. young children, adults, people with a Grade 12 education). Included in this should be consideration of whether the measure is to be used in a multicultural context and, if so, which cultural groups it could be used with;
- whether the measure can be individually administered and/or administered in a group context;
- whether the measure is **paper-based** or **computer-based**; and
- whether it is a **normative** measure (where an individual's performance is compared to that of an external reference or norm group), an **ipsative** measure (where intra-individual as opposed to inter-individual comparisons

are made when evaluating performance), or a **criterion-referenced** measure (where an individual's performance is interpreted with reference to performance standards associated with a clearly specified content or behavioural domain such as managerial decision-making or academic literacy).

6.1.1.2 **Defining the content of the measure**

The content of a measure is directly related to the purpose of the measure. How does a test developer decide on the domains of content to include in a measure?

Firstly, the construct (content domain) to be tapped by the measure needs to be operationally defined. For tests used in clinical settings, this can be done by undertaking a thorough literature study of the main theoretical viewpoints regarding the construct that is to be measured (this is known as the rational method). In educational settings, learning outcomes in specific learning areas or programmes form the basis for defining the constructs to be tapped. In organizational settings, test developers base the operational definition of the construct to be tapped on a job analysis that identifies the competencies (i.e. knowledge, skills or tasks, and attitudes) needed to perform a job successfully (McIntire and Miller, 2000). In this regard, competency sets have been developed for a number of jobs, which could provide a useful starting point before customizing the competencies for a specific organizational context. For example, Nikolaou (2003) delineates the generic work competencies for managers and discusses the development of a measure to evaluate them in Greece. Whether the dimensions of the construct are identified in a theoretical review, through an analysis of learning outcomes, or a job analysis, it is important that the construct is comprehensively defined. Wilson (2004) recommends that a construct map be developed to ensure that the construct is well-defined, which will make it easier to operationalize more concretely.

Secondly, the purpose for which the measure is developed must be considered. If the measure needs to discriminate between different groups of individuals, for example to identify high risk students who need extra attention, information will have to be gathered about the aspects of the construct on which these groups usually differ (this is known as **criterion keying**). For example, when it comes to a construct such as academic aptitude, high risk students find it very difficult to think critically, while low risk students have less difficulty in this regard. Therefore, if a measure aims to identify high risk students, items related to critical thinking should be included in it.

A test developer rarely uses only one approach when it comes to operationalizing the content domains of a measure. The more rational or analytical approach is often combined with the empirical criterion keying approach to ensure that the resultant measure is theoretically grounded, as well as being linked to an important criterion. Furthermore, when the items are tried out in the subsequent phases, factor analysis can be used to assist in refining the underlying dimensions (constructs) being tapped by the measure.

Foxcroft (2004c) points out that when a measure is developed for use with multicultural and multilingual groups, it is critical that the construct to be tapped is explored in terms of each cultural and language group's understanding of it as well as its value for each group. For example, if a test of emotional intelligence is to be developed for all cultural and language groups in South Africa, the test developer needs to explore through focus group and individual interviews how each group understands the concept 'emotional intelligence' to see whether or not there is a shared understanding of the concept. A further example can be found in the way in which the South African Personality Inventory (SAPI) is being developed (Meiring, 2006). For the SAPI Project a broad range of 'everyday' adults were interviewed across all the 11 official language groups in South Africa to get information on the descriptors that they use to describe personality. From this, the common and unique personality dimensions of the different language groups are being distilled, from which the SAPI will be developed. To read more about this project consult www.meiringd.co.za/sapi project.htm.

6.1.1.3 Developing the test plan (specifications)

The format of the test needs to be considered. **Test format** consists of two aspects: 'a *stimulus* to which

a test taker responds and a *mechanism for* response' (McIntire and Miller, 2000, p. 192). Test items provide the stimulus and the more common item formats are the following:

- **open-ended items**, where no limitations are imposed on the response of the test-taker;
- **forced-choice items**, for example, multiple-choice items, where careful consideration needs to be given to the distracters (alternative options) used, and true-false items, where the test-taker responds to each individual item. However, in an alternative forced-choice format, namely an **ipsative** format, the test-taker has to choose between two or more attributes for each item (e.g. 'Do you prefer science or business?'). In this instance, the relative preference for each attribute can be determined and rank-ordered for an individual, but the absolute strength of each attribute for an individual cannot be determined;
- **sentence completion items**; and
- **performance-based items** such as where apparatus (e.g. blocks) needs to be manipulated by the test-taker, a scientific experiment needs to be performed, an essay must be written, an oral presentation must be prepared, or a work-related competency must be demonstrated through solving complex realistic problems via innovative interactive computerized activities (Linn and Gronlund, 2000; Williamson, Bauer, Steinberg, Mislevy, Behrens, and DeMark, 2004). Such items test problem identification and problem solving, logical thinking, organizational ability, and oral or motor performance, for example. Traditionally, some performance-type items (e.g. an essay) have been more difficult to score objectively but modern computer technology has enhanced the objective scoring of computer-based performance-type tasks.

While the choice of item format is linked to what is to be measured, practical considerations also have a bearing on the choice of format. For example, if the measure is to be administered in a group context and large numbers of people are to be evaluated on it, it needs to be easily scored. This implies that the use of fixed response items (e.g. true/false, multiple-choice) would be a better choice than an essay-type or open-ended format for a paper-based test.

When it comes to the method of responding to an item, there are also various formats such as the following:

- **objective formats** where there is only one response that is either correct (e.g. in multiple choice options and in matching exercises), or is perceived to provide evidence of a specific construct (e.g. in true-false options, or the value assigned to a statement along a rating scale).
- **subjective formats** where the test-taker responds to a question verbally (e.g. in an interview) or in writing (e.g. to an open-ended or essay-type question) and the interpretation of the response as providing evidence of the construct depends on the judgement of the assessment practitioner (McIntire and Miller, 2000). **Projective tests** such as the Rorschach Inkblot test or the Thematic Apperception Test (see Chapter 12) are examples of a subjective answer format. In these tests, ambiguous pictures are presented (stimulus) to which test-takers must respond by either describing what they see or by telling a story.

Linked to the response to an item stimulus is whether or not a **time limit** is imposed. While all **speed tests** are timed, many cognitive tasks and especially performance-type items as well as measures administered in group contexts normally also have time limits. If a test is to be timed, this will place restrictions on the number of items that can be included. However, it is interesting to note that Kennet-Cohen, Bronner and Cohen (2003), working in a multicultural context, found that for the Psychometric Entrance Test used in Israeli universities, setting and overall time limit for the test battery of 150 minutes was more effective than setting time limits for the individual subtests and that predictive validity increased by 20% in this instance. The Centre for Access Assessment and Research at the Nelson Mandela Metropolitan University have found that the assessment of university applicants in a multicultural group context is enhanced if all time limits are removed as this provides a more accurate picture of the proficiencies of applicants (Foxcroft, 2008).

Bias can unintentionally be introduced through either the item stimulus or the mode of response. It is critically important to pay attention to the potential for **method** and **response bias**, especially when the measure is developed for use with multicultural test-takers (Foxcroft, 2004c; Hambleton, 1994, 2001). For example, Owen (1989a) found that black and white South African children performed differently on story-type items. Such items should thus be avoided if the aim is to develop a test for use with black and white children. When she developed the LPCAT, de Beer (2005) developed only non-figural verbal items (figure series, figure analogies and pattern completion) as such item types are 'recommended for the fair assessment of general reasoning ability in multicultural contexts' (p. 723). As regards response bias, this aspect is extensively dealt with in Chapter 14 when we discuss the impact of computer familiarity on computer-based test performance.

Other than method and response bias, test-takers are a potential source of bias themselves as they might respond by using a specific style or **response set** (e.g. by agreeing with all the statements) that might result in false or misleading information. Response sets are discussed more fully in Chapters 4, 12 and 17. However, test developers should try to minimize the possibility of response sets influencing the test results through the way that they construct the test items.

Another potential source of bias relates to the language in which the measure is developed and administered in. If the measure is intended to be used in a multilingual context, then only having the measure available in isiXhosa, for example, could be a potential source of bias for test-takers who only speak English or Afrikaans. In this instance, it would be better to have multiple language versions of the measure. How to deal with issues related to language in test development and administration will be discussed in Chapters 7 and 9.

The eventual length of the measure also needs to be considered at this stage. The length is partly influenced by the amount of time that will be available to administer the measure. The length also depends on the purpose of the measure. A measure that is developed to tap a variety of dimensions of a construct should have more items than a measure that focuses on only one dimension of a construct, or else the reliability of the measure could be problematic.

Having taken into account all the aspects related to the dimensions of the construct to be tapped, item and response format, whether time limits will be set for the responses, test length, and number of items, the test developer now has a clear conceptualization of the specifications for the measure. This is formalized in a **test plan** (specifications) that specifies the specific content domains to be included and the number of items that will be included in each one. For example, part of a test plan for an emotional intelligence test could indicate that four aspects of the construct will be covered, namely, interpersonal relations, intrapersonal functioning, emotional well-being, and stress management, and that there will be ten items per aspect.

6.1.2 Item writing

6.1.2.1 Writing the items

Usually a team of experts writes or develops the items. The purpose of the measure and its specifications provide the constant guiding light for the item developers. A variety of sources can be consulted for ideas for items: existing measures, theories, textbooks, curricula, self-descriptions, anecdotal evidence in client files, and so on.

Depending on the type of measure being developed, a few important pointers for item writing are the following:

- Wording must be clear and concise. Clumsy wording and long, complex sentences could make it difficult for test-takers to understand what is required of them.
- Use vocabulary that is appropriate for the target audience.
- Avoid using negative expressions such as 'not' or 'never', and double negatives in particular.
- Cover only one central theme in an item.
- Avoid ambiguous items.
- Vary the positioning of the correct answer in multiple-choice measures.
- All distracters for multiple-choice response alternatives should be plausible (i.e. the distracters should be as attractive as the correct answer).

As far as the number of alternative response choices is concerned, Linn and Gronlund (2000) suggest that it is best to provide four answer choices. This implies that three good distracters need to be developed, which they feel can be reasonably achieved. However, for children, they suggest that three alternatives are used to reduce the amount of reading required.

- True and false statements should be approximately the same length and the number of true statements should be approximately equal to the number of false statements.
- The nature of the content covered should be relevant to the purpose of the measure (e.g. you would not expect a personality measure to contain an item asking what the capital of Kenya is).

When it comes to writing items for children's measures, the stimulus material should be as colourful and attractive as possible. Varied types of tasks should be included, and where stimulus materials have to be manipulated, the child should be able to manipulate them without difficulty (e.g. blocks and form board shapes for young children should be large).

As some of the items will be discarded during the test development, item analysis, and refinement phase, provision needs to be made for including many more items in the experimental version than will be required in the final version. As a general rule of thumb, test developers usually develop double the number of items that they require in their final item pool (Owen and Taljaard, 1996). At least one third of the items are usually discarded when the item analysis is performed.

6.1.2.2 Reviewing the items

After a pool of items has been developed, it should be submitted to a panel of experts for review and evaluation. The expert reviewers will be asked to judge whether the items sufficiently tap the content domain or dimensions of the construct being assessed. They will also be asked to comment on the cultural, linguistic, and gender appropriateness of the items. The wording of the items and the nature of the stimulus materials will also be closely scrutinized by the panel of experts.

The pool of items could also be administered to a small number of individuals from the intended target population to obtain qualitative information regarding items and test instructions that they have difficulty understanding.

Based on the review panel's recommendations as well as data gathered from trying out the items, certain of the items in the pool may have to be revised or even re-written.

6.1.3 Assembling and pre-testing the experimental version of the measure

In getting the measure ready for its first experimental administration, several practical considerations require attention.

6.1.3.1 Arranging the items

The items need to be arranged in a logical way in terms of the construct being measured. Furthermore, for paper-based tests, items need to be grouped or arranged on the appropriate pages in the test booklet.

6.1.3.2 Finalizing the length

Now that the experimental item pool is available, the length of the measure needs to be revisited. Although sufficient items have to be included to sample the construct being measured, the time test-takers will need to read items also has to be considered. The more test-takers have to read, the longer it will take them to complete the measure. Thus, if the measure has time constraints, and there is quite a bit to read, either some items will have to be discarded to allow the measure to be completed in a reasonable time period, or the amount that has to be read will have to be adjusted.

6.1.3.3 Answer protocols

For paper-based tests, decisions need to be made as to whether items will be completed in the test booklet, or whether a separate answer sheet (protocol) needs to be developed. Care should be taken to design the answer protocol in such a way that it aids the scoring of the measure and that it is easy to reproduce.

6.1.3.4 Developing administration instructions

Care needs to be taken in developing clear, unambiguous administration instructions for the experimental try-out of the items. It is usually advisable to pre-test the instructions on a sample of people from the target population. Furthermore, the assessment practitioners who are going to administer the experimental version of the measure need to be comprehensively trained. If care is not taken during this step of the test development process, it could have negative consequences for performance on the items during the experimental pre-testing stage. For example, badly worded administration instructions, rather than poorly constructed items, can cause poor performance on the item.

6.1.3.5 Pre-testing the experimental version of the measure

The measure should now be administered to a large sample (approximately 400 to 500) from the target population. Besides the quantitative information regarding performance on each item gathered during this step, those assisting with the administration should be encouraged to gather qualitative information. Information about which items test-takers generally seemed to find difficult or did not understand, for example, could be invaluable during the item refinement and final item selection phase. Furthermore, information about how test-takers responded to the stimulus materials, the ordering or sequencing of the items, and the length of the measure could also prove to be very useful for the test developer.

6.1.4 Item analysis phase

The item analysis phase adds value to the item development and the development of the measure in general. Simply put, the purpose of item analysis is to examine each item to see whether it serves the purpose for which it was designed. Item analysis helps us to determine how difficult an item is, whether it discriminates between good and poor performers, whether it is biased against certain groups, and what the shortcomings of an item are. Certain statistics are computed to evaluate the characteristics of each item. Two statistical approaches can be followed in that the characteristics of items can be analysed using classical test theory or item response theory (IRT) or both (e.g. de Beer, 2005). The resultant statistics are then used to guide the final item selection and the organization of the items in the measure.

6.1.4.1 Classical test theory item analysis

Determining item difficulty (p)

The difficulty of an item (*p*) is the proportion or percentage of individuals who answer the item correctly. That is,

$$p\text{-value} = \frac{\text{Number of people who answered the item correctly}}{\text{Number of people who took the measure}}$$

The higher the percentage of correct responses, the easier the item; the smaller the percentage of correct responses, the more difficult the item. However, *p* is a behavioural measure related to the frequency of choosing the correct response, and therefore tells us nothing about the intrinsic characteristics of the item. Furthermore, the difficulty value is closely related to the specific sample of the population to which it was administered. A different sample might yield a different difficulty value. Nonetheless, one of the most useful aspects of the *p*-value is that it provides a uniform measure of the difficulty of a test item across different domains or dimensions of a measure. It is for this reason that difficulty values are often used when selecting final items for a measure.

Determining discriminating power

One of the purposes of item analysis is to discover which items best measure the construct or content domain that the measure aims to assess. Good items consistently measure the same aspect that the total test is measuring. Consequently, one would expect individuals who do well in the measure as a whole to answer a good item correctly, while those who do poorly on the measure as a whole would answer a good item incorrectly. The discriminating power of an item can be determined by means of the **discrimination index** and **item-total correlations**.

To compute the **discrimination index (D)**, the method of extreme groups is used. Performance on an item is compared between the upper 25 per cent of the sample and the lower or bottom 25 per cent of the sample. If the item is a good discriminator, more people in the upper group will answer the item correctly.

To compute the discrimination index, the upper and lower 25 per cent of test-takers need to be identified. Next, the percentage of test-takers in the upper and lower groups who passed the item is computed and the information is substituted in to the following formula:

$$D = \frac{U}{n_u} - \frac{L}{n_l}$$

where:

U = number of people in the upper group who passed the item

n_u = number of people in the upper group

L = number of people in lower group who passed the item

n_l = number of people in the lower group.

A positive *D*-value indicates an item that discriminates between the extreme groups, while a negative *D*-value is indicative of an item with poor discriminatory power.

An **item-total correlation** can be performed between the score on an item and performance on the total measure. A positive item-total correlation indicates that the item discriminates between those who do well and poorly on the measure. An item-total correlation close to zero indicates that the item does not discriminate between high and low total scores. A negative item-total correlation is indicative of an item with poor discriminatory power. In general, correlations of 0.20 are considered to be the minimum acceptable discrimination value to use when it comes to item selection.

The advantage that using item-total correlations brings with it is that correlation coefficients are more familiar to people than the discrimination index. Furthermore, the magnitude of item-total correlations can be evaluated for practical significance (e.g. 0.4 = moderate correlation) and can be expressed in terms of the percentage of variance of the total score that an item accounts for (e.g. if $r = 0.40$ the item accounts for 16 per cent of the total variance).

There is a direct relationship between item difficulty and item discrimination. The difficulty level of an item restricts the discriminatory power of an item. Items with *p*-values around 0.5 have the best potential to be good discriminators.

6.1.4.2 **Item response theory (IRT) item analysis**

By using item response theory, the difficulty level and discriminatory power of an item can be even more accurately determined. In IRT the item parameters are sample invariant. That is, the parameters are not dependent on the ability level of the test-takers responding to the item and are thus 'a property of the item and not of the group that responded to it' (de Beer, 2005, p. 723).

In IRT an item-response curve (see Figure 7.1 in Chapter 7) is constructed by plotting the proportion of test-takers who gave the correct response against estimates of their true standing on a latent trait (e.g. ability) (Aiken, 2002). The estimates are derived through logistic equations, with the specific equations used varying according to the estimation procedures used. In the one-parameter or Rasch model, an item-response curve is constructed by estimating only the item difficulty parameter (b). In the two-parameter model, both difficulty (b) and discrimination (a) parameters. This is the most popular model especially since it makes it possible to compare the difficulty level and discriminating power of two items, for example (Aiken, 2002). The three-parameter model allows for variations among the items in terms of difficulty level (b), discrimination (a) and for guessing (c) on multiple choice items (de Beer, 2005).

Especially when you are developing a measure in a multicultural, multilingual country such as South Africa, it is useful to investigate **item bias** in the early stages of developing a measure. IRT also makes it possible to explore **differential item functioning** (DIF) in a much more sophisticated way to identify items that may be biased or unfair for test-takers from certain groups. One of the common procedures for detecting DIF is to calculate the area between the item characteristic curves for two groups (e.g. males and females, or Xhosa and Zulu speakers). The larger the area, the more likely it is that the item shows DIF. However, as de Beer (2005) points out, it remains a subjective decision regarding how large the area should be for DIF to be evident. Usually a combination of visual inspection and empirically estimating cut-off points is used to flag items that exhibit DIF. Kanjee (2007) also points out that DIF procedures are only applicable

when two groups are compared. He thus suggests that logistic regression can be used to simultaneously explore bias when multiple groups need to be compared. If you are interested to read more about how IRT is used for item analysis purposes during test development, de Beer (2005) provides an example of how the items of the LPCAT were analysed and refined using IRT. DIF will also be discussed in more detail in Chapter 7.

6.1.4.3 **Criteria used for item selection**

Classical test theory, IRT and DIF analyses can be used to determine item parameters based on which items should be included in the final version of the measure or discarded. Available literature should be consulted to set item parameter values that must be met for inclusion or exclusion. For example, if the three-parameter IRT model is used, a-values should fall between 0.8 and 2.0 while c-values should fall between 0.0 and 0.3 for an item to be included (Hambleton and Swaminathan, 1985).

A word of caution, however, is necessary. Item analysis is a wonderful aid that the test developer can use to identify good and bad items and to decide on the final item pool. Performance on an item is, however, impacted on by many variables (e.g. the position of an item or the administration instructions). Consequently, item analysis statistics should not necessarily replace the skill and expertise of the test developer. At times, the item characteristic statistics may be poor, but the test developer could motivate the inclusion of the item in the final pool on logical or theoretical grounds. In a similar vein, the item statistics may be very impressive, but on closer inspection of the item, the test developer may feel that there is no logical or theoretical reason for retaining the item.

6.1.5 **Revising and standardizing the final version of the measure**

Having gathered quantitative and qualitative information on the items and format of the experimental version of the test, the next phase focuses on revising the items and test and then administering the final version of the test to a large sample for standardization purposes.

6.1.5.1 Revising the items and test

Items identified as being problematic during the item analysis phase need to be considered and a decision needs to be made for each one regarding whether it should be discarded or revised. Where items are revised the same qualitative review process by a panel of experts as well as experimental try-outs of the item should be done.

6.1.5.2 Selecting items for the final version

The test developer now has a pool of items that has been reviewed by experts and on which empirical information regarding item difficulty, discrimination, and bias has been obtained. Based on this information, the selection of items for the final measure takes place. After the selection of items, the existing database can be used to check on the reliability and validity coefficients of the final measure, to see whether they appear to be acceptable.

6.1.5.3 Refining administration instructions and scoring procedures

Based on the experience and feedback gain during the pre-testing phase, the administration and scoring instructions might need to be modified.

6.1.5.4 Administering the final version

The final version is now administered to a large, representative sample of individuals for the purposes of establishing the psychometric properties (validity and reliability) and norms.

6.1.6 Technical evaluation and establishing norms

6.1.6.1 Establishing validity and reliability

The psychometric properties of the measure need to be established. Various types of validity and reliability coefficients can be computed, depending on the nature and purpose of the measure. We dealt with the different types of validity and reliability and how they are established in detail in Chapters 4 and 5.

6.1.6.2 Establishing norms, setting performance standards or cut-scores

If a norm-referenced measure is developed, appropriate norms need to be established. This represents the final step in standardizing the measure. An individual's test score has little meaning on its own. However, by comparing it to that of a similar group of people (the norm group), the individual's score can be more meaningfully interpreted. Common types of norm scales were discussed in Chapter 3. If a criterion-referenced measure is used, cut-scores or performance standards need to be set to interpret test performance and guide decision-making. We discussed cut-scores and performance standards in Chapter 3.

6.1.7 Publishing and ongoing refinement

Before a measure is published, a test manual must be compiled and it should be submitted for classification. Once a measure has been published and ongoing research into its efficacy and psychometric properties is conducted, revised editions of the manual should be published to provide updated information to assessment practitioners.

6.1.7.1 Compiling the test manual

The test manual should:
- Specify the purpose of the measure.
- Indicate to whom the measure can be administered.
- Provide practical information such as how long it takes to administer the measure, whether a certain reading or grade level is required of the test-taker, whether the assessment practitioner requires training in its administration, and where such training can be obtained.
- Specify the administration and scoring instructions.
- Outline, in detail, the test development process followed.
- Provide detailed information on the types of validity and reliability information established, how this was done, and what the findings are.
- Provide information about the cultural appropriateness of the measure and the extent to which test and item bias has been investigated.
- Provide detailed information about when and how norms were established and norm groups were selected. A detailed description of the

normative sample's characteristics must be provided (e.g. gender, age, cultural background, educational background, socio-economic status, and geographic location).

- Where appropriate, provide information about how local norms and cut-off scores could be established or augmented by assessment practitioners to enhance the criterion-related or predictive validity of the measure.
- Indicate how performance on the measure should be interpreted.

6.1.7.2 **Submitting the measure for classification**

As the use of psychological measures is restricted to the psychology profession, it is important that a measure be submitted to the Psychometrics Committee of the Professional Board for Psychology so that it can be determined whether the measure should be classified as a psychological measure or not. In Chapter 8 we will elaborate on the reasons for classifying a measure and the process followed.

6.1.7.3 **Publishing and marketing the measure**

Finally, the measure is ready to be published and marketed. In all marketing material, test developers and publishers should take care not to misrepresent any information or to make claims that cannot be substantiated. For example, if the norms for a measure have not been developed for all cultural groups in South Africa, the promotional material should not claim that the measure can be administered to all South Africans. A clear distinction should also be made between marketing and promotional material and the test manual – they are not one and the same thing. As outlined in Section 6.1.7.1, the test manual must contain factual information about the measure, rather than act as a selling device that tries to put the measure in a favourable light.

As the use and purchase of psychological measures is restricted to the psychology profession in South Africa (see Chapter 8), test developers and publishers need to market the measures to the appropriate target market. Furthermore, promotional material should not provide examples of actual test items or content, as this could invalidate their use if this information were to be released in the popular media.

Increasingly, test developers and publishers are beginning to set standards for those who purchase and use their measures. Such standards could include insisting that assessment practitioners undergo special training in the use of the measure, as well as follow-up activities whereby test developers and publishers check that the assessment practitioners are using and interpreting the measure correctly and fairly.

6.1.7.4 **Ongoing revision and refinement**

There is no rule of thumb regarding how soon a measure should be revised. It largely depends on the content of the measure. When item content dates quickly, more frequent revisions may be necessary. A further factor that influences the timing of revisions is the popularity of a measure. The more popular a measure, the more frequently it is researched. From the resultant database, valuable information can be obtained regarding possible refinements, alterations in administration and scoring procedures, etc. Test developers usually wait until a substantial amount of information has been gathered regarding how the measure needs to be revised before they undertake a full-scale revision and renorming process.

>> **CRITICAL THINKING CHALLENGE 6.1**

Construct a flow diagram of the steps involved in developing and publishing a measure.

6.2 **Evaluating a measure**

Test developers and publishers have the responsibility of ensuring that measures are developed following a rigorous methodology and of providing information to verify the measure's validity and reliability. Assessment practitioners have the responsibility of evaluating the information provided about a measure and weighing up whether the measure is valid and reliable for the intended purpose. Assessment practitioners can use the information provided in Section 6.1 on the development of a measure to identify the key technical and psychometric aspects that they should keep in mind when they evaluate a measure. When evaluating a measure, assessment practitioners should, among other things, consider the following:

- How long ago a measure was developed, as the appropriateness of the item content and the norms changes over time.
- The quality and appeal of the test materials.
- The quality of the manual contents (e.g. does it indicate the purpose of the measure, who it should be applied to, what the limitations are, how to administer, score, and interpret the measure).
- The clarity of the test instructions (especially where there are different language versions).
- The cultural appropriateness of the item content and the constructs being tapped (e.g. has there been an empirical investigation into item bias, differential item functioning, and construct equivalence for different groups).
- If the measure is to be used in a multicultural and/or multilingual context, whether bias investigations provide evidence that the performance of various groups on the measure is equivalent.
- The adequacy of the psychometric properties that have been established.
- The nature of the norm groups and the recency of the norms.

Assessment practitioners should use available information, both local and international, to develop their own rules of thumb when it comes to assessing the quality of assessment measures. Consult the web site of the European Federation of Psychologist Associations (www.efpa) or that of the British Psychological Society's Psychological Testing Centre (PTC) (www.psychtesting.org.uk) for information on a detailed test review system.

>> **CRITICAL THINKING CHALLENGE 6.2**

Develop your own set of guidelines to use when evaluating psychological assessment measures. Try to develop your guidelines in the form of a checklist, as this will be more practical and save you valuable time in practice.

CHECKING YOUR PROGRESS 6.1

6.1 In educational assessment, test plans are based on the content of a chapter or module. Develop a test plan for a multiple choice measure that covers the content of this chapter. Your test plan should include:
- Definitions of the constructs (learning outcomes) to be measured.
- The content to be covered.
- The number of questions per learning outcome.
- The item and response format.
- How the test will be administered and scored.

How's the journey going? There's only one more stop left in the *Foundation Zone*. In the last stretch of uphill climbing for a while, you will be introduced to issues related to the development and adaptation of measures in cross-cultural contexts.

Cross-cultural test adaptation, translation and tests in multiple languages

ANIL KANJEE AND CHERYL FOXCROFT

CHAPTER OUTCOMES

The adaptation of assessment measures is essential in a multicultural and multilingual society like South Africa if test results are to be valid and reliable for all test-takers. In practice, this implies that test-takers from different cultural, language, and/or socio-economic backgrounds should be given the same opportunity to respond to any test item. For example, companies regularly require prospective employees to undertake various assessment tasks to assess the suitability of the applicant for a specific position. If prospective applicants speak different languages or come from different cultural backgrounds, the assessment tasks selected should accommodate the different languages and cultural backgrounds of the applicants. This is certainly a daunting and challenging task that is not only costly and time-consuming, but also requires high levels of expertise in translating and adapting measures. In this chapter, we will discuss the process of adapting measures as well as issues related to test bias impacting on this process. In addition, the challenges in adapting measures for the multilingual South African context will be highlighted and some solutions will be posed. In addition, the possibility of developing indigenous multiple language versions of a measure using a simultaneous multicultural approach will be explored. By the end of this chapter you will be able to:

> list reasons why assessment measures are adapted;
> describe the process followed when adapting measures;
> explain the concepts of equivalence and bias, which are fundamental to understanding the different designs and methods used to adapt measures;
> understand both the statistical and judgemental designs used to adapt measures, as well as their associated advantages and disadvantages;
> discuss the issue of test bias and describe methods of detecting bias;
> understand the steps involved in maximizing success in test adaptations;
> discuss obstacles and problems in adapting measures in South Africa and suggest possible solutions; and
> describe the simultaneous multicultural test development process.

7.1 **Reasons for adapting measures**

Before we explain the reasons for test adaptation, we need to clarify some terminology. **Test translation** refers to the process of converting a measure from one language to one or more other languages (e.g. from English to Setswana), while still retaining the original meaning. **Test adaptation,** on the other hand, is also based on retaining the original meaning but refers to that process of making a measure more applicable to a specific context while using the same language. In adapted tests, the language remains the same but the words, context, examples, etc. are changed to be more relevant and applicable to a specific national, language, and/or cultural group. For example, in a South African adaptation of a test, references to the British pound would be changed to the South African rand or a sports example that uses ice hockey would be changed to a sport that is more familiar to all South Africans, such as soccer. For the purpose of this chapter, the terms adaptation and translation will be used interchangeably.

Some of the most important reasons for adapting assessment measures include the following:

- To enhance **fairness** in assessment by allowing persons to be assessed in the language of their choice. Thus possible bias associated with assessing individuals in their second or third best language is removed and the validity of results is increased.
- To **reduce costs** and **save time**. It is often cheaper and easier to translate and adapt an existing measure into a second language than to develop a new measure. In addition, in situations where there is a lack of resources and technical expertise, adapting measures might be the only alternative for ensuring a valid and reliable measure.
- To **facilitate comparative studies** between different language and cultural groups, both at an international and national level. This has become especially relevant in recent years with the growing contact and cooperation between different nations in economic, educa-

tional, and cultural spheres. This has resulted in an increased need for many nationalities and groups to know and learn more from and about each other and for multinational organizations to assess people from diverse backgrounds for selection and training purposes.

- To **compare** newly developed measures to existing norms, interpretations, and other available information about established and respected measures (Brislin, 1986). For example, comparing a recently developed personality inventory with the established 16 Personality Factor questionnaire. This adds some sense of security that established and respected measures provide.

With increased diversification of cultures in countries and the globalization of world trade, Casillas and Robbins (2005) observe that there has been a marked increase in cross-cultural assessment and test adaptation. They report that in the period from 1964 to 1983 only 20 articles were published that focused on various aspects of cross-cultural assessment, whereas in the period 1984 to 2004 some 198 articles were published.

7.2 **Important considerations when adapting measures**

The adaptation of measures must be viewed within the overall context of the use of assessment in a cross-cultural setting, and should not focus only on the adaptation process. Besides the technical methods, other aspects of the adaptation process include test administration, item formats used, and time limits of the measure.

7.2.1 **Administration**

The validity of a measure can be seriously compromised if there are any communication problems between the assessment practitioner and the test-takers, for example, if instructions are misunderstood due to language difficulties. To overcome this problem, it is important for assessment practitioners to:

- be familiar with the culture, language, and dialect of the test-takers;

- have adequate administration skills and expertise; and
- possess some measurement expertise (Hambleton and Kanjee, 1995).

7.2.2 **Item format**

Item format refers to the type of questions (items) used in any measure, for example, multiple-choice, true/false, essays (see Chapter 6). In a cross-cultural context, it cannot be assumed that all test-takers will be equally familiar with the specific item formats used in the measure. For example, students in South Africa are more familiar with essay-type questions while those in the United States of America are more familiar with multiple-choice questions. The use of specific item formats can therefore place some individuals at an advantage over others. A possible solution to this problem is to include a balance of different item formats in the measure. Another solution, especially with multiple-choice items, is to include practice items that would allow test-takers some opportunity to familiarize themselves with the unfamiliar format.

7.2.3 **Time limits**

The concept of speed as a function of intellectual ability is a common foundation of many measures. For example, in some cultures it is commonly accepted that the better or brighter students are the ones who complete tasks first. However, in other cultures, answering questions quickly and blurting out a response is often regarded as rude or impolite. Instead, intellectual ability is associated with thoughtfulness and careful consideration of your response. Consequently, in such cultures the concept of speed is not seen to be a significant factor in cognitive ability. Thus measures that have time restrictions can place some test-takers at a severe disadvantage. The best solution to this problem is to minimize test speed as a factor when assessing test-takers by ensuring that there is adequate time for completion of the measure.

7.3 **Designs for adapting measures**

In this section we discuss the different designs for adapting measures for use in cross-cultural/lingual settings. Specifically, judgemental and statistical designs used, as well as the associated advantages and disadvantages, are presented. However, we will first focus on the concept of equivalence, which is fundamental to understanding the various adaptation designs.

7.3.1 **Equivalence in cross-cultural comparisons**

The attainment of equivalent measures is perhaps the central issue in cross-cultural comparative research (Van de Vijver and Leung, 1997). For measures to be **equivalent**, individuals with the same or similar standing on a construct, such as learners with high mathematical ability, but belonging to different groups, such as Xhosa- and Afrikaans-speaking, should obtain the same or similar scores on the different language versions of the items or measure. If not, the items are said to be **biased** and the two versions of the measure are non-equivalent. If the basis of comparison is not equivalent across different measures, valid comparisons across these measures and/or groups cannot be made, as the test scores are not directly comparable. In such a situation, it is uncertain whether these scores represent valid differences or similarities in performance between test-takers from different cultural groups, or merely measurement differences caused by the inherent differences in the measures themselves.

Measures therefore have to be equivalent if comparisons are to be made between individuals belonging to different subgroups. To ensure that measures are equivalent, they are adapted using judgemental and/or statistical designs. However, it must be noted that even if scores are comparable, it cannot be assumed that the measure is free of any bias. This issue of bias is discussed in Section 7.4.

7.3.2 **Judgemental designs for adapting measures**

Judgemental designs for establishing equivalence of adapted measures are based on a decision by an individual, or a group of individuals, on the degree to which the two measures are similar. Usually judges are individuals who have relevant experience and expertise in test content and measurement issues and are familiar with the culture and language of the groups under consideration. The common designs used are **forward-translation** and **back-translation**.

7.3.2.1 Forward-translation designs

In this design, the source version of a measure, which is referred to as the original language source, is translated into the target language (i.e. the language that the measure is translated into) by a single translator or a group of translators. In one version of this design, a sample of target test-takers answer the target version of the measure and are then questioned by judges about the meaning of their responses. Judges decide if the responses given reflect a reasonable representation of the test items in terms of cultural and linguistic understanding. If a high percentage of test-takers present a reasonable representation of an item (in the target language), the item is then regarded as being equivalent to the source language. The main judgement here is whether test-takers in the target language perceive the meaning of each item on a measure in the same way as the source language test-takers (Hambleton, 1993). Relevant changes to the measure, if any, can be made based on information provided by the judges. The advantage of this design is that valuable information about the functioning of any item is provided directly by the test-takers. Such information is otherwise unavailable when test-takers only respond to questions on paper. The disadvantage, however, is that there are many factors (e.g. personal, cultural, linguistic) that play a role during the interaction between test-takers and judges that can quite easily interfere with the results (Hambleton and Kanjee, 1995). For example, judges can easily misinterpret, misunderstand, and/or misrepresent responses of target test-takers. Another disadvantage of this design is that it is very labour intensive and time consuming, compared to other judgemental designs.

In a more common variation of this design, instead of having target group test-takers answer the translated version of the instrument, individual (or preferably a group of) different bilingual experts (judges) compare the source and target versions of the measure to determine whether the two versions are equivalent. These comparisons can be made on the basis of having the judges do the following:

- simply look the items over;
- check the characteristics of items against a checklist of item characteristics that may indicate non-equivalence; or
- attempt to answer both versions of the item before comparing them for errors (Hambleton and Bollwark, 1991).

This design, however, also has certain disadvantages:
- it is often difficult to find bilingual judges who are equally familiar with the source and target languages and/or culture;
- due to their expertise and experience, bilingual judges may inadvertently use insightful guesses to infer equivalence of meaning; and
- bilingual judges may not think about the item in the same way as the respective source and target language test-takers and thus the results may not be generalizable.

7.3.2.2 Back-translation designs

In back-translation designs, the original measure is first translated into the target language by a set of translators, and then translated back into the original language by a different set of translators (Brislin, 1986). Equivalence is usually assessed by having source language judges check for errors between the original and back-translated versions of the measure. For example, a test is translated from Zulu to Setswana, back-translated in Zulu by different translators, and the two Zulu versions are assessed for equivalence by a group of judges with expertise in Zulu. The main advantage of this design is that researchers who are not familiar with the target language can examine both versions of the source language to gain some insight into the quality of the translation (Brislin, 1986). Also, this design can easily be adapted such that a monolingual researcher (assessment or subject specialist) can evaluate and thus improve the quality of the translation after it has been translated into the target language, but before it is back-translated into the source language.

The main disadvantage of this design is that

the evaluation of equivalence is carried out in the source language only. It is quite possible that the findings in the source language version do not generalize to the target language version of the measure. Another disadvantage is that the assumption that errors made during the original translation will not be made again during the back-translation is not always applicable (Hambleton and Bollwark, 1991). Often skilled and experienced translators use insight to ensure that items translated are equivalent, even though this may not be true. This, however, can be controlled by either using a group of bilingual translators or a combination of bilinguals and monolinguals to perform multiple translations to and from the target and source languages (Bracken and Barona, 1991; Brislin, 1986). For example, Brislin (1986) suggests the use of monolinguals to check the translated version of the measure and make necessary changes before it is back-translated and compared to the original version. Once the two versions of a measure are as close as possible, Bracken and Barona (1991) argue for the use of a bilingual committee of judges to compare the original or back-translated and the translated version of the measure to ensure that the translation is appropriate for the test-takers.

7.3.3 **Statistical designs for assessing equivalence**

The statistical designs used to assess the equivalence of translated measures are dependent on the characteristics of participants, that is, monolingual, bilingual, or multilingual speakers, as well as on the version of the translated instrument, that is, original, translated, or back-translated (Hambleton and Bollwark, 1991). We will discuss three statistical designs in this section: bilingual, both source and target language monolinguals, and source language monolinguals.

7.3.3.1 **Bilingual test-takers**

In this design, both the source and target versions of the measures are administered to test-takers who speak both the source and target languages, before comparing the two sets of scores. The advantage of this design is that, since the same test-takers take both versions of the measure, differences in the abilities of test-takers that can confound the evaluation of translation equivalence will be controlled (Hambleton and Bollwark, 1991). The disadvantage of this design is that, due to time constraints, test-takers might not be able to take both versions of the instruments. A variation of this design that overcomes the problem of time is to split the bilingual sample and randomly assign test-takers to only one version of the measure. Results for items and overall performance on the measure of the randomly equivalent groups can then be compared. Differences between the test-takers with respect to their level of bilingualism and/or level of biculturalism could still violate the assumption of equal abilities between test-takers (Hambleton, 1993). A more serious problem, however, is that the results obtained from bilingual test-takers may not be generalizable to the respective source language monolinguals (Hambleton, 1993).

7.3.3.2 **Source and target language monolinguals**

In this design, source language monolinguals take the source version and target language monolinguals take the target version of a measure (Brislin, 1986; Ellis, 1989; 1991). The source version can either be the original or back-translated version of the measure (Brislin, 1986). The two sets of scores are then compared to determine the equivalence between the two versions of the measure. The main advantage of this design is that, since both source and target language monolinguals take the versions of the measure in their respective languages, the results are more generalizable to their respective populations. A major problem, however, is that the resulting scores may be confounded by real ability differences in the groups being compared, since two different samples of test-takers are compared (Hambleton, 1993). However, alternative steps can be taken to minimize this problem (Bollwark, 1992).

Firstly, test-takers selected for the groups should be matched as closely as possible on the ability/abilities of interest and on criteria that are relevant to the purpose of assessment. For example, scores from measures that assess related tasks/abilities could be used for matching purposes. If such information is unavailable, test-taker samples should be chosen using available information about the ability level of each sample, for example, information based on years and type of schooling and/or demographic data. Secondly, conditional statistical techniques that take into account the ability of test-takers when comparing test scores on a measure can also be used to control for differences in ability between the source and target test-taker samples. Methods based on item response theory and/or logistic regression, for example, can be used. Lastly, factor analysis or any other statistical technique where no common scale is assumed is often used in conjunction with this design. For example, in factor analysis, scores of the two groups are separately analysed to determine the similarity of the factor structures across the two groups. The disadvantage is that, since factor analysis is based on classical item statistics, the results are sample dependent (Hambleton and Bollwark, 1991). Still, researchers must, at a minimum, check that the ordering of item difficulties is the same in the two versions of the measure.

7.3.3.3 Source language monolinguals

In this design, equivalence of the measure is based on the scores of source language monolinguals who take both the original and the back-translated versions of the measure. The advantage is that the same sample of test-takers is used and scores are therefore not confounded by test-taker differences. A major problem, however, is that no data on the performance of target language individuals, nor the translated version of the measure is collected. Information about possible problems concerning the target group version is therefore not available, causing this design to have very limited validity.

7.4 Bias analysis and differential item functioning (DIF)

By definition, the bias analysis process implies an unfair advantage/disadvantage to one or more groups. Thus, when developing or adapting any measure, it is essential to eliminate any unfair advantage or disadvantage to any test-taker, irrespective of their cultural, social, economic, and/or linguistic background. This is especially relevant to cross-cultural settings and must begin at the test conceptualization phase. When developing or adapting any measure, the various differences among the population for whom the measure is intended must be recognized and taken into account. Thus, item writers need to be selected not only because they are competent and experienced in the content area and knowledgeable in measurement issues, but also because they are representative of and sensitive to the cultural, linguistic, and socio-economic differences of the population for whom the measure is intended.

As was discussed in Chapter 6, once a measure has been developed, additional analyses are conducted to identify specific items that could disadvantage one or more groups of individuals in terms of the test results. For example, some items may be biased against females or test-takers from rural areas and these test-takers would therefore probably obtain lower scores. Usually this analysis takes two forms: judgemental and statistical. A **judgemental analysis** is conducted before a measure is administered and involves a group of experts reviewing the measure for any items that could cause bias, as well as ensuring that the content, for example, language, examples, and pictures, would not be offensive to any groups or individuals. A **statistical analysis**, on the other hand, is conducted using the data obtained from administering the measure and involves the use of statistical methods for flagging those items that might or might not result in bias.

7.4.1 Differential item functioning (DIF)

When **differential item functioning (DIF)** is investigated, statistical procedures are used to compare test results of test-takers who have the same ability but who belong to different cultural (or language) groups. Hambleton, Swaminathan, and Rogers (1991) note that the accepted definition of **DIF** is as follows:

> an item shows DIF if individuals having the same ability, but from different groups, do not have the same probability of getting the item right.

The ability level of test-takers is a critical factor since statistical procedures are based on the assumption that test-takers with similar ability levels should obtain similar results on the measure. In addition, it is unreasonable to compare test-takers with different levels of ability since their test scores will inevitably differ, irrespective of their cultural or linguistic backgrounds. Stated technically, equivalence cannot be determined using unequal comparisons.

In practice, statistical methods cannot detect bias as such. Rather, these methods merely indicate that an item functions differently or that it provides different information for test-takers with the same ability but who belong to different subgroups, for example male and female (Holland and Thayer, 1988). To determine whether any bias exists, those items flagged need to be further investigated to identify possible reasons for functioning differently. Therefore, the term *item bias* has been replaced by the less value-laden term *differential item functioning (DIF)*. Thus, an item that exhibits DIF may or may not be biased for or against any group unless specific evidence indicates otherwise.

It is important to note that the identification and elimination of DIF from any measure increases the reliability and validity of scores. Test results from two or more groups from which DIF items have been removed are more likely to be equivalent and thus comparable.

7.4.2 Statistical methods for detecting DIF

A discussion of the various methods for detecting DIF is beyond the scope of this chapter. However, we will discuss the Mantel-Haenszel procedure and the item response theory (IRT) approach. Other popular methods include factor analysis, item difficulty, chi-square, and logistic regression (Kanjee, 1992, 2007).

7.4.2.1 Mantel-Haenszel procedure

The **Mantel-Haenszel procedure** is based on the assumption that an item does not display any DIF if the odds of getting an item correct are the same for two groups of test-takers across all different ability levels. In this procedure, the odds-ratio is used to compare two group where:

- test-takers are first matched into comparable groups, based on ability levels; for each ability level separately, the pass/fail data are tabulated for the two matched groups in a two-by-two table, and then
- the matched groups are compared on every item on the measure for each of the ability groups. The null hypothesis, that is, that the odds of a correct response to the item are the same for both groups on all ability levels, is tested using the chi-square statistic with one degree of freedom.

7.4.2.2 Item response theory

Item response theory (IRT) is a test theory used to develop and assemble test items, detect bias in measuring instruments, implement computerized adaptive tests, and analyse test data. IRT is an extremely powerful theory that is especially useful for large-scale testing programmes. By applying IRT, it is possible to analyse the relationship between the characteristics of the individual (e.g. ability) and responses to individual items (Hulin, Drasgow, and Parsons, 1983; Lord, 1980; Thissen and Steinberg, 1988). A basic assumption of IRT is that the higher an individual's ability level is, the greater the individual's chances are of getting an item correct. This makes sense as good students generally obtain higher marks.

This relationship is graphically represented (see Figure 7.1) by the **item characteristic curve** (ICC). The X-axis in Figure 7.1 represents the ability level of test-takers while the Y-axis represents the probability of answering an item correctly. The difficulty level of an item is indicated by the position of the curve on the X-axis as measured by that point on the curve where the probability of answering an item correctly is 50 per cent. The slope of the curve indicates the discriminating power. The steeper the slope, the higher the discriminating power of an item. Item 1 displays a curve for an item of moderate difficulty that is highly discriminating, while the curve for Item 2 implies that the item is a difficult item with very little discrimination.

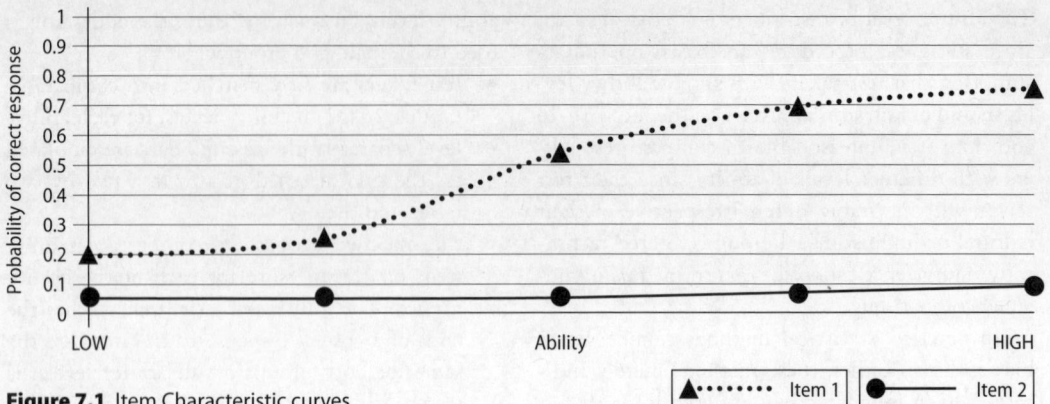

Figure 7.1 Item Characteristic curves

▲········ Item 1   ●——— Item 2

The disadvantage of IRT, however, is that relatively large sample sizes are required for analysing the data. In addition, the complex mathematical calculations require the use of sophisticated software, which can be costly to purchase.

7.4.2.3 **IRT and DIF detection**

The detection of DIF using IRT is a relatively simple process. Once item characteristics and test-taker ability measures are calculated, the item characteristic curves (ICCs) of the groups under investigation can be directly compared. This can be done graphically or statistically and involves determining whether any significant differences exist between the respective ICCs. Figure 7.2 contains two ICCs for a group of test-takers with the same ability levels. Since the ability levels of both

groups are equal, the ICCs for both groups should be the same. These ICCs, however, are clearly different, indicating that the item is functioning differently for each of the groups. If many of the items in a measure produce the same DIF picture, Group 2 will obtain lower test scores, and the measure would not be measuring the construct as well for Group 2 as it would for Group 1 (due to the lower discriminatory power for Group 2). Once the existence of DIF is confirmed, the next step involves ascertaining the probable reasons for the DIF detected. Generally, items detected as DIF are revised if possible, or removed from the measure. Possible reasons for DIF can usually be traced to the use of unfamiliar, inappropriate, or ambiguous language, concepts, or examples; test speededness; and unfamiliar item format.

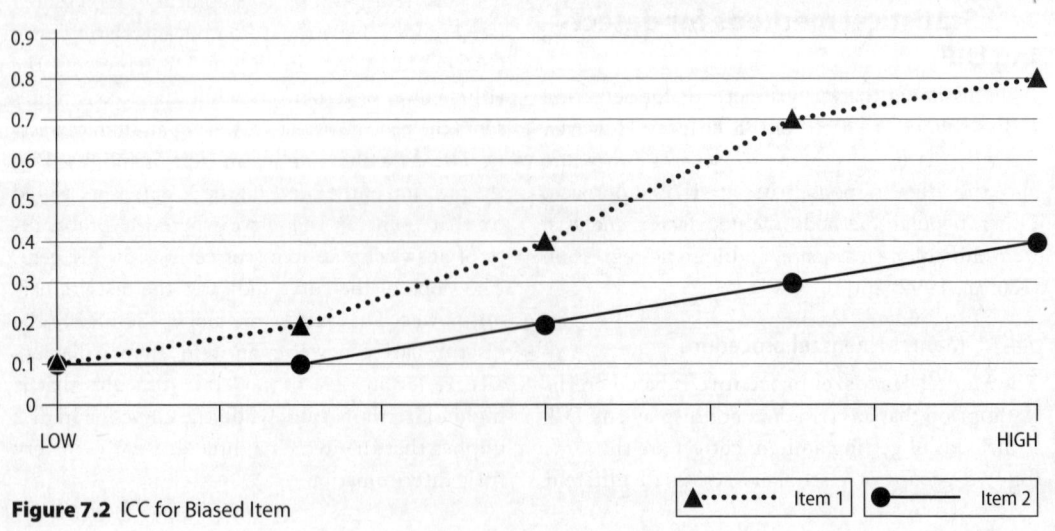

Figure 7.2 ICC for Biased Item

▲········ Item 1   ●——— Item 2

»   CRITICAL THINKING CHALLENGE 7.1

Look at the ICCs in Figure 7.2. Assume that Group 1 represents the ICC for males and Group 2 the ICC for females for an item. Explain to a friend why this item is biased against females.

7.5 Steps for maximizing success in test adaptations

The International Test Commission provides a comprehensive set of 22 guidelines for improving the translating and adapting of educational and psychological instruments (available at www. intestcom.org). The guidelines fall into four main categories: those concerned with the cultural context, those concerned with the technicalities of instrument development and adaptation, those concerned with test administration, and those concerned with documentation and interpretation. Hambleton (2004) summarized these guidelines and notes the following nine key steps that should be addressed when adapting or translating any assessment instrument:

• Review construct equivalence in the languages and cultures of interest.
• Decide whether test adaptation/translation is the best strategy.
• Choose well qualified translators.
• Translate/adapt the instrument using the appropriate design.
• Review the adapted version and make necessary changes.
• Conduct a small tryout of the adapted test.
• Conduct a validation investigation.
• Place scores of both the translated and the original test on a common scale.
• Document the process and prepare the manual for test users.

7.6 Challenges related to test adaptation in South Africa

While the previous sections in this chapter have outlined the 'why' and 'how' of test adaptation in theory, you might want to know more about the practice of test adaptation in South Africa. This section will outline some of the challenges being experienced, the reasons for them and some potential solutions will be suggested.

7.6.1 Language choice for assessment

It could be argued that test adaptation in South Africa in terms of developing multiple language versions of measures has not flourished as it should have. Why? There is a widely held assumption that as the majority of South Africans are educated in English from Grade 4 onwards, and as English is the language of instruction at most higher education institutions and in the work place, assessing test-takers in English is acceptable (Foxcroft and Aston, 2006). It is argued that if test-takers cannot perform well on measures administered in English, they will not be able to cope with English as the language of instruction at a higher education level or in the work place. Consequently, despite the great diversity of languages in South Africa, it has not become standard practice to have multiple language versions for all measures. However, various South African researchers (e.g., Foxcroft and de Bruin, 2008; Koch, 2005; Meiring, 2007, Saunders, 2002) have been critical of this assumption for a number of reasons. For example, Watson, Davies and Foxcroft (2006) have shown that merely being educated through the medium of English is no guarantee that learners are sufficiently proficient in English as a second language at the end of Grade 12. In fact, the majority are not proficient. In this instance it violates the standards set for the ethical and fair practice of assessment if the test-taker is assessed in a language in which he/she is not proficient. Furthermore, where second language English speakers are assessed on a measure developed for first language English speakers, there needs to be evidence that the measure is assessing comparable constructs for the two groups and that language is not a 'nuisance factor' that impacts negatively on test performance. In terms of the latter, a number of South African studies have highlighted language proficiency as a potential source of bias on South African measures for both cognitive (e.g. Foxcroft and Aston, 2006; van Eeden and van Tonder, 1995) and personality measures (Abrahams and Mauer, 1999b; Joseph and van Lill, 2008; Meiring, van de Vijver, and Rothmann, 2006; Meiring, van de Viyver, Rothmann and Barrick, 2005). It would thus seem that if English proficiency is important for higher education studies and in the work place, the solution does not lie in making English the preferred language of assessment as this can have a negative impact on the test performance of non-English mother tongue speakers on the construct being assessed (e.g., cognitive ability, personality). Instead, two solutions can be suggested. One solution is to determine the English proficiency level for a measure (e.g., a Grade 8 level) and then to administer an English proficiency test to see whether the test-taker achieves the desired level of proficiency. If he/she is not appropriately proficient, then the measure cannot be administered in English. If he/she is found to be appropriately proficient, then administering the measure in English could still result in an unbiased assessment of the construct. The other solution lies in administering an English proficiency test to assess language proficiency and then assessing the other competencies/proficiencies/constructs in the language in which the test-taker is most proficient in. The implication of both solutions is that there needs to be multiple language versions of tests to achieve fair assessment in South Africa. Is this feasible and will it not be too costly and time-consuming to undertake in a country with 11 official languages?

The need for multiple language versions of a measure is not a uniquely South African one. Hambleton and De Jong (2003, p. 130) have observed that 'Growing recognition of multiculturalism has raised awareness of the need to provide for multiple language versions of tests and instruments intended for use within a single national context'. Indeed there are numerous examples of multiple language versions of a test being available in other multilingual countries. Take Israel, for example. Beller, Gafni and Hanani (1999) report that the Psychometric Entrance Test (PET) is used for admission to universities in Israel. Although it was originally developed in Hebrew, it has been translated into Arabic, Russian, French, Spanish and English. Furthermore, the English version provides the questions in both English and Hebrew and is administered to applicants whose home language is English or who are not proficient in any of the languages available for the PET. For this version, an innovative feature is that there is a short dictionary at the bottom of each page, which contains a translation of some of the key words in the more frequent languages of the test-takers such as German, Hungarian, and Italian. All applicants who are not tested on the Hebrew version of the PET are also required to take a Hebrew proficiency test given that the medium of instruction at Israeli universities is Hebrew. Beller, Gafni and Hanani (1999) acknowledge that considerable effort, resources and research has gone into ensuring that the translation methods used were sound and that while the construct-equivalence of the various versions is acceptable, more investigations are needed before it can be unequivocally concluded that the versions are equivalent. However, despite all the effort that has gone into adapting/translating and researching the different language versions of the PET, Beller, Gafni and Hanani (1999) assert that 'the alternative of testing non-Hebrew speakers in Hebrew would seem to constitute a much less fair solution' (p. 18).

In the South African context, measures such as the Raven's Coloured Progressive Matrices (e.g. Vaas, 2002; Knoetze, Bass, and Steele, 2005), the 16 Personality Factor Questionnaire Fifth Edition (16PF5) (e.g. van Eeden and Mantsha, 2007) and the Kaufman Assessment Battery for Children (K-ABC) (Jansen and Greenop, 2008) have been translated and adapted for different language/cultural groups. Furthermore, the Paper and Pencil Games (PPG) can be administered in all 11 official languages as multiple language versions are available. De Beer (2005) approaches the choice of language for administering the Learning Potential Computerized Adaptive Test (LPCAT) in an innovative way. Two versions of the LPCAT have been developed. In the first version all instructions, feedback and explanations are provided on the screen, whereas in the second version, instructions, feedback and explanations are read to the test-taker and do not appear on the screen. For the second version, test instructions are available in the 11 official South African languages. Test instructions are available in English and Afrikaans for the first version. De Beer (2002a) recommends that an English or Afrikaans Grade 6 reading level is needed if the first version is administered. To screen the reading proficiency of test-takers four items are included to test whether the test-taker has any difficulty with four very easy language items. If a test-taker fails more than one of these items, it is possible that he/she might not have understood some of the terms used in the instructions, feedback and training which could have affected the results negatively. In such an instance, it is recommended that the test-taker by re-assessed on the second version of the measure where the instructions are read in a language that he/she might be more proficient in.

So, in answer to the question posed above, it is possible to develop multiple language versions of tests. The international and South African examples cited above serve to substantiate this assertion. While considerable effort and resources go into developing multiple language versions, in accordance with Beller, Gafni and Hanani's (1999) conclusion, it remains a worthwhile investment as it is far fairer to assess test-takers in a language which they are proficient in than in their second or third language.

A note of caution needs to be sounded in relation to the fact that given that the majority of South Africans are not educated in their mother tongue, it is not always easy to determine the one language that test-takers are most proficient in for assessment purposes. In many instances **bilingual assessment** might be more appropriate as they may be able to comprehend and respond to items that draw on previously learned knowledge by using the language that they were educated in but find it easier to respond to novel problem-solving items using their mother tongue. However, to be able to use bilingual assessment, assessment practitioners will have to be proficient in both languages being used to administer the measure. At present the majority of assessment practitioners are not sufficiently proficient in a black language to be able to undertake bilingual assessment on their own. However, they could use a fellow practitioner who is proficient in a black language or a translator, for example, to assist them during test administration.

7.6.2 **Translation and adaptation challenges**

The task of adapting measures and translating them into multiple languages provides researchers in South African and elsewhere in the world with a number of challenges. For example, van Eeden and Mantsha (2007) highlight a number of translation difficulties encountered when translating the 16PF5 into Tshivenda from English using the back-translation method. Among the difficulties were:

- the fact that there is not an equivalent term for a concept in the target language. For example, there is no Tshivenda term for 'depression' which made the literal translation of the item 'I don't let myself get depressed over little things' problematic. Other researchers have similarly found that restricted vocabularly makes it difficult to translate personality descriptors into isiXhosa (Horn, 2000) and Xitsonga (Piedmont, Bain, McCrae and Costa, 2002);
- that idiomatic expressions cannot be translated literally; and
- use of the negative form (e.g. 'I don't let myself get depressed') which often confuses test-takers.

According to van Eeden and Mantsha (2007) such translation difficulties could result in inaccuracies that change the meaning of an item and make it difficult for the test-taker to understand the item. Van Eeden and Mantsha (2007, p. 75) also note that 'it is clear that the problems experienced at the item level when testing in a multicultural context are not merely related to language but also involve a cultural component.' This is an important reminder that the content of items could be culture bound and that constructs could manifest differently in different groups. Furthermore, even when international measures are adapted for use in the multicultural South African context and biased items are removed and language issues addressed, Meiring, van de Vijver and Rothmann (2006) found that although bias was reduced for the adapted version of the Fifteen Factor Questionnaire (15FQ+), internal consistencies remained low for the black sample, which is problematic. Consequently, in the domain of personality assessment in particular, in an attempt to find a measure that is appropriate for the different cultures in South Africa, attention is shifting to the development of an indigenous measure. As was pointed out in Chapter 6, a team of researchers have started the process of developing the South African Personality Inventory (SAPI) which aims to include both universal and unique dimensions of personality (Meiring, 2006). Suggestions related to the development of measures that will be used in multicultural and multilingual contexts are covered in the next sub-section. Aspects of the SAPI project will be highlighted.

7.7 Multicultural test development

According to Tanzer (2005) there are two main approaches followed when making measures available for use in multicultural contexts, namely, a successive and a simultaneous multicultural approach. The most popular one is the **successive approach**. In successive test development the measure is developed for a mono-cultural/mono-lingual context. When the measure proves to be useful, it is adapted and translated for use in other cultural/language groups. Examples of where the successive approach has been used in South Africa are the adaptation of the WAIS- III for South Africa (see Chapter 10) and the adaptation and translation of the 16PF5 and the 15FQ+ (see 7.6.2). While this approach is the one of choice to adapt widely used international measures for the South African context, the main drawbacks with it are that the constructs measured in the original and adapted versions might not be equivalent and the way in which the construct is operationalised might not be as relevant or appropriate for the cultural group that it is being adapted for.

Tanzer (2005) makes a strong case for the advantages of using a simultaneous multicultural approach when developing tests to be used in multiple cultures and languages. As was discussed in Chapter 2, when this approach is used, a multicultural and multi-disciplinary panel or committee of experts is assembled. Panel members need to have expertise in test development and psychometrics,

in psychology and in cross-cultural psychology in particular, in linguistics, in relation to the cultures and language groups for whom the measure is being developed, and in terms of the construct being assessed (e.g. personality). While it is not necessary that each expert possesses all this expertise, the panel or committee must collectively reflect this expertise. In the South African Personality Inventory (SAPI) project (Meiring, 2006), which is being developed using a simultaneous multicultural approach, a core panel of national and international experts in personality test development and cross-cultural psychology have spearheaded the development of the SAPI. In addition, masters' and doctoral students from various South African cultural and language groups have interacted closely with the core panel to develop the data collection and analysis methods. Other experts such as linguists, sociologists and anthropologists have been consulted and brought into the core panel at appropriate points in the test development process. The value of having such a diverse array of experts involved in developing a measure such as the SAPI is that the way in which the construct is operationalized as well as the content of the measure is more likely to be appropriate for use in the multiple cultures for which it is being developed than is the case with the successive approach. A further interesting feature of the development of the SAPI is that in the first phase of its development, ordinary adults across the age and socio-economic spectrum, from rural and urban areas provided descriptions of personality, which were clustered and categorized to uncover the personality dimensions for each of the 11 language groups in South Africa. This should further ensure that the operationalization of the personality construct should be appropriate for the diverse cultural and language groups in South Africa.

Once the construct has been delineated in the simultaneous approach, the test specifications need to be determined and the items need to be developed. Items can be developed by the expert panel or committee. As the panel or committee includes language and cultural experts they can ensure that the items do not contain culturally loaded content or idiomatic expressions that will only be meaningful for one cultural or language group. Another approach is to establish various test development teams, with each team having expertise in one of the cultures and language groups for whom the test is being developed. In this instance, careful planning is required. Solano-Flores, Turnbull and Nelson-Barber (2002) report that in order for multiple test development teams to generate items that contribute to the overall measure, 'shells' need to first be developed. A 'shell' is a framework or a template that specifies the characteristics of 'families' or types or problems that makes it possible for the test development teams to generate items of a similar structure and complexity level. Items developed in one language can then be translated using the techniques described earlier in this chapter into the other languages that the measure is being developed in. When the different language versions are administered, they need to be researched to ensure that equivalent constructs are being tapped across the various versions and that the reliabilities are acceptable.

7.8 **Conclusion**

In the context of a multicultural society like South Africa, the adaptation of measures and the detection and elimination of bias from measures plays a vital role in the transformation process. To this end, it is important that rigorous methods and designs (such as those outlined in this chapter) are used if the information obtained from assessment measures is to be valid and reliable. As we pointed out in Chapters 1 and 2, assessment practitioners must accept responsibility for ensuring that the development and use of measures, and the interpretation and reporting of information are non-discriminatory, unbiased, and fair towards all South Africans.

And so ... you have finished the long climb through the *Foundation Zone*. You should give yourself a little check up to see if you have mastered the basic concepts that will be used in the remainder of this book. This set of questions will help you check that you can move with confidence to the *Assessment Practice Zone*. If, however, you stumble over a few of these questions, do some backtracking down the hill, just to familiarize yourself again with some of the more difficult concepts.

CHECKING YOUR PROGRESS **7.1**

7.1 What is a psychological measure/test?

7.2 What are the main characteristics of a psychological measure/test?

7.3 Why must a psychological measure be reliable?

7.4 What are the different forms of reliability that can be established?

7.5 Why must a psychological measure be valid?

7.6 What are the different types of validity that can be established?

7.7 Why are norms used?

7.8 What different types of norms can be established?

7.9 List the steps involved in developing a measure.

7.10 Why do we need to translate and adapt measures?

7.11 What methods/designs can be used when translating and adapting measures?

7.12 What are the major pitfalls (historical and current) associated with using psychological measures in the multicultural South African context?

The last question (7.12) sets the scene for the next zone of our journey, and our next stop in particular.

Assessment Practice Zone (1)

Now that we are out of the Foundation Zone, things are going to become a little less theoretical and a little more practical or applied. In the first stretch (Part 1) of the Assessment Practice Zone you will get a view of good assessment practices in general, as well as the administration of measures in particular.

Part

2

The practice of psycho-logical assessment: Controlling the use of measures, competing values, and ethical practice standards

CHERYL FOXCROFT, GERT ROODT AND FATIMA ABRAHAMS

Chapter

8

CHAPTER OUTCOMES

In this chapter you will learn more about who is legally allowed to use psychological assessment measures in South Africa, why the use of assessment measures needs to be controlled, and the ethical practice standards to which assessment practitioners should aspire. Please note: In this chapter the term 'use' relates to whoever may administer, score, interpret, and report on assessment measures and the outcome of assessment, and not to other users of assessment information such as human resource managers, teachers, and so on.

By the end of this chapter you will be able to:

> give reasons why the use of psychological measures should be controlled;
> explain the statutory control of psychological assessment in South Africa;
> list the different categories of assessment practitioners in South Africa, indicate the types of measures they are allowed to use, and discuss their training and registration requirements;
> understand why and how psychological measures are classified; and
> describe good, ethical assessment practices and the roles and responsibilities of the various stakeholders.

8.1 Statutory control of the use of psychological assessment measures in South Africa

8.1.1 Why should the use of assessment measures be controlled?

Assessment measures are potentially valuable tools that aid decision-making, as we saw in Chapter 1. However, the item content of some psychological assessment measures might tap into very personal information. This might cause psychological trauma to the individual being assessed if a professionally trained, caring professional is not on hand to work through any traumatic reactions during the course of assessment. Furthermore, feedback regarding psychological assessment results needs to be conveyed to the person being assessed in a caring, sensitive way, so that he/she does not suffer any emotional or psychological trauma. We also pointed out in Chapter 1 that assessment measures and their results can be misused, which can have negative consequences for those being assessed. In view of the potentially sensitive nature of some of the item content and the feedback, and given that assessment measures can be misused, the use of assessment measures needs to be controlled so that the public can be protected. Controlling the use of psychological measures by restricting them to appropriately trained professionals should ensure that:

- the measures are administered by a qualified, competent assessment practitioner and that assessment results are correctly interpreted and used;
- the outcome of the assessment is conveyed in a sensitive, empowering manner rather than in a harmful way;
- the purchasing of psychological assessment measures is restricted to those who may use them and that test materials are kept securely (as it is unethical for assessment practitioners to leave tests lying around) – this will prevent unqualified people from gaining access to and using them;

- test developers do not prematurely release assessment materials (e.g. before validity and reliability have been adequately established), as it is unethical for assessment practitioners to use measures for which appropriate validity and reliability data have not been established;
- the general public does not become familiar with the test content, as this would invalidate the measure. Should a measure be published in the popular press, for example, it would not only give members of the public insight into the test content, but could also give them a distorted view of psychological assessment.

> **» CRITICAL THINKING CHALLENGE 8.1**
>
> As a psychologist, you find yourself testifying in court at a murder trial. You assessed the person accused of the murder on a battery of measures, which included a measure of general intelligence as well as a personality measure. While you are testifying regarding your assessment findings, the judge asks you to show some of the intelligence test items to the court so that they can get a more concrete idea of what was assessed. How would you respond to this request? What factors would you weigh up in your mind to help you to formulate your response?

8.1.2 How control over the use of psychological assessment measures is exercised in South Africa

8.1.2.1 Statutory control

In South Africa, the use of psychological assessment measures is under **statutory control.** What does this mean?

A law (statute) has been promulgated that restricts the use of psychological assessment measures to appropriately registered psychology professionals. According to the **Health Professions Act**, Act 56 of 1974, the following acts are defined in Section 37(2) (a), (b), (c), (d), and (e) as 'specially pertaining to the profession of a psychologist:

(a) the evaluation of behaviour or mental processes or personality adjustments or adjustments of individuals or groups of persons, through the interpretation of tests for the determination of intellectual abilities, aptitude, interests, personality make-up or personality functioning, and the diagnosis of personality and emotional functions and mental functioning deficiencies according to a recognized scientific system for the classification of mental deficiencies;

(b) the use of any method or practice aimed at aiding persons or groups of persons in the adjustment of personality, emotional or behavioural problems or at the promotion of positive personality change, growth and development, and the identification and evaluation of personality dynamics and personality functioning according to psychological scientific methods;

(c) the evaluation of emotional, behavioural and cognitive processes or adjustment of personality of individuals or groups of persons by the usage and interpretation of questionnaires, tests, projections or other techniques or any apparatus, whether of South African origin or imported, for the determination of intellectual abilities, aptitude, personality make-up, personality functioning, psychophysiological functioning or psychopathology;

(d) the exercising of control over prescribed questionnaires or tests or prescribed techniques, apparatus or instruments for the determination of intellectual abilities, aptitude, personality make-up, personality functioning, psychophysiological functioning or psychopathology;

(e) the development of and control over the development of questionnaires, tests, techniques, apparatus or instruments for the determination of intellectual abilities, aptitude, personality make-up, personality functioning, psychophysiological functioning or psychopathology.'

Therefore, according to Act 56 of 1974, the use of measures to assess mental, cognitive, or behavioural processes and functioning, intellectual or cognitive ability or functioning, aptitude, interest, emotions, personality, psychophysiological functioning, or pyschopathology (abnormal behaviour), constitutes an act that falls in the domain of the psychology profession. Does this imply that only registered psychologists may use psychological assessment measures? The answer is 'No'. Within the psychology profession, there are various categories of professionals who may use psychological measures to varying extents. Furthermore, with the permission of the Professional Board for Psychology, various other professionals (e.g. occupational therapists, speech therapists) may be permitted to use certain psychological measures. Let us consider these different categories of users in greater detail.

8.1.2.2 The different categories of psychology professionals who may use psychological measures

There are currently five categories of professionals within the profession of psychology in South Africa, namely, **Psychologists, Registered Counsellors, Psychometrists (independent practice), Psychometrists (supervised practice),** and **Psychotechnicians.** However, the categories of Psychotechnician and Psychometrist (supervised practice) are being phased out: no new psychotechnicians or psychometrists (supervised practice) will be added to the register and those who were registered before the register was closed may continue to practice in their capacity as a psychotechnician or psychometrist (supervised practice). The extent to which each of these categories of practitioners may use psychological assessment measures, as well as the training requirements of each has been summarized in Table 8.1.

The Professional Board for Psychology has decided to introduce a further professional category at a specialist level. The first two specialist areas will be in clinical neuropsychology and forensic psychology. The scope of practice and training of such specialists is still being delineated, but when it comes to assessment, these specialists will

Table 8.1 Psychology professionals who may use psychological measures

ASPECT OF TEST USE	Range of measures and specialized assessment	Purchase of measures	Private practice and billing	Training requirements
PSYCHOLOGIST	Administer, score, interpret, and report on all measures and may perform specialized assessments (e.g. forensic, neuro-psychological) provided that appropriate training has been received.	May purchase psychological assessment measures.	Can set up private practice and bill clients for assessment.	Coursework Masters degree and 12-month internship; 70% for national exam set by Professional Board; mandatory continuing professional development.
REGISTERED COUNSELLOR	Administer, score, interpret, and report on certain measures (i.e. measures trained in and may not use projective personality measures, specialist neuropsychological measures, or measures for diagnosis of psychopathology).	May purchase some psychological assessment measures.	Can set up a private practice and may bill clients for assessment.	B.Psych; 720 hours in a supervised practicum; 70% for national exam set by Professional Board.
PSYCHOMETRIST (INDEPENDENT PRACTICE)	Administer, score, interpret, and report on certain measures (i.e. measures trained in and may not use projective personality measures, specialist neuropsychological measures, or measures for diagnosis of psychopathology).	May purchase certain psychological assessment measures.	Can set up a private practice and may bill clients for assessment.	BPsych or equivalent with a psychometry focus that includes 720 hours in a supervised practicum, or a psychometrist (supervised practice) can work under a psychologist for three years to log 720 hours of supervised practical training; 70% in a national exam set by Professional Board
PSYCHOMETRIST (SUPERVISED PRACTICE)	Administer, score, and provisionally interpret measures under a psychologist's supervision (excludes projective and specialist measures). Can participate in feedback and co-sign the report.	May not purchase psychological assessment measures.	Cannot practice independently; must work under a psychologist.	BPsych or equivalent with a psychometry focus; 720 hours of practical assessment work; 70% in a national exam set by Professional Board.

PSYCHO-TECH-NICIAN	Administer, score, and interpret standardized group or individual screening-type tests. May not perform specialized assessments.	May not purchase psychological assessment measures.	Must work under supervision and may not bill clients for assessment.	Bachelors degree in psychology; 6-month internship; pass a national exam set by Psychometrics Committee.

conduct specialized clinical neuropsychological and forensic assessments respectively and it is possible that the use of certain measures will be restricted for use by specialists. You should thus follow the development of the specialist categories and how this might impact on the scope of assessment that psychologists can perform by consulting the web site of the Health Professions Council of South Africa (http://www.hpcsa.org.za).

In Chapter 1, we pointed out that, as far as integrating and synthesizing assessment information in particular are concerned, the assessment practitioner has to draw on all his/her knowledge and experience in the field of psychology and not just experience in assessment. Therefore, all the psychology professionals described in Table 8.1, apart from completing modules in assessment, have to be in possession of a degree in which they studied psychology in depth as well as related disciplines (e.g. statistics). This provides them with a broader knowledge base on which to draw during the assessment process.

8.1.2.3 Other professionals who use psychological measures

Speech and occupational therapists use some assessment measures that tap psychological constructs (e.g. measures of verbal ability or visual-motor functioning). You will remember from Section 8.1.2.1, that we looked at what is legally considered to be a psychological act. By administering measures that tap psychological constructs, speech and occupational therapists are performing psychological acts which fall outside of the scope of their profession. Nevertheless, these measures are essential tools that assist them in making appropriate diagnoses and developing interventions. A practical solution to this problem thus had to be found. Fortunately, through the process of test classification, which we will discuss in the next

section, the conditions under which a measure may be used can be relaxed. The Professional Boards for Speech Therapy and Occupational Therapy thus interact with the Psychometrics Committee of the Professional Board for Psychology to obtain lists of measures that may tap psychological constructs which they use. The relevant boards and the Psychometrics Committee discuss these lists and reach agreement on the prescribed list of tests for the various professionals, as well as the nature of the psychometrics and assessment training which trainees should receive. It is also possible that other professionals (e.g. social workers, paediatricians) might use measures in the course of their work that might tap psychological constructs. A similar process of engagement as described above will then have to be entered into with such professionals to see whether, under specified conditions, the Professional Board for Psychology will make it possible for them to use psychological measures.

8.1.2.4 The classification of psychological measures

Classification is a process whereby a decision is made regarding the nature of a measure and, consequently, who may use it. There are two main reasons why measures need to be classified in South Africa. Firstly, as there are many assessment measures of which only some qualify as being psychological assessment measures, measures have to be subjected to a classification process to determine whether or not they should be classified as a psychological measure. Secondly, as you saw in Section 8.1.2.2, various categories of psychology professionals may use psychological measures to varying extents, and certain other professionals can also be permitted to use psychological measures in the course of their assessment (see Section 8.1.2.3). The other purpose of classifying measures is therefore to determine which categories of practitioners may administer, score, interpret, and report on a particular measure.

Who undertakes the classification of measures in South Africa? In Chapter 1, we pointed out to you that the **Psychometrics Committee** of the **Professional Board** has been tasked with psychological assessment matters, including the classification of psychological measures, amongst others. The Psychometrics Committee only assumed this function in 1996. Prior to this, the Test Commission of the Republic of South Africa (TCRSA) undertook the classification of measures on behalf of the Professional Board for Psychology. According to the system of classification used by the TCRSA, measures were classified as 'not a psychological test', an A-level test (achievement measures), a B-level test (group tests of ability, aptitude and interest), or a C-level test (individually administered intelligence and personality-related measures). The classification decisions made by the TCRSA were based on the content domain tapped by the measure, the nature of the administration and scoring, and the extent to which the person being assessed could suffer psychological trauma. After a few years of adopting the same system, the Psychometrics Committee found that not only was the ABC classification no longer in widespread use internationally, but also that it unnecessarily complicated both practitioners' and the public's perception of what a psychological measure is. The Psychometrics Committee then developed a simplified classification system whereby a measure is simply labelled as either a psychological measure or not.

How is it determined whether a measure is a 'psychological measure'? According to the Psychometrics Committee's *Guidelines for Reviewers*, 'the simple rule of thumb is that a test is classified as being a psychological test when its use results in the performance of a psychological act' (Professional Board for Psychology, Psychometrics, November 1999b, p. 1). It is therefore not important whether a measure is of South African origin or is imported; is administered individually, in a group context, or via a computer; whether or not the test instructions are highly structured; whether the scoring procedure is objective, requires psychological judgement, or is computerized; whether the

interpretation is straightforward, requires professional expertise, or is generated via computer. The main criterion is whether or not use of the measure results in the performance of a psychological act.

A second aspect considered during the classification process is the fact that the test content and the outcome of the assessment might have a negative impact on the person being assessed (see Section 8.1.1). For this reason, the process of classifying a measure also takes into consideration whether the nature of the content of the measure and the results from it may have negative psychological consequences for the individual. This will imply that the administration and feedback should be handled in a supportive, sensitive way which, in turn, assists in the determination of the category of practitioner who may use the measure.

Test developers should, as a matter of course, send any new measures to the Psychometrics Committee to be classified. The Psychometrics Committee also has the right to request a test developer or publisher to submit a measure for classification. The Human Science Research Council (HSRC) assists the Psychometrics Committee by conducting a review. Independent reviewers reach their decision based on classification guidelines which are provided to them. Reviewers are also asked to comment on the quality of the test materials and the manual, the psychometric properties of the measure, the cultural appropriateness of the content, and the appropriateness of the norm groups. The test developer or publisher is then asked to comment, if they so wish, on the classification decision suggested. Thereafter, the Psychometrics Committee considers the independent reviewers' reports, together with the comments from the test developer or publisher and the HSRC, in order to reach an informed classification decision. The classification decision is indicated on the classification certificate which is issued by the Psychometrics Committee and must be published in the manual.

On an annual basis, the Psychometrics Committee should publish a list of measures that have been classified as being psychological measures, as well as a list of measures that are in the process of being classified or developed. You can visit the web site of the Health Professional Council of South Africa to access the list of measures that have been classified (http://www.hpcsa.org.za). Assessment practitioners are encouraged by the Professional Board to use only measures that have been classified.

One final point about classification: many people, particularly test developers and publishers, are concerned that the process of classifying a measure as a psychological measure restricts its use to psychology professionals and robs them of their livelihood. However, classification of a measure by the Psychometrics Committee does not impose any new restrictions on it. It is the Health Professions Act, Act 56 of 1974, which restricts the use of a measure that taps psychological constructs to the domain of psychology. In fact, the classification process can allow for the relaxing of conditions under which a measure can be used thus making it possible for an assessment practitioner other than a psychologist to use it. Consequently, the classification process could actually result in the measure being used more freely than it would have been otherwise.

8.1.2.5 The Professional Board for Psychology and the protection of the public

As we pointed out in Chapter 1, one of the main functions of the **Professional Board for Psychology** is to protect the public. In view of the statutory regulation that restricts the use of psychological measures to appropriately registered assessment practitioners, the public's interests are served in two ways.

Firstly, members of the public may contact the Professional Board directly if they feel that assessment practitioners have misused assessment measures or have treated them unfairly or unprofessionally during the course of assessment. The Professional Board will then contact the assessment practitioner to respond to the complaint. Thereafter, the Professional Board will decide whether or not to convene a disciplinary hearing. Should an assessment practitioner be found guilty of professional misconduct, he/she could be fined, suspended, or even struck off the roll, depending on the severity of the offence. Assessment practitioners are well advised to take out malpractice insurance as members of the public are increasingly becoming aware of their right to lodge a complaint, which may or may not be valid, but which, nevertheless, needs to be thoroughly investigated and which may involve costly legal council.

Secondly, the Professional Board serves the interests of the public by laying down training and professional practice guidelines and standards for assessment practitioners. The Psychometrics Committee of the Professional Board has drafted competency-based training guidelines for assessment practitioners. Training institutions are regularly inspected to ascertain whether they are adhering to the training guidelines. As regards ethical practice standards, the Professional Board has adopted the International Test Commission's *International Guidelines for Test Use* (Version 2000). Furthermore, an updated ethical code of professional conduct was also released by the Professional Board at the end of 1999. In the next section, we will focus on ethical, fair assessment practices and standards.

> **>> CRITICAL THINKING CHALLENGE 8.2**
>
> Benni is a psychometrist (supervised practice) who works for a psychologist. Benni's friend approaches him with a problem. She needs to have her son's intellectual functioning assessed and a report needs to be forwarded to his school. The problem, however, is that she cannot afford to pay the psychologist's fees. She thus asks Benni to do the assessment on her son as a favour and to send a report on the assessment to the school. Advise Benni regarding whether or not he should agree to his friend's request. Tell him what the implications would be if he performed the assessment and sent a report to the school on his own, without the knowledge of the psychologist who employs him.

8.2 Fair and ethical assessment practices

8.2.1 What constitutes fair and ethical assessment practices?

Based on the International Test Commission's *International Guidelines for Test Use* (Version 2000), one could define fair assessment practices as involving:

- the appropriate, fair, professional, and ethical use of assessment measures and assessment results;
- taking into account the needs and rights of those involved in the assessment process;
- ensuring that the assessment conducted closely matches the purpose to which the assessment results will be put; and
- taking into account the broader social, cultural, and political context in which assessment is used and the ways in which such factors might affect assessment results, their interpretation, and the use to which they are put.

By implication, to achieve the fair assessment practices outlined above, assessment practitioners need to:

- have adequate knowledge and understanding of psychometrics, testing, and assessment which informs and underpins the process of testing;
- be familiar with professional and ethical standards of good assessment practice that affect the way in which the process of assessment is carried out and the way in which assessment practitioners treat others involved in the assessment process;
- have appropriate knowledge and skills regarding the specific measures which they use;
- have appropriate contextual knowledge and skills which include knowledge of how social, cultural, and educational factors impinge on test scores and how the influence of such factors can be minimized; knowledge regarding appropriate selection of measures in specific contexts; knowledge about policies regarding the use of assessment and assessment results;
- have appropriate interpersonal skills to establish rapport with test-takers and put them at ease, to maintain the interest and cooperation of the test-takers during the test administration, and to provide feedback of the assessment results in a meaningful, understandable way; and
- have oral and written communication skills which will enable them to provide the test instructions clearly, write meaningful reports, and interact with relevant others (e.g. a selection panel) as regards the outcome of the assessment.

8.2.2 Why assessment practitioners need to ensure that their assessment practices are ethical

Simply put, an assessment context consists of the person being assessed and the assessment practitioner. However, viewed from another vantage point, there are, besides the test-taker and the assessment practitioner, other role players with a vested interest in the assessment process, such as organizations, educational institutions, parents, and test developers, publishers, and marketers. We will first focus on developing an understanding of the reason why the assessment practitioner needs to adhere to ethical assessment practices and what the rights and responsibilities of test-takers are. In Section 8.3, we will highlight the responsibilities of some of the other role players as regards fair assessment practices.

The relationship between the person being assessed and the assessment practitioner in many ways reflects a power relationship. No matter how well test-takers have been prepared for the assessment process, there will always be an imbalance in power between the parties concerned where assessment results are used to guide selection, placement, training, and intervention decisions. Assessment practitioners hold a great deal of power as they have first-hand knowledge of the assessment measures and will directly or indirectly contribute to the decisions made on the basis of the assessment results. Although test-takers hold some power in terms of the extent to which they perform to their best ability, there is a definite possibility that test-takers can perceive the assessment situation to be disempowering. It is precisely due to the power that assessment practitioners have over test-takers that assessment practitioners should ensure that this power is not abused through the use of unfair or unethical assessment practices. What are some of the important things that psychological assessment practitioners should do to ensure that their assessment practices are professional and ethical?

8.2.3 Professional practices that assessment practitioners should follow

The good assessment practices that assessment practitioners should follow in every assessment context include:

- informing test-takers about their rights and the use to which the assessment information will be put;
- obtaining the **consent of test-takers** to assess them, to use the results for selection, placement, or training decisions and, if needs be, to report the results to relevant third parties. Where a minor child is assessed, consent must be obtained from the parent or legal guardian;
- treating test-takers courteously, respectfully, and in an impartial manner, regardless of culture, language, gender, age, disability, and so on;
- being thoroughly prepared for the assessment session;
- maintaining **confidentiality** to the extent that it is appropriate for fair assessment practices;
- establishing what language would be appropriate and fair to use during the assessment and making use of bilingual assessment where appropriate;
- only using measures that they have been trained to use;
- administering measures properly;
- scoring the measures correctly and using appropriate norms or cutpoints or comparative profiles;
- taking background factors into account when interpreting test performance and when forming an overall picture of the test-taker's performance (profile);
- communicating the assessment results clearly to appropriate parties;
- acknowledging the subjective nature of the assessment process by realizing that the final decision that they reach, while based at times on quantitative test information, reflects their 'best guess estimate';
- using assessment information in a fair, unbiased manner and ensuring that anyone else who has access to this information also does so;
- researching the appropriateness of the measures that they use and refining, adapting, or replacing them where necessary; and
- securely storing and controlling access to assessment materials so that the integrity of the measures cannot be threatened in any way.

Contracts between assessment practitioners and test-takers are often implicit. It is, however, important that contracts should be more explicitly stated in writing, and that test-takers should be thoroughly familiarized with the roles and responsibilities of the assessment practitioners, as well as what is expected of the test-takers themselves. By making the roles and responsibilities clear, the possibility of misunderstandings and costly litigation will be minimized.

8.2.4 **Rights and responsibilities of test-takers**

According to Fremer (1997), test-takers have the right to:

- be informed of their rights and responsibilities;
- be treated with courtesy, respect, and impartiality;
- be assessed on appropriate measures that meet the required professional standards;
- be informed prior to the assessment regarding the purpose and nature of the assessment;
- be informed whether the assessment results will be reported to them, as well as the use to which the assessment results will be put;
- be assessed by an appropriately trained, competent assessment practitioner;
- know whether they can refuse to be assessed and what the consequences of their refusal may be; and
- know who will have access to their assessment results and the extent to which confidentiality will be ensured (see also Chapter 16).

According to the International Test Commission's *International Guidelines for Test Use* (version 2000), test-takers have the responsibility to:

- read and/or listen carefully to their rights and responsibilities;
- treat the assessment practitioner with courtesy and respect;
- ask questions prior to and during the assessment session if they are uncertain about what is required of them, or about what purpose the assessment serves, or how the results will be used;
- inform the assessment practitioner of anything within themselves (e.g. that they have a headache) or in the assessment environment (e.g.

noise) that might invalidate their assessment results;
• follow the assessment instructions carefully; and
• represent themselves honestly and try their best during the assessment session.

8.2.5 Preparing test-takers

Among the important characteristics of South African test-takers which can potentially impact negatively on test performance is the extent to which they are 'test wise' (Nell, 1997). Given the differential educational experiences that South African people were exposed to in the past, 'taking a test' is not necessarily something that is within the frame of reference of all South Africans. Therefore, if we wish to employ fair assessment practices to provide all test-takers with an equal opportunity to perform to the best of their ability on assessment measures, we have to prepare test-takers more thoroughly prior to assessing them. By having either **practice examples**, completed under supervision, for each measure in the battery, or **practice tests** available, test-takers can be prepared more thoroughly, not only for the nature of the assessment questions, but also for what to expect in the assessment context in general. Where computerized testing is used, test-takers need to be familiarized with the computer keyboard and/ or mouse and need to be given the opportunity to become comfortable with a computer before they are expected to take a test on it (see Chapter 14).

Preparing all test-takers prior to a test session should not be confused with the related, yet somewhat different, concept of **coaching**. A great amount of literature has been produced on coaching and the positive impact it has on certain test scores, especially for some achievement (especially mathematics) and aptitude tests that have 'coachable' item types (Gregory, 2007). **Coaching** includes providing extra practice on items and tests similar to the 'real' tests, giving tips on good test-taking strategies, and providing a review of fundamental concepts for achievement tests. Coaching, however, has drawbacks: it not only invalidates test scores as they are no longer a true representation of a test-takers level of functioning, but, because coaching is often done by private companies outside of the assessment context, it is unaffordable

for less privileged test-takers. The solution to the problems brought about by coaching is to make self-study coaching available to all test-takers so that everyone is given the opportunity to familiarize themselves with the test materials.

8.3 Multiple constituents and competing values in the practice of assessment

8.3.1 Multiple constituency model

We pointed out in Section 8.2.2 that the parties who play a role in the psychological assessment context include:
• the person being assessed (or the test-taker),
• the assessment practitioner (as well as a psychologist, should the assessment practitioner not be a psychologist),
• other parties with a vested interest in the process and outcome of the assessment (such as an organization, human resources managers and practitioners, parents, labour unions, government departments, the Professional Board for Psychology, schools, and teachers), and
• the developers, publishers, and marketers of measures.

The assessment context, then, consists of a complex set of interrelated parties who might have different needs and values regarding the necessity for and the outcome of the assessment. The relationship between the role players involved in the assessment context is illustrated in Figure 8.1 in terms of a model that may be aptly named a multiple constituency model of psychological assessment. This model was adapted from the competing-values model of organizational effectiveness developed by Quinn and Rohrbaugh (1981).

8.3.2 Competing values: An example from industry

The utility value of psychological assessment for the multiple constituents involved in the assessment context is largely dictated by their own goals, needs, and values. By way of example, Table 8.2 provides information about some of the more

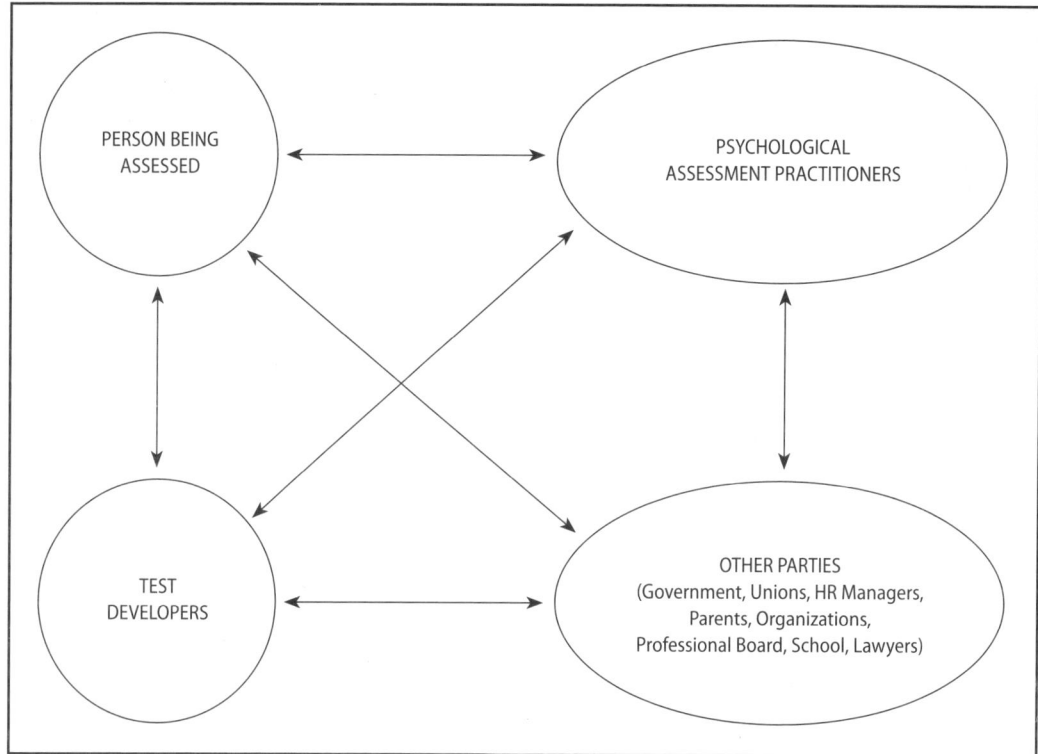

Figure 8.1 A multiple constituency model of psychological assessment (adapted from Schmidt, 1997).

important needs and values of different parties when assessment is performed in industry or occupational settings. This example is used as the Employment Equity Act, Act 55 of 1998, has led to the growing realization of the large number of role players who have a stake in the use of assessment measures and assessment results in industry.

You will realise from Table 8.2 that there is some overlap between the goals and values of the role players in assessment contexts in industry, but perhaps for different underlying reasons (motives). For example, all role players involved in assessment value accurate, valid, and reliable assessment. However, assessment practitioners value valid assessment measures as the use of such measures helps them to pursue good practice standards; test developers and publishers, on the other hand, value valid assessment measures because assessment practitioners are more likely to buy such measures.

Given their differing values and motives, tensions might potentially arise between the constituents. For example:

- Test developers may sell measures that are suspect with regard to their validity and reliability and this will anger assessment practitioners and organizations. On the other hand, assessment practitioners may use measures for inappropriate purposes and then claim that the measures are invalid, which will irritate the test developers.

- On the one hand, test-takers may claim that they were not informed about the purposes of the assessment, while on the other hand assessment practitioners may suggest that test-takers are intentionally trying to discredit the assessment.

- Assessment practitioners may claim that Government regulations are forcing them to employ incompetent personnel, thus affecting their organization's profitability, while the government may retaliate by claiming that organizations are practising discriminatory employment practices.

Table 8.2 The utility value of psychological assessment for stakeholders / role-players in industry

ROLE PLAYERS	DIRECTING GOAL	GUIDING VALUES	UNDERLYING MOTIVE
Assessment Practitioners, Psychologists, HR Managers	Generating valid and reliable assessment information.	Professionalism. Ethical conduct. Unbiased decisions. Promoting fairness and equity. Enhancing the contribution of assessment to company performance.	Professional and ethical conduct.
Assessment, or Business, or Employer Organizations	Making valid and reliable decisions regarding selection, job placement, and training.	Assessment must be practical (easy to administer) and economical (as regards costs and time). Fair assessment practices must be followed.	Understanding and improving individual or organizational functioning, performance, or development.
Test-taker	To present an accurate picture of themselves.	To be treated fairly. To be given the best chance of performing to their capabilities.	To gain employment, or promotion, or to get an opportunity to further their development.
Unions	Pursuit of non-discriminatory personnel decisions.	Fairness. Equity. Unbiased decisions.	Enhancing fairness and equity.
Professional Board, Government	Serving the interests of the public.	Fairness. Equitable assessment practices. Non-discriminatory practices. Setting standards. Controlling practices.	Protecting the public and promoting the well-being of all citizens.
Developers, publishers, and marketers of measures	Developing valid and reliable measures.	Scientific and theoretical integrity in the development of measures. Obtaining and keeping their share of the market.	Developing empirically sound measures. Selling assessment measures to make a living.

You will find more information on fair assessment practices, issues, and competing values when assessing children, people with physical or mental disabilities and information on the organizational, forensic, psychodiagnostic, and educational contexts in Chapter 15.

8.3.3 **Responsibilities of organizations as regards fair assessment practices**

In Section 8.2 we looked at the responsibility of the assessment practitioner in ensuring that ethical assessment practices are followed. Increasingly,

attention is also being focused on the responsibility of organizations as regards fair assessment practices.

The organization *inter alia* has the responsibility of ensuring that:

- it has an **assessment policy** in place that reflects fair, ethical practices;
- it employs assessment practitioners who are competent, who have been appropriately trained in the specific measures that they need to use, and who are mentored and supervised where necessary (especially when they are inexperienced);

- valid assessment measures are used for appropriate purposes;
- assessment results are used in a non-discriminatory manner;
- it has support mechanisms in place to assist assessment practitioners to build a research database that can be used to establish the fairness and efficacy of the measures used and the decisions made; and
- it regularly monitors the extent to which its assessment policy is being put into effect 'on the ground' and revises it where necessary.

Which aspects should an assessment policy cover? The International Test Commission's *International Guidelines for Test Use* (version 2000) (www.intest-com.org), suggests the following:

> A policy on testing will need to cover most if not all the following issues:
> - proper test use;
> - security of materials and scores;
> - who can administer tests, score, and interpret tests;
> - qualification requirements for those who will use the tests;
> - test user training;
> - test taker preparation;
> - access to materials and security;
> - access to test results and test score confidentiality issues;
> - feedback of results to test takers;
> - responsibility to test takers before, during, and after test session;
> - responsibilities and accountability of each individual user' (p. 22).

If an organization adopts an assessment policy, an individual should be given the authority to see to it that the policy is implemented and adhered to. Normally, one would expect this person to be a qualified, experienced assessment practitioner who probably has at least managerial level status in the organization.

>> CRITICAL THINKING CHALLENGE 8.3

You are working as a psychologist in a large organization. You tested all the trainee managers in your organization when you were developing and testing items for a new leadership test a year ago. As a result of this testing, the content of the test was considerably refined as it was found that many of the original items had questionable validity and reliability. The Human Resources Director now approaches you with the following request: 'Please forward me the leadership scores for each of the trainee managers whom you tested a year ago, as we want to appoint the ones with the most leadership potential as managers now.' Write a memo to the Human Resources Director in response to this request. Motivate your response clearly.

You have now completed your first stop in the *Assessment Practice Zone*. You have probably realized that there are many different aspects to consider when you are trying to develop an understanding of what constitutes good and fair assessment practices.

CHECKING YOUR PROGRESS 8.1

8.1 Explain the following statement: 'psychological assessment in South Africa is under statutory control'.

8.2 Explain why psychological tests need to be kept securely.

8.3 Explain why organizations should have an assessment policy and the key aspects that such a policy should contain.

8.4 List the professionals who may use psychological tests in South Africa as well as their qualifications and the restrictions placed on their use of the tests.

8.5 Tell your friend in your own words why it is so important that assessment practitioners follow fair and ethical practices.

Administering psychological assessment measures

LOURA GRIESSEL, JENNY JANSEN AND LOUISE STROUD

Chapter

9

CHAPTER OUTCOMES

No matter how carefully an assessment measure is constructed, the results will be worthless unless it is administered properly. The necessity of following established procedures or guidelines for administering and scoring psychological and educational assessment measures is one of the hallmarks of sound psychological measurement. During this stop on our journey through the *Assessment Practice Zone*, we will explore what an assessment practitioner should do to ensure that a measure is administered in the optimal way so as to achieve valid and reliable results. By the end of this chapter, you will be able to:

> understand the importance of administering psychological assessment measures correctly;

> describe the assessment practitioner's duties before administering a psychological assessment measure;

> describe the main duties of an assessment practitioner during an assessment session;

> describe the assessment practitioner's duties after the assessment session; and

> understand the assessment challenges related to assessing young children and people with disabilities.

9.1 Introduction

The basic rationale of assessment involves generalizing the sample of behaviour observed in the testing situation to behaviour manifested in other non-test situations. A test score should help to predict, for example, how the test-taker will achieve or how he/she will perform on the job. However, assessment measurement scores are influenced by many factors. Any influences that are specific to the test situation constitute error variance and may reduce test validity. Moreover, when scores are obtained, there is a tendency to regard the observed score as being representative of the true ability or trait that is being measured. In this regard, the concepts of reliability and measurement error are mostly concerned with random sources of error that may influence test scores. In the actual application of assessment measures, many other **sources of error** should be considered, including the **effects of test-taker characteristics, characteristics of the assessment practitioner and the testing situation** (see also Chapter 17).

The procedure to be followed in administering an assessment measure depends not only on the kind of assessment measure required (individual or group, timed or non-timed, cognitive or affective), but also on the characteristics of the people to be examined (chronological age, education, cultural background, physical and mental status). Whatever the type of assessment measure, factors related to the individuals, such as the extent to which the test-takers are prepared for the assessment and their level of motivation, anxiety, fatigue, health, and test wiseness, can affect performance (see also Chapter 17).

The skill, personality, and behaviour of the assessment practitioner can also affect test performance. Administration of most assessment measures requires that the assessment practitioner be formally accredited with the Health Professions Council of South Africa. Such requirements help to ensure that assessment practitioners possess the requisite knowledge and skills to administer psychological assessment measures.

Situational variables, including the time and place of assessment and environmental conditions such as noise level, temperature, and illumination, may also contribute to the motivation, concentration, and performance of test-takers.

In order to systematically negotiate these variables and the role they play in administering assessment measures, we will discuss the **administering of psychological assessment measures** in **three stages**. Firstly, we will discuss the variables that the assessment practitioner has to take into account **prior** to the assessment session, secondly, the practitioner's duties **during** the assessment

session, and finally, the duties of the assessment practitioner **after** the assessment session (see Figure 9.1). Our discussion will deal mainly with the common rationale of test administration rather than with specific questions of implementation.

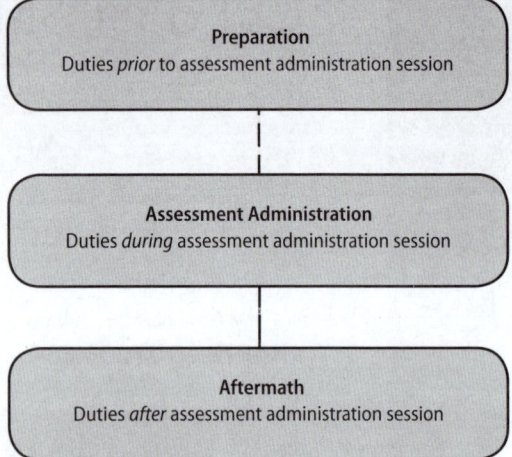

Figure 9.1 Stages in administering psychological assessment measures

9.2 Preparation prior to the assessment session

In the following sections we will highlight the most important aspects that should be taken care of during the various stages of administering psychological measures. Good assessment practices require the assessment practitioner to prepare thoroughly for an assessment session.

9.2.1 Selecting measures to include in a test battery

Various factors influence the measures that the assessment practitioner chooses to include in a **test battery**. Among these are:

- the purpose of the assessment (e.g., selection, psychodiagnostic, neuropsychological), the competencies or constructs that need to be assessed, and the types of decisions that need to be made based on the outcome of the assessment;
- demographic characteristics of the test-taker (e.g., age, culture, education level, home language);

- whether the test-taker has a mental disability. When assessing mentally challenged individuals, it is important to choose a measuring instrument that fits the mental age range of that person;
- whether the test-taker is differently-abled (e.g., is partially sighted or deaf) and consequently the assessment needs to be adapted and tailored;
- the amount of time available to perform the assessment;
- the psychometric properties (validity and reliability) of available measures and the suitability of such measures for the particular test-taker or the purpose for which the assessment is being conducted; and
- whether the assessment practitioner has the necessary competencies to administer the measures selected and whether he/she is permitted to use these measures given the scope of practice for the professional category that the practitioner falls into (see Chapter 8).

Examples of the types of measures to include in a test battery for specific purposes (e.g., selection of managers) or for assessing specific psychological, neuropsychological and chronic disorders are available and assessment practitioners could consult these to get an idea of what measures they could include in the battery that they must compile. The block below provides an example of a test battery to assess the neuropsychological functioning of people with HIV/Aids that was compiled on the basis of research.

Research has indicated that neurological deficits which include motor dysfunction, cognitive decline, and behavioural changes may occur in up to 50 per cent of persons with HIV/Aids. In order to identify neuropsychological functions most affected, an assessment battery needs to be constructed that would be sensitive towards early detection of deficiencies. Based on previous research, an assessment battery would include some of the following measures:

- **Depression Scale (Hamilton Depression Scale or Beck Depression Scale)**
  The HIV Virus often compromises mood and emotional status. Depression could also be the result of an emotional response to the disease and could affect any other testing. For this reason, a measure to assess depression needs to be included in such a battery.
- **Trail-Making Test**
  This assessment measure assesses motor functioning, attention, processing of information, and visual perception. It is especially the first three functions that are compromised in HIV/Aids-related neuropsychological impairment.
- **Co-ordination (SAT 78 or DAT)**
  This subtest is part of the Senior Aptitude Test (SAT) battery. It is used to assess the domain of psychomotor speed, with an emphasis on eye-hand co-ordination. This test was specifically developed for the South African context, with norms available for learners in Grade 10, 11, 12, and adults.
- **Rey Osterrieth Complex Figure Test (ROCF)**
  Mental slowing is characteristic of neuropsychological impairment, and, in later stages of the dementing process, affects both memory functions and the ability to learn new information. To enable an examiner to assess these abilities, this measure should be included in such a test battery.
- **Tower of London Procedure (TOL)**
  A characteristic of neuropsychological impairment in the disease process is the reduced speed of information processing. This measure can be included in a neuropsychological test battery as it assesses motor planning, processing of information, and executive functioning. Although South African norms are not available at present, norms for adults are suggested by Krikorian, Barlok, and Gay (1994).
- **Folstein's Mini Mental Status Examination**
  This is a screening test to assess cognitive functioning. The test assesses special and temporal orientation, concentration, memory, comprehension, and motor functions. It identifies signs of impairment, but does not provide a diagnosis. This assessment measure is the most widely used brief screening measure for dementia and can be used on a large variety of population groups.

• **Adult Neuropsychological Questionnaire**
This measure was initially designed to screen for brain dysfunction. The items are designed to obtain information regarding subjectively experienced neuropsychological functioning reported by the patient. As it is a screening measure, no normative data is available. Responses obtained are classified into domains representative of possible neuropsychological deficits.

By using a basic battery, trends in neuropsychological functioning can be identified which could facilitate a better understanding of the deficits. This could, in turn, assist employees, caretakers, and the persons living with HIV/Aids with managing the illness through its various stages. This battery can be extended or reduced depending on the condition of the patient as well as the reason for such an assessment

9.2.2 Checking assessment materials and equipment

It is advisable to make a list of the number of booklets, answer sheets, pencils, and other materials required, so that it will be easy to check beforehand whether the correct materials and the correct quantities are available. It is also advisable to have approximately 10 per cent more than the required quantity of the materials at hand, in case extra material is needed for one reason or another: a poorly printed page in a book, pencil points that break, etc.

The assessment booklets and answer sheets should be **checked** for any mistakes (e.g. misprints, missing pages, blank pages) as well as for pencil marks that might have been made by previous test-takers so that they can be erased or the booklet can be replaced.

If an individual with a disability is to be assessed, assessment practitioners should consult someone who has experience in working with people who have such a disability to find out whether the test materials need to be adapted in any way. For example, for a partially sighted test-taker the test instructions and verbal items that the test-taker must read him-/herself need to be presented using a large-size font.

9.2.3 Becoming familiar with assessment measures and instructions

Advance preparation for the assessment sessions concerns many aspects. However, becoming thoroughly familiar with the general instructions, as well as the specific instructions for the various subsections of the measure, is one of the most important aspects.

The assessment practitioner should ensure that he/she **knows all aspects** of the material to be used. He/she should know which different forms of the assessment measure will be used, how the materials should be distributed, where the instructions for each subtest or measure in the assessment battery can be located in the manual, and the sequence of the subtests or measures that comprise the assessment battery.

Memorizing the exact verbal instructions is essential in most individual assessments. Even in a group assessment in which the instructions are read to the test-takers, some prior familiarity with the statements to be read prevents misreading and hesitation, and permits a more natural, informal manner during assessment administration.

9.2.4 Checking that assessment conditions will be satisfactory

The assessment practitioner should ensure that seating, lighting, ventilation, temperature, noise level, and other **physical conditions** in the assessment venue and surroundings are appropriate. In administering either an individual or a group assessment measure, **special provisions** may have to be made for physically challenged or physically different (e.g. left-handed) test-takers.

9.2.4.1 Assessment rooms

The choice of the assessment room is important and should comply with certain **basic requirements**. The room should be in a quiet area that is relatively free from disturbances. An 'Assessment in progress – Do not disturb' sign on the closed door of the assessment room may help to eliminate interruptions and other distractions.

The **room** should be **well-lit** and properly **ventilated**, since physical conditions can affect the achievement of the test-takers. There should be a **seat** available for every test-taker as well as an **adequate writing surface.** Where young children are being assessed, it will be necessary to have small tables and small chairs.

Where **group testing** is conducted, the **size** of the **assessment room** should be such that **every** test-taker **can hear** the assessment practitioner without difficulty, and **can see him/her** and any writing apparatus he/she might use – blackboards, flip charts, and so on – **without interference.** Large rooms are not suitable for group assessment unless assessment assistants are used. In large rooms where there are several people together, test-takers are often unwilling to ask questions concerning unclear instructions or problems they experience. The **availability of assistants** can help to alleviate this problem. There should be **sufficient space** around the **writing desks** so that the assessment practitioner and assistants can move about freely and reach each test-taker to answer questions or to check their work, particularly during the practical exercises, so as to ensure that they have understood and are following the instructions correctly. There should also be **enough space between the test-takers to ensure that they cannot disturb one another** and to eliminate cheating.

Telephones should be taken off the hook or should be diverted to the switchboard. Test-takers should be asked to **switch off their cell phones** and assessment practitioners and assessment assistants should do likewise.

As wall charts, sketches, or apparatus may sometimes help or influence test-takers, there should be **no aids on the walls** or in the room that have any relation to the content of the assessment measure.

9.2.4.2 Minimizing cheating during group assessment and using assessment assistants

There are various ways of minimizing cheating during group assessments, including the following: **seating arrangements** (e.g. leave an adequate space between test-takers); preparing **multiple forms of the assessment measure** and distributing different forms to adjacent test-takers; and using **multiple answer sheets**, that is, answer sheets that have different layouts. The presence of several **roving assessment assistants** further

discourages cheating and unruliness during assessment. These assistants, who should be suitably trained beforehand, can also:

- provide extra assessment material when necessary, after assessment has started;
- answer individuals' questions about instructions which are not clearly understood;
- exercise control over test-takers; for example, ensure that pages are turned at the correct time, see that the test-takers stop when instructed to, and ensure that they adhere to the instructions and that dishonesty does not occur.

Assessment assistants are best equipped to help if they have studied the assessment measure and the instructions, and have also had the opportunity to apply them. They should be informed in advance of possible problems that may be encountered when the assessment measures are administered.

It is very important that assessment assistants should be well informed about what will be expected of them, so that there will be no uncertainty about their role in relation to that of the assessment practitioner in the assessment situation. The assessment practitioner is ultimately in charge of the assessment situation. However, the assessment practitioner's attitude towards the assessment assistants should be such that the latter do not get the impression that they are fulfilling only a minor routine function without any responsibility. Therefore, through his/her conduct, the assessment practitioner should always make assistants aware of the importance of their tasks.

Under no circumstances should an assessment practitioner and his/her assessment assistants stand around talking during the assessment session, as this will disturb the test-takers. An assessment practitioner should never stand behind a test-taker and look over his/her shoulder at the test booklet or answer sheet. This kind of behaviour could make some test-takers feel very uncomfortable or even irritable.

9.2.5 Personal circumstances of the test-taker and the timing of assessment

The **activities** that test-takers are engaged in preceding the **assessment situation** may have a critical impact on their performance during assessment, especially when such activities have led to emotional upheaval, fatigue, or other perturbing conditions. Studies have found, for example, that when military recruits are assessed shortly after intake – that is, after a period of intense adjustment due to unfamiliar and stressful situations – their scores are significantly lower than when assessed later, once their situations have become less stressful and more familiar (Gordon and Alf, 1960). Studies have also suggested that when students and children are subjected to depressing emotional experiences, this impacts negatively on their assessment performance. For example, when children and students are asked to write about the worst experience in their lives versus the best thing that ever happened to them, they score lower on assessment measures after describing a depressing emotional experience than when they describe more enjoyable experiences (McCarthy, 1944).

A person's **physical well-being** at the time of assessment is very important. If a child has a head cold, or is suffering from an allergy (e.g. hay fever), he/she will find it very difficult to concentrate and perform to the best of his/her capabilities on the assessment measures. In such instances it would be wise to re-schedule the assessment when the person being assessed feels better. It is well-known that medication can impact on levels of alertness (e.g. creating drowsiness), as well as cognitive and motor functioning. The assessment practitioner thus needs to know beforehand whether the test-taker is on any medication and how this may impact on test performance.

The time of day when an assessment session is scheduled is also very important. Young children, elderly people, and those who have sustained head injuries often tire easily and should thus be assessed fairly early in a day, before other activities have sapped their energy. For example, if a child attends a pre-school all morning, and he/she is only assessed in the afternoon, the assessment practitioner will have great difficulty eliciting cooperation, and being irritable, the child won't give of his/her best.

Where a person has an **emotional, behavioural, or neurological condition or disorder,** the timing of assessment is critical if valid assessment data is to be obtained. The motor and men-

tal functions of a person suffering from depression may be slower as a result of the depression. A hyperactive child may be so active and distractible that it is impossible for him/her to complete the assessment tasks. In such instances, it is better to first treat the mood or behavioural disorder before the individual is assessed, as the presence of the disorder will contaminate the assessment results. In cases where a person has sustained a head injury or suffered a stroke (cerebrovascular accident), comprehensive assessment immediately after the trauma is not advised, as there can be a rapid change in brain functioning during the acute phase following the brain trauma. Comprehensive assessment of such individuals should only take place three to six months after the trauma, when their condition has stabilized.

Assessment practitioners thus need a **thorough knowledge of the individuals** whom they assess, prior to assessing them. This information can then help assessment practitioners to plan the best time to assess them as well as any intervention that might be required before assessment can take place.

9.2.6 **Planning the sequence of assessment measures and the length of assessment sessions**

Where a battery of measures is to be administered, care should be taken to **sequence** the measures in an appropriate way. A measure that is relatively easy and non-threatening is usually administered **first**. This will help the test-takers to settle in and not feel overwhelmed at the beginning of the assessment. It will also give them the opportunity to gain more self-confidence before having to face the difficult tasks. Having successfully negotiated the first measure, test-takers often relax and appear to be less anxious. Measures that require **intense concentration, complex reasoning, and problem-solving** are usually placed towards the **middle** of an assessment battery. Placing them at the beginning of an assessment session could be very threatening to the test-takers. Placing them at the end, when they are tired, could result in the assessment practitioner not being able to elicit the best possible effort and performance from the test-takers. The **final** measure in the battery should also be a relatively easy, non-threatening measure, which paves the way for the test-takers to leave the assessment session on a positive note.

The length of an assessment session should be planned thoroughly in advance. The **length depends** mainly on the **level of development and mental and physical status** of the test-takers. Care should be taken, however, to ensure that the length of the assessment session is planned in such a way that fatigue resulting from too many assessment measures in succession does not play a detrimental role in performance.

The assessment period should seldom be longer than **forty-five minutes to one hour** for preschool and primary school children and **one-and-a-half hours** for secondary school learners, as this corresponds to the period of time that they can remain attentive to assessment tasks. Concentration may be a problem for many children and adults with chronic illnesses (e.g. epilepsy, asthma, diabetes, cardiac problems. This needs to be taken into account during assessment by providing sufficient breaks and by having reasonably short assessment sessions. More than one session may thus be required for administering longer assessment batteries to children, as well as to adults with emotional or neurological disorders, a mental disability or a chronic illness.

9.2.7 **Planning how to address linguistic factors**

South Africa is a **multilingual country**. Ideally, one would argue that every test-taker has a right to be assessed in his/her home (first) language. However, as was discussed in Chapter 7, various **complications** arise when trying to put this ideal into practice in South Africa. The most important among these are that:

- for the foreseeable future the majority of measures will still be available in English and Afrikaans as it will take a **number of years to adapt and translate measures** into the different African languages; and
- many South Africans have been or are being educated in their second or third language, either by choice or as a result of apartheid educational policies of the past. Particularly in instances where a measure taps previously learned

knowledge (e.g. certain subtests of intelligence measures), it **may be fairer to assess test-takers in the language medium in which they were or are being educated**, instead of in their first language or to perform **bilingual assessment**.

In view of the dilemma faced by assessment practitioners, the Psychometrics Committee of the Professional Board for Psychology has suggested that the following:

- A test-taker should be assessed in a language in which he/she is **sufficiently proficient**. The assessment practitioner thus firstly has to determine the test-taker's proficiency in the language in which the measure will be administered.
- If a measure is administered in a **test-taker's second or third language**, the assessment process should be designed in such a way that **threats to the reliability and validity** of the measures are minimized. In this regard, the assessment practitioner or a trained interpreter could make use of bilingual communication when giving test instructions, so as to ensure that the instructions are understood and the best possible performance is elicited. For example, the instructions could be given in English. The test-taker could then be asked to explain what they are expected to do. If there is any confusion, the instructions could be repeated in the home language of the test-taker, via an interpreter if necessary.
- A measure should only be administered by an assessment practitioner who possesses a **sufficient level of proficiency** in the language in which it is being administered.

Prior to an assessment session, assessment practitioners thus need to carefully consider in which language the assessment should be conducted. Where necessary, an interpreter or assessment assistant will need to be trained to give the instructions, if the assessment practitioner is not proficient in that particular language.

9.2.8 **Planning how to address test sophistication**

The **effects of test sophistication (test wiseness)**, or sheer test-taking practice, are also relevant in this connection. In studies with alternate forms of the same test, there is a tendency for the second score to be higher. The implication is that if a test-taker possesses **test-sophistication** and especially if the assessment measure contains susceptible items, the combination of these two factors can result in an **improved score**; in contrast, a test-taker **low in test-sophistication** will tend to be **penalized** every time he/she takes a test that includes test-wise components. Individuals lacking exposure to specific test materials or test formats may be at a disadvantage.

Brescia and Fortune (1989) have reported that children from a Native American culture may not exhibit behaviours conducive to successful test taking due to a lack of experience. This includes not reading tests items accurately or not having opportunities to practice tasks required by the test. Test scores are therefore meaningless if the test-taker has not had exposure to an optimal educational environment (Willig, 1988) associated with specific test taking. A test-taker who has had prior experience in taking a standardized test thus enjoys a certain advantage in test performance over one who is taking his/her first test.

It has been proven that **short orientation and practice sessions** can be quite effective in equalizing test sophistication. Such familiarization training reduces the effects of prior differences in test-taking experiences as such. Issues of test sophistication become imperative in a multicultural and diverse South Africa where individuals may have had differing experiences with standardized testing procedures. Orientation sessions should be distinguished from **coaching** sessions (see Section 8.2.5) or training in broad cognitive skills (Anastasi and Urbani, 1997).

9.2.9 Informed consent

Test-takers should be informed well in advance about when and where the assessment measure is to be administered, what sort of material it contains, and what it will be assessing. Test-takers deserve an opportunity to prepare intellectually, emotionally, and physically for assessment. Furthermore, by providing test-takers with sufficient information about the assessment, they are in a better position to judge whether they want to consent to assessment.

Informed consent is an **agreement** made by an agency or professional with a particular person, or his/her legal representative, to permit the administration of a psychological assessment measure and/or obtain other information for evaluative or psychodiagnostic purposes. The nature of the agreement reached should be **captured in writing**, usually by making use of a pre-designed consent form. The consent form usually specifies the purposes of the assessment, the uses to which the results will be put, the test-taker's, parents', or guardians' rights, and the procedures for obtaining a copy of the final report, as well as whether oral feedback will be provided.

Obtaining informed consent is not always a straightforward matter and it may pose some challenges to the assessment practitioner. For example, from whom should consent be obtained if the child to be assessed lives with his/her grandparents in an urban area while his/her parents work on a farm in a rural community? How do you go about obtaining informed consent from people living in deep rural areas to whom the concept of taking a test is completely unknown? Readers are referred to Foxcroft (2002) for a discussion on issues related to informed consent within an African context.

Figure 9.2 provides a summary of the assessment practitioner's duties prior to the assessment session.

>> **CRITICAL THINKING CHALLENGE** 9.1

Thembi, a psychologist, is preparing to administer a self-report personality questionnaire to a group of Grade 9 learners in a secondary school. Discuss and outline the nature of her duties as she prepares to administer this group assessment measure. Apply your knowledge of group testing in a practical way to this case example.

9.3 The assessment practitioner's duties during assessment administration

9.3.1 The relationship between the assessment practitioner and the test-taker

PREPARATION

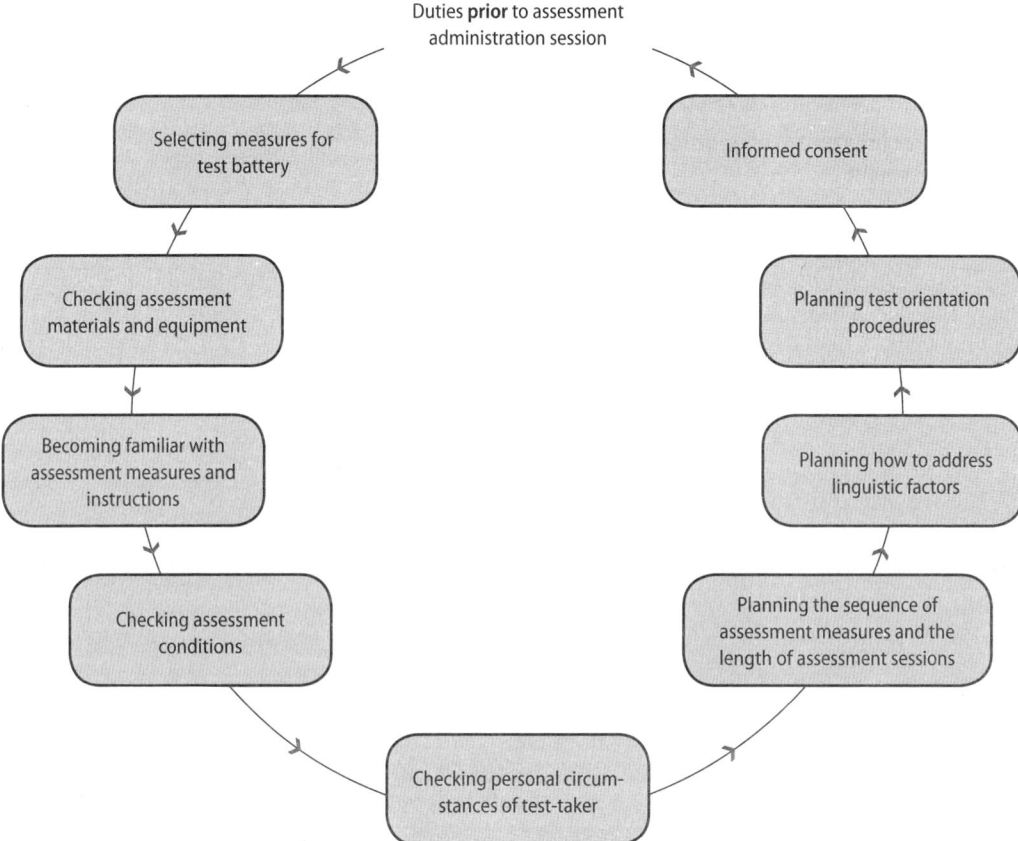

Duties **prior** to assessment administration session

Selecting measures for test battery

Checking assessment materials and equipment

Becoming familiar with assessment measures and instructions

Checking assessment conditions

Informed consent

Planning test orientation procedures

Planning how to address linguistic factors

Planning the sequence of assessment measures and the length of assessment sessions

Checking personal circumstances of test-taker

Figure 9.2 Preparation prior to the assessment session

9.3.1.1 **Adopting a scientific attitude**

The assessment practitioner should adopt an **impartial, scientific, and professional attitude** when administering an assessment measure. It sometimes happens that an assessment practitioner wants to help some individuals, or adopts a different attitude towards them because he/she knows them and unconsciously urges them to do better. Under no circumstances should this be allowed to happen. Indeed, it is the assessment practitioner's duty to ensure that every test-taker does his/her best, but he/she may not assist anyone by means of encouraging facial expressions, gestures, or by adding words of encouragement to the instructions, etc.

The **race** of the assessment practitioner as well as the **effects** it might have, have generated considerable attention due to concern about **bias and impartiality**. However, Sattler (1988) found that the effects of assessment practitioner's race are **negligible**. One of the reasons so few studies show effects of the assessment practitioner's race on results is that the procedures for **properly administering measures** are so **strict and specific**. Thus, assessor (examiner) effects might be expected to be greatest when assessors are given more discretion in how they use assessment measures. Even though most standardized assessment measures have a very strict administration procedure, there are numerous ways in which assessment practitioners can communicate a hostile or friendly atmosphere, or a hurried or relaxed manner. These effects may not be a function of the race of the assessment practitioner *per se* but may be reflected in strained relationships between members of different groups.

9.3.1.2 Exercising control over groups during group assessment

The assessment practitioner should exercise proper control over the assessment group. The test-takers should obey the test instructions explicitly. They should respond immediately and uniformly. Discipline should be maintained throughout, but in such a way that test-takers will still feel free to ask questions about aspects that are not clear to them. As the assessment practitioner is in command, he/she alone gives instructions or answers questions, unless assessment assistants are being used. The assessment practitioner should issue an instruction only when every test-taker is able to comply with it. He/she should wait until an instruction has been carried out by everyone before giving the next one and should ensure that everyone in the group is listening and paying attention before giving an instruction.

9.3.1.3 Motivating test-takers

An important aspect in the administration of an assessment measure is the test-takers' motivation to do their **best.** To motivate test-takers positively is, however, not easy, since no direct reward can be offered to them for good achievement and no procedure can be prescribed as to how they can best be motivated. Furthermore, no single approach can be used to ensure that each and every test-taker will be equally motivated. The assessment practitioner needs to learn from experience which techniques or approaches will ensure the greatest degree of cooperation and motivation on the test-takers' part. When poorly motivated, test-takers soon reveal symptoms of listlessness and lack of attention.

One way of motivating test-takers, is to ensure that they will **benefit** in one way or another from the assessment. The point of departure should be that the assessment is being conducted for the sake/benefit of the individual. If test-takers know that the results of psychological assessment will

yield something positive, they will be better motivated to do their best. Where assessment measures are used for the purpose of selecting the most suitable candidate for employment, the candidates are usually self-motivated, simplifying the assessment practitioner's task.

Assessment practitioners should be aware of the **effects of expectancy** and of **reinforcing responses** when motivating test-takers. A well-known line of research in psychology has shown that data obtained in experiments sometimes can be affected by what an experimenter expects to find (Rosenthal and Rosnow, 1991). This is called the **Rosenthal effect**. Even though studies on expectancy effects are often inconsistent, it is important to pay careful attention to the potentially biasing effect of expectancy. The effect of reinforcement on behaviour is also well-known. Several studies have shown that reward can have an important effect on test performance (Koller and Kaplan, 1978). As a result of this potency, it is very important to administer tests under controlled conditions.

9.3.1.4 Establishing rapport

In assessment administration, rapport refers to the assessment practitioner's efforts to **arouse the test-takers' interest** in the assessment measure, to elicit their **cooperation**, and to **encourage** them to respond in a manner appropriate to the objectives of the assessment measure. In ability assessment, this objective calls for careful concentration during the test tasks so that optimal performance can be achieved. In self-report personality measures, the objective calls for frank and honest responses to questions about one's usual behaviour, while in certain projective techniques, it calls for full reporting of associations evoked by the stimuli, without any censoring or editing of content. Other kinds of assessment may require other approaches. But, in all instances, the assessment practitioner must endeavour to motivate the test-takers to follow the instructions as fully and conscientiously as they can. Normally, the **test manual** provides guidelines for establishing rapport. These guidelines standardize this aspect of the assessment process, which is essential if comparable results are to be obtained from one test-taker to the next. Any deviation from the standard suggestions for establishing rapport should be noted and taken into account in interpreting performance.

In general, test-takers understand instructions better and are better motivated, if the assessment practitioner gives instructions fluently, without error, and with confidence. A thorough knowledge of the instructions is conducive to self-confident behaviour on the part of the test-taker. Uncertainty causes a disturbing and uncomfortable atmosphere. The consequences of a poor knowledge of instructions and a lack of self-confidence can give rise to unreliable and invalid data, as well as a decrease in rapport between the assessment practitioner and the test-taker or group of test-takers.

An assessment practitioner who does not have a good relationship with test-takers will find that they do not pay attention to the instructions, become discouraged easily when difficult problems are encountered, become restless, criticize the measures, etc. A good relationship can be fostered largely through the calm, unhurried conduct of the assessor.

Although rapport can be more fully established in individual assessment, specific steps can also be taken in group assessment to motivate test-takers and relieve their anxiety. Specific **techniques** for establishing rapport vary according to the nature of the assessment measure and the age and characteristics of the persons to be assessed. For example, **pre-schoolers** tend to be shy in the presence of strangers, are more distractible, and are less likely to want to participate in an assessment session. For this reason, assessment practitioners should not initially be too demonstrative but should rather allow for a 'warming up' period. Assessment periods should be brief and contain varied activities which are introduced as being 'games' to arouse the child's curiosity. The game approach can usually also be used to motivate children in the early grades of school. Older **school-age children** can be motivated by appealing to their competitive spirits as well as their general desire to do well on tests.

When assessing individuals from an **educationally disadvantaged background**, the assessment practitioner cannot assume that they will be motivated to excel at test tasks that might appear to be academic in nature. Special rapport and mo-

tivational problems may also be encountered when assessing **prisoners or juvenile delinquents**. Such persons are likely to manifest a number of unfavourable attitudes such as suspicion, fear, insecurity, or cynical indifference, especially when examined in institutions.

Negative past experiences of test-takers may also adversely influence their motivation to be assessed. As a result of early failures and frustrations in school, for example, test-takers may have developed feelings of hostility and inferiority toward academic tasks, which psychological assessment measures often resemble. The experienced assessment practitioner will make a special effort to establish rapport under these conditions. In any event, he/she must be sensitive to these special difficulties and take them into account when interpreting and explaining assessment performance.

When assessing individuals, one should bear in mind that every assessment measure presents a potential threat to the individual's prestige. Some reassurance should therefore be given from the outset. For example, it is helpful to explain that no one is expected to finish or to get all the items correct. The test-taker might otherwise experience a mounting sense of failure as he/she advances to the more difficult items or is unable to finish any subsection within the time allowed.

Adult assessment, which is most often used in industry, presents additional problems. Unlike the school child, the adult is less likely to work hard at a task without being convinced that it is necessary to do so. Therefore, it becomes more important to sell the purpose of the assessment to the adult. The cooperation of the adult test-taker can usually be secured by convincing them that it is in their own interests to obtain a valid score – that is, to obtain a score that accurately indicates what they can do, rather than one that overestimates or underestimates their abilities. Most people will understand that an incorrect decision, which might result from invalid assessment scores, could mean subsequent failure, loss of time, and frustration for them. This approach can serve not only to motivate test-takers to try their best on ability measures, but can also reduce faking and encourage frank reporting on personality measures, as test-takers realize that they would be the losers otherwise. It is certainly not in the best interests of individuals to be admitted to a career or job where they lack the prerequisite skills and knowledge, or are assigned to a job they cannot perform, based on inaccurate assessment results.

Assessment results may thus be influenced by the assessment practitioner's behaviour during the assessment. For example, controlled investigations have yielded significant differences in intelligence assessment performance as a result of a 'warm' versus a 'cold' interpersonal relation between the assessment practitioner and the test-taker, or a rigid or aloof versus a natural manner on the part of the assessment practitioner. Moreover, there may be significant interactions between assessment practitioner and test-taker characteristics in the sense that the same assessment practitioner characteristics or manner may have a different effect on different test-takers as a function of the test-taker's own personality characteristics. Similar interactions may occur with task variables, such as the nature of the assessment measure, the purpose of assessment, and the instructions given to test-takers.

9.3.2 Dealing with assessment anxiety

Assessment anxiety on the part of the test-takers may have a detrimental effect on performance. During assessment, many of the practices designed to enhance rapport also serve to reduce anxiety. Procedures which dispel surprise and strangeness from the assessment situation and which reassure and encourage the test-taker will help to lower anxiety. The assessment practitioner's own manner, as well as how well-organized he/she is and how smoothly the assessment proceeds, will contribute towards the same goal.

Studies indicate that achievement and intelligence scores yield significant negative correlations with assessment anxiety (Sarason, 1961). Of course, such findings do not indicate the direction of causal relationships. It is possible that students develop assessment anxiety because they have experienced failure and frustration in previous assessment situations. It appears likely that the relation between anxiety and assessment performance is non-linear in that a slight amount of anxiety is beneficial, while a large amount is detrimental. It is undoubtedly true that chronically high anxiety levels exert a detrimental effect on school learning and intellectual development. Anxiety interferes with both the acquisition and the retrieval of information. However, it should also be mentioned that studies have called into question common stereotypes of the test-anxious student who knows the subject matter but freezes when taking an assessment. This research has found that students who score high on an assessment anxiety scale obtain lower grade-point averages and tend to have poorer study habits than those who score low on assessment anxiety (Hill and Sarason, 1966).

Research on the nature, measurement, and treatment of assessment anxiety continues at an ever-increasing pace. With regard to the nature of assessment anxiety, two important components have been identified: **emotionality and concern**. The emotionality component comprises feelings and physiological reactions, such as tension and increased heartbeat. The concern or cognitive component includes negative self-orientated thoughts, such as an expectation of doing poorly, and concerns about the consequences of failure. These thoughts draw attention away from the task-orientated behaviour required by the assessment measure and thus disrupt performance.

Considerable effort has been devoted to the development and evaluation of methods to treat assessment anxiety. These include behaviour therapy, which focuses on procedures for reducing the emotional component of assessment anxiety. The results generally have been positive, although it is difficult to attribute the improvement to any particular technique as a result of methodological flaws in the evaluation studies. Performance in both assessment and course work is more likely to improve when treatment is directed to the self-orientated cognitive reactions. Available research thus far suggests that the best results were obtained from combined treatment programmes, which included the elimination of emotionality and concern, as well as the improvement of study skills (Hagtvet and Johnsen, 1992). Assessment anxiety is a complex phenomenon with multiple causes, and the relative contribution of different causes varies with the individual. To be effective, treatment programmes should be adapted to individual needs.

While assessment contexts may be perceived to be stressful in general, for a child or adult suffering from asthma or epilepsy, it is possible that a perceived stressful situation could elicit an asthma or epileptic attack. It is thus important that the assessment practitioner establishes a relationship with the child prior to the assessment so as to make the assessment situation as unstressful as possible. However, the practitioner should be alert to possible signs of stress and/or of an asthma/epileptic attack throughout the session. Practitioners should also receive the necessary First Aid training to know how to respond appropriately when someone has an asthma/epileptic attack.

9.3.3 **Providing assessment instructions**

Assessment instructions, which have been carefully **rehearsed** beforehand, should be read slowly and clearly. Providing instructions is the **most important task** the assessment practitioner has to perform in the whole process of assessment. The purpose of a standardized assessment measure is to obtain a measurement that may be **compared** with measurements made at other times. It is imperative that the assessment practitioner gives the directions in **precisely the way that they are presented in** the manual. The assessment practitioner's task is to follow the printed directions, reading them word for word, without adding or changing anything. It is of the utmost importance that there should be no deviation from the instructions, so that each test-taker will have exactly the same opportunity to understand what is to be done, and to work according to the same instructions. Only if assessment measures are administered strictly according to the prescribed instructions can test-takers' scores be compared.

Whether in an individual context, or a group context, the assessment practitioner should position himself/herself in such a way that interaction with test-takers is facilitated. After each instruction, the assessment practitioner should check to ensure that the test-taker understands the instructions and has not misinterpreted any aspect. Although test-takers should always be given the opportunity to ask questions, the experienced assessment practitioner always tries to avoid unnecessary questions by giving the instructions as fully and clearly as possible. Questions should always be answered on the basis of the guidelines provided in the manual.

9.3.4 **Adhering to time limits**

Assessment practitioners should always **adhere strictly** to the stipulated assessment times. Any deviation from these times will render the **norms invalid**. When assessment measures that have time limits are administered, a stopwatch should be used in order to comply with time limits strictly.

When assessment measures are administered to large groups, it is advisable to tell the test-takers to put down their pencils when the command to stop is given and to sit back in their seats. In this way, it will be easier for the assessment practitioner to ensure that there is close adherence to the time limit.

Where the instructions stipulate that test-takers should be given a break, the **length of the breaks** should also be strictly adhered to. These breaks are an integral part of the standardization of the assessment measure and should not be omitted, even when an assessment practitioner notices that time is running out in relation to the period of time set aside for the assessment session. If sufficient time is not available, the assessment measure should rather be administered on a subsequent day.

9.3.5 **Managing irregularities**

The assessment practitioner should always be alert to any **irregularities and deviations** from standardized procedures that might arise. The assessment practitioner should be aware of signs related to low motivation, distractibility, and stress in the test-taker. Close attention should be paid to signs of excessive nervousness, illness, restlessness, and indifference, and the assessment practitioner may have to intervene if it appears that these factors are resulting in the test-taker not being able to perform optimally. If the assessment practitioner knows that a test-taker has a chronic condition and how this condition could impact on the test-taker's concentration and motivation levels, plans can be put in place to combat this in order to obtain maximum participation. For example, a diabetic child may need to eat during the assessment.

The assessment practitioner should also be alert

to any strange happenings in the assessment environment (e.g. a phone ringing, loud noises, noisy laughter). He/she should keep a careful record of factors related to the test-taker as well as environmental and situational factors that could impact on test performance and should take these factors into account when interpreting the results.

9.3.6 Recording assessment behaviour

Assessment practitioners should keep a **close record of a test-taker's behaviour** during an assessment session. Which tasks seemed to cause the most anxiety? Which tasks seemed to be the easiest? How well was the test-taker able to attend to the assessment tasks? Was it easy or difficult to establish rapport with the test-taker? How effectively was the test-taker able to communicate the answers to the assessment questions? How did the test-taker solve complex problems? To answer this question, the assessment practitioner will have to ask the test-taker how he/she set about solving a problem presented during the assessment session. All the information gained by observing assessment behaviour should be used to amplify and interpret the assessment findings.

Figure 9.3 provides a summary of the assessment practitioner's duties during an assessment session.

9.3.7 Specific suggestions for assessing young children and individuals with physical and mental disabilities

While a general overview of the assessment practitioner's duties with respect to the administration of assessment measures has been provided above, the assessment of young children and individuals with physical and mental disabilities poses challenges for the assessment practitioner. Some suggestions are provided below to assist practitioners who assess young children and differently-abled individuals.

9.3.7.1 Specific suggestions for assessing young children

Your skills as an assessment practitioner are tested to the limit when you find yourself trying to assess a hyperactive three-year-old. What are some of the special skills that an assessment practitioner needs

to effectively assess a young child?

- The assessment practitioner has to literally get down to the child's level. By bending or kneeling you can look the child in the eye. In this way you will immediately get the child's attention and you will send a strong non-verbal message to the child about his/her importance. Do not begin the assessment immediately. Spend some time getting to know the child first. This can also serve the purpose of allowing the child to become familiar with the assessment environment. The more comfortable the child feels and relaxed he/she is, the more likely it is that he/she will cooperate and give of his/her best.

- Introduce the assessment to the child as a series of games to be played. This usually sounds attractive to children and helps them to understand what might happen in an assessment session. The assessment practitioner needs to stimulate a desire on the child's part to give his/her best effort. A friendly approach is important, and the assessment practitioner needs to show flexibility and adaptability when encouraging a child to demonstrate his/her talents, even when they are quite limited.

- Young children require a specific and clear structure in an assessment situation. The child needs to know exactly what is expected of him/her. The assessment practitioner needs to maintain eye contact with the child and ensure that he/she is listening to the test instructions. It is important that the assessment practitioner establishes exactly what is expected before the test task is performed. To ensure that the child gives his/her best possible response, the assessment practitioner should not hesitate to repeat the instructions or amplify them where necessary.

- Children often say 'I don't know how to do that', especially regarding test tasks that they find difficult. The assessment practitioner should make every effort to elicit a positive effort from the child.

- Children often want to erase their writing or drawings. In such an instance they delete very important diagnostic information. It is suggested that children should not be permitted to use rubbers. Instead, give them another sheet of paper if they want to re-draw something.

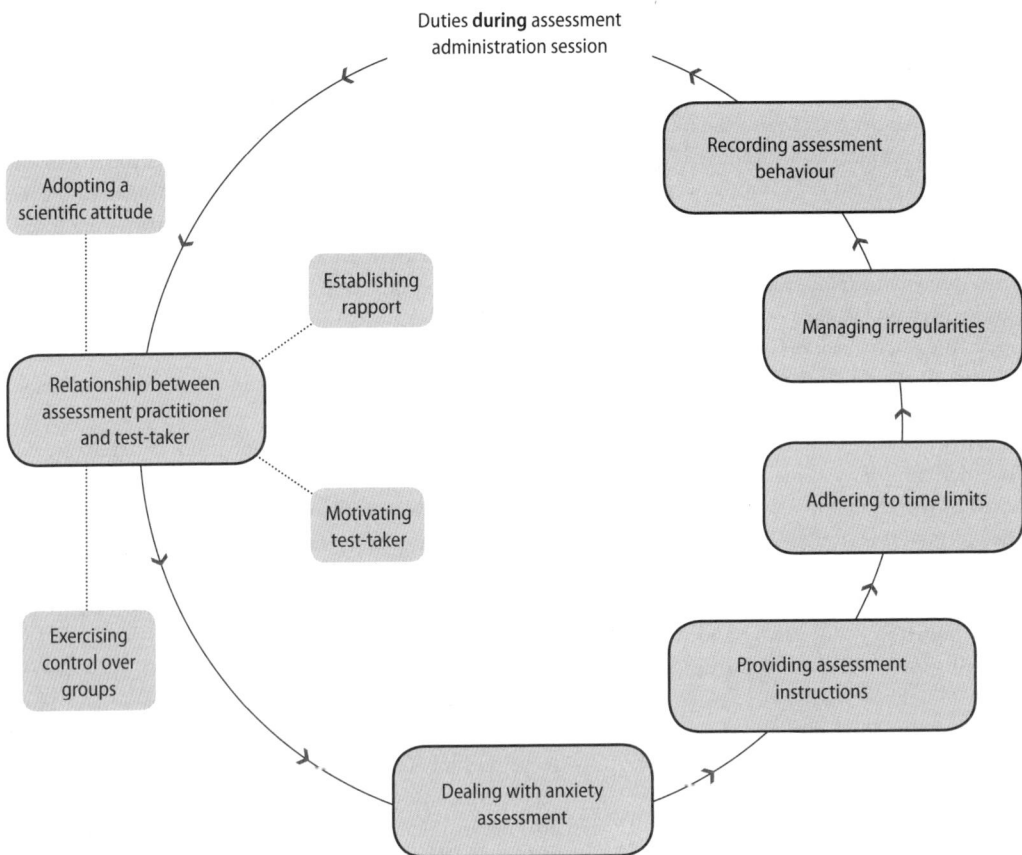

Figure 9.3 Assessment administration

- When an assessment practitioner notices that a child's attention is beginning to wander, a direct verbal challenge, such as 'I want you to listen carefully to me', might be useful. Frequent breaks and short assessment sessions make it easier for children to sustain their attention.

9.7.3.2 **Assessment of individuals with physical disabilities**

Whatever their age, the assessment of individuals with physical disabilities (e.g. motor, visual and hearing disabilities) poses special challenges for the assessment practitioner as regards administering the measures and interpreting performance in an unbiased way. Simple guidelines that can be followed to ensure that measures are administered fairly to disabled people do not seem to exist.

Essentially the assessment needs to be adapted and tailored by modifying the test items, content, stimuli, material, or apparatus, adjusting or abandoning time limits, and choosing the most appropriate medium (e.g. visual, auditory, or tactile) to use. The assessment practitioner has to make decisions regarding how to adapt or modify a measure for use with disabled individuals and should consult the manual to see whether any information has been provided in this regard. National disability organizations as well as assessment practitioners that specialize in assessing individuals with disabilities can also be consulted.

Given the lack of empirical information about how disabled people perform on assessment measures, whether or not they have been modified, it is often more ethical and fair to use the assessment results in a qualitative way. Assessment results can be used to gain an indication of a particular characteristic being assessed. This information can then be augmented by collateral information and observations from, and interviews with, teachers and caregivers who deal with the individual everyday. Ideally, the assessment of disabled individuals should take place within a multidisciplinary team context involving various professionals such as paediatricians, medical specialists, ophthalmologists, psychologists, occupational therapists, educationalists, and so on.

While individual assessment can be tailored in relation to the capabilities of the individual being assessed, group assessment, which is often used in industry and educational settings, is more difficult to tailor. It is very difficult to modify the mode of administration for disabled individuals when they form part of a group of people being assessed. Furthermore, if the time limit is lengthened for disabled people, they become conscious that they are being treated differently and those without a disability may feel that disabled people are being given an unfair advantage.

There are thus unresolved psychometric and ethical issues regarding the assessment of individuals with disabilities. To an extent, some of the issues may never be resolved, as each individual presents a unique combination of capabilities, disabilities, and personal characteristics (Anastasi and Urbina, 1997). Nonetheless, there is a growing body of information regarding how to assess disabled people. Furthermore, technological advances, such as voice synthesizers and computer-controlled electronic devices, present interesting possibilities for the innovative assessment of individuals with disabilities (Anastasi and Urbina, 1997).

9.7.3.3 Assessment of mental disability

The intellectual level used to demarcate mental disability is an IQ score of 70 to 75. Why an IQ score of 70 to 75? Well, think back to the discussion of test norms in Chapter 3 and the fact that you were made aware in the same chapter that the mean score on an intelligence test is 100 with a standard deviation of 15. An IQ score of 70 to 75 represents approximately two standard deviations below the mean, which is well below (i.e. sub) average.

The purpose of assessing mentally challenged people is to be able to design and place them in appropriate training programmes that could optimize their potential. If information can be gathered from a variety of professionals (e.g. occupational therapists) and teachers, the assessment data will provide a more comprehensive picture of the individual and what he/she is capable of in his/her everyday life. If an individual is attending a special school or training centre, teacher or therapist observations need to form part of the assessment. An occupational therapy assessment with a view to further placement after school is vital. Job evaluation is an integral part of a mentally challenged individual's assessment.

The use of information from different people dealing with the child is necessary as parents are not always objective when providing information regarding their mentally disabled child. When interviewing parents, the assessment practitioner should ask what the child can do rather than a direct question such as 'Can he feed himself?' This type of question can give the assessment practitioner inaccurate information. Parents also often blame the child's inabilities during assessment to lack of sleep, to being hungry, or in an unfamiliar environment. It is thus important to make sure that there are not too many people around or that the child is not frightened or sleepy. Home assessment, if possible, can cancel out some of the variables used as excuses for the child's poor performance.

When assessing mentally challenged individuals, it is important to choose a measuring instrument that fits the mental age range of that person. The diagnostic and screening developmental measures and individual intelligence measures discussed in Chapters 10 and 15 can all be used to determine whether intellectual functioning falls in the mentally disabled range. Measures of adaptive behaviour in everyday situations (e.g. the Vineland Adaptive Behaviour Scales) are also typically included in an assessment battery for mentally challenged persons. It is important to start the assessment with items that will elicit success. Concentration is usually problematic and assessment needs to be scheduled over a few sessions.

9.4 **The assessment practitioner's duties after assessment administration**

9.4.1 **Collecting and securing assessment materials**

After administering assessment measures, the assessment practitioner should **collect and secure** all materials. The booklets and answer sheets must be counted and collated, and all other collected materials checked to make certain that nothing is missing.

The **safekeeping** of assessment measures and results is closely related to the confidential nature of the assessment process itself. In Chapter 8, the reasons for control over psychological measures were provided. Psychological assessment measures are confidential and potentially harmful if they are used by unqualified people. They should thus be safely locked away (e.g. in a strong cabinet or safe) when not in use. The keys of such a cabinet should be available only to authorized assessment practitioners.

9.4.2 **Recording process notes, scoring, and interpreting the assessment measures**

Having administered the measures, the assessment practitioner should write up the **process notes** immediately, or as soon as possible after the session. The process notes should contain the date on which the assessment took place, which measures were administered, as well as any important

observations made about the behaviour of the test-taker during the session and any other important information that will assist in the interpretation of the findings.

The assessment measures also need to be scored, norm tables need to be consulted (where appropriate), and the findings need to be interpreted. These aspects will be covered in greater detail in Chapter 16.

Figure 9.4 provides a summary of the assessment practitioner's duties after the assessment session.

CHECKING YOUR PROGRESS 9.1

9.1 When administering tests, what actions on the part of the assessment practitioner could tend to make the test-takers' scores less valid?

9.2 How does the role of the assessment practitioner giving an individual test differ from that of a medical technician collecting a blood sample for analysis?

9.3 What principles should guide the person who, for purposes of legal procedures, is assigned to administer a test to an uncooperative adult?

9.4 In assessing a group of potential applicants who have indicated that they are all fluent in English, the assessment practitioner finds that an applicant is having great difficulty following the English instructions. The applicant asks many questions, requests repetitions, and seems unable to comprehend what is desired. What should the assessment practitioner do?

9.5 In preparing for an assessment session where

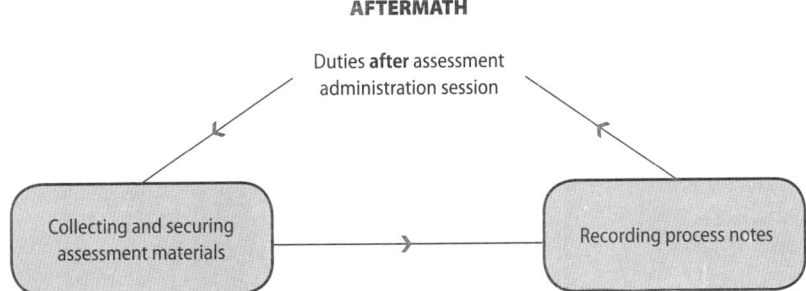

Figure 9.4 The assessment practitioner's duties after assessment

a diverse group of applicants have to be tested as part of an organization's selection procedure, you find that some of the applicants have never had exposure to group standardized testing whereas some of them have had considerable exposure to tests. How would you manage this situation?

9.6 Explain to a trade union leader whether, as is mandated by the Employment Equity Act, assessment measures can be used in a fair, non-discriminatory way with job applicants who have a physical or mental disability.

9.7 What are some of the important things to keep in mind when you are assessing young children?

9.8 What are some of the important things to keep in mind when assessing people with physical or mental disabilities?

We have travelled a little way through the *Assessment Practice Zone* now. You should have a broad understanding of what fair assessment practices are, as well as some of the specific practices that need to be adhered to when administering measures. Before we journey further into assessment practice territory, we first need to gain some insight into the different types of measures that are available. So, we will be crossing into the *Types-of-Measures Zone* for a while. Once we have visited the different types of measures, we will return to the *Assessment Practice Zone* and consider issues related to interpreting measures, reporting, factors that affect assessment outcomes, as well as looking ahead to the future of assessment.

>> ENRICHMENT ACTIVITY 9.1

If you want to know more about test administration visit the following web sites:
www.intestcom.org/orta
www.era.org.in/Library/Best20practicePsychometrics.pdf

Types-of-Measures Zone

In this zone you will be introduced to a variety of measures that can be used to assess psychological constructs. You will be making a number of stops along the way. Look out for the following signposts:

Part

3

Assessment of cognitive functioning

RENÉ VAN EEDEN AND MARIÉ DE BEER

CHAPTER OUTCOMES

After studying this chapter you should be able to:
> explain the meaning of cognitive test scores;
> discuss issues related to the use of cognitive measures;
> define the different types of cognitive measures;
> describe each type of measure and indicate where and how it is used; and
> give examples of cross-cultural cognitive research.

What do we mean by cognitive functioning, how do we go about measuring it, and how should we interpret the scores? These are some of the key issues in the somewhat controversial field of cognitive assessment discussed in this chapter. The measurement of cognitive functioning has been an integral part of the development of Psychology as a science. Although measurement has a much longer history, the main body of cognitive assessment and measurement procedures as we know it today developed since the beginning of the last century. Some argue that the lack of theoretical consensus on intelligence and, consequently, also on the measurement of cognitive ability and in particular the cross-cultural measurement of cognitive ability, endangers the status of this field as a science (Helms-Lorenz, Van de Vijver and Poortinga, 2003). Also, the fact that different measures provide different scores has often been used as evidence in attacks on cognitive measures in particular. However, the fact that, even in the physical sciences, there are still differences of opinion after centuries of research (Eysenck, 1988) should guide and inspire the theory and practice of cognitive assessment. In other words, much can be achieved that is useful, even if the ideal situation has not yet been reached.

10.1 Theories of intelligence: A brief history and overview

10.1.1 Background

A clear cyclical or pendulum movement can be traced throughout the history of cognitive ability assessment. Initially, the focus was mainly on psychophysical measures with the emphasis on objective methods of measuring simple sensory processes. The work of Galton and Wundt's psychological laboratory in 1879 is a good example of this era in testing (Gregory, 2007). Cattell introduced these types of measures in the United States, focusing on the measurement of differences in reaction time. Interestingly enough, since the early 1980s there has been a revival in the measurement of reaction time as a measure of cognitive ability. Of course, the more recent methods of measurement are much more sophisticated and also include use of computers in assessment. Other approaches that focus on physical and biological measures have some support too, and results generally correlate positively with measures of intelligence (Eysenck, 1986; Vernon and Jensen, 1984).

The French psychologist, Binet, took a different approach. He used more complex tasks of reasoning and thinking to measure intelligence when he was commissioned in 1904 to develop techniques for identifying children in need of special education (Locurto, 1991) (as was pointed out in Chapter 2). According to Gould (1981), Binet wanted the test scores to be used as a practical device and not as the basis for a theory of intellect. He wanted them to be used to identify children who needed special help and not as a device for ranking children according to ability. Lastly, he hoped to emphasize that intellectual ability can be improved and modified through special training. However, this was not the way in which Binet's measure was interpreted and used in practice. Recently there has been a renewed focus on Binet's more applied approach to cognitive assessment. For example, the approach known as **dynamic assessment**, where the focus is on identifying potential and providing learning opportunities to help individuals improve their level of functioning, has become an important field of study in psychological assessment today (Grigorenku and Sternberg, 1998; Lidz, 1987; Murphy and Maree, 2006; Sternberg and Grigorenku, 2002).

Another modern method which reflects Binet's approach to assessment is **computerized adaptive assessment**. As we will point out in Chapter 14, in adaptive assessment the difficulty level of items is calculated beforehand and the items are then interactively selected during assessment to match the estimated ability level of the test-taker. A South African test that utilizes this technology is the Learning Potential Computerized Adaptive Test (LPCAT) (De Beer, 2005). The modern version of this approach is based on Item Response Theory and the use of interactive computer programs. However, in principle, Binet applied these same principles and used the assessment practitioner's judgement to decide which entry-level item the child should get first. He made use of a ceiling level by terminating the measure if a certain number of items at a specific level were answered incorrectly (Reckase, 1988).

Another recurring pattern is the controversy between Spearman's and Thurstone's theories, namely the question of whether intelligence is influenced by a single general factor or by multiple factors. Both theories are still actively used in current research today (Carroll, 1997; Helms-Lorenz et al., 2003; Johnson, Bouchard, Krueger, McGue and Gottesman, 2004). The measurement of emotional intelligence (EQ), which represents the area in which cognitive and personality assessment are combined, has also been receiving a lot of attention in recent years (Matthews, Zeidner and Roberts, 2002).

On the social front, there is still active and ongoing debate on cognitive ability assessment, the interpretation of test scores, and particularly the differences between groups. Every now and again, a new publication appears and, once again, controversy flares up. One recent example is Herrnstein and Murray's book *The bell curve* published in 1994. Some earlier books that have had a similar effect are Gould's *The mismeasure of man* (1981), Fancher's *The intelligence men* (1985) and Eysenck and Kamin's book *The intelligence controversy* (1981).

Here in South Africa, our country is adapting to the integration of different cultures and guidelines on equity and affirmative action have been introduced in our legislation. In practice, this legislation also affects the use of psychological assessment. During the next decade, we may well see a repeat of the American pattern, that is, a movement away from and subsequent return to assessment, as well as legal battles over the fairness of measures for various groups.

10.1.2 Defining intelligence

Why has the study of intelligence, or the measurement of cognitive functioning, involved so many problems and controversies? We need to start by looking at the theoretical underpinning of the construct. It may surprise you to learn that, even today, psychologists do not agree on how to define cognitive functioning or intelligence, how to explain exactly the way in which it functions, or how it should be measured. This complicates efforts to understand the concept of cognitive functioning and also makes it difficult to build theories or construct procedures and methods to measure intelligence. Interestingly enough, there are parallels in physics, where people still manage to live with such unclear issues. For instance, in the case of gravity or heat, there are no unilaterally accepted definitions, theories, or measuring devices. However, this has not caused the controversy that we find with the measurement of intelligence (Eysenck, 1988).

In general, we can distinguish different types of intelligence, for instance, biological intelligence, psychometric intelligence, and social (or emotional) intelligence. When we discuss biological intelligence, we focus on the physical structure and functioning of the brain in ways that can be measured objectively. For example, we measure reaction times to physical stimuli, although using much more sophisticated methods

than those used in the early measurement laboratories. **Psychometric intelligence** implies that we use mainly standardized psychological tests to measure levels of functioning on psychologically defined constructs. According to the psychometric view, intelligence is defined as 'what intelligence tests measure', which seems to be a confusing way to define a construct. These measures make use of various types of items and the assumption is that the ability to display the type of behaviour needed to work with these items reflects some form of intelligent behaviour. It is always important to remember that all these measures base their final scores on a limited sample of behaviour of the people being assessed. The **social or contextual (emotional) view of intelligence** defines the construct of intelligence in terms of adaptive behaviour and argues that we must define intelligent behaviour within the particular context where we find it.

10.1.3 Theories of intelligence

Many different theories of intelligence have developed over the decades, together with many different approaches to the measurement of intelligence. Although each of these theories contributes to our general understanding of intelligence in its own way, each has both supporters and critics – this highlights the controversial nature of dealing with and trying to understand and explain human cognitive functioning. Plomin and Petrill (1997) summarize the essence of this dilemma when they emphasize that, although all men are created equal, this does not necessarily mean that all men are created the same. We have to be aware that the framework or perspective that we use to view people will affect the way in which we interpret our observations and measurement results.

One general factor (g)

Spearman was the first person to suggest that a single general (*g*) factor could be used to explain differences between individuals. This view is based on the fact that different measures of cognitive ability correlate positively with each other, indicating that they measure some shared ability or construct. Even when multiple factors are identified, second order factor analysis usually indicates some underlying general factor. On the other hand, factors specific to a particular activity can also be identified and are known as specific (*s*) factors. As a result, we have the well-known two-factor theory of intelligence that allows for both a general factor (*g*) and specific factors (*s*) (Gregory, 2007). Cattell later maintained that Spearman's *g* could be split into two distinct *g*'s which he called g_f or fluid intelligence and g_c or crystallized intelligence (Gregory, 2007; Owen, 1998). Carroll (1997) reiterates the general agreement among experts that some general factor exists and maintains that there is ample evidence to support this view (Helms-Lorenz et al., 2003; Johnson et al., 2004).

Multiple factors

Thurstone was the main proponent of the multiple factor theory. He identified seven primary mental abilities, namely verbal comprehension, general reasoning, word fluency, memory, number, spatial, and perceptual speed abilities (Anastasi and Urbina, 1997). Although there was lively debate between supporters of the one factor theory of intelligence and supporters of the multiple factor theory, Eysenck (1988) points out that the proponents of these two opposing theories of intelligence were eventually forced to agree on a similar view of the structure of intellect.

Biological measures (reaction time and evoked potential)

Different physical and biological measures are often correlated with intelligence scores, and strong evidence exists that a significant correlation exists between these measures and performance on standardized intelligence measures. According to Vernon (1990), there is little doubt that speed of information processing forms an integral part of general intelligence. Because these measures do not rely on past learning, they can be administered to persons in a very wide range of age and level of mental abilities. The biological approach was one of the first recorded approaches, and Wundt's laboratory, where a variety of physical measurements was recorded, served as the starting point.

Multiple intelligences

Gardner (1983) identified several mental skills, talents, or abilities making up what he defines as intelligence. These are musical, bodily kinaesthetic, logical-mathematical, linguistic, spatial, interpersonal, and intrapersonal skills. This approach broadened the view of intelligence by including a variety of different facets that are considered to be part of intelligence, however, practical considerations limit the application of this view.

Stages of cognitive development

Piaget, a Swiss psychologist, developed a theory that is based on four different stages of cognitive development that can be identified (Gregory, 2007). The four stages are the sensorimotor (birth to two years); pre-operational (2 to 6 years); concrete operational (7 to 12 years) and formal operational (12 years and older). According to Piaget, each of the four stages are qualitatively different from the others and characterized by distinctive patterns of thought (Gregory, 2007).

Contextual intelligence

Sternberg (1984) proposes that intelligence be seen in terms of the contexts in which it occurs rather than seeing it only as something we obtain from test results (Brody, 2003a, 2003b; Sternberg, 2003). Socio-cultural factors and context should also be taken into consideration. The individual's ability to adapt to real-world environments is important and Sternberg therefore emphasizes real-world behaviour, relevance of behaviour, adaptation, shaping of environments as well as adapting to them, and purposeful or goal-directed behaviour. He proposed a triarchic theory of intelligence; which includes Componential (analytical) intelligence, Experiential (creative) intelligence and Contextual (practical) intelligence (Gregory, 2007). The Sternberg Triarchic Abilities Test (STAT) is based on this theory (Brody, 2003a, 2003b; Gottfredson, 2003, Sternberg, 2003). Let us take an example from nature and look at the queen bee: although it has a limited range of activities, it nevertheless plays a crucial role within that context. Although certain behaviours may fall short of what is prescribed as the norm when they are measured objectively, these same behaviours may very well be representative of highly adaptive behaviour.

Conceptual intelligence and the systems or information processing approach

What was initially known as the information processing approach has since become known as the cognitive processing approach to the measurement of cognitive ability (Naglieri, 1997). According to this approach, intelligence is seen as based on three components, namely attentional processes, information processes, and planning processes. The PASS (Planning, Attention, Simultaneous, and Successive) theory is an example of this approach (Das, Naglieri and Kirby, 1994).

Dynamic assessment

Dynamic assessment is a specific approach to assessment which incorporates training into the assessment process in an attempt to evaluate not only the current level of cognitive ability, but also the potential future level of ability. It is based on Vygotsky's theory (Vygotsky, 1978) which distinguishes between the level of functioning a person can reach without help and the level of functioning a person can reach with help. Therefore, Vygotsky's theory incorporates the view that lack of educational or socio-economic opportunities affects cognitive functioning and may prevent some people from reaching their full potential. It makes provision for the effect of differences in educational and social opportunities and focuses on the measurement of learning potential. Grigorenko and Sternberg (1998) give an extensive overview of the work that has been done in this field. Many different approaches exist, some of which attempt to change the level of functioning (Feuerstein, Rand, Jensen, Kaniel, and Tzuriel, 1987), while others attempt in various ways to modify test performance only and monitor the help that is required to reach certain predetermined levels of functioning (Budoff, 1987; Campione and Brown, 1987). In many of these studies, standard cognitive measures are used in a dynamic way. More recently, measures have been specifically developed for the purpose of dynamic assessment. In South Africa, Taylor (1994) has developed a family of measures (APIL-B, TRAM1, TRAM2) based on his approach to measurement of learning potential, and De Beer (2000 a and b, 2006) developed the LP-CAT, a dynamic, computerized adaptive measure for the measurement of learning potential. These tests provide not only information on the current level of performance achieved by the individual, but by incorporating a learning experience as part of the assessment, are also able to provide information on the projected future (potential) levels of achievement that could be attained by the individual if relevant learning opportunities can be provided. By providing a learning opportunity as part of the assessment, it takes into account that individuals can differ considerably in terms of their educational and socio-economic background – factors that are known to influence cognitive performance – and attempts to provide an opportunity for individuals to indicate their potential levels of performance irrespective of their background.

Emotional intelligence

The measurement of **emotional intelligence** refers to the behavioural and interpersonal adjustment of the individual to a particular environment or situation.

Goleman (1995) argues that our traditional way of looking at intelligence is much too narrow and does not allow for the role that our emotions play in thought, decision-making, and eventually also in our success. He challenges the narrow view that intelligence is merely 'what intelligence tests measure' or IQ, and argues that aspects such as self-control, zeal, and persistence, as well as the ability to motivate oneself, are important factors determining success in life. A distinction can be made between the socio-emotional approach to the study of emotional intelligence (a broad model that includes abilities as well as a series of personality traits) and the view that links emotions with reasoning (a view that focuses on abilities only). The first approach includes the initial work by Salovey and Mayer (1990), and the work by Goleman (1995) and Bar-On (1997), while the latter refers to the adaptations by Mayer and Salovey (1997). Examples of measures of emotional intelligence include objective measures such as the **Multifactor Emotional Intelligence Scales** (MEIS) and the **Mayer, Salovey and Caruso Emotional Intelligence Test** (MSCEIT), and self-report measures such as the Bar-On Emotional Quotient Inventory (EQ-I).

10.2 Interpreting the intelligence score and diversity issues

10.2.1 The meaning of the intelligence score

Misconceptions about interpreting and using cognitive test results have been at the core of many controversies in this field. Owen (1998) warns against the danger of:

- viewing results as if they represent an inherent and unchangeable ability;
- the expectation that results are 100 per cent accurate; or
- the view that results are infallible and perfectly reliable.

In the preceding sections, the concept, theories, and measurement of intelligence were discussed in the broad sense, including different ways of defining and measuring intelligence. The use of intelligence measures to obtain a score that reflects a person's intellectual ability has traditionally been associated with the measurement of intelligence. Accepting that this is one way of defining and measuring intelligence, we will now describe the intelligence score and explain what is meant by the term.

An individual's mental level or mental age corresponds to the age of normal children or adults who perform similarly on a measure. The term **Intelligence Quotient (IQ)** was introduced by the German psychologist, Stern, in 1912 in an attempt to enable us to compare scores among and between different age groups. The IQ, which is obtained by dividing mental age by chronological age, represents a relationship between mental age and chronological age. It provides a measure of an individual's relative functioning compared to his/her age group and makes allowance for the development of cognitive ability over time.

If **standardized scores** are used, performance on a measure can also be compared across age groups. Based on the mean and standard deviation of performance of a specific age group, raw scores can be converted to standard scores or normal-ized scaled scores (these concepts were discussed in more detail in Chapter 3). It is now possible to determine how an individual's test performance compares with that of his/her age group. Because the same scale is used for all age groups, the meaning of a particular score also remains constant from one age group to the next. In the case of intelligence tests, the intelligence score is often expressed on a scale with a mean of 100 and a standard deviation of 15. Although this is a standard score and not a quotient, the term **Deviation IQ** is used to describe it.

We can explain what intelligence scores mean by using height as an example. We know that children grow in height from birth until approximately eighteen years of age. By looking at the height of a child, we can to some degree guess his/her age, thereby acknowledging that there is a mean or standard height for children of specific ages. Although we do acknowledge that a great variety of different heights exist within each age bracket, most children of a certain age are similar in height. If we were to obtain the average height of each age group, we could compare any child of a certain age with the average height of his/her age group and then decide whether this child was average in height, above the average (taller), or below the average (shorter). Because the average heights of the different age groups would not be the same, we would have difficulty comparing children of different ages with each other. However, if we standardized the height measurement by taking into account that the height changes for the different age groups, we would then be able to compare the height of children of different ages. In this way, we could compare children in the same age group, but we could also compare children of different age groups directly with each other. The same is done with intelligence test scores.

We must remember that an IQ or intelligence score is a theoretical concept and it cannot reflect intelligence in all its diversity. The way in which intelligence is defined will determine the type of tasks included in a measure, which should be taken into account in the interpretation of the score obtained. In addition, psychological measures are not as accurate as physical measures like height, and this contributes to the difficulty and controversy surrounding the measurement of cognitive functioning. The inaccuracy of measurement in the social sciences is partly due to the fact that we measure constructs, entities that are not directly visible or directly measurable and which have to be measured in some roundabout manner. We have to take a sample of behaviour and on the basis of performance of particular tasks that have been set, evaluate current performance and make predictions about future performance in real-life activities. There are also various factors other than cognitive ability that could affect test results. These factors are discussed in more detail in Chapter 17.

10.2.2 **Individual differences and cultural diversity**

People in general, and psychologists in particular, have always been, and will probably always be, interested in cognitive differences (and at times similarities too) between people – this is probably part of the human legacy. The fact that individuals differ from each other forms the basis of the entire field of psychology. South Africa's multicultural society has an eventful history. Its inhabitants, both individuals and groups, are in various stages of adaptation to a generally Western society, made up of the interesting but complicating diversity of all the people who live here. The spectrum of differences is certainly fascinating, but, for test developers and assessment practitioners, it presents an unenviably complex task. Shuttleworth-Jordan (1996) notes 'signs of a narrowing and possibly disappearing gap across race groups on cognitive test results in association with a reduction in socio-cultural differences' and takes this as indicative of similarities between people in terms of cognitive processes (p. 97). Claassen (1997) reports the same pattern of change and decreasing differences in scores when comparing English-speaking and Afrikaans-speaking whites over the last fifty years. This indicates quite clearly that differences in test results of various cultural groups can often be attributed to the general level of acculturation of a group, compared to the norm group for which the measures are constructed and against whose results comparisons are made. Similar patterns have been found in the United States, where differences between children of different cultural groups are

markedly different from those found between adults of the same groups. This indicates that 'differences are in a very real sense a barometer of educational and economic opportunity' (Petrill, Pike, Price and Plomin, 2004; Vincent, 1991, p. 269).

Cross-cultural assessment of cognitive ability (and other psychological constructs) has received a lot of attention in recent years. Researchers consider different aspects when investigating the cross-cultural equivalence of measures (Helms-Lorenz et al., 2003). The three aspects that Van de Vijver (2002) specifically refers to are construct equivalence, method equivalence, and item equivalence (also refer to Chapter 7 in this regard). **Construct equivalence** refers to the fact that one needs to investigate and ensure that the construct being measured is equivalent across different subgroups. One way of doing this is to make use of factor analysis, to indicate that the underlying pattern(s) of the construct(s) being measured is (are) similar for various subgroups. Another way to investigate this aspect is to compare the results of different measuring instruments that measure the same construct. In terms of **method equivalence**, reference is made to the way in which measures are applied – ensuring that the contextual and practical application of measures do not lead to differences between subgroups. Aspects such as test sophistication, language proficiency, and so on, are relevant here. Lastly, on an item level, for **item equivalence** one also needs to ensure that different subgroups do not respond to a particular item differently due to the way that it has been constructed and not related to the construct being measured. In this regard the use of **IRT (item response theory)** and **DIF (differential item functioning)** methods are powerful tools in detecting differences in the performance of groups on particular items (De Beer, 2004).

You now have some background to the way we define and think about intelligence, how we go about measuring it, and how the scores can be interpreted. We will now provide some information on specific measures of cognitive ability and use examples to illustrate the different types of measures. You can obtain information on specific measures from local test publishers or sales agents for international test companies.

10.3 Measures of general cognitive functioning

10.3.1 Individual intelligence measures

> A young boy has been living in a shelter for two years. A social worker has now been able to place him in a school that is also prepared to provide accommodation for him. However, they need to know if this child has the general ability to benefit from mainstream education and/or if he has special needs.

This is an example of the type of situation where an individual intelligence measure can be used to obtain an indication of a person's level of general intelligence. General ability is also taken into account in career counselling and if a person is not performing well at school or in the workplace, individual intelligence measures can provide information to guide further psychodiagnostic assessment (see Chapter 15). These measures typically consist of a number of verbal and non-verbal subtests that together provide an indication of general intelligence. If a more comprehensive picture of an individual's functioning is required, performance on the different subtests can also be analysed.

10.3.1.1 Description and aim

The measures commonly used in South Africa are based on the psychometric model of testing. This model assumes that the individual's ability to perform a variety of tasks that require intelligence (in accordance with a specific theoretical definition) represents his/her level of general intelligence (Wechsler, 1958). Therefore, the items included in these measures cover a wide field and the different tasks are related to different cognitive abilities. For example, in one of the types of items in the Junior South African Individual Scales (JSAIS), the assessment practitioner reads out a series of numbers which the test-taker must repeat in the same order. The cognitive ability measured by this type of item is attention and immediate auditory recall for numbers (remembering something that one has heard rather than something that one has read) (Madge, 1981).

Items in an intelligence measure can be classified and described according to item type and the specific abilities measured. In a test such as the Individual Scale for General Scholastic Aptitude (ISGSA) a variety of items are arranged in ascending order of difficulty (i.e. becoming more difficult) (Robinson, 1996). Together they measure general ability. However, it is also possible to group relatively homogeneous (similar) items into subtests. Box 10.1 contains a description of the subtests of the Senior South African Individual Scale – Revised (SSAIS-R) (Van Eeden, 1991). The items in each subtest are arranged in ascending order of difficulty. Scores are also provided for groups of subtests that have mental abilities in common (i.e. factors such as verbal comprehension, spatial ability, and so on). In Box 10.1 we show how nine of the eleven subtests of the SSAIS-R are grouped together in a Verbal Scale and a Non-verbal Scale. We assume that the total score on all subtests represents an underlying general factor of intelligence (Spearman's g factor). The Global Intelligence Scale of the JSAIS also renders four subscales, namely a Verbal IQ Scale, a Performance IQ Scale, a Numerical Scale and a Memory Scale each consisting of a number of subtests (Madge, 1981). The 14 subtests of the Wechsler Adult Intelligence Scale – Third Edition (WAIS-III) are grouped in a similar manner to obtain either a Verbal IQ, a Performance IQ, and a Full Scale IQ, or alternatively a Verbal Comprehension Index, a Perceptual Organization Index, a Working Memory Index, and a Processing Speed Index (Claassen, Krynauw, Holtzhausen, and wa ga Mathe, 2001). In Box 10.2 descriptions of the Griffiths Scales of Mental Development (Griffiths, 1954, 1970), which were recently revised and are now known as the Griffiths Mental Development Scales – Extended Revised (GMDS-ER) (Luiz, Barnard, Knoesen, Kotras, Horrocks, McAlinden, Challis, and O'Connell, 2006); the Grover-Counter Scale of Cognitive Development (GCS) (HSRC, 1994) and the McCarthy Scales of Children's Abilities (McCarthy Scales) (McCarthy, 1972) illustrate the unique combinations of tasks used in diagnostic measures for young children to assess the functions associated with the developmental stages of this phase.

BOX 10.1 SCALES AND SUBTESTS OF THE SSAIS-R

Verbal Scale

Vocabulary: This subtest consists of five cards with four pictures on each card. For each card the assessment practitioner reads ten words and the test-taker is asked to indicate the picture that is most relevant for a given word. The subtest measures language development and usage.

Comprehension: The test-taker is asked fifteen questions about everyday social situations. Knowledge of conventional standards of behaviour and the ability to use this information are important.

Similarities: For each of fifteen items the test-taker must indicate what two concepts (objects or ideas) have in common. He/she must be able to distinguish important from unimportant resemblances. The abilities measured include abstract reasoning and verbal concept formation.

Number Problems: The subtest consists of twenty arithmetical problems read by the assessment practitioner. The last nine items are also presented on cards. In addition to basic mathematical skills, mental alertness and concentration are also important for success.

Story Memory: The assessment practitioner reads a short story and the test-taker is asked to repeat what he/she can remember about the story. This subtest measures short-term auditory memory.

Non-verbal Scale

Pattern Completion: Four practice examples and fifteen items consisting of partially completed patterns are presented. Each item consists of three figures and the test-taker must deduce a pattern in order to draw the fourth figure. Visual perception is important but the test-taker should also be able to reason by means of analogies.

Block Designs: The test-taker must reproduce a model (two items) and two-dimensional geometric designs presented on cards (thirteen items) by using three-dimensional coloured blocks. The abilities measured include perceptual organization, spatial orientation, and visual-motor coordination.

Missing Parts: For each of the twenty pictures the test-taker must indicate the important part that is missing from the picture. The subtest involves comprehension of familiar situations, and perceptual and conceptual abilities are important.

Form Board: The test consists of a board with six figures. Each figure is constructed out of three or four loose parts with a distinguishing colour and the test-taker has to fit the parts into the relevant figure. This measures visual perception and organization as well as visual-motor coordination. The test-takers must be able to see the underlying relations between objects.

Additional subtests

Memory for Digits: The assessment practitioner reads aloud a series of numbers that the test-taker has to repeat in the same order (Digits Forward – eight items) or in reverse order (Digits Backward – seven items). This subtest measures auditory short-term memory for numbers, and attention and concentration are also important.

Coding: A list of digits from 1 to 9, each with an accompanying symbol, is shown to the test-taker. He/she is then given a series of ninety-one random digits and must then draw the appropriate symbol below the correct digit. This subtest requires immediate learning of an unfamiliar task. Attention and concentration, short-term memory, and visual-motor integration and coordination are important.

BOX 10.2 GRIFFITHS MENTAL DEVELOPMENT SCALES, THE GCS AND THE MCCARTHY SCALES

Griffiths Mental Development Scales – Extended Revised

The Griffiths Mental Development Scales are used for children from birth to eight years of age. It comprises six separate scales: Locomotor (Subscale A) which allows the examiner to observe certain physical weaknesses or disabilities; Personal-Social (Subscale B) which gives opportunity to assess personal and social development; Language (Subscale C) which gives opportunity to study the growth and development of language; Eye and Hand Coordination (Subscale D) which consists of items relating to the manual dexterity and visual-motor ability of the child; Performance (Subscale E) which enables the examiner to observe and measure skill in manipulation, speed of working, and precision; and Practical Reasoning (Subscale F) which records the earliest indications of arithmetical comprehension and the realization of the simplest practical problems.

The GCS

The Grover-Counter Scale of Cognitive Development (GCS) is based on Piagetian theory and was developed according to Piaget's stages of development. It consists of five domains, each measuring a stage in a person's development. Section A consists of simple recognition of shapes and colours. Section B assesses the ability to reconstruct patterns from memory. Section C assesses the ability to copy a model made by the tester. Section D assesses the ability to produce and complete patterns from a design card within a time limit.

McCarthy Scales

The McCarthy Scales are used for children between the ages of three years six months and eight years six months. There are eighteen separate tests which are grouped into five scales: Verbal, Perceptual Performance, Quantitative, Motor, and Memory. When the Verbal, Quantitative and Perceptual Performance Scales are combined, an overall measure of the child's intellectual functioning is obtained.

The administration and scoring procedures of individual intelligence measures are usually standardized. This means that there is a written set of instructions that should be followed to ensure a uniform (standardized) method of administration and scoring. However, individualized administration also enables the assessment practitioner to interact with the test-taker. Depending on the reason for referral (why the individual needs to be tested), individual measures might therefore be more suitable than group measures. For example, if a referral is made where underlying emotional problems affect academic or work performance, the assessment practitioner has to put such a person at ease and develop rapport to ensure that performance on the measure reflects his/her ability. Any non-cognitive factors that could influence performance on the measure, such as anxiety, are observed, noted, and taken into account when interpreting the results. Another example is the referral of children with learning problems. If a child has trouble reading or

writing, scholastic aptitude and other group measures might underestimate his/her ability. In an individualized situation, test behaviour also provides clues to possible reasons for the learning difficulties, such as distractibility (see Chapters 9 and 15).

10.3.1.2 The application of results

Different measures have been developed for different age groups. Measures with South African norms include the Bayley Scales of Infant Development (1 month to 30 months), the JSAIS (3 years to 7 years 11 months), the SSAIS-R (7 years to 16 years 11 months) and the WAIS-III (16 years to 69 years 11 months). These measures are used for the following reasons:

- to determine an individual's level of general ability in comparison with his/her age group, and
- to compare a person's own performance on the different scales and subtests of a measure in order to gain an understanding of his/her unique intellectual functioning.

General ability

The raw scores on individual intelligence measures are converted to standard scores or normalized scaled scores. This implies that an individual's performance on a specific test or subtest is expressed in terms of the performance of a fixed reference group called the norm group. The individual's overall performance on the intelligence measure (the Full Scale score or the Global Scale score), as well as his/her performance on subscales (e.g. the Verbal Scale score, the Performance or Non-verbal Scale score, the Numerical Scale score, and so on), can therefore be compared with the performance of others in the particular norm group – often specified in terms of age. This information is used in educational and occupational counselling, as well as in the selection and placement of students, and in personnel selection (see Chapter 15). You should keep in mind that decisions are not based on a single test score. Biographical information, academic and work performance, and results from other measures are also taken into account (see Chapter 1). In a survey by van der Merwe (2002), organizations that used individual scales as part of their assessment process indicated that they used testing not only for selection purposes. Psychometric tests are used for placement, promotion, transfers and, more importantly in terms of individual intelligence measures, for the identification of potential and training needs, performance counselling and career development. However, these measures are more suitable for individual counselling (see below) and group tests of intelligence are regarded as more suitable for generalised used in industry.

Profile of abilities

Working with standard scores also implies that scores on the same scale are expressed in comparable units. In addition to comparison with the norm group, it is possible to compare a person's own performance on the different scales (e.g. to see how the use of words and symbols on the Verbal Scale compare with the ability to handle objects and perceive visual patterns on the Non-verbal Scale) and in the various subtests. If someone obtains a relatively higher score for a subtest, some of the abilities measured by that subtest can be regarded as strengths. Similarly, relatively lower scores could indicate weaknesses. (Refer to Box 10.1 for an example of the types of subtests included in intelligence measures and the abilities measured by the various tasks.) This information is used to formulate hypotheses about an individual's problems, to suggest further assessment, and even help in planning intervention and remediation. This process requires experience as well as comprehensive knowledge of the theory that relates to the abilities measured by a test and the research that has been done on these abilities (Kaufman, 1979).

The following are important considerations when using individual intelligence measures (as well as the other measures discussed in this chapter):

*   the reliability and validity of a measure for a specific context (the concepts of reliability and validity are explained in Chapters 4 and 5), and
*   how suitable the measure is for cross-cultural use.

The test manuals of tests standardized in South Africa (including the JSAIS, the ISGSA, the SSAIS-R, and the WAIS-III) contain information on reliability and construct validity, and usually also report on how the results can be used to predict academic

performance. Results are mostly satisfactory for the standardization samples. It is also important to consult literature on research in this area. There are a number of studies on the use of South African individual intelligence tests in different contexts. The results of two studies indicated that the SSAIS (in particular the Non-verbal Scale) is suitable for assessing hearing-disabled children (Badenhorst, 1986; Du Toit, 1986). Robinson and Hanekom (1991) found that the JSAIS is valid for the evaluation of school readiness at the stage of school entrance. The Number and Quantity Concepts subtest of the JSAIS is also useful to identify children who are at risk for under-achievement in mathematics at school entry level (Roger, 1989). Robinson (1986) determined a characteristic pattern of JSAIS scores for learning-disabled children with reading problems that distinguishes them from 'normal' children. A correlational study with the JSAIS and the Griffiths Scales of Mental Development provided additional proof of the construct validity of the JSAIS, and Luiz and Heimes (1988) also made some suggestions for the early diagnosis of problems in young children and their subsequent treatment. Extensive research relating to the reliability, validity, and clinical use of the original Griffiths Mental Development Scales has also been conducted in South Africa (e.g. Luiz, Foxcroft and Povey, 2006; Luiz, Foxcroft and Stewart, 1999; Luiz, Foxcroft, Worsfold, Kotras and Kotras, 2001). Such research includes pilot normative studies on three- to eight-year-old black, coloured, Asian, and white children (Allan, 1992). Some South African research has been conducted on the Griffiths Mental Development Scales – Extended Revised (GMDS-ER) (e.g., van Heerden, 2007; van Rooyen, 2005) in which normal South African children were compared with their counterparts in the standardization sample in the United Kingdom. Given that the GMDS-ER has changed from being a criterion-referenced to a norm-referenced test, van Heerden's (2007) study raises serious questions about the applicability of the norms developed in the United Kingdom for South African children. Before assessment practitioners can use the GMDS-ER with confidence in South Africa, South African normative studies need to be conducted. The manual of the Grover-Counter Scale of Cognitive Development (GCS) was revised in 2000 and a growing body of research is developing on the scale (e.g. Dickman, 1994), which has proved its clinical use in South Africa.

It is also important to take account of the cultural or language group for which norms were originally determined. Equivalent individual intelligence measures have been constructed for South Africans whose home language is English or Afrikaans (i.e. ISGSA, JSAIS, and SSAIS-R). A slightly modified version of the WAIS-III has been standardized for English-speaking South Africans and for the first time blacks were included in the norm group along with Indians, coloureds, and whites (Claassen et al., 2001). Measures have also been constructed in African languages, for example, the Individual Intelligence Scale for Xhosa-speaking Pupils (Landman, 1989) and both the Bayley Scales of Infant Development and the McCarthy Scales of Children's Abilities have been adapted and normed for black South Africans (Richter and Griesel, 1988, 1991). However, no South African norms are available for the revised Bayley scales or Bayley II. Although similar, these measures cannot be regarded as equivalent to the English versions. On the other hand, testing a person in a language other than his/her home language raises questions about the influence of language proficiency on test performance as seen in studies on the SSAIS-R and the WAIS-III (Claassen et al., 2001; Van Eeden, 1993; Van Eeden and Van Tonder, 1995). Foxcroft and Aston (2006) critically examined the suitability of the WAIS-III for different cultural and language groups and concluded that some bias might exist for English second language speakers. However, because the language of education is often English, assessing individuals in an African language might also disadvantage them (Van den Berg, 1996). Nell (1999a) refers to studies in which African language speakers scored lower in both verbal and performance subtests, indicating that more than just language alone should be considered when determining the cross-cultural validity of individual intelligence measures. Demographic variables, especially test wiseness as determined by education, urbanization, and socio-economic level, also affect performance (Nell, 1999a; Shuttleworth-Edwards, Kemp, Rust, Muirhead, Hartman, and Radloff, 2005).

In some cases, the same measures have been standardized for different population groups and separate norms have been developed for each group, for example, the JSAIS for Indian students (Landman, 1988) and for coloured students (Robinson, 1989). Van Eeden and Visser (1992) report that although the SSAIS-R can be regarded as reliable and valid for white, coloured, and Indian students, some variations in factor structure and with regard to the predictive value of scores should be taken into consideration when making comparisons across groups. Environmental deprivation was shown to explain part of the variance in performance on the SSAIS-R (Van Eeden, 1991) and the ISGSA (Robinson, 1994). Consequently, separate norms for these tests were developed for non-environmentally disadvantaged children. Although reliability and validity were similar, substantial differences between the ethnic subpopulations of the English-speaking norm sample of the WAIS-III were attributed to quality of education experienced (Claassen et al., 2001). It is suggested that education, amongst other variables, should be considered on a case-to-case basis when interpreting results (refer to Chapter 15). Given the complexity of cross-cultural testing, the practice has developed where a combination of instruments suitable to the purpose – including tests not standardized locally such as the Wechsler Intelligence Scale for Children – Revised (WISC-R) – is used. Although such a battery is often of value to the informed user (Shuttleworth-Jordan, 1996), issues on the suitability of measures should be kept in mind (refer to Chapter 15). Using the measuring instruments discussed here in a multicultural context places a great responsibility on the psychologist in the application of assessment in practice. This provides further justification for considering alternatives in contexts where more general indications of ability are required, for example using a competency-based testing in industry.

10.3.2 Group tests of intelligence

Every year, large numbers of students who have just finished school apply for admission to higher education institutions such as universities and universities of technology. Government funds these institutions on the basis of the number of students who pass, so they prefer to admit students who will be successful in their studies. Admission testing programmes are often used to select students who are most likely to benefit from what is offered educationally and who are most likely to meet the criteria of success as defined by each institution.

General intellectual ability is one of the aspects often evaluated in selection decisions for admission to educational institutions and training, as well as for placement in industry. Where large numbers are to be assessed, it is more convenient to use a group measure of intelligence rather than the individual measures discussed in the previous section. Furthermore, group tests are designed to assess cognitive abilities that are relevant to academic achievement. Usually, a combination of verbal and non-verbal subtests provides a total ability score. However, some group measures contain only verbal or non-verbal content. The development of culture-fair measures, for example, focuses on non-verbal measures of general intelligence.

10.3.2.1 Description and aim

Similar to the position with individual measures, the main consideration when selecting items for group measures is that each type of item should provide a good indication of a person's level of general intelligence. Variation in item content is necessary to measure a general factor of intelligence (Spearman's g). Items in group intelligence measures commonly measure the ability to solve problems that involve figures, verbal material (words and sentences), and numbers. Box 10.3 contains a practice example from the Word Analogies subtest of the General Scholastic Aptitude Test (GSAT) Senior Series (Claassen, De Beer, Hugo, and Meyer, 1991, p. 12). This is an example of a verbal item. Box 10.4 contains an example of a non-verbal item, namely a practice example from the Pattern Completion subtest of the GSAT Senior (Claassen, De Beer, Ferndale et al., 1991, p. 19; Claassen, De Beer, Hugo et al., 1991, p. 18).

BOX 10.3 GSAT SENIOR: WORD ANALOGIES PRACTICE EXAMPLE

mouse : squeak : frog : ?

A	B	C	D	E
swim	cheese	croak	screech	jump

We call the sound that a MOUSE makes a SQUEAK and the sound that a FROG makes a CROAK. MOUSE stands to SQUEAK as FROG stands to CROAK. CROAK should therefore go in the place of the question mark. The letter above CROAK is C, therefore the answer to Question 1 is C.

SOURCE: Copyright © by the Human Sciences Research Council. Reproduced by permission.

BOX 10.4 GSAT SENIOR: PATTERN COMPLETION PRACTICE EXAMPLE

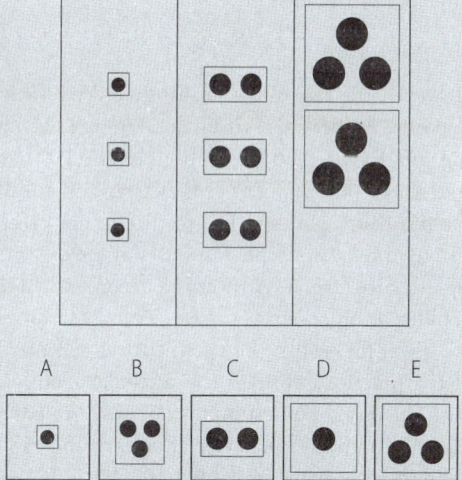

In the first row, in the first square there is a small square with one small dot, then a slightly bigger square with two dots, and then an even bigger square with three dots in it. The second row looks exactly like the first, and the third row also begins like the first two rows. We therefore expect that this row should look like the other two rows. In the third square we therefore need a large square with three dots, and that is E.

SOURCE: Copyright © by the Human Sciences Research Council. Reproduced by permission.

Items are grouped together according to item type in homogeneous subtests and the items in each subtest are arranged in increasing order of difficulty. In the GSAT Senior (Claassen, De Beer, Hugo et al., 1991) for example, subtests are also grouped into verbal and non-verbal subscales and scores are provided for these subscales. It is now possible to see if there is a difference in the individual's ability to solve problems with verbal and non-verbal content. The total score is assumed to represent an underlying general factor of intelligence. A computerized adaptive version of the GSAT is also available (Van Tonder, 1992).

Some group tests provide only a verbal or a non-verbal measure of general intelligence. In the LPCAT (De Beer, 2000, 2006), for example, the test-taker analyses sets of figures and deduces basic relations. This is therefore a measure of non-verbal reasoning ability and provides an index of an individual's general intellectual ability without the influence of verbal skills.

Group measures are designed to be administered simultaneously to a number of persons. However, the size of the group should be limited to ensure proper supervision and rapport. According to Claassen, De Beer, Hugo et al. (1991), an assessment practitioner needs assistance if a group exceeds thirty persons. The test items are printed and require only simple responses or are of a multiple-choice format. Answers are recorded in a test booklet or on an answer sheet. Practice examples are given for each type of item. After completion of the practice examples the test-taker continues with the test or subtest on his/her own. An advantage of group measures is that the scoring can be done objectively and quickly (often by computer).

The administration procedure is standardized and the assessment practitioner is only required to read the instructions and make sure that time limits are adhered to. The testing conditions are more uniform than in the case of individual measures, but the opportunity for interaction between the assessment practitioner and test-takers is limited. We mentioned that some individuals might score below their ability owing to anxiety, motivational problems, and so on; these non-cognitive factors that could influence test performance are more difficult to detect in a group situation. In addition,

group measures assume that the persons being tested have normal reading ability. If an individual has reading problems, his/her score in a group measure should not be regarded as a valid estimate of his/her ability. It should be noted that group measures can also be administered to individuals. For example, the Cognitive Process Profile (CPP) was developed to measure thinking processes and styles. The measure is a self-administering (but supervised) computerized assessment technique and as the role of the assessment practitioner is minimized it can be categorised as a group test. However, some practitioners prefer the CPP when assessing individuals, especially at higher organizational levels, due to its culture fair item content and the fact that it provides an indication of both current functioning and learning potential as well as diagnostic information that can be used for placement and development purposes (Jopie van Rooyen & Partners, 2007).

10.3.2.2 The application of results

Group measures are used at different stages in the educational and career counselling process. The range of difficulty covered by a measure should be suitable for the particular age, grade, or level of education for which it is intended. Different forms of a measure for different ability levels normally provide continuity in terms of content and the nature of the abilities measured. Therefore, it is possible to retest a person and compare his/her score over several years. Different age groups or grade groups can also be compared. For example, the General Scholastic Aptitude Test has a Junior Series (9 years to 11 years), an Intermediate Series (11 years to 14 years), and a Senior Series (14 years to 18 years) (Owen and Taljaard, 1996). The Paper and Pencil Games (PPG) can be used for younger children (Grades 2 to 4) (Claassen, 1996).

The scores on group measures of general ability are expressed as standard scores and an individual's performance can be compared with that of a reference group (the norm group). This gives an indication of the individual's level of reasoning ability or problem-solving ability. Because this information is relevant to his/her academic achievement, these measures can be used for educational counselling as well as for the selection and placement of students at school and at tertiary institutions. For example, students who could benefit from special education (gifted individuals or those with learning problems) can be identified. Although further testing, for instance with individual intelligence measures, would be necessary to obtain a differential picture of abilities, this initial screening helps to limit the number of persons involved. Group measures can also be used as part of the selection process in industry.

Similar to individual intelligence measures, the content of group measures is culture specific, and knowledge of and familiarity with the material could influence test results. Claassen and Schepers (1990) found that mean differences on the GSAT Intermediate for different population groups were related to differences in socio-economic background. In addition, test wiseness (i.e. being accustomed to testing) may play a somewhat greater role than in the case of individual measures (Anastasi and Urbina, 1997). Claassen, De Beer, Hugo et al. (1991) consequently prefer the term 'scholastic aptitude' to 'general intelligence' and these authors maintain that the GSAT measures 'a student's present level of reasoning ability in respect of scholastic material' (p. 25). Only in the case of students who are not environmentally disadvantaged can this score also be interpreted as an intelligence score.

Lack of knowledge of the language used also influences test results if a person is not assessed in his/her mother tongue. This effect seems less significant in the case of non-verbal measures (Hugo and Claassen, 1991; Claassen and Hugo, 1993). According to De Beer (2006) the LPCAT makes provision for differences between culture groups amongst other reasons due to its non-verbal item content. It is generally assumed that non-verbal measures cannot be used as successfully as verbal scores to predict academic achievement. However, De Beer (2006) found that the predictive validity of the LPCAT is generally acceptable at school and at junior tertiary levels with lower correlations with academic performance found for postgraduate students. The construct validity of the measure is acceptable irrespective of age or attained level of education. Holburn (1992) reports very little bias for the non-verbal Figure Classification

Test when comparing different population groups. The Raven Progressive Matrices (RPM) is an overseas non-verbal measure regarded as suitable for cross-cultural use, and Owen (1992) compared the performance of white, coloured, Indian, and black students in Grade 9 for the standard form of the RPM. He found that the measure 'behaves in the same way for the different groups', but that large mean differences between the white and black groups in particular imply that common norms cannot be used (p. 158). The author suggests that children from the different groups do not necessarily use the same solution strategies. In the case of the PPG, instructions are presented in the mother tongue (Claassen, 1996). If the same set of test norms is used for different groups, it is important to establish whether the same construct is measured and if a common regression line predicts academic achievement equally well for each group (see, for example, Claassen's (1990) study on the comparability of GSAT scores for white, coloured, and Indian students).

10.4 **Measures of specific abilities**

10.4.1 **Aptitude measures**

A major car manufacturer appoints persons who have completed ten years of schooling as apprentices. They are then trained to become motor mechanics. When selecting these apprentices, level of general intelligence, academic achievement, previous experience, etc. are taken into account. In addition, an apprentice should have above-average mechanical aptitude.

The term aptitude is used to describe a specific ability. It refers to the individual's ability to acquire, with training, a specific skill or to attain a specific level of performance. According to Owen (1996), the abilities measured by aptitude measures correspond to the intellectual abilities measured by tests of general ability. The difference is that the items and subtests of measures of general cognitive functioning are selected primarily to provide a unitary measure, and not to provide an indication of differential abilities. In addition, certain areas of functioning relevant to guidance in educational and occupational contexts are not covered by measures of general cognitive functioning (e.g. mechanical and clerical skills).

10.4.1.1 Description and aim

The abilities measured by different aptitude measures include reasoning on the basis of verbal, non-verbal, and quantitative material, language comprehension, spatial ability, perceptual speed, memory, coordination, and so on. Tasks that measure the same ability are grouped together in homogeneous tests. For example, each item in the Mechanical Insight test of the Differential Aptitude Tests Form R (DAT-R) consists of a drawing representing a mechanical apparatus or portrays a mechanical or physical principle. This test measures mechanical ability or the ability to perceive mechanical principles and to understand the functioning of apparatus based on these principles (Claassen, van Heerden, Vosloo, and Wheeler, 2000).

A special aptitude test focuses on a single aptitude. There are a variety of special aptitude tests that measure a comprehensive range of work skills at different levels, for example, the Acer Mechanical Reasoning Test (MRT) (Jopie van Rooyen & Partners, 2007). Tests of specific abilities are used in combination to assess the specific abilities relevant to a job. SHL (2007) suggests batteries consisting of tests, questionnaires, and assessment centre exercises that focus on specific abilities but that in combination are relevant to certain types of jobs and job levels. Among the abilities measured are verbal, numerical, accuracy and checking, spatial reasoning, working with systems and rules, mechanical reasoning, manual dexterity, problem solving, idea generation and managerial judgement. For example, the Critical Reasoning Test Battery (CRTB) is suggested for use with the job categories 'Management and graduates' and 'Junior managers and supervisors'. It consists of Verbal Evaluation, Interpreting Data and Diagrammatic Series. Another example is the Information Technology Test Series (ITTS) used for the category 'Information technology staff' that consists of Verbal reasoning, Number Series, Computer Checking,

Syntax Checking, Diagramming, and Spatial Reasoning. The Psytech (2007) batteries are similar but correspond to a greater extent with what is known as multiple aptitude batteries. A multiple aptitude battery consists of a number of homogeneous tests, each of which measures a specific ability. The Psytech batteries were designed in terms of a recommended minimum level of education and include the Graduate and General Reasoning Tests (GRT1 and GRT2), different levels of the Critical Reasoning Test (CRTB1 and CRTB2), the Technical Test Battery (TTB2) and the Clerical Test Battery (CTB2). The latter, for example, consists of Clerical Checking, Spelling, Typing, Verbal Reasoning, Numerical Ability and Filing. The Critical Reasoning Skills Series (CRSS) (Jopie van Rooyen & Partners, 2007) is another example of a battery used for graduates and managers. The homogeneous tests are, in certain instances, also grouped to obtain measurements in more general aptitude fields. For example, the nine tests of the Differential Aptitude Tests Form K (DAT-K) are grouped into six aptitude categories that can be more easily related to specific occupations than the individual tests (see Table 10.1) (Coetzee and Vosloo, 2000, p. 44).

The administration and scoring procedures are similar to those for group measures and the same advantages and limitations apply. Although most items are multiple-choice or require only simple responses, tests such as those measuring coordination and writing speed involve more complex responding and scoring procedures. Some tests can be administered on a computer, for example the specialized ability tests included in the Vienna Test System (Schuhfried, 1999), which is a fully computerized system. An aptitude test can also be administered as an individual test. For example, we can administer the Aptitude Tests for School Beginners (ASB) individually in a context where it is often helpful to observe the child's behaviour, work methods, and other non-cognitive factors that could influence performance (Olivier and Swart, 1974).

10.4.1.2 The application of results

The scores for each measure in a multiple aptitude battery are converted to standard scores so

Table 10.1 Grouping of the tests of the DAT-K in aptitude fields

APTITUDE	TESTS
Verbal Aptitude	Vocabulary Verbal Reasoning Reading Comprehension Memory (Paragraph)
Numerical Aptitude	Calculations
Visual-spatial Reasoning	Non-verbal Reasoning: Figures Spatial Visualization 3D
Clerical Aptitude	Comparison
Memory	Memory (Paragraph)
Mechanical Aptitude	Mechanical Insight

the individual now has a set of scores for different aptitudes. His/her profile of aptitudes can be compared with that of others in the norm group, or the individual's strengths and weaknesses can be identified. As indicated there is an aptitude test for school beginners. The DAT is primarily used in an educational context and it consists of a standard form (Form R) and an advanced form (Form S) for grades 7 to 10 as well as a standard form (Form K) and an advanced form (Form L) for grades 10 to 12. As discussed, aptitude tests and multiple aptitude batteries used in industry are also often graded in terms of a minimum educational level and/or a suitable job level (or levels).

Educational context

The Aptitude tests for School Beginners (ASB) (HSRC, 1994) measures level of development with regard to a number of aptitudes that are important to progress at school. This test battery is used to determine if children are ready to enter school. It aims to obtain a comprehensive picture of specific aptitudes of the school beginner and evaluates the cognitive aspects of school readiness. The ASB comprises eight tests: Perception, Spatial, Reasoning, Numerical, Gestalt, Coordination, Memory, and Verbal Comprehension. The ASB is an educationally focussed screening measure that, simi-

larly to measures designed to assess global developmental progress and delays, are used to identify children who are potentially at risk for developmental difficulties. These children are then further assessed using diagnostic measures (see Box 10.2). The aptitude profile on the DAT is used together with results from other tests and information on academic performance for guidance on decisions regarding which type of secondary school children should attend (e.g. academic or technical), subject choice, the level at which a subject should be taken, and the field of study after school. Combinations of aptitudes are considered when making these decisions and conclusions are not based on a single score. For example, if a boy in Grade 12 scores above average on Numerical Aptitude and Visual-spatial Reasoning on the DAT-K, he could consider a technical or scientific field of study or occupation depending on his performance in Mathematics at school.

Industrial context

Different aptitudes and aptitude fields are also important for success in different occupations. A number of aptitude tests and multiple aptitude batteries have been developed to aid in selection and placement in industry. For example, the ITTS referred to earlier is suitable for the selection, development, and promotion of staff working in information technology such as software engineers, system analysts, programmers, and database administrators. However, the level of skill that a person may reach also depends on his/her general intellectual ability, interests, personality traits, attitude, motivation, and training. This was confirmed by Van der Merwe's (2002) survey on tests used in a number of organizations. Psychological assessment measures from all categories were included. However, the measures of cognitive functioning identified were primarily aptitude tests with limited use of individual intelligence measures and group tests of intelligence. Considering some of the measures of cognitive functioning commonly used in the training of psychometry interns it is clear that, although the WAIS III is generally included, emphasis needs to be placed on measures of learning potential (APIL-B, CPP, LPCAT, Raven's Progressive Matrices and TRAM1/2) and the wide range of aptitude measures discussed in the previous section.

When aptitude profiles are compared, it is assumed that everyone being assessed has more or less the same level of experience with regard to the different aptitudes. This is not necessarily true in a context where people's backgrounds might not be the same. The composition of the norm group with regard to language and culture should, therefore, be taken into account when interpreting results. In 1994, norms were established on the ASB for all South Africans (HSRC, 1999/2000). Instructions have also been translated into numerous languages (Northern Sotho, Tswana, Xhosa, and so on). In a study with the Junior Aptitude Tests (JAT), Owen (1991) found differences in mean test performance for white, coloured, Indian, and black students, despite the fact that the test measured the same psychological constructs for these groups. He suggests that factors such as language could have been a source of bias, especially in the case of the black students who were tested in English. Some forms of the DAT have been standardized for all population groups. In the case of the tests referred to that are used in an industrial context, cross-cultural research and norming for samples representative of the South African population are taking place on a continuous basis.

10.4.2 Measures of specific cognitive functions

> A twenty-five-year-old woman was involved in a motor accident. She complains that she is not functioning as well at home or at work as she used to before the accident, and she is referred for neuropsychological assessment. The clinician needs to determine which cognitive functions have been affected by the accident and to what extent. This will help him/her to explain behaviour deficits and to plan rehabilitation.

From Box 10.1 it should be clear that the subtests of an individual intelligence test measure not only general ability but also specific cognitive functions. Hypotheses about areas in which an individual might be experiencing problems (or in which he/she is expected to do well) can therefore be based on performance in combinations of subtests. However, tests constructed to measure particular functions should be used to confirm these hypotheses.

Tests for specific cognitive functions can be grouped in a number of categories. The scope of this textbook does not allow for a comprehensive discussion of all the categories. Only measures of language, perceptual functions, spatial and manipulatory ability, and motor performance are briefly discussed in this section. Tests of attention and concentration, memory, and executive functions are not covered.

10.4.2.1 Description and aim

The aspects measured by **measures of verbal functions** include speech, reading, writing, and comprehension of spoken language. With less serious problems, standardized language-related scholastic achievement measures that are discussed in the next section can be used to obtain information about the nature of a problem and to recommend steps for remediation. In the case of language dysfunctions caused by brain damage (called aphasia), a more comprehensive assessment by a specialist is necessary. The Token Test is an example of a screening measure for aphasia (Lezak, 1995). The test material consists of tokens – shapes (circles and squares) in two sizes (big and small) and five colours. The test items require the test-taker to follow relatively simple instructions such as: 'Touch the yellow circle with the red square' (this is not an actual item). To do this, the test-taker must understand what 'circle' and 'square' mean and must also know the meaning of the verbs and prepositions in the instructions. The Token Test is sensitive to deviations in language performance related to aphasia. However, once a person is known to be aphasic, a more comprehensive diagnostic measure or test battery should be administered.

Perceptual measures deal with visual, auditory, and tactile functions – that is, vision, hearing, and touch. For example, line bisection tests provide an indication of unilateral visual inattention, in other words, failure to perceive individual stimulation (Lezak, 1995). One or more horizontal lines are presented and the test-taker is asked to divide the line by placing a mark at the centre of the line. The face-hand tests and the finger recognition tests are examples of measures of tactile functions (Gregory, 2007). These measures consist of simple tasks: in the first type of measure the assessment practitioner touches the subject on the hand and/or the cheek and the subject must then indicate where he/she felt the touch. Finger recognition tests require identification (pointing or verbally) of the finger or set of fingers touched. In both these types of measures a series of touches is presented while the test-taker's eyes are either open or closed, depending on the measure used.

Measures of constructional performance assess a combination of perceptual functions (more specifically, visuoperceptual functions), spatial ability, and manipulatory ability or motor responses (Lezak, 1995). The activities included in these measures involve either drawing (copying or free drawing) or assembling. The Bender-Gestalt Test is a widely used drawing test (Anastasi and Urbina, 1997). It consists of relatively simple designs or figures that are presented to the test-taker one at a time. He/she has to copy each design as accurately as possible. Drawings are evaluated to determine if the performance is more typical of the brain-impaired than that of 'normal' individuals. For example, it is noted whether a figure was rotated, if a hand tremor is evident, or if separate

designs overlap. If a measure that involves assembling tasks (see the Block Designs subtests of the SSAIS-R described in Box 10.1) is also included as part of the evaluation process, the assessment practitioner will be able to discriminate better between visual and spatial components of constructional problems.

Measures of motor performance assess manipulative speed and accuracy (Lezak, 1995) among other things. The Purdue Pegboard Test was developed to measure dexterity when selecting employees for manual jobs such as assembly, packing, and operation of certain machines. The test-taker has to place a number of pegs into holes with the left hand, right hand, and both hands simultaneously. The score is the number of pegs placed correctly in a limited time (thirty seconds for each trial). In the Grooved Pegboard test each peg has a ridge along one side and the subject has to rotate the peg in order to fit it into a slotted hole. This test measures both manual dexterity and complex coordination.

Measures of specific cognitive functions are administered individually and qualitative interpretation of responses and test behaviour are important sources of information. The assessment practitioner should have the experience to accommodate test-takers with mental and/or physical handicaps. In addition, there are a large number of measures available for measuring the different cognitive functions. The assessment practitioner should study the test manuals and other relevant literature on the administration and scoring procedures for a specific measure.

10.4.2.2 The application of results

Depending on a person's complaints and reasons for referral, the assessment practitioner can use a combination of relevant tests to measure a number of different cognitive functions. This is an individualized approach and implies a different set of tests for each client. Alternatively, the assessment practitioner can use a standardized test battery, which consists of a fixed set of subtests, each measuring a specific function or an aspect of a function. By using the same set of tests, the assessment practitioner can compare the results of different persons.

Measures of specific cognitive functions are used in neuropsychological assessment to detect brain impairment and to determine which functions have been affected and to what extent. The specific aspect of a function with which a person is experiencing problems can also help to identify and localize the impaired brain area. A person's score on a particular measure is evaluated in terms of research information available for that measure. This will show how his/her performance compares with what can be expected from a 'normal' person, and possible brain damage can be identified. A qualitative analysis of responses also provides more information on the nature of the problem. An example is the inability of brain-damaged individuals to process as much information at once as normal individuals can. This can be seen in brain-damaged individuals' disorganized approach to copying complex figures. As a result of the diversity of disorders and the corresponding behavioural manifestations, experience is required to identify problems and plan rehabilitation. Therefore, a team of specialists is usually involved in the assessment process and various factors other than the test scores (e.g. medical history, interview information) are also taken into account (see also Chapter 15).

As yet, many of the measures referred to in this section have not been adapted or standardized for South Africa. Research on local use is also limited, especially with regard to cross-cultural issues. Nevertheless, these and similar measures are frequently administered in South Africa as part of neuropsychological assessment, and assessment practitioners make inferences using normative data that is based on foreign populations. Various authors argue in favour of locally developed normative data (Tollman and Msengana, 1990; Viljoen, Levett, and Tredoux, 1994). Tollman and Msengana (1990) discuss problems in interpreting test results if culture, language, and education are not taken into account. Their study deals with an adaptation of Luria's Neuropsychological Investigation to accommodate Zulu-speakers. Viljoen et al. (1994) found significant differences when comparing the Bender-Gestalt test performance of a group of Zulu-speaking children with that of the foreign normative sample. They recommend further studies on the clinical value and applicability of this test when used for other groups. Based on cross-cultural experience and empirical results, Nell (1999b) has recommended a battery of existing psychological and neuropsychological measures that can be used for persons with less than twelve years of education. Instructions for this battery are available in a number of African languages.

10.5 **Scholastic tests**

Although the focus of this book is on psychological assessment measures, scholastic measures are often used in conjunction with psychological measures in educational settings. Standardized scholastic tests measure current attainment in school subjects or fields of study. There are three categories of scholastic tests, namely proficiency tests, achievement tests, and diagnostic tests. Proficiency tests overlap with aptitude tests, but, whereas aptitude tests measure a number of cognitive abilities, proficiency tests are more focused in terms of defined fields of study or school subjects (e.g. English language proficiency test for a specific school grade). Proficiency tests are not limited to syllabus content. On the other hand, achievement tests are syllabus-based and the items of these tests should cover syllabus content (e.g. mathematics). In addition, diagnostic tests measure performance in subsections of a subject domain. This enables the assessment practitioner to determine specific areas of a subject where a child experiences problems. The use of scholastic tests are not limited to the school context, for example, the English Literacy Skills Assessment (ELSA) are suitable for use in work and training environments (Jopie van Rooyen & Partners, 2007).

10.6 **Conclusion**

To understand why the theories and measurement of cognitive functioning have sparked such intense debate and emotional reactions, we have to consider the psychosocial issues involved. In most Western societies, either directly or indirectly, various 'advantages' are associated with a specific level of cognitive functioning – 'intelligence' as it is defined in psychometric terms. These include aspects such as a good education, a corresponding higher level of employment, higher standing in the society, a higher level of income, and so the list goes on. However, after studying this chapter, you should realize that measures of cognitive functioning differ in terms of the underlying assumptions. The interpretation of results is limited to what each test measures and should always be used in the context for which a specific measure was intended. Technical features, such as the reliability and validity of the measure, should be considered, as well as the population or norm group for whom the measure was standardized. In addition, research on differences within and between groups should make us aware of the need to invest in people through social or educational programmes.

CHECKING YOUR PROGESS **10.1**

10.1   Critically discuss the meaning of an intelligence score.

10.2   Discuss the different aspects that need to be considered when investigating the cross-cultural equivalence of measures.

10.3   Discuss the use and application of measures of general cognitive functioning.

10.4   Discuss the use and application of measures of specific abilities.

10.5   What factors will you consider when selecting a cognitive measure to be used in a specific situation?

10.6   You are working in the human resources department of a mining company that has an active personnel development programme. Your job is to identify individuals with the potential to benefit from an administrative training course, a language course, and/or a technical course. What type of measure(s) would you use? Justify your answer.

When you have finished responding to the questions, it will be time to continue your travels through the *Types-of-Measures Zone*. At the next stop, you will have an opportunity to investigate measures of affective functioning.

Measures of affective behaviour, adjustment, and well-being

CAROLINA HENN AND NICOLENE BARKHUIZEN

CHAPTER OUTCOMES

This stop follows a similar pattern to the first two stops in the Types-of-Measures Zone. In what way is the pattern similar? You will first be provided with some theoretical perspectives and issues, after which you will be introduced to various measures. After completing this chapter, you will be able to:

> understand well-being as a broad concept within psychology;
> understand the impact of well-being in the world of work; and
> name and describe the assessment tools that can be utilized to measure various constructs related to well-being.

11.1 **Well-being**

The overriding impression one gets from reading the available literature on well-being, is of the vastness of the concept. Different authors provide different definitions, and also emphasize different aspects of well-being. Roodt (1991) attributes this to the numerous disciplines that investigate well-being. These disciplines include psychology, sociology, medicine and economics. He also points out that the use of numerous terms (including well-being, psychological well-being, life satisfaction, happiness and quality of life) further complicate understanding of well-being. There does seem to be consensus, however, that well-being is a multi-dimensional construct with numerous domains. Moreover, these different domains exercise mutual influence on each other. In terms of schools of thought within psychology, well-being is most at home within positive psychology.

In the following sections attention will be given to providing a fairly inclusive definition of well-being, explaining its attachment to positive psychology, and discussing some of the domains of well-being.

11.1.1 **Defining well-being**

The World Health Organization (WHO) defines health as 'a state of complete physical, mental and social well-being and not merely the absence of disease or infirmity' (Preamble to the Constitution of the World Health Organization, p. 100). It is interesting to note that this definition has remained unchanged since 1948, when it was first entered into force. In addition, the WHO also provides a definition of mental health, namely 'a state of well-being in which every individual realizes his or her own potential, can cope with the normal stresses of life, can work productively and fruitfully, and is able to make a contribution to her or his community' (WHO, 2008: Online Question and Answer: What is mental health?, para.1). This definition encompasses both subjective elements (i.e. within the individual) such as coping with stress, as well as objective elements (i.e. between the individual and his environment) such as making a contribution to the community.

Literature on well-being supports the above definitions by focusing on two key elements of well-being, namely an absence of disease/illness on the one hand and the presence of physical and emotional health on the other. In many writings the term 'psychological well-being' is utilized to refer to this absence of negative aspects such as illness, and the presence of positive factors such as happiness. Despite the 'psychological' prefix, the term is still applied in a broad sense that encompasses both emotional and physical aspects.

Diener, Kesebir and Lucas (2008) highlight that well-being refers to the full range of aspects that contribute to an individual's assessment of his/her quality of life, including social aspects, physical and mental health, and feelings of happiness and safety. In addition, they distinguish between non-specific well-being indicators such as life satisfaction, and more specific ones such as job satisfaction. Blanchflower and Oswald (2004) refer to the former as 'context-free' well-being and the latter as 'context-specific' well-being (p.1360). A person may thus rate his overall well-being as positive, but single out a specific aspect (e.g. physical fitness) as negative.

11.1.2 **Positive psychology and well-being**

It is most probably the second element of well-being, namely the presence of positive aspects of functioning, that places it within the domain of positive psychology. Positive psychology emphasizes that psychology is not merely about disease and finding cures, but also about positive aspects of living such as happiness and virtue (Seligman, 2003). Keyes and Haidt (2003) point out that positive psychology is about helping people to not merely exist, but to flourish. However, they are also quick to mention that positive psychology's view of life and people is realistic and balanced. In other words, they do not deny the existence of challenging and daunting life circumstances and negative affect such as sadness.

This view is also expressed by Peterson (2006) who states quite succinctly that 'everyone's life has peaks and valleys, and positive psychology does not deny the valleys' (p. 4). The focus remains, though, on the fact that people are generally resilient and manage to cope with life's difficulties, sometimes in ways that astound those around them. Ryff and Singer (2003) refer to the many well-documented empirical findings of individuals who were able to preserve and even improve their well-being despite difficult challenges. One is reminded, for example, of South Africa's paralympic gold medallist swimmer, Natalie du Toit, who lost a leg in a motor cycle accident at a time when she was already a swimmer with extremely good prospects. Despite this loss and obvious adaptations she had to make, she continues to aspire to ever greater achievements. By doing so, she is serving as a source of inspiration for numerous other people.

11.1.3 **Domains of well-being**

Deci and Ryan (2008) indicate that research on well-being generally falls within one of two traditions: the **hedonistic** tradition and the **eudaimonic** tradition. The hedonistic view on well-being focuses on subjective experiences of well-being, such as happiness, and positive and negative affect. The eudaimonic perspective is concerned with maximizing one's full potential and living 'as one was inherently intended to live' (Deci and Ryan, 2008, p. 2). In addition, there are also other fields of study, such as Economics, that evaluates well-being in terms of economic indicators such as employment and income.

11.1.3.1 Subjective well-being

Discussions on the experience of subjective well-being (SWB) are best placed within the hedonistic tradition. Diener, Sapyte and Suh (1998) defines SWB as an individual's evaluation of his/her quality of life. This valuation can be in terms of cognitive judgements (e.g. marital satisfaction) as well as affect (e.g. the presence of positive emotions and the absence of negative emotions). There is an abundance of literature on various determinants of SWB. A few of these determinants that feature prominently, are:

- **Quality of Life (QoL)**
  According to Roodt (1991) quality of life can be determined in two ways. Firstly, social indicators such as crime – and unemployment rates can be utilized to judge quality of life. Secondly, quality of life is determined by individuals' subjective perceptions of different aspects of their lives. He also ranks QoL as an overarching concept that encompasses psychological well-being. It is interesting to note that, although QoL is generally considered to be a subjective indicator of well-being, it does contain an objective component as well, which is expressed in, amongst others, social factors such as neighborhood and crime. Ring, Hofer, McGee, Hickey and O'Boyle (2007) point out that empirical findings strongly indicate the specific nature of QoL (in other words, there is much variation in terms of individuals' perceptions thereof).

- **Happiness**
  In some writings, happiness is used interchangeably with subjective well-being (cf. Deci and Ryan, 2008) whereas Roodt (1991) considers happiness to be a subcomponent of psychological well-being. Veenhoven (1991) defines happiness as 'the degree to which an individual judges the overall quality of his life-as-a-whole favourably' (p. 1). He further proposes that this global appraisal consists of an affective component (which refers to the degree to which emotions experienced are considered pleasant), and a cognitive component (which is determined by a person's perceptions of having his/her expectations met). Argyle and Crossland (1987) identified three key components of happiness, namely a high frequency of positive affect, the absence of negative feelings and a high average level of satisfaction over time. Diener et al. (2008) present the following empirical findings on the benefits of happiness: improved relationships, higher income, improved health, increased behaviours that benefit the community such as volunteering, etc. In short, according to them, 'happiness fosters effective functioning across a variety of domains' (p. 44).

- **Life Satisfaction**
  According to Bekhet, Zauszniewski and Nakhla (2008), life satisfaction is 'similar to happiness but lacks any reference to a state of mind' (p. 16), This implies that happiness has an emotional component attached to it that satisfaction may not necessarily have. Roodt (1991) lists life satisfaction as a subcomponent of psychological well-being. Life satisfaction can be divided into two separate components, namely overall life satisfaction and domains-of-life satisfaction (i.e. satisfaction in specific areas of your life, e.g. such as finances, physical health and relationships).

- **Positive and negative affect**
  Happiness/life satisfaction on one hand, and a balance between positive and negative affect on the other, are considered the two legs on which subjective well-being rests (cf. Busseri, Sadava and DeCourville, 2007; Deci and Ryan, 2008; Ryff and Keyes, 1995). Descriptions of positive affect include joyful, happy, pleased and enjoyment/fun, and descriptions of negative affect includes worried/anxious, depressed, frustrated, angry/hostile and unhappy (cf. Diener and Emmons, 1984). Research has indicated that certain personality traits are related to the experience of affect (for example, the relationship between personality traits such as extraversion and optimism on the one hand, and emotional well-being on the other (Reis,

Sheldon, Gable, Roscoe and Ryan, 2000). It is generally known that consistent experiencing of negative emotions such as stress are contributing factors to illnesses such as cancer, cardiovascular disease and numerous other health problems. In addition, research findings into the benefits of positive emotion, has indicated that it can promote health and longevity, and can lead to more likelihood of success in careers (Diener et al., 2008).

- **Social and economic determinants of subjective well-being**
Social and economic factors that can be expected to impact an individual's perception of well-being include crime rate, neighborhood, income and unemployment. In their research on the experience of well-being over time in Europe and the United States of America, Blanchflower and Oswald (2004) found that women, married people, highly educated people and those with parents whose marriages are still intact, are the happiest. Higher income was also associated with greater happiness, and happiness levels were low amongst unemployed people. These findings indicate that external factors do impact on well-being.

11.1.3.2 **Other dimensions of well-being**

Carol Ryff's model of well-being is one of the best-known within the eudaimonic tradition. She developed this six-dimensional model as a response to the emphasis placed on subjective experiences of well-being in research. The six dimensions in her model are described as follows (Ryff and Keyes, 1995):

- **Self-Acceptance**
Possessing a positive attitude towards oneself; acknowledging and accepting all aspects of oneself, including good and bad qualities; and feeling positive about one's past life.
- **Positive relations with others**
Having warm, trusting relationships with other people; being concerned about the welfare of others; being capable of empathy, affection and intimacy; the ability to give and take in relationships.
- **Autonomy**
Self-determination and being independent; internal locus of control; can resist social pressure

to think and act in specific ways; can evaluate oneself in terms of one's own standards.
- **Environmental mastery**
Competent management of the environment; controlling diverse and complex activities within the environment; can choose contexts suitable to personal needs and aligned with personal values.
- **Purpose in life**
Having goals in life and a sense of direction; finding meaning in life (past and present); holds beliefs that provides purpose in life.
- **Personal growth**
Feels that one is developing continuously; can see improvement within oneself and in behaviour over time; openness to new experiences; experiencing a sense of achieving and optimizing one's potential; changing in ways that are indicative of increased self-knowledge and effectiveness.

In a criticism of Ryff's model, Diener et al. (1998) commends her for focusing on positive aspects of well-being, and accedes that some of the characteristics outlined by her (e.g. purpose, mastery and positive self-regard) do contribute to subjective well-being. They strongly criticize her model, though, for under-estimating the importance of subjective well-being. Ryff developed her theoretical framework of well-being, and its dimensions, through a comprehensive literature review including psychological theories (e.g. the humanistic theories of Maslow and Rogers) and philosophical understandings of the 'good life' (Dierendonck, Diaz, Rodriguez-Carvajal, Blanco and Moreno-Jimenez, 2008, p. 474). It is exactly this way in which she arrived at her multi-dimensional model that forms a considerable part of Diener et al's (1998) critique, as she does not incorporate an individual's own definition of well-being in these dimensions. Ryff and Keyes (1995), on the other hand, are of the opinion that too much emphasis has been placed on positive affect and happiness as determinants of well-being, at the cost of other important aspects of functioning such as meaning in life and realizing one's potential. Diener et al. (2008) counters this argument by emphasizing research findings that subjective feelings, such as happiness, do in fact facilitate behaviours that foster meaning in life and the actualization of potential, such as increased trust, ethical behaviour and volunteering (i.e. outcomes that contribute positively to society).

In conclusion, it can be said that a discussion of well-being is better served by a 'both ... and' approach than an 'either ... or' approach. In other words, both the hedonistic and eudaimonic traditions serve to enhance and broaden our understanding of well-being.

You may have noticed that the foregoing sections on well-being did not include a discussion of physical and mental illness, other than mentioning the absence thereof as an indicator of health and well-being. We will, however, discuss this in the following section when we look at the impact of well-being on the business world.

> » **CRITICAL THINKING CHALLENGE 11.1**
>
> Think of a person that you know that, in your opinion, exemplifies well-being in all its aspects. Based on your knowledge of and experiences with this person, develop a model of well-being that encompasses both hedonistic and eudaimonic understandings and perceptions thereof. Your model should also indicate the interrelatedness of concepts of well-being.

11.2 Well-being in the workplace

It is a logical deduction that happy people are most likely also happy employees, which will in turn benefit the companies they work for (for example as measured by productivity). In the following sections, we will present several prominent aspects of the relationship between well-being and the workplace. In corporate jargon the term 'wellness' appears to be preferred over 'well-being, although the two concepts have essentially the same meaning. In our discussion we will thus also use the two terms interchangeably.

11.2.1 Why well-being matters

There are two main reasons why employers should take cognisance of their employees' well-being. Firstly because healthy employees are generally

better employees, which in turn impacts positively on productivity, thus leading to improvement of the company bottom-line (profit) (cf. Foulke and Sherman, 2005). Loeppke (2008) emphasizes the importance of making 'strategic investments in health care' (p. 106) so as to ensure that companies can maintain a 'workforce that is both able and available to employers competing in a global economy' (p. 106). Research findings indicate that employers can save money by investing in the well-being of their employees. For example, according to Johnson & Johnson the company have saved $154 in healthcare costs per participant in their wellness programme, after deducting the cost of the programme (Mason, 1994). It is also estimated that, for every £1 spent on employing someone it costs double that amount when the employee is absent (Cotton, 2004). Thus, caring about the wellness of employees makes economic sense. Secondly, employers have a moral and ethical responsibility to support their employees. This is, in part, due to the fact that some illnesses such as stress, can be caused by working conditions and job demands. It is also part of an employers' overall community responsibility to assist in improving quality of life of people, and one's own employees seems to be a logical starting point. In this regard, Loeppke (2008) stresses the need to invest in health as individuals, families, employers, communities and nations.

11.2.3 The cost of ill-health

Numerous sources indicate the cost of ill-health to employers. A study done by AIC Insurance in South Africa estimates that absenteeism costs companies in South Africa approximately R12 billion rand annually (Lilford, 2008). Of this amount, between R1,8 billion and R2,2 billion is due to HIV/Aids (Moodley, 2005). The Corporate Absenteeism Management Solutions (CAMS) survey found the cost to be even higher, namely R19 billion rand per year (Encouraging corporate wellness maintenance, 2007). At the average company, approximately 4,5% of employees are absent on any given day, in some companies this rate is as high as 18%.

Mental illness (depression, in particular) and HIV/Aids appear to be the most prevalent wellness-related issues that are currently confronting companies, not only globally, but especially in South Africa.

HIV/Aids

Given the high infection rate of HIV/Aids in South Africa (11,4%) (Shisana, 2002) there can exist no doubt that the epidemic will have a negative impact on companies. The following findings underscore this impact:

- The findings presented by Rosen, Vincent, MacLeod, Fox, Thea and Simon (2004) in terms of the costs of HIV/Aids to businesses in Southern Africa (South Africa and Botswana) are indeed sobering: HIV prevalence among employees ranged from 7,9% to 25%; HIV/Aids among employees, adds 0,4–5,9% to the companies' annual salary and wage bills; the value of an HIV infection ranges from 0,5 to 3,6 times the annual salary of the employee.
- In addition, they also found that employees who ultimate terminate employment due to AIDS took between 11–68 more days of paid sick leave in their last year of service; supervisors also estimate that employees who die or go on disability due to Aids are approximately 22–63% less productive in the last year they became ill.
- According to Rosen, Simon, Thea and Vincent (2000) the direct costs of HIV to the employer include pension and provident fund contributions, death and funeral benefits, health clinic use, recruitment and training. Indirect costs are typically incurred through absenteeism and presenteeism (reduced productivity on the job).
- According to AIC Business Insurance (Moodley, 2005) companies lose as much as one month's worth of work for every employee with advanced HIV/Aids. The absenteeism rate for employees with HIV/Aids is about three times higher than for those not infected.
- As far back as 1999 a senior official at Anglo Coal estimated that HIV/Aids would be costing the company R156 million over the next decade (Simon, 1999).
- Despite these dire findings, the Business Coalition found that only 27% of companies have attempted to assess the risk of HIV/Aids to their business (Reed, 2003).

Mental illness

As far as mental illness is concerned (Gelman et al., 1987 p. 42), most findings seem to indicate that depression, known for many years as the 'common cold of mental illness', is still the psychological disorder with the most severe impact on employers. The following findings regarding mental health, and specifically depression, show us why mental health should be an important focus of the business world:

- Health24 (SA: 1 in 3 mentally ill, 2007) reports the findings of the first South African Stress and Health Study that was publicized in 2007: about one-third of South Africans will have a psychiatric disorder at some point in his/her life; anxiety disorders are most prevalent, followed by substance abuse and mood disorders, particularly major depression; 75% of sufferers do not receive treatment for the disorder.
- Sanderson and Andrews (2006) found that simple phobia and depression are the most prevalent disorders in the workplace. They also found that depression and anxiety is more consistently associated with presenteeism (being at work, but with lowered productivity) than absenteeism.
- The WHO (2004) reports that alcohol abuse costs South Africa about R8,7 billion annually, due to medical costs, lost productivity, violence and crime. It is interesting to note, though, that Foster and Vaughan (2005) found that the cost of substance-abuse related absences to employers is negligible, and at best an incidental cost that does not justify corporate investment in the prevention and treatment thereof. Such a viewpoint, however, does not take the moral responsiblity of the employer into account.
- Dewa, McDaid and Ettner (2007) cite statistics indicating that depression will be the second leading cause of disability by 2020 (with chronic heart disease being the number one cause) globally.
- They also cite the findings of several research projects indicating that depression is associated with more work-related loss than most chronic medical conditions. Employees in the USA lose about an hour per week in depression-related absenteeism as opposed to four

hours lost weekly in depression-related presenteeism. In addition, depressed employees also seem to experience more workplace conflict.

- Adler, McLaughlin and Rogers (2006) found that depressed workers had significantly greater deficits in managing time and output tasks, even after improvement of their symptoms. In support of their findings, Wang et al. (2004) also found major depression to be significantly associated with decrements in productivity and task focus. They also found depression to be more consistently related to poor work performance than any of the other chronic conditions in their study (i.e. allergies, arthritis, back pain, headaches, high blood pressure and asthma).

11.2.4 **Determinants of wellness in the workplace**

As mentioned previously in this chapter, employee well-being can be approached from two different perspectives: from a positive well-being and negative un-well-being perspective (Schaufeli and Bakker, 2004). These two states are not antipodes, but rather complement each other. Therefore it is important to identify those aspects of work that can either abate (job demands) or enhance (job resources) the well-being of the employee.

Every job has demands that require some physical and mental effort from the employee. These demands can be a result of (Cartwright and Cooper, 2002; Cooper and Dewe, 2004):

- *Work relationships:* poor or unsupportive relationships with colleagues and/or superiors; isolation and unfair treatment; and people not pulling their weight;
- *Work-life balance:* work interferes with home and personal life; long working hours; work unsocial hours;
- *Overload:* unmanageable workloads; and time pressures;
- *Control:* lack of influence in the way work is organised and performed, not involved in decisions; and ideas and suggestions not taken into account;
- *Resources and communication:* adequate training for the job; proper equipment; and performance feedback;

- *Job insecurity:* skills become redundant; and fear of job loss;
- *Pay and benefits*
- *Other aspects:* unpleasant physical work conditions; difficult customer/client relationships; and constant organisational change.

Job demands however, are associated with a certain level of costs (Schaufeli and Bakker, 2004). When these costs become too high, in the absence of balancing resources, employees cannot cope with them. Such experiences are most likely to result in different physical (i.e. heart disease) and psychological (i.e. stress, burnout) symptoms (Cooper and Dewe, 2004) and cause withdrawal behaviour and negative job attitudes such as reduced job satisfaction and organizational commitment (Mauno, Kinnunen, and Ruokolainen, 2006). For the organization, incidences of employee stress has been implicated as a causal factor for impaired work performance, decreases in productivity, absenteeism, propensity to leave and high staff turnover (Cooper and Dewe, 2004). Eventually, stress can become a major determinant of the overall quality of life, including family life.

Job resources are the physical, social and organizational resources that assist employees in carrying out their jobs (Bakker and Demerouti, 2008). These resources may reduce job demands and the associated physical and psychological costs attached to it. For example, social support from supervisors, colleagues and friends may have a protective effect on the potentially harmful consequences of stressful encounters on the individual's well-being. Job resources can further be functional in achieving work goals (extrinsically motivating) and stimulating personal growth and development (intrinsically motivating) (Bakker and Demerouti, 2008). Therefore job characteristics such as role clarity, task variety, independence, opportunities for learning and participation, effective communication, advancement, remuneration and good relationships with superiors and colleagues are needed to enhance employee well-being (Frey, Jonas and Greitemeyer, 2003; May, Gilson, and Harter, 2004) and hence organizational performance and profitability (Harter, Schmidt, and Hayes, 2002).

11.2.5 **Wellness programmes**

Interest in well-being, and wellness at work specifically, has spread rapidly in the last years (cf. Loeppke, 2008; Wicken, 2000). Thus, many companies have introduced wellness programmes for their employees. There is more than enough evidence testifying to the effectiveness of these programmes. Numerous companies report favourable outcomes (cf. Bloom, 2008; Mason, 1992; Mason, 1994). These outcomes include, amongst others: decreased absenteesim, reductions in health risks, increased quality of work life and increased morale. In a review of several independent studies, Cascio (2006) concludes that wellness programmes do reduce health-risks, that these reductions are maintained over the long term and that the costs of illness are reduced. The benefits, therefore, seem to justify the expense.

Despite the positive outcomes reported, low employee participation in wellness programmes is a cause for concern (cf. Busbin and Campbell, 1990; Marquez, 2008). Busbin and Campbell (1990) suggest the following explanations for low participation: (1) people may rationalize their health problems and believe that it 'will happen to someone else', (2) they may be resistant to such a change in the employer-employee relationship, (3) they may not be willing to make the necessary lifestyle changes and (4) they may believe that a good medical aid is sufficient thus relying on treatment interventions rather than preventative actions.

A typical wellness programme will ideally comprise activities encompassing all the essential elements of well-being, particularly health awareness and promotion, chronic disease management and preventative programmes. Furthermore, both mental and physical health will receive attention in a wellness programme. Occupational health and safety concerns are also addressed in these programmes. Specific aspects include, amongst others, screenings for certain cancers, high cholesterol and elevated blood sugar levels; on-site gymnasiums; support groups for substance abusers and chronic disease management (for diseases such as HIV/Aids and diabetes). An important component of a Wellness Programme is the Employee Assistance Programme (EAP). This programme offers specific support to employees who, for example, have been traumatized by crime; who are recently divorced or are experiencing other family-related problems; and who suffer from stress and burnout. Companies will typically utilize counsellors and psychologists (at no cost to the employee) to provide this support. The service may be offered on-site or off-site (cf. Cascio, 2006). Examples of other activities include support with time management, disability support and financial life skills training. You can clearly see from the above examples that a wellness programme encompasses all aspects of an employee's well-being.

>> **CRITICAL THINKING EXERCISE 11.2**

Imagine you are an industrial psychologist working in the Human Resources Division of a South African university. Develop a programme for a 'Wellness Week' to be held at your institution. Be sure to include activities that relate to all the key components of wellness at work.

11.3 **Measures of well-being**

In this section you will be introduced to measurement tools that can be utilized to measure various constructs relating to well-being. The section is divided into two parts. The first part contains measuring instruments that are applied to assess aspects of well-being in diverse contexts. The second part focuses on measurement tools that measures aspects of well-being at work.

11.3.1 **Assessment of well-being in diverse contexts**

The following measuring instruments are used to assess different aspects of well-being:

Personal, Home, Social and Formal Relations Questionnaire (PHSF)

The purpose of the 180-item PHSF is to determine the level of adjustment of high school pupils, students and adults on four levels as indicated in the title (Fouche and Grobbelaar, 1971). The following components are grouped under each of these levels:

- *Personal relations:* self-confidence, self-esteem, self-control, nervousness, health

- *Home relations:* family influences, personal freedom
- *Social relations:* sociability-G (a need for participation in social interaction), sociability-S (a need for interaction with a specific person from the opposite sex), moral sense
- *Formal relations:* formal relations
- *Desirability:* a validity scale indicating the honesty with which questions were answered

Norms are available, for grade and gender, for white, black, coloured and Indian adolescents in Grades 11–12. Unfortunately these norms are outdated as they were developed in the 1970s.

Interpersonal Relations Questionnaire (IRQ)

The IRQ is basically the same as the PHSF, and contains similar scales, but is utilized with younger adolescents (Grades 7, 8 and 9). The short form version contains 100 items and the full-length version contains 260 items (Joubert, 1981). The full-length scale measures the same 12 components of adjustment measured by the PHSF.

Institute for Personality and Ability Testing Anxiety Scale (IPAT)

The IPAT (Cattell and Scheier, 1961) is a 40-item questionnaire aimed at providing an assessment of **free-floating manifest anxiety** (in other words, anxiety that is not linked to specific situations). It has been adapted for use in South Africa (Cattell, Scheier and Madge, 1968). It has been standardized for use in some South African populations and norms are available for white English – and Afrikaans speaking adolescents and first-year university students. Although not yet standardized for black South Africans, it has been used successfully in multicultural samples (cf. Hatuell, 2004; Mfusi and Mahabeer, 2000).

State-Trait Anxiety Inventory (STAI)

The STAI consists of 40-items and measures anxiety as a state and as a trait (Spielberger, Gorsuch and Lushene, 1970). **State anxiety** refers to the 'transitory feelings of fear or worry that most of us experience on occasion', whereas **trait anxiety** refers to 'the relatively stable tendency of an individual to respond anxiously to a stressful predicament' (Gregory, 2007, p. 384). The two terms

are related, as a person's trait anxiety is indicative of the likelihood that he/she will experience state anxiety (Gregory, 2007). No norms for the STAI have been established in South Africa as yet, which considerably limits its use. In addition Gregory (2007) mentions that results of the STAI should be interpreted cautiously as it is highly face valid, which makes it easy to fake responses.

The Affectometer-2 Scale (AFM2)

The Affectometer-2 Scale (AFM2) was developed by Kammann and Flett (1983) to measure general happiness or well-being by evaluating the balance between positive and negative recent feelings. The 40 items of the scale are divided into two 20-item subscales. There are ten negative and ten positive items in each subscale. Subtotal scores are obtained for Negative Affect (NA) and Positive Affect (PA). An overall score is obtained by subtracting the NA score from the PA score. Overall scores higher than 40 indicate positive subjective well-being (i.e. happiness), while scores below 40 indicate lower levels of subjective well-being (i.e. unhappiness). Aspects of its psychometric properties have been researched in South Africa.

Beck Depression Inventory (BDI)

The BDI is a 21-item self-report inventory aimed at assessing the severity of depressive symptoms in adults and in children from 13 years of age onwards (Beck, Steer and Brown, 1996). The items in the inventory are aligned with the diagnostic criteria for depression as listed in the *Diagnostic and Statistical Manual of Mental Disorders* (fourth edition) (DSM-IV). It is not yet standardized for use with different populations in South Africa, but studies are underway (e.g. Steele and Edwards, 2002).

Sense of Coherence (SOC)

The SOC (Antonovsky, 1987), is a 29-item scale that measures sense of coherence in the areas of comprehensibility, manageability, and meaningfulness. The SOC utilizes a 7-point Likert-type scale with two anchoring responses of different descriptors. Examples of questions are 'When you talk to people, do you have the feeling that they don't understand you?' (1 = *never have this feeling*, 7 = *always have this feeling*) and 'When you have a difficult problem, the choice of the solution is ...' (1 = *always confusing and hard to find*, 7 = *always completely clear*). Responses to items are summed, with higher scores indicating a stronger sense of coherence. For more information on the SOC, refer to Antonovsky (1979, 1987, 1996), Fourie, Rothmann and Van de Vijver (2008), and Strümpfer and Wissing (1998).

The Satisfaction with Life Scale (SWLS)

The Satisfaction with Life Scale (SWLS), is a five-item measure and is used to measure life satisfaction (Diener, Emmons, Larsen, and Griffin, 1985). The SWLS is designed around the idea that one should ask respondents about the overall judgement of their life in order to measure the concept of life satisfaction. Scores on the SWLS range from 5 to 35, with higher scores indicating greater life satisfaction. For South African studies view Heyns, Venter, Esterhuyse, Bam and Odendaal (2003) and Westaway and Maluka (2005).

The Life Orientation Test – Revised (LOT-R)

The LOT-R, a 10-item measure, was developed by Scheier, Carver and Bridges (1994) to measure individual differences in generalised optimism versus pessimism. Six items contribute to the optimism score and four items are fillers. The LOT-R measures a continuum of high, average and low optimism/pessimism. The LOT-R has been used in South African studies and showed acceptable internal consistencies (see Coetzer and Rothmann, 2004).

Experience of Work and Life Circumstances Questionnaire (WLQ)

This scale was developed in South Africa to measure stress levels, as well as causes of stress, in individuals with reading and writing skills equivalent to a Grade 10 level (Van Zyl and Van der Walt, 1991). The WLQ consist of three scales: Scale A measures levels of stress; Scale B measures possible sources of stress at work (including physical working conditions, fringe benefits and career matters) and Scale C measures 16 possible sources of stress outside of an individual's work (for example, family problems, phase of life and financial issues). This questionnaire has been used successfully in research with multicultural samples (Nell, 2005; van Rooyen, 2000).

Adult Coping Scale (ACS)

The ACS (Frydenburg and Lewis, 1993) is aimed at identifying ways in which an individual typically deals with stressful life situations. It is mostly utilized in counselling/therapy, for psychodiagnostic, purposes and in research. There is also a version aimed at adolescents (Adolescent Coping Scale). It is interesting to note that the last question on the questionnaire is open-ended, and allows test-takers to describe any personal coping strategies not covered in the questionnaire. Although the scale has been found suitable for use in white South African adults further research is necessary to determine its suitability for other population groups.

The Coping Resources Inventory (CRI)

The CRI (Hammer and Marting, 1988) is aimed at measuring coping resources in five domains, namely cognitive, social, emotional, spiritual/philosophical and physical. Although findings in terms of the suitability of the CRI in the South African context are promising (cf. Brown, 2002; Madhoo, 1999) it has not yet been standardized for a South African population.

The Locus of Control Inventory (LCI)

The LCI (Schepers, 2005) is a normative scale measuring locus of control. The scale consists of 65 items and measures three constructs, namely internal control, external control and autonomy. Internal control refers to a person's belief that his/her behaviour is self-determined. Persons with high internal control believe, amongst others, that they determine the outcomes of matters and that their achievements are the result of hard work and commitment. People with high external control believe that aspects such as random events and fate determine their behaviour. Such persons believe, for example, in fatalism and that their life is to a large extent influenced by coincidence. Autonomy refers to the fact that individuals 'seek control of situations that offer possibilities of change, take initiative in situations requiring leadership, prefer to work on their own and choose to structure their own work programme' (Schepers, 2005, p. 25).

Psychometric properties of the scale are very good and Afrikaans, English and Zulu versions are available. The available norms are suitable for all four population groups, namely black, white, coloured and Indian South Africans. It is also suitable for use amongst students and adults.

McMaster Health Index Questionnaire (MHIQ)

This questionnaire is a result of an attempt to develop a measure that assesses quality of life of medical patients that conforms to the World Health Organization's definition of health (cf. Chambers, 1993). The MHIQ includes physical, emotional and social aspects in its assessment of an individual's quality of life. The measure has not yet been standardized for use with South African populations.

11.3.2 Assessment of well-being in the work context

The following measurement tools can be utilized to assess various aspects of well-being that relate to the world of work.

Sources of Work Stress Inventory (SWSI)

The SWSI (De Bruin and Taylor, 2005) is a South African developed questionnaire aimed at measuring occupational stress as well as identifying possible source of work stress. The first section (General Work Stress Scale) assesses the extent of work itself as a source of stress. The second section (Sources of Job Stress Scale) consists of nine sources of job stress. These sources are (De Bruin and Taylor, 2005):

- *Role ambiguity:* stress experienced due to, for example, aspects such as constant change in expectations and vague job specification.
- *Relationships:* stress experienced due to, for example, poor relationships with colleagues and supervisors.
- *Workload:* stress experienced due to, for example, a perceived inability to cope with work demands.
- *Autonomy:* stress experienced due to inadequate empowerment.
- *Bureaucracy:* stress experienced due to rigid and strictly controlled rules, procedures and protocols.

- *Tools and equipment:* stress experienced due to broken down machinery, complex, machinery and inadequate or inappropriate tools to do the job.
- *Physical environment:* stress caused by factors such as extreme temperatures and high noise levels.
- *Career advancement/Job security:* stress caused by a perceived lack of chance to further one's career (career advancement) or uncertainty in terms of an individual's future at his place of work (job security).
- *Work/Home interface:* stress experienced due to aspects such as insufficient social support at home.

Maslach Burnout Inventory (MBI)

The MBI measures the burnout of individuals. Three versions of the MBI exist, namely the MBI-GS (General Survey), The MBI-ED (Educators) and the MBI-HSS (Human Services Survey). The General survey measures burnout in a broad range of professions, whereas the ED and HSS-versions of the MBI measures burnout in the human services and education contexts respectively (Naude & Rothmann, 2004). The MBI-GS consists of 16 items and measures burnout in terms of Exhaustion, Cynicism and Professional Efficacy. The MBI-ED and MBI-HSS consists of 22 items and measures Emotional Exhaustion, Depersonalisation and Personal Accomplishment. Together these subscales provide a three-dimensional perspective on burnout. High scores on Exhaustion/ Emotional Exhaustion and Cynicism/Depersonalisation and low scores on Professional Efficacy/Personal Accomplishment is indicative of burnout. Although the MBI has been utilized in several South African studies, it has not been standardized yet. It is thus mostly utilized for research purposes. For more information on the MBI see Maslach, Jackson and Leiter (1996) and Worley, Vassar, Wheeler and Barnes (2008).

The Utrecht Work Engagement Scale (UWES)

The UWES measures the levels of work engagement of university students and adults (Schaufeli and Bakker, 2003). Three dimensions of work engagement can be distinguished, namely Vigour,

Dedication and Absorption. Vigour is characterised by high levels of energy and mental resilience while working, the willingness to invest effort in one's work and the persistence even in the face of difficulties. Dedication is characterised by a sense of significance, enthusiasm, inspiration, pride and challenge. Absorption is characterised by being totally and happily immersed in one's work, to the extent that it is difficult to detach oneself from it. Engaged individuals are characterized by high levels of Vigour and Dedication and also elevated levels of Absorption. Three versions of the UWES exist, depending on the number of items to be used in research. This includes the UWES-17, UWES-15 and UWES-9. The UWES has been used in several South African studies. For more information on the UWES visit the following website: http://www.schaufeli.com/.

Minnesota Satisfaction Questionnaire (MSQ)

The MSQ (Weiss, Dawis, Engand and Lofquist, 1967) is used in the assessment of job satisfaction. It taps affective responses to various aspects of one's job. A person can be relatively satisfied with one aspect of his/her job while being dissatisfied with one or more of the other aspects. The revised MSQ form measures intrinsic job satisfaction and extrinsic job satisfaction, using questions like: 'The chance to be "somebody" in the community' (intrinsic), 'The chance to do something that makes use of my abilities' (intrinsic), 'The way my supervisor handles his/her workers' (extrinsic), and 'The working conditions' (extrinsic) (Hirschfeld, 2000). The item content is of such a nature that it can be applied to a variety of organizations and occupational positions.

Work Locus of Control Scale (WLCS)

The WLCS consists of 16 items and was developed by Spector (1988) to measure the work locus of control of individuals. The measure is composed of eight items designed to tap internal control and eight items tapping external control. A sample internal control item is 'A job is what you make of it.' A sample external control item is 'Getting the job you want is mostly a matter of luck.' High scores are indicative of an external locus of control. The scale has also been utilized in South African studies and showed acceptable internal consistency (see Botha and Pienaar, 2006).

CHECKING YOUR PROGRESS 11.1

11.1 Differentiate between, and describe, eudaimonic and hedonistic conceptions of well-being

11.2 Explain the importance of well-being from the side of the employer, as well as from the employee's side.

11.3 Name and describe measurement tools that can be utilized to assess the various constructs related to well-being

---

Did you find this an interesting stop in the *Types-of-Measures Zone*? The next stop should prove to be just as interesting as you will be given an opportunity to explore how personality functioning can be assessed. Assessing what makes people tick (personality make-up) is fundamental to the discipline and profession of psychology, so it is something that most psychology students are very keen to learn more about.

Personality assessment

GIDEON P DE BRUIN AND NICOLA TAYLOR

CHAPTER OUTCOMES

The aim of this chapter is to provide a brief introduction to the field of personality assessment. Psychologists in industrial, psychodiagnostic, forensic, educational, and other contexts are often requested to assess an individual's personality (see Chapter 16). Usually the purpose of such an assessment is to understand the uniqueness of the individual. Psychologists also use personality assessment to identify the individual's characteristic strengths and weaknesses and his/her typical way of interacting with the world and the self. There are many different methods and procedures that psychologists may use for personality assessment. The choice of method usually depends on (a) the reason for the assessment, (b) the psychologist's theoretical orientation, and (c) the psychologist's preference for particular methods and procedures. In this chapter you will be introduced to assessment measures that psychologists typically use in practice. By the end of this chapter you will be able to:

> have a conceptual understanding of personality and personality assessment;
> distinguish between structured and projective personality assessment methods;
> critically describe the main assumptions underlying the use of the structured assessment methods and discuss the problems associated with the cross-cultural use of such methods; and
> critically describe the main assumptions underlying the use of projective tests such as the TAT and discuss the problems associated with the cross-cultural use of the TAT.

12.1 A conceptual scheme for personality assessment

The American personality psychologist, Dan Mc-Adams, argued that personality can be described and understood on at least three levels (McAdams, 1995). Briefly, the first level focuses on personality traits or basic behavioural and emotional tendencies, and refers to the stable characteristics that the person has. The second level focuses on personal projects and concerns, and refers to what the person is **doing** and what the person **wants to achieve**. This level is, to a large degree, concerned with an individual's motives. On the third level, the focus falls on the person's life story or narrative and refers to how the person constructs an **integrated identity**. These three levels are not necessarily related to each other and do not neatly fold into each other. As the different levels are also not hierarchically arranged, all the levels have equal importance (McAdams, 1994). For a full understanding of a person it is probably necessary to focus on all three levels as set out in McAdams' scheme.

This scheme provides a comprehensive framework for personality assessment. Depending on which level of description the psychologist wishes to focus, different assessment techniques or measures may be selected. In this chapter we focus on the first two levels of McAdams' scheme. It is only on these two levels that the assessment measures and techniques that psychologists typically use for personality assessment are relevant. The third level focuses on the individual's identity and life story. Assessment on this level refers to the way in which the individual constructs his/her identity and falls outside the domain of what is commonly thought of as personality assessment.

Structured methods of personality assessment usually refer to standardized questionnaires, inventories, or interviews that contain a fixed set of statements or questions. Test-takers often indicate their responses to these statements or questions by choosing an answer from a set of given answers, or by indicating the extent to which the statements or questions are relevant to them. Structured methods are also characterized by fixed scoring rules. In this chapter structured methods are used to illustrate assessment on the first level in McAdams' scheme.

Projective assessment techniques are characterized by ambiguous stimuli, and individuals are encouraged to provide any response to the stimuli that comes to mind. It is assumed that these responses reflect something of the individual's personality. Projective techniques are often scored and interpreted in a more intuitive way than structured personality questionnaires and inventories and are used to assess the second level of personality as set out by McAdams.

One potentially major advantage of projective techniques is that the person who is being assessed may find it very difficult to provide **socially desirable responses**. This is often a problem in structured personality measures, because it may be obvious from the content of the items or the questions what the psychologist is attempting to assess and what the socially desirable or appropriate answer would be. For example, when being assessed with regards to your suitability for a job, you are asked to respond either 'Yes' or 'No' to the following item on a personality measure: 'I tell lies sometimes'. You will feel fairly pressurized to answer 'No', as you will reason that your potential employers are not looking to employ someone who lies. If you succumb to the pressure and answer 'No', you would have responded in a socially desirable way. Furthermore, if you continue to respond in this way on the measure, a pattern of socially desirable answers will be discernible (this is often referred to as a **response set**). Another response set that can be problematic in objective personality measures is that of acquiescence. This is the tendency to agree rather than to disagree when you doubt how best you should respond to a question.

Due to limited space, it is not possible to discuss all assessment procedures and instruments that are available in South Africa. Rather than providing a superficial overview of all available measures, we will focus on measures and techniques that (a) are commonly used both in South Africa and internationally, (b) have potential for use with all cultural groups, and (c) illustrate important methods of personality assessment.

>> CRITICAL THINKING CHALLENGE 12.1

Describe what is meant by a socially desirable response set. Then write five true/false items that you think will provide a good measure of this response set.

12.2 Level 1: The assessment of relatively stable personality traits

This level of understanding and describing personality focuses on basic tendencies, attributes, or **traits**. Some personality psychologists prefer to regard such basic tendencies or traits as predispositions to behave in particular ways. From this perspective, someone with a trait of, for instance, aggressiveness will be predisposed to behave in an aggressive way. Likewise, somebody with a trait of extraversion will be predisposed to seek out environments where, for example, a great amount of social interaction is to be found.

Trait psychologists focus on internal factors that influence the way in which people behave. It is assumed that these internal factors influence behaviour across a variety of situations and over time. From the above it can be seen that trait psychologists are interested in describing consistencies in people's behaviour. Trait psychologists are also interested in stable differences between people. Trait researchers ask questions such as 'What are the basic dimensions of personality in terms of which people differ from each other?' and 'Why is it that people show relatively stable differences in terms of traits such as aggressiveness and extraversion?' Trait psychologists are also interested in the real-life implications of such differences between people. Accordingly, they attempt to demonstrate that traits can be important predictors of criteria such as psychopathology, leadership, marital and job satisfaction, career choice, and academic and work success.

One of the problems with which trait psychologists are confronted is the identification of a fundamental set of attributes or traits that may be used to provide an economical but comprehensive description of personality. Any casual perusal of a diction-

ary may reveal that there are thousands of words descriptive of personality. It is also possible to think of thousands of different sentences in which personality may be described. However, many of these words and sentences show a substantial amount of overlap and many refer to similar behaviours. This overlap suggests that it may be possible to reduce the large number of words and sentences that describe personality to a smaller number of dimensions that contain most of the information included in the original words and sentences. Similarly, it is possible that many of the traits or attributes that might be used to describe people may overlap and hence be redundant. In such a case it may be possible to reduce the number of traits to a smaller number of more fundamental traits without much loss in information.

Trait psychologists rely heavily on a technique called **factor analysis** to identify basic dimensions that underlie sets of related variables (such as overlapping words or sentences that may be used to describe personality). Factor analysis is a powerful statistical technique that can be used to reduce large groups of variables to a smaller and more manageable number of dimensions or factors. In this sense, factor analysis can be used as a summarizing technique. As an example, consider the following short list of words: talkative, social, bold, assertive, organized, responsible, thorough, and hardworking. Each of these words may be used to describe personality. Based on our observations we could say, for example, 'Mr X is very talkative and social, but he is not very organized and responsible'. We could also rate Mr X in terms of the eight words in our list on, for instance, a three-point scale. On this hypothetical three-point scale, a rating of three indicates that the word is a very accurate descriptor, two indicates that the word is a reasonably accurate descriptor, and one indicates that the word is an inaccurate descriptor. By rating many different people in terms of these words, one may begin to observe certain patterns in the ratings. In our example it is likely that people who obtain high ratings for **organized** will also obtain high ratings for **responsible**, **thorough**, and **hardworking**. It is also likely that people who obtain high ratings for **assertive** will also obtain high ratings for **talkative**, **bold**, and **social**.

It therefore seems as if the original eight variables cluster into two groups and that the original variables may be summarized in terms of two basic or fundamental dimensions. These could perhaps be described as Extraversion (Outgoing) and Methodical.

In our example we used only eight variables and even a casual glance at the words suggested they could be grouped according to two dimensions. However, when the aim is to identify a comprehensive set of basic personality dimensions, a much larger number of variables that are representative of the total personality domain is needed. In such a study it will not be possible to identify basic personality dimensions by visual inspection of the variables alone. Factor analysis helps researchers to identify statistically the basic dimensions that are necessary to summarize the original variables. **Factor analysis** also helps in understanding the nature of the dimensions that underlie the original variables. This is achieved by inspecting the nature or meaning of the variables that are grouped together in the dimension or factor. Although the aims of factor analysis can be relatively easily understood on a conceptual level, the mathematics underlying the procedure is quite complex. Fortunately, computers can perform all the calculations, although researchers should have a thorough knowledge of the mathematical model in order to use factor analysis properly. Interested readers are referred to Gorsuch (1983) and Kline (1994).

>> CRITICAL THINKING CHALLENGE 12.2

Consult a dictionary and write down fifty adjectives that refer to traits or characteristics of personality. Try to choose a mixture of positive and negative terms and be careful not to include adjectives that are synonyms (similar in meaning) or antonyms (opposites). Put the list in alphabetical order and then tick each adjective that you think would describe characteristics of your personality.

Summarize the information by trying to group together adjectives (which you have ticked) that seem to share something in common and then try to find one overarching name for each grouping. How accurately do you think that these groupings describe your personality? What has been left out?

12.2.1 The 16 Personality Factor Questionnaire (16PF)

One of the most prominent trait psychologists of the twentieth century was Raymond B. Cattell (see Chapter 2). He made extensive use of factor analysis and identified a list of about twenty primary personality traits. These traits are also often called factors. Cattell selected sixteen of these traits to be included in a personality questionnaire for adults, which he called the 16 Personality Factor Questionnaire (16PF). The 16PF has established itself as one of the most widely used tests of normal personality in the world (Piotrowski and Keller, 1989). The traits that are measured by the 16PF are listed in Table 12.1. You should note that all the traits are bipolar, that is, at the one pole there is a low amount of the trait and at the other pole there is a high amount of the trait.

The 16 primary personality traits or factors are not completely independent of each other. By factor analyzing the patterns of relationships between the 16 primary traits, personality researchers have identified at least five well-established second-order factors that underlie the 16 primary factors (Aluja and Blanch, 2004; Krug and Johns, 1986; Van Eeden and Prinsloo, 1997). A sixth second-order factor is also sometimes identified, but this factor is usually defined only by Scale B, which measures reasoning rather than a personality trait. These factors are called second-order factors because they are derived from the relationships between primary or first-order factors. The second-order factors are listed in Table 12.1. This table also shows the primary factors that define the second-order factors. The second-order factors are more general and relate to a broader spectrum of behaviours than the primary factors. However, what is gained in generality is lost in predictive power. Mershon and Gorsuch (1988) and Paunonen and Ashton (2001) showed that primary factors or lower level personality traits allow for better prediction of future behaviours than do second-order factors or higher level personality traits.

An important aspect to take note of is that the development of the 16PF was not guided by any particular psychological theory. Items and scales were not selected because they correlated with

Table 12.1 Personality factors measured by the 16PF

FACTOR	LOW SCORE	HIGH SCORE
Primary factors		
A: Warmth	Reserved	Warm
B: Reasoning	Concrete	Abstract
C: Emotional Stability	Reactive	Stable
E: Dominance	Cooperative	Dominant
F: Liveliness	Restrained	Lively
G: Rule-Consciousness	Expedient	Rule-conscious
H: Social Boldness	Shy	Socially bold
I: Sensitivity	Utilitarian	Sensitive
L: Vigilance	Trusting	Suspicious
M: Abstractedness	Practical	Imaginative
N: Privateness	Forthright	Private
O: Apprehension	Self-assured	Apprehensive
Q1: Openness to Change	Traditional	Open to change
Q2: Self-Reliance	Group-orientated	Self-reliant
Q3: Perfectionism	Unexacting	Perfectionistic
Q4: Tension	Relaxed	Tense
Second-order factors		
EX: Extraversion	Introverted	Extraverted
AX: Anxiety	Low anxiety	High anxiety
TM: Tough-Mindedness	Receptive	Tough-minded
IN: Independence	Accommodating	Independent
SC: Self-Control	Unrestrained	Self-controlled

Note: The factor labels and descriptors were taken from the 16PF Fifth Edition (Conn and Rieke, 1998).

important external criteria such as psychopathology or leadership. Rather, the scales were chosen and refined because they were identified through factor analysis as representing important and meaningful clusters of behaviours. This strategy of test development is called the factor analytic strategy.

The most recent version of the 16PF to be standardized in South Africa is the 16PF Fifth Edition, which has largely replaced the earlier Forms A, B, and SA92. The 16PF Fifth Edition is used with adults who have completed at least Grade 12 or its equivalent. Earlier forms of the

16PF were often criticized for the low reliabilities of the 16 primary factor scales. In response to these criticisms the reliabilities and general psychometric properties of the 16PF Fifth Edition are much improved (Aluja and Blanch, 2004; Schuerger, 2002).

Form E of the 16PF is designed for use with adults who have reached an educational level of Grade 4 to Grade 11. Prinsloo (1992) explains that Form E fills the need for a personality questionnaire that can be used with people whose formal level of education is lower than Grade 12. The vocabulary and the format of Form E have been simplified to make it more accessible for adults who may find the reading level of Forms A and B too difficult. Prinsloo (1992) reports that the internal consistency reliabilities of the scales can be regarded as satisfactory.

The primary and second order factors of the 16PF are interpreted on a sten scale, with a mean of 5.5 and a standard deviation of 2. Generally, scores that deviate more than two stens from the mean are regarded as practically significant; that is, if a person obtains a score of eight on scale Q4, it may be interpreted that he/she is experiencing significantly more tension than other people similar to the norm group.

There are many different potential uses for the 16PF. It has become well established as an instrument used in personnel selection. It is also widely used in career counselling and academic counselling (Schuerger, 2002). The 16PF can also be profitably used in personal development programmes where the aim is to develop deeper self-understanding and psychological growth. In psychotherapy the 16PF may help the client and psychotherapist to understand relatively stable patterns of behaviour that may contribute to the client's difficulties. The 16PF may also reveal strengths in the client's psychological make-up that may be emphasized and built on in psychotherapy. Lastly, the 16PF may also be used to evaluate whether any changes in stable behaviour patterns are occurring as a result of psychotherapy.

A number of sources provide detailed information on the interpretation of the 16PF (e.g. Cattell, 1989; Golden, 1979; Karson and O'Dell, 1976; Krug, 1981; Schuerger, 2002). Users of the 16PF are encouraged to consult these sources in order to obtain a deeper understanding of each of the traits that are measured by the 16PF. In addition to the 16PF, Cattell also developed the High School Personality Questionnaire (HSPQ) for high school children and the Children's Personality Questionnaire (CPQ) for primary school children. These measures provide similar scores to the 16PF and are also interpreted in a similar way.

Although the 16PF has been used extensively with all population groups in South Africa, the evidence in support of the cross-cultural use of the earlier versions of the questionnaire is not very strong. Abrahams and Mauer (1999a, 1999b) reported that

many of the 16PF SA 92 items appear to be biased. Their qualitative analysis demonstrated that the meaning of many of the English words included in the 16PF items is not clear to individuals who do not use English as their first language. Van Eeden and Prinsloo (1997) also concluded in their study into the cross-cultural use of the 16PF that the 'constructs measured by the 16PF cannot be generalized unconditionally to the different subgroups' (p. 158) in their study. The subgroups to which they referred were (a) individuals using English and Afrikaans as their first language and (b) individuals whose first language is an African language.

The 16PF Fifth Edition (16PF5; Cattell, Cattell, and Cattell, 1993) has recently been adapted into South African English and Afrikaans versions (Institute for Personality and Ability Testing, 2006), and research into a Zulu adaptation is underway. The factor structure of the 16PF5 appeared to replicate well in the South African version, indicating alignment with the international versions. Schepers and Hassett (2006) investigated the relationship between the 16PF5 and the Locus of Control Inventory, and found three significant canonical correlations between the two assessments that were interpreted as Ascendancy, Emotional stability, and Rule-consciousness. Six global factors were found for the 16PF5 that were identified as Liveliness, Perfectionism, Dominance, Tension, Abstractedness, and Warmth. De Bruin, Schepers, and Taylor (2005) recently reported that the second-order factor structure of the 16PF5 is very similar for Afrikaans, English, Nguni, and Sotho groups, suggesting that it measures the same broad personality traits across the different languages. This holds promise for the cross-cultural use of the 16PF in South Africa.

12.2.2 The Big Five model of personality traits

During the last two decades many personality researchers have come to the conclusion that the domain of personality traits may be accurately described and summarized in terms of five broad traits. These traits are often labelled as **Extraversion**, **Neuroticism** or Emotional stability, **Agreeableness**, **Conscientiousness**, and **Openness to Experience** or Intellect or Culture. This conclusion is based on the observation that the factor analysis of different personality scales and personality descriptive adjectives mostly result in a five-factor solution which corresponds with the factors just listed. These factors, which are jointly referred to as the **Big Five model of personality**, have also been identified in many different cultures. However, attempts to identify the Big Five structure in South Africa have yielded mixed results. De Bruin (2000) found support for the Big Five factors among white Afrikaans-speaking participants, whereas Heaven, Connors and Stones (1994), Heaven and Pretorius (1998), and Taylor (2000) failed to find support for the factors among black South African participants. Recently, Taylor and De Bruin (2004) reported support for the Big Five factors among the responses of Afrikaans, English, Nguni, and Sotho speakers to the Basic Traits Inventory, which is a newly constructed South African measure of the Big Five model. This finding shows that measures of personality that take local conditions into account may yield more satisfactory results than imported measures that fail to take local conditions into account.

12.2.3 **The Basic Traits Inventory**

The development of the Basic Traits Inventory (BTI) started in 2002. At that stage there were no cross-culturally appropriate, locally developed personality inventories available in South Africa. Taylor and De Bruin (2005) decided to develop a new measure of personality for South Africa, using the Big Five factors that have been shown to have cross-cultural applicability worldwide (McCrae et al., 2004). The intention was to ensure the construct validity of the BTI from the outset, which demanded the specification of precise definitions of the five factors. Each of the five factors is divided into five facets, except for the Neuroticism factor, which has only four facets. The items in the BTI were then written in the form of statements with a five-point Likert-type scale. The items are grouped according to their respective facets, and these are presented together for each factor, instead of in random order. Contrary to convention, the items are all keyed positively in the direction of their dimension.

The five factors of the BTI have consistently shown good internal consistency reliability, and the factor structure has been replicated in a number of different contexts and across gender, ethnic, and language groups (De Bruin et al., 2005; Taylor, 2004; Taylor and De Bruin, 2006). Ramsay, Taylor, De Bruin and Meiring (2008) showed that the BTI functioned equally well across Nguni, Sotho, and Pedi language groups, providing further evidence for the cross-cultural transportability of the Big Five model of personality, as well as the use of the BTI in different language groups. The BTI can be used for academic and career counselling, individual development, recruitment and selection, and is often used in research projects as an indicator of the Big Five. The development of a short version of the BTI is currently underway. The BTI is also available in Afrikaans.

12.2.4 **The Occupational Personality Questionnaire**

Recently, the Occupational Personality Questionnaire (OPQ) has become a popular personality assessment tool in the workplace. The OPQ exists in a variety of forms, of which the most recent is the OPQ32. The OPQ32 measures 32 work-related personality characteristics, and is used in industry for a wide variety of purposes, namely personnel selection, training and development, performance management, team building, organizational development, and counselling.

The OPQ is not based on any particular personality theory. The authors adopted an eclectic approach and included personality traits studied by other psychologists such as Cattell, Eysenck, and Murray. In addition, personality traits and characteristics deemed important in the workplace were added. Items were written for each of the traits or characteristics and the scales were then refined through item and factor analyses. Note that in contrast to the 16PF, factor analysis was used to refine scales rather than to identify constructs. The reliabilities of the 32 scales for a representative South African sample ranged between 0.69 and 0.88 and in general appear to be satisfactory. Visser and Du Toit (2004) recently demonstrated that the relations between the 32 scales may be summarized in terms of six broad personality traits. These were labelled as Interpersonal, Extraversion, Emotional stability, Agreeableness, Openness to experience, and Conscientiousness. You will note that the last five of these factors correspond to the factors of the Big Five model of personality traits.

12.2.5 The Myers Briggs Type Indicator

Another popular standardized personality questionnaire is the Myers Briggs Type Indicator (MBTI). This measure is based on Jung's theory of psychological types. It consists of four bipolar scales, namely Introversion-Extraversion (E-I), Thinking-Feeling (T-F), Sensing-Intuition (S-N), and Judgement-Perception (J-P). People scoring high on **Extraversion** tend to direct their energy to the outside world and seek interaction with other people. **Introverts** direct their energy to their inner world of ideas and concepts and tend to value privacy and solitude. **Sensing** individuals rely on information gained through the senses and can be described as realistic. **Intuitive** individuals rely on information gained through unconscious perception and can be described as open-minded. People scoring high on **Thinking** make decisions in an impersonal and rational way, whereas **Feeling** individuals prefer decisions made on subjective and emotional grounds. Those showing a preference for **Thinking** may be described as tough-minded, and those showing a preference for **Feeling** may be described as tender-minded. Individuals with a preference for **Judgement** seek closure and an organized environment, while individuals with a preference for **Perception** are characterized by adaptability and spontaneity (Lanyon and Goodstein, 1997).

By combining the four poles of the scales, it is possible to identify sixteen personality types. One such a type might, for example, be **ENTP**. People who are assigned this type show preferences for extraversion, intuition, thinking, and perception. Another type might be **ISFJ**. Individuals who are assigned this type show preferences for introversion, sensing, feeling, and judgement. In contrast to the 16PF, where the emphasis falls on determining a person's position in terms of each of the primary and second order traits, the emphasis in the MBTI falls on assigning the individual to one of sixteen different types of people. People who are assigned the same type are assumed to share similar characteristics. The manual of the MBTI and several other publications provide detailed descriptions of the characteristics associated with each of the sixteen types. The MBTI is used widely for career counselling, team building, and for organizational and personal development (McCaulley, 2000). It is assumed that different personality **types** function better in different environments and ideally a match between the individual and the environment should be sought. The MBTI may also be profitably used as an indicator of the roles that people are likely to play in work-related teams. One attractive feature of the MBTI is that no single type is considered superior to the other types. It is assumed that each one of the sixteen types has something positive to offer in different contexts. Similarly, the two poles of each of the four scales are presumed equally desirable. The result is that individuals can always receive positive feedback with an emphasis on their strengths rather than weaknesses.

The manual of the MBTI provides evidence that the scales provide internally consistent scores (Myers and McCaulley, 1985). Factor analyses of the MBTI items have also provided support for the validity of the four scales (De Bruin, 1996). However, there is disagreement about the factor structure, with some factor analysts holding the view that the factor structure of the MBTI items does not support the validity of the four scales. The manual also provides evidence in support of the criterion-related validity of the MBTI. However, most of the research was conducted in the United States of America and more research of this kind is needed in South Africa. The MBTI is available in English and Afrikaans versions.

12.2.6 The Minnesota Multiphasic Personality Inventory (MMPI)

Unlike the 16PF which was developed by following a factor analytic approach, and the MBTI which was developed by following a theoretical or construct approach, the Minnesota Multiphasic Personality Inventory (MMPI) was developed using a criterion-keying approach (see Chapter 6). The test-taker is confronted by a number of statements (e.g. 'I think that people are all out to get me'), to which the response choice has to be either 'Yes' or 'No'. The MMPI was originally developed to assess personality characteristics indicative of psychopathology (DeLamatre and Schuerger, 2000). Items were developed and included in the final version of the MMPI based on their ability to discriminate between psychiatric patients and normal people. The 550 items were grouped into ten clinical scales as well as three validity scales. The clinical scales are as follows: Hypochondriasis, Depression, Hysteria, Psychopathic Deviate, Masculinity-Femininity, Paranoia, Psychasthenia, Schizophrenia, Mania, and Social Introversion. The validity scales were included to provide information about test-taking behaviour and attitudes and response sets (e.g. carelessness, malingering, acquiescence, answering in socially desirable ways). By studying the validity scales, it can be determined whether the person is 'faking good' (deliberately putting themselves in a favourable light) or 'faking bad' (deliberately putting themselves in a negative light) – both of which could be indicative of malingering.

As the MMPI was designed to identify pathological personality characteristics, it was used widely in mental hospitals and for psychodiagnostic purposes, but was not considered to be as a useful measure of 'normal' personality traits. Thus, when the MMPI was revised, the brief was to broaden the original item pool to make it more suitable for 'normal' individuals as well. Added to this, the revision focused on updating the norms, revising the content and language of the items to make them more contemporaneous and non-sexist, and on developing separate forms for adults and adolescents. The end result was the publication of the MMPI-2 (Hathaway and McKinley, 1989). The MMPI-2 consists of 567 true/false questions, requires a reading level of at least Grade 8, and takes about ninety minutes to complete. The first 370 statements are used to score the original ten clinical and three validity scales. The remaining 197 items, of which 107 are new, are used to score an additional 104 validity, content, and supplementary scales and subscales.

The MMPI has been adapted for use in South Africa and has been translated into Afrikaans and Xhosa. Preliminary interpretative profile data are available for various groups of South Africans (Shillington, 1988). Research is currently under-

way to adapt the MMPI-2 and to translate it into various black languages as well as Afrikaans.

The Minnesota Multiphasic Personality Inventory-Adolescent (MMPI-A) was developed specifically for use with adolescents. While it is similar to the MMPI and MMPI-2 in terms of its basic clinical (ten) and validity scales (three), it is shorter (478 items), and covers areas that are relevant to adolescents. The usefulness of the MMPI-A, both internationally as well as in South Africa, is still being determined through research.

The Personality Inventory for Children (PIC) was constructed using a similar methodology to that of the MMPI. As was the case with the MMPI, it has been revised and the revised version is known as the PIC-R. It can be used with children and adolescents from three to sixteen years of age. However, parents or other knowledgeable adults complete the true/false items, not the children. Thus, the PIC and PIC-R are not self-report measures. Rather, they rely on the behavioural observation of a significant person in the child's life. Parents, however, can also be biased. The inclusion of validity scales in the PIC and PIC-R provide some indication of the truthfulness and trustworthiness of the responses. The assessment practitioner is advised to combine the information obtained from the PIC and PIC-R with personal observations and other collateral information.

A parallel version of the PIC-R, the **Personality Inventory for Youth (PIY)**, has been developed for nine- to eighteen-year-olds. Interesting information can be obtained from the self-profile obtained from the child or adolescent on the PIY and the profile obtained on the PIC-R, which the parents completed.

While the PIC-R has been adapted, translated, and researched in South Africa with pre-school and Grade 1 samples, no research has been conducted with the PIY. The PIC-R research suggests that it can be used cross-culturally in South Africa, but that the large proportion of double negatives in the items is problematic (Kroukamp, 1991).

12.2.7 Cross-cultural use of structured personality assessment measures

It is common practice for psychologists to take an assessment measure developed in one culture and to translate it for use in another culture (see Chapter 7). Psychologists often use such measures to make cross-cultural comparisons. One important precondition for cross-cultural comparisons with structured assessment measures, such as personality questionnaires and inventories, is that the constructs that they measure must have the same meaning in the two cultures. This is not always easily achieved and assessment instruments can often be said to be biased. One way of defining bias is to say that the measure does not measure the same construct in the different cultures, and therefore no valid comparisons between people of the different cultures can be drawn (see Chapter 7). The assessment of bias is usually done by examining the patterns of interrelationships between the items included in the measure. If these relationships are not the same in the different cultures, the conclusion can be drawn that the measure is not measuring the same constructs and that the measure is therefore biased (Huysamen, 2004; Paunonen and Ashton, 1998).

Paunonen and Ashton (1998) pointed out that if an assessment measure does not measure exactly the same construct in different cultures all is not lost. What is required for valid interpretation is that the psychologist should know what the meaning of particular constructs (as represented by scores for personality measures) is in the culture where he/she intends to use it. However, much research needs to be done before psychologists will be able to state confidently what scores on the 16PF, BTI, MMPI-2, MBTI, and so on, mean for different groups in South Africa.

12.3 Level 2: Assessment of motives and personal concerns

McAdams (1994) argues that knowledge of stable personality traits is not enough to know a person completely. Traits provide a decontextualized picture of an individual, that is, a picture of how the person generally behaves across many different situations. This view does not acknowledge the importance of the context in which behaviour takes place. It also does not give insight into the motives that underlie behaviour. Traits also do not provide any information about a person's dreams or about what a person wishes to achieve. Winter, Stewart, John, Klohnen and Duncan (1998) argue that motives cannot be measured and assessed in the same way as traits. Motives need to be assessed by means that access implicit aspects of personality. Motives 'involve wishes, desires or goals' (Winter et al., 1998, p. 231) and are often unconscious or implicit. Hence, it is necessary to use indirect methods to assess motives. These motives refer to the second level of personality as set out by McAdams (see Section 12.1).

Implicit motives are measured by making use of **projective** assessment techniques (see Section 12.1). One of the most widely used methods of gaining insight into unconscious motives is the Thematic Apperception Test (TAT). This measure is also one of the most widely used psychological measures in clinical and psychodiagnostic contexts (Watkins, Campbell, Nieberding and Hallmark, 1995). The TAT is discussed in the following section.

12.3.1 The Thematic Apperception Test (TAT)

Morgan and Murray (1935) developed the TAT as a way of gaining insight into implicit motives. This test requires of respondents to 'make up stories about a series of vague or ambiguous pictures' (Winter, Stewart, John, Klohnen and Duncan, 1998, p. 232). These stories can be presented orally or in writing. Respondents are instructed to make their stories as dramatic as possible. Each story is to include a description of what led up to the event in the picture, what is happening at the moment, and what the outcome of the story will be. Respondents are also encouraged to describe the thoughts and feelings of the characters in the stories.

The assumption is made that the individual will project his/her own wishes, needs, and conflicts into the story that he/she tells. Hence, the TAT can be used to gain insight into aspects and themes of personality that relate to basic needs and conflicts that are partially hidden. It is assumed that the characteristics of the main characters in the stories reflect tendencies in the respondent's own personality. It is further assumed that the characteristics of the main characters' environments reflect the quality of the respondents' environment (Lanyon and Goodstein, 1997).

In interpreting TAT stories, the psychologist should consider the motives, trends, and feelings of the hero of the story (McAdams, 1994). The interpreter should also focus on the forces in the main character's environment, because this might provide insight into the way that the respondent perceives his/her world. By focusing on the outcomes of the TAT stories, the psychologist may also gain insight into the extent to which the respondent believes his/her needs will be met. Psychologists should also try to note combinations of needs and environmental situations that may constitute significant themes in the respondent's life. One such a theme might be a need for achievement that is constantly undermined by unsupportive parents. Lastly, the TAT may also reveal significant interests and sentiments, that is, the respondent's feelings about particular kinds of people and aspects of the environment (McAdams, 1994).

McAdams (1994) argues that the TAT is most useful as an indicator of motives. Murray generated a list of twenty needs. However, several of these needs overlap. It appears that the TAT measures three major motives, namely need for intimacy, need for achievement, and need for power. Objective scoring systems have been devised to score respondents' TAT stories in terms of the three major motives. McClelland and his colleagues devised the best-known system for the scoring of the **achievement motive** (McClelland, Atkinson, Clark and Lowell, 1953; McClelland, 1985). This motive refers to a need to do better. McAdams (1994) notes that individuals who are high in achievement motivation tend to be interested in entrepreneurship and careers in business. High achievement motivation is also associated with success and promotion in business, although this relationship may only hold for promotions at relatively junior levels. At higher levels, qualities and skills other than achievement motivation may be more important predictors of promotion (McClelland and Boyatzis, 1982).

The **power motive** refers to a need for making an impact on other people. The most popular scoring system for this motive was devised by Winter

(1973). Several studies have shown that individuals who adopt leadership positions are high in the power motive (McClelland and Boyatzis, 1982; Winter, 1973). Interestingly, research suggests that women high in power motivation tend to have happy relationships and marriages, while the opposite is true of men high in power motivation (Veroff, 1982; Veroff and Feld, 1970).

The **intimacy motive** refers to a need to feel close to other people. McAdams devised a scoring system for this motive (McAdams, 1980, 1982). It appears that people high in intimacy spend more time thinking about relationships and make more warm contact with other people than people low in intimacy motivation.

Although objective scoring systems for the TAT are available, most clinicians tend to take an intuitive and impressionistic approach in interpreting people's responses to the stimuli. This has led many researchers to voice their concern over the reliability and validity of the TAT. When objective scoring systems are used, the inter-scorer reliability of the TAT seems satisfactory (Murstein, 1972). However, the test-retest reliability of the TAT does not measure up to conventional psychometric standards. Winter and Stewart (1977) and Lundy (1985) investigated the effects of different assessment instructions on the test-retest reliability of the TAT. They found that most people assume that it is expected of them to tell different stories at the retest and that this may account for the low test-retest reliabilities. When respondents were told that is not a problem if their stories are similar to their previous stories, test-retest reliabilities were substantially improved.

Personality researchers and theorists hold different views on the validity of the TAT. It appears that the best evidence in support of the criterion validity of the TAT is centred on the three major motives, namely need for achievement, need for power, and need for affiliation. Groth-Marnat (2003) points out that the motives measured by the TAT influence long-term behaviours rather than short-term behaviours. Hence, it is not expected that the TAT will correlate with specific acts or immediate behaviour (McClelland, Koestner and Weinberger, 1989). In a recent meta-analysis,

Spangler (1992) reports that the TAT does predict long-term outcomes, such as success in a person's career. Recently, item response theory methods have been applied to the scoring of the TAT, with the results providing support for the need for achievement motive (Tuerlinckx, De Boeck and Lens, 2002).

12.3.2 Cross-cultural use of the TAT

Retief (1987) pointed out that successful cross-cultural use of thematic apperception tests requires that 'the constructs chosen and the signs or symbols used in the stimulus material' (p. 49) should not be unfamiliar or alien to individuals of the 'new' culture. This means that the stimulus materials often need to be adapted for cross-cultural use. The stimuli of the original TAT reflect symbols and situations associated with westernized contexts. If these stimuli are presented to individuals from a different culture, the stimuli may take on different meanings, which would lead to difficulty in interpreting the responses to the stimuli. Because the nature and quality of the stimulus material influence the richness and the meaning of the stories or responses they stimulate, it is important that great attention should be paid to the selection of people, situations, and symbols that are included in the pictures of thematic apperception tests.

Psychologists in southern Africa have attempted to counter this problem by specifically devising thematic apperception tests for use with black populations. Early attempts at establishing thematic apperception tests for black southern Africans include those of Sherwood (1957), De Ridder (1961), Baran (1972), and Erasmus (1975). However, Retief (1987) commented that some of these measures appear to be biased and to reflect cultural and racial stereotypes that may be offensive to some people.

In addition to the unsuitability of many of the original TAT cards for black South Africans, the stimuli may also seem outdated and unfamiliar for many white, coloured, and Indian South Africans. It seems that psychologists in South Africa are in need of a thematic apperception test that reflects the contemporary cultural complexity and richness of its society.

12.3.3 Other projective methods of personality assessment

Other popular projective methods that may provide useful information on implicit or unconscious aspects of personality include the **Rorschach Inkblot Test**, the **Draw-A-Person test**, and **sentence completion tests**. In the Rorschach test, individuals are shown pictures of inkblots. The task of the test-taker is to report what he/she sees in the inkblots. Several sophisticated scoring methods have been developed for the Rorschach Inkblot Test. In the Draw-A-Person test, the individual is generally instructed to draw a picture of a person. The individual may thereafter be instructed to draw a picture of someone of the opposite sex than the person in the first picture. Some psychologists may also request the individual to draw himself/herself. In therapeutic situations, psychologists may proceed by asking the individual questions about the picture(s) that the test-taker has drawn. Sentence completion tests require the individual to complete sentences of which only the stem has been given, such as 'I get upset when ...'. With all three methods described above, the assumption is made that the individual will project aspects of his/her personality into his/her responses. However, the same psychometric criticisms directed against the TAT are also directed against these methods. For a more comprehensive discussion of these methods, interested readers are referred to Groth-Marnat (2003).

12.4 Conclusion

In order to understand the uniqueness of the individual, it is necessary to examine personality on all three levels of McAdams' scheme. The first level of the scheme provides insight into the individual's typical ways of interacting with the world and characteristic patterns of behaviour. Structured personality assessment tools such as the 16PF, BTI, OPQ, and MMPI may help psychologists to understand and describe these typical patterns of interaction and behaviour. The information gained by using such tools may also be useful in predicting how an individual is likely to behave in the future. However, these assessment measures do not provide insight into the reasons or motives for a person's behaviour. In order to achieve this, psychologists need to move to the second level of McAdams' (1995) scheme where the focus falls on personal concerns, projects, and motives. Projective techniques, such as the TAT, may be useful in gaining insight into implicit and unconscious aspects of personality. This may provide insight into the reasons for a person's behaviour. By combining information gained on both these levels and by integrating it with an individual's life story, the psychologist can construct an integrated and rich picture of the person who is being assessed.

CHECKING YOUR PROGRESS **12.1**

12.1   Draw a distinction between structured and projective methods of personality assessment.

12.2   Discuss potential problems with cross-cultural use of structured personality assessment methods.

12.3   How was factor analysis used in the development of the 16PF?

12.4   What criticisms are commonly directed at projective methods of personality assessment?

12.5   Discuss potential problems with the cross-cultural use of the TAT.

There have been quite a few stops to make in the *Types-of-Measures Zone*. You only have two left. At the next stop in this zone, you will take a look at some of the measures used in career assessment.

Career counselling assessment

GIDEON P DE BRUIN AND KARINA DE BRUIN

Chapter

13

CHAPTER OUTCOMES

Once you have studied this chapter you will be able to:
> identify the central theoretical concepts and assumptions of the person-environment-fit, developmental and systems approaches to career counselling assessment;
> identify the major differences between the person-environment-fit, developmental, and systems approaches to career counselling assessment;
> identify points of criticism against the approaches; and
> name the most important measures and techniques associated with each of the three approaches to career counselling assessment.

13.1 **Introduction**

Career counselling can be defined broadly as the process in which a professional career counsellor helps an individual or a group of individuals to make satisfying career-related decisions. A **career** can be defined as the totality of work one does in a lifetime (Sears, 1982).

Crites (1981) divides the career counselling process into three stages, namely diagnosis, process, and outcome. In the diagnosis phase, the career counsellor and client often need to determine the following:
• what the client wishes to achieve through the career counselling;

• why the client cannot (or chooses not to) make the career decision on his/her own;
• what the client's relative work-related strengths and weaknesses are; and
• what the client's work-related preferences are.

In order to make an accurate diagnosis with regards to these factors, career counsellors often make use of psychological assessment measures. In this chapter we aim to provide an overview of career counselling assessment from three different theoretical points of view. The first two, namely the person-environment-fit approach and the developmental approach, represent traditional assessment approaches. The third, namely the systems approach to career counselling assessment, is strongly influenced by constructivism and represents a qualitative assessment approach.

There are at least three general reasons why assessment in career counselling is important: '(1) to stimulate, broaden, and provide focus to career exploration, (2) to stimulate exploration of self in relation to career, and (3) to provide what-if information with respect to various career choice options' (Prediger, 1974, p. 338). These three roles of assessment in career counselling are likely to be important irrespective of which theoretical approach the career counsellor follows. However, as you will see in the sections that follow, each of the theoretical approaches emphasizes different aspects of the assessment process. Individual career counsellors often have a preference for certain assessment tools and techniques. Some find the use of **standardized** psychological tests useful, whereas others may feel more comfortable with qualitative methods. For others, a combination of standardized psychological tests and qualitative assessment techniques may be more appealing. To provide for the needs of the client, a comprehensive and collaborative approach to career assessment – including both standardized psychological tests and **qualitative assessment** procedures – is often the most desirable approach.

13.2 **The person-environment-fit approach**

Early in the twentieth century Parsons (1909) stated the basic principles of the trait-and-factor approach to career counselling, which has since evolved into the **person-environment-fit approach**. According to Parsons, the individual has to do three things when choosing a career:

- the individual must know himself/herself;
- the individual must know the world of work; and
- the individual must find a fit between his/her characteristics and the world of work.

This approach to career counselling was enthusiastically espoused by applied psychologists and psychologists interested in individual differences. Differential psychologists developed psychological tests and questionnaires that could be used to indicate differences in intelligence, specific abilities, personality traits, and interests. Using such tests and questionnaires, counselling psychologists and career counsellors could determine the relative 'strengths' and 'weaknesses' of their clients in terms of abilities, personality traits, and interests. The task of the career counsellor became one of helping the client to better understand his/her abilities, personality traits, and interests. The next step was to match the acquired self-knowledge with knowledge about the world and work and to choose an appropriate occupation.

This approach to career counselling is still very widely used, although contemporary writers emphasize the dynamic aspects of person-environment-fit (Swanson, 1996). This approach focuses on the fact that successful work adjustment depends on correspondence between an individual's characteristics and the characteristics of the working environment. Every person has needs that have to be met and skills that he/she can offer to the working environment. Similarly, every working environment has needs and reinforcers to offer to the individual. Ideal work adjustment will take place if the individual's skills correspond to the needs of the working environment and the reinforcers of the working environment correspond to the needs of the individual (Dawis and Lofquist, 1984).

Next, we will discuss several domains that form an important part of assessment from a person-environment-fit approach.

13.2.1 **Assessing intelligence**

Although intelligence measures have been formally used for almost a hundred years, there still is no consensus among psychologists about what **intelligence** really is (see Chapter 10). However, psychologists do know that scores on well-constructed intelligence measures are powerful predictors of academic success and work performance (De Bruin, De Bruin, Dercksen and Hartslief-Cilliers, 2005; Kuncel, Hezlett and Ones, 2004; Ree and Earles, 1996; Schmidt and Hunter, 1998). Therefore, it should come as no surprise that intelligence measures have often formed part of career counselling assessment batteries from a person-environment-fit perspective.

Intelligence measures can be used profitably in career counselling contexts. However, although the total IQ score is a powerful predictor of academic- and work-related achievement, career counsellors should keep in mind that many other factors also play important roles in the prediction of achievement. Such factors may include socio-economic status, quality of schooling, test anxiety, and measurement error. Another important factor in multicultural contexts is that measures may provide biased scores when used with groups that differ from the standardization sample (see Chapter 7). Therefore, it is not wise to base any decision on whether a person will be able to cope with the cognitive demands of any particular academic or training course or occupation on a total IQ score alone. Career counsellors should seek additional information that may confirm the scores on the intelligence measure, such as reports of previous academic or work performance. Career counsellors should also explore the role of factors such as language and socio-economic status in an individual's performance on an intelligence measure.

Both **individual** and **group** intelligence measures lend themselves to being used in career assessment contexts. You were introduced to a variety of these measures in Chapter 10. The most widely used group intelligence measure for career counselling purposes in South Africa is probably the General Scholastic Ability Test (GSAT; Claassen, De Beer, Hugo and Meyer, 1991). The Raven Progressive Matrices (Raven, 1965) are also popular as they are non-verbal measures (De Bruin et al., 2005). The Senior South African Individual Scale – Revised (SSAIS-R; Van Eeden, 1991) is often used for individual assessment purposes.

13.2.2 **Assessing aptitude**

Career counsellors have long relied on measures of specific abilities or **aptitudes** to try and match clients with specific occupations. The assumption is that different occupations require different skills. Measures of specific abilities may be used to assess whether an individual has the potential to be successful in an occupation. According to Zunker

(2006), 'aptitude test scores provide an index of measured skills that is intended to predict how well an individual may perform on a job or in an educational and/or training program' (p. 192). Other authors maintain that an aptitude refers to an individual's potential to acquire a new skill or to learn some specialized knowledge (Isaacson and Brown, 1997). Because most aptitude measures are multidimensional (i.e. they are designed to measure several different aptitudes), they may also be used to identify relative cognitive strengths and weaknesses. All of the aptitude measures discussed in Chapter 10 lend themselves to being used in career counselling contexts.

13.2.3 **Interest questionnaires**

An individual's scores on an interest inventory reflect his/her liking or preferences for engaging in specific occupations (Isaacson and Brown, 1997). MacAleese (1984) identified three general purposes of interest inventories in career counselling:

- to identify interests of which the client was not aware;
- to confirm the client's stated interests; and
- to identify discrepancies between a client's abilities and interests.

The first widely used interest inventory was developed in the United States of America by Strong (1927). His measure, the Strong Interest Inventory, has been revised several times and remains one of the most researched and widely used interest inventories in the United States of America.

Let us now look at two interest inventories that have been developed and standardized in South Africa or adapted for the South African context.

13.2.3.1 **The Self-Directed Search (SDS)**

The Self-Directed Search (SDS) is one of the best-known interest inventories in the world. This inventory is based on the theory of John L. Holland (1985) and was adapted for South African conditions by Du Toit and Gevers (1990). The SDS was standardized for all South African groups and can be used with high school students and adults. The SDS measures interests for six broad interest fields, namely **Realistic** (practical), **Investigative** (scientific), **Artistic**, **Social**, **Enterprising** (business), and **Conventional** (clerical). Factor analyses of many different interest inventories have revealed that these six broad fields provide a satisfactory summary of all the important fields of interest (De Bruin, 2002). These six fields can also be used to describe working environments. According to Holland (1997), individuals should strive to choose careers that will lead to congruence between an individual's interests and the characteristics of the working environment.

Holland's (1985) theory also describes the relationships between the six interest fields. Specifically, Holland predicts that the interest fields are ordered in a hexagonal fashion. Fields that lie next to each other on the hexagon are assumed to be more closely related than fields that lie further apart. This structural ordering of the interest fields allows the career counsellor to assess the consistency of an individual's interests. If the client achieves high scores in the interest fields that lie next to each other, it can be said that his/her interest pattern is high in consistency. However, if the client achieves high scores in interest fields that are not next to each other on the hexagon, the interest pattern is low in consistency. Although this aspect of the SDS is potentially very useful, it makes the assumption that the hexagonal ordering of the six fields is valid. Unfortunately, there is evidence that the proposed hexagonal structure of the SDS is not valid for black South African high school students (Du Toit and De Bruin, 2002) and other non-westernized samples (Rounds and Tracey, 1996). Therefore, career counsellors should be cautious when interpreting the SDS scores for these groups.

13.2.3.2 **MB-10**

Several other interest inventories have been developed in South Africa. One of the most popular measures is the MB-10 (Meyer, 1998), which is a revised version of the KODUS Interest Inventory (Meyer, 1980). This instrument measures interests for ten different fields, namely working with individuals, working with groups, business, numbers, reading and writing, art, handicraft and machine work, science, animals, and plants. The MB-10 was standardized for the following groups: high school learners that are representative of the total

Western Cape population, and first-year students at the University of Stellenbosch.

There are two important differences between the SDS and the MB-10. The first difference lies in the item format. For the SDS, the test-taker has to indicate whether he/she likes an activity or occupation or not by answering YES or NO to the item. In contrast, for the MB-10, the test-taker must choose one of two activities that are presented simultaneously. The item format of the MB-10 is called a forced choice or **ipsative format**, because the client must always choose which of two options he/she will like best (see Chapter 6).

The second major difference lies in the way in which the scores are used. For the SDS, six total scores are obtained and each of the scores represents the test-taker's interest in one of the six fields. The three highest scores are generally taken to reflect the test-taker's career interests. The forced-choice item format of the MB-10 leads to ipsative interpretation. This means that the test-taker is compared with him-/herself and not with a norm group (see Chapter 6).

13.2.4 **Assessment of values**

Zunker (2006) emphasizes the importance of value clarification in career counselling assessment. Values arise from people's needs: because we need something, we start to value that particular thing (Super, 1995). Values may be considered as important motivators of behaviour, because people strive to achieve or obtain the things that they value and to move away from the things that they do not value. Dawis and Lofquist (1984) emphasized the consideration of values for work adjustment and job satisfaction. According to them, job satisfaction depends on the degree of correspondence between an individual's values and the reinforcers offered by a particular job.

13.2.4.1 **The Values Scale**

The Values Scale (Langley, Du Toit and Herbst, 1992a) may be used to assess the relative importance that an individual places on activities. This scale is based on a scale developed by Nevill and Super (1986) and formed part of the international Work Importance study (Super, Sverko and Super, 1995). The scale measures twenty-two different values. Factor analysis of the twenty-two scales showed that they can be grouped in six broad clusters, namely **Inner Orientation, Material Orientation, Autonomous Life-Style, Humanism** and **Religion, Social Orientation,** and **Physical Orientation** (Langley, 1995). Carvalho (2005) repeated the factor analysis of the twenty-two scales and found support for all these broad clusters in a group of South African university students, except for Material Orientation. The Values Scale is standardized for English, Afrikaans, and African language groups in South Africa.

13.2.5 **Assessment of personality**

Like the assessment of abilities and interests, the assessment of personality is also an important component of career counselling from a person-environment-fit point of view. The aim of personality assessment is to identify an individual's salient personality characteristics and to match these characteristics to the requirements of occupations. For example, if a person is extroverted and group dependent, occupations that allow a person to have social contact and to work in groups may be more desirable than occupations where the person has no social contact. The assumption is made that personality traits reflect basic and relatively stable tendencies to behave in certain ways (Larsen and Buss, 2002), (see Chapter 12). Individuals also seek out environments that correspond with their personality traits, for example, extroverts seek out situations with lots of social activity, whereas introverts seek out situations where they can avoid social contact. The role of personality in terms of career decision behaviour has recently attracted research attention and is increasingly taken into account in designing career counselling programmes (cf. Betz, 2007; Borgen and Betz, 2008). We will discuss four standardized personality measures that may be employed fruitfully in the career counselling context next.

13.2.5.1 **The 16 Personality Factor Questionnaire**

The 16 Personality Factor Questionnaire (16PF; Cattell, Eber and Tatsuoka, 1970) as well as the version for high school students, the High School Personality Questionnaire (Cattell and Cattell, 1969), which were discussed in Chapter 12, have

been used widely for career counselling purposes (De Bruin, 2002; Schuerger, 2000). Several personality profiles have been developed for different occupations, and an individual's profile is then compared to these profile types. If the individual's profile fits the profile type for a specific occupation, it would suggest that this occupation may be worth exploring further. Similarly, if the individual's profile differs significantly from the profile type for a certain occupation, the individual may want to explore alternative options. However, career counsellors should keep in mind that, even within a particular occupation, there can be large differences between people in terms of personality traits. To assume that there is one particular configuration of personality traits for any particular occupation is an oversimplification. The 5th edition of the 16PF was recently adapted for the South African population.

13.2.5.2 **The Myers-Briggs Type Indicator and Jung Personality Questionnaire**

The Myers-Briggs Type Indicator (MBTI; Myers and McCaulley, 1985) aims to categorize people into one of sixteen different personality types based on their scores for four bipolar scales. It is assumed that people who belong to the same personality type share the same personality characteristics and that they differ from individuals who belong to another type in important ways (McCaulley, 2000). A further assumption is that different personality types are differentially suited for different occupations. The task of the career counsellor and the client becomes one of exploring the client's personality type and identifying environments that correspond with this type. The validity of the MBTI for different groups in South Africa is currently being investigated.

The Jung Personality Questionnaire (JPQ; Du Toit, 1983) is a South African version of the MBTI that was developed for use with high school students. Unfortunately, the research literature on the JPQ is limited and more research is needed especially with regards to evaluating its usefulness with black, coloured, and Indian students. (We discussed both the MBTI and the JPQ in more detail in Chapter 12.)

13.2.5.3 **The Basic Traits Inventory**

The Basic Traits Inventory (BTI; Taylor and de Bruin, 2006) was developed to assess the Big Five personality factors in the South African population. The five factors that are measured are: **Neuroticism, Extroversion, Openness to Experience, Agreeableness and Conscientiousness.** The construct validity of the five-factor model has received empirical support in the South African context (Heuchert, Parker, Stumpf and Myburgh, 2000; Taylor and De Bruin, 2006).

13.2.6 **The validity of the person-environment-fit approach to assessment**

The **person-environment-fit approach** rests on the assumption that, if an individual knows himself/herself and the world of work, the individual should be able to make a satisfying career choice by selecting a work environment that fits his/her abilities, interests, and personality (Sharf, 2006). However, this approach does not recognize that individuals may be differentially ready to make career choices. Some individuals can benefit from a self-exploration exercise and can readily integrate information about the world of work, while others are not mature enough (in a career decision-making sense) to usefully implement such information. The person-environment-fit approach also assumes that people are free to choose from a variety of available career options. However, in many developing countries such as South Africa, job opportunities are scarce and few individuals have the privilege to choose a career from the available options. The majority do not have a choice in this regard and may be forced to take any career opportunities that may come their way. Therefore, taking several psychological measures in order to identify salient abilities, interests, and personality characteristics may be of limited value for many individuals. Lastly, assessment from a person-environment-fit perspective can only be useful if the psychological tests and questionnaires used in the assessment provide reliable and valid scores. Due to the differences in language, socio-economic status, beliefs, and educational background, it cannot just be taken for granted that measures developed for one group can be used with other groups. In this regard, psychom-

etricians have to do the following:
- demonstrate that the measures tap the same characteristics for different groups; or
- develop new measures that measure the same characteristics for the different groups (see Chapter 7).

Despite the above criticisms, the person-environment-fit approach has been a dominant force in career counselling and several important psychometric instruments have been developed specifically for career counselling purposes.

13.3 **The developmental approach to career counselling assessment**

During the 1950s, Donald Super introduced the concept of career maturity and, by doing so, placed career decision-making within the context of human development (Crites, 1981). From a developmental perspective, career choice is not viewed as a static event but, rather, as a developmental process that starts in childhood and continues through adulthood. According to Super (1983), career maturity refers to the degree to which an individual has mastered the career development tasks that he/she should master in his/her particular developmental stage. By assessing an individual's level of career maturity, the career counsellor may identify certain career development tasks with which the individual has not dealt successfully. These tasks may then become the focus of further counselling.

13.3.1 **Assessing career development**

Super (1990) described a model for developmental career counselling assessment. The model consists of four stages: preview, depth-view, assessment of all the data, and counselling. During the first stage, the career counsellor reviews the client's records and background information. Based on this review as well as a preliminary interview with the client, the counsellor formulates a plan for assessment. In the second stage, the counsellor assesses the client's work values, the relative importance of different life roles, career maturity, abilities, personality, and interests. During the third stage, the client and career counsellor integrate all the information in order to understand the client's position in terms of the career decision-making process. The last stage involves counselling with the aim of addressing the career-related needs identified during the assessment process.

The assessment of interests, values, personality, and abilities were already discussed in the previous section. We will discuss two measures that may be used for the assessment of career maturity and role saliency next.

13.3.1.1 Career Development Questionnaire

After a comprehensive review of the literature on career development, Langley (1989) identified five components of career maturity:

- self-knowledge;
- decision-making;
- career information;
- the integration of self-knowledge with career information; and
- career planning.

Langley (1989) emphasized that the career counsellor should not only assess whether the client knows himself/herself and the world-of-work, but also whether the individual is able to integrate this material in a meaningful way. The Career Development Questionnaire (CDQ; Langley, Du Toit and Herbst, 1992b) may be used to assess the career maturity of black, coloured, Indian, and white high school students and university students. If the CDQ indicates that a client lacks self-knowledge, career information, or the ability to integrate the two, then he/she may not be ready to make a responsible career choice. Langley's (1989) model of career maturity also emphasizes the importance of assessing an individual's career decision-making ability. If the individual lacks career decision-making skills, the counsellor and individual may agree to make this a focus point of the career counselling process before a decision about a career is made. The last component of Langley's (1989) model focuses on the degree to which an individual has engaged in career planning. Individuals who have done more future career planning

are generally more career mature than individuals who have done less planning.

13.3.1.2 Life Role Inventory

The importance of the work role is another important aspect of career counselling assessment from a developmental perspective. Super (1983, 1994) has emphasized that the role of worker is not equally important to everybody and that the assessment of work role salience should form an important part of the career counselling process. Career counselling may only be successful if both the client and the counsellor understand how important the worker role is relative to other roles. Super distinguishes between five major arenas in which an individual's life roles are played:

- the workplace;
- the community;
- the family;
- the academic environment; and
- the leisure environment.

The Life Role Inventory (LRI; Langley, 1993) was designed to measure the relative importance of each of these five roles. This measure is based on the Role Salience Inventory (Nevill and Super, 1986). The LRI was standardized for white and black South African high school students. Nevill and Super (1986) have pointed out that the importance of the five life roles may vary with age. In late adolescence, when a career decision has to be made, the salience of the work role has important implications for career counselling. Specifically, for adolescents who attach low importance to the role of worker, career counselling should focus on their readiness to make a career choice. However, it should be kept in mind that for adolescents the roles of worker and student are likely to be intertwined. A factor analysis of the LRI by Foxcroft, Watson, De Jager and Dobson (1994) indicated that it is not possible to distinguish psychometrically between these two roles for South African university students.

13.3.2 **Evaluation of the developmental approach to career counselling assessment**

The validity of the developmental approach to career

counselling in the South African context has been questioned by several authors (De Bruin and Nel, 1996; Naicker, 1994; Stead and Watson, 1998). The developmental approach adds to the person-environment-fit approach in that it emphasizes the developmental nature of career decision-making. The developmental approach also emphasizes the need to focus on an individual's specific career counselling needs. However, the developmental approach makes certain assumptions that are of questionable value in the context of a developing country characterized by poverty, unemployment, and crime. These assumptions are as follows:

- that career development follows a predictable path with clearly defined stages;
- that the developmental stages associated with every stage have to be successfully completed before the client can move on to a next stage; and
- that if a person is career mature he/she will be able to make a successful career choice.

These assumptions do not hold in developing countries where individuals often do not have the financial resources to complete their schooling, where schooling is often disrupted by social and political unrest, and where job opportunities are very scarce. In such countries individuals are often forced to find any employment that may be available, without considering how well the characteristics of the working environment can be integrated with their interests, values, and abilities. Also, some individuals may be highly career mature and may still find it very difficult to find any employment.

13.4 **The systems approach to career counselling assessment**

Constructivism has recently started to show its influence in career theory and counselling. As a result, the counselling process has become more collaborative with the counsellor and client as more equal partners in the process. According to McMahon and Watson (2008), constructivism has also informed the development of the Sys-

tems Theory Framework (STF) of career development. Therefore an important goal of qualitative career assessment is to identify 'connections between client's experiences and various elements from their system of influences ... including the past, present and future' (McMahon, Patton and Watson, 2003).

This theoretical framework includes both the content influences and process influences on the career development of individuals. Both these influences are set within a time system of past, present and future. The past influences the present and both the past and present have an influence on the future.

Content influences refer to the intrinsic personal characteristics and the effect of the context in which the individual lives. These subsystems are interconnected and include the individual, other people, organizations and the society and environment (McMahon and Watson, 2008). The individual system includes intrapersonal influences such as age, gender, interests, personality and abilities. The individual system forms part of a larger contextual system – accommodating the social system and the environmental-societal system. The social system refers to other people systems, for example family, friends and educational institutions. The individual system and the social system are nested in the environmental-societal system (including politics, technological developments and globalization) which may have a significant influence on the individual's career development. These systems can change and are constantly interacting with one another – implicating a process of dynamic open systems.

Process influences include three aspects: recursiveness, change over time, and chance. Recursiveness refers to the interaction of the various influences. Changes in one system will have an influence on and may lead to changes in another subsystem. Secondly, the nature and degree of influence change as time goes by. With reference to change, career development of individuals can no longer be planned, logical and predictable. Chance events, including unexpected happenings such as illness, downsizing and natural disasters, may also hugely impact the individual's career development (McMahon and Watson, 2008).

13.4.1 **My System of Career Influences**

McMahon et al. (2003) provided suggestions to guide the development of qualitative career assessment instruments. These suggestions include the need to ground the assessment process in theory, the testing of the process, completing the process in a realistic time frame, understandable instructions for the client, providing for a flexible process, cooperation between the counsellor and client and a debriefing process. These suggestions were adhered to in the development of the *My System of Career Influences* reflection activity (MSCI; McMahon, Watson and Patton, 2005). This tool is grounded in the Systems Theory Framework (Patton and McMahon, 1999) which 'takes into account broad-based contextual influences as well as intrapersonal influences' on the career development process (McMahon et al., 2005, p. 477). The MSCI consists of a booklet in which the individual is required to reflect on his/her current career situation. According to McMahon and Watson (2008, p. 280), it helps individuals 'to explore the systemic influences on their careers and, in so doing, to tell their career stories'. Finally, they summarize these reflections to construct their own unique MSCI diagrams. Clients can complete the process on their own; however it may be more beneficial to them if a counsellor is available to provide support and clarify aspects where necessary. The instrument is useful across cultures.

13.4.2 **Evaluation of the systems approach to career counselling assessment**

Constructivism in career theory and counselling has influenced career counsellors to increasingly adopt qualitative methods of career assessment in addition to, or as an alternative to, standardized psychological testing. The systems approach to career counselling assessment has resulted in the Systems Theory Framework and the development of the My System of Career Influences. The theory and accompanying assessment and counselling in-

strument is useful because it is flexible and can be used with clients from diverse backgrounds. The assessment also actively involves the client in the process and provides an avenue along which the meaning that clients attach to their career development can be explored (McMahon et al., 2003).

Individuals cannot be separated from their environments – their behaviour should be understood within the context that it occurs. The approach also provides for the creativity of the counsellor to develop his/her own assessment techniques and processes.

An emphasis on qualitative assessment at the expense of traditional psychological inventories and questionnaires may be seen as limiting in the career assessment process. The purpose of career assessment may be seen as the enhancement of self-awareness. Traditional tools such as interest inventories and values scales may serve this purpose very well. Typically, interest inventories cover a wide range of occupational activities, including some that clients may not even be aware of. In this sense the mere act of completing an interest inventory and becoming aware of new occupations facilitates the development of self-awareness. In addition, being able to compare the strength of one's interests with those of others may provide clients and counsellors with useful information for discussion in the career assessment process. Similarly, in the hands of a skilled counsellor, a client's profile obtained from a personality inventory may serve as a powerful tool with which to enhance self-awareness. In keeping with a constructivist approach the information gained from the inventory is not taken as absolute and fixed, but as information that must be given meaning within the broader system of influences wherein a client is situated.

> **» CRITICAL THINKING CHALLENGE 13.1**
>
> James Mhlangu is eighteen years old and in Grade 12. He comes from the rural areas of KwaZulu-Natal. He wants to study at a university. What career assessment approach would you follow and which measures may help you and James in the career counselling process? State why you would use the measures that you choose.

13.5 **Career counselling in a changing environment**

We described two more traditional approaches as well as one emerging approach to career counselling assessment in this chapter. Each one of these approaches has a different emphasis. The person-environment-fit approach emphasizes the fit between a person and his/her environment. The developmental approach adds to this by emphasizing the readiness of an individual to make a career choice. The systems approach provides for the influence of various subsystems on the individual's career development.

All three approaches can be valuable in the career counselling context, depending on the particular needs of a client. Career counsellors are encouraged to further explore these approaches (and also other approaches); in that way they will be able to tailor their assessment and interventions according to what is best for the client, and not according to that with which they are most comfortable and familiar.

Career counsellors are also encouraged to recognize the pervasive social and technological changes that are influencing the way in which work is structured and perceived. In the future it is unlikely that individuals will enter organizations and devote their entire career to that organization. It is expected that individuals will not only change from one organization to another, but sometimes also change to whole new fields of work during their career. Workers will have to be multi-skilled and flexible. Career counselling assessment can be valuable in this regard by helping individuals recognize their work-related strengths, skills, and abilities that can be applied in many different contexts. Values and interests will also remain important, because workers will probably still seek to find working environments that satisfy their psychological needs.

CHECKING YOUR PROGRESS 13.1

13.1 What are the basic features of the person-environment-fit approach?

13.2 Which intelligence measures are often used in the career counselling situation?

13.3 Discuss the Self-Directed Search and the MB-10 as interest inventories.

13.4 Why are assessments of values and personality important in career counselling?

13.5 Discuss the Career Development Questionnaire and the Life Role Inventory as career development assessment measures from the developmental approach.

13.6 Which subsystems are accommodated in the Systems Theory Framework and how can the influence of these on the career development of the individual be explored?

13.7 Evaluate the person-environment-fit, developmental and systems approaches to career counselling in the South African context.

Computer-based and Internet-delivered assessment

CAROLINE DAVIES, CHERYL FOXCROFT, LOURA GRIESSEL, AND NANETTE TREDOUX

CHAPTER OUTCOMES

In this chapter we will outline the rise of computer-based assessment, the advantages of computer-based and Internet testing, the ethical, cross-cultural, and practical issues that arise when using computer-based and Internet testing, as well as highlight good practices that should be followed.

By the end of this chapter you will be able to:

> distinguish between computer-based and Internet-delivered assessment;
> understand how computer-based and Internet-delivered testing and assessment developed internationally as well as in South Africa;
> describe the advantages and disadvantages of computer-based and Internet-delivered testing and assessment;
> describe the advantages and disadvantages of computer-based test interpretation;
> understand the ethical and legal issues in computer-based and Internet-delivered testing and assessment as well as the guidelines available to deal with such issues; and
> understand how continual technological advances expand the horizons of computer-based and Internet-delivered testing and assessment.

14.1 **Introduction**

The increasingly sophisticated applications of computer technology have revolutionized all aspects of the field of testing and assessment. For example, according to Gregory (2007), computers and computer technology are used in assessment to:

- design tests more efficiently;
- individually tailor tests during testing based on feedback on test performance;
- present items that range from being straightforward (e.g. reading text on the screen) to those that use multimedia technology (e.g. simulations and dynamic item formats), which often makes the latter items more engaging and realistic for test-takers;
- deliver tests over the Internet, a function which has become increasingly useful for multinational companies who need to test applicants using the same measure at any location in the world;
- score tests more accurately and in a shorter space of time;
- interpret test results according to various rules and hypotheses;
- generate test reports, which can be used when providing feedback to clients; and
- interview clients in order to obtain case histories and information on a current problem and symptoms, by storing a set of questions in a programme and using conditional branching strategies whereby, once an answer is given to a question, the computer decides which question to ask next.

Before we go any further, we need to define some of the important terms that you will find in this chapter. Simply stated, a **computer-based test** refers to a test that is administered and scored using a computer. Sometimes a test has both a paper-based and a computer-based version. However, a test is often available in a computerized format only as the item types used, for example, cannot be replicated in a paper-based format. When a computer-based test is used, the resultant type of testing is referred to as **computer-based testing (CBT)**. **Computerized adaptive testing (CAT)** is a special type of computer-based testing, which uses a set of statistical procedures that make it possible to tailor the test for the individual being assessed on the basis of their responses and which allows for more accurate and efficient measurement. Many computer-based tests have **computer-based test interpretation (CBTI)** systems which aid assessment practitioners in interpreting test performance and provide hypotheses related to understanding the test-taker better, making a diagnosis, and suggesting treatment possibilities. **Internet-delivered testing (IDT)** represents a method of administering computer-based tests via the World Wide Web. This method enhances the speed with which tests can be delivered to assessment practitioners and the security that can be exercised over such tests, and also enables test-takers to be assessed on the same measure almost anywhere in the world.

14.2 **Brief historical overview of computer-based and Internet-delivered testing**

14.2.1 **Internationally**

The technical innovation of the high-speed scanner to score test protocols in the 1950s and 1960s (viewed as the first use of computer technology in testing) increased the use of interest questionnaires (e.g. the Strong Vocational Interest Blanks) and personality tests (e.g. the Minnesota Multiphasic Personality Inventory) in particular. This invention, coupled with greater use of multiple-choice item formats led to the increased efficiency of, and a reduction in, the cost of testing (Clarke, Madaus, Horn, and Ramos, 2000).

In 1962 the first computer-based test interpretation (CBTI) system was developed at the Mayo Clinic for the MMPI (Swenson, Rome, Pearson, and Brannick, 1965). This was followed by the development of a system for the computer-based interpretation of the Rorschach Inkblot Test in 1964 (Gregory, 2007). The 1970s witnessed the first automation of the entire assessment process at a psychiatric hospital in Utah and the introduction of computerized adaptive testing (CAT), which is considered to be one of the greatest contributions of computer-based testing (see Section 14.3.1).

Until the 1980s, the role of the computer in testing was restricted mainly to recording answers and computing test scores (Murphy and Davidshofer, 1998. The first original applications of computerized testing involved the computerization of the items of paper-and-pencil tests, for both administration and scoring purposes (Bunderson, Inouye and Olsen, 1989; Linn, 1989). This continued until the early 1980s when the emergence of advanced computer technology and the possibilities this presented for the design, administration, and scoring of tests had a large impact on all aspects of the testing industry (Clarke, Madaus, Horn, and Ramos, 2000).

The advent of computer-based tests meant that computers became an integral part of the process of testing (administration, scoring, and reporting), rather than simply providing the means of scoring the tests as they did initially. Computer-based testing differs from the conventional paper-based testing primarily in that test-takers answer the questions using a computer rather than a pencil and paper (Clarke, Madaus, Horn, and Ramos, 2000). Computer technology also made it possible to develop different types of items. For example, in 1994 the first multimedia assessment batteries were developed to assess real-life problem-solving skills in prospective employees (Gregory, 2007).

During the 1990s and at the first decade of the twenty-first century, computer-based testing and its delivery over the Internet have brought more flexibility to the testing arena. Individuals are now able to register by email or telephone and can be tested by appointment in a designated testing centre and receive their scores at the end of the test session. Testing organizations are furthermore able to exchange questions and test-taker responses electronically with test centres, and send scores to institutions in a similar fashion (Clarke, Madaus, Horn, and Ramos, 2000). This has enhanced the efficiency of test delivery.

The advent of the computer and the Internet has also enhanced test development. Expert item writers from all over the world can be contracted to develop items and can be linked to each other electronically. This not only facilitates the item development process but also the item refinement process. The process of assessment generation can

now be done through item engines, which encapsulate a model of the intended assessment, and take the form of software that writes the test at the touch of a key. Artificial intelligence has further enhanced these engines by enabling the software to 'learn' in the act of production, which enhances the production of subsequent items and other versions of a test (Professional Affairs Board Steering Committee on Test Standards, British Psychological Society, 2002). The use of computers has also helped test developers to re-envision what test items look like and how they are scored and reported (Zenisky and Sireci, 2002).

Despite the advances that computer-based and Internet-delivered testing has brought to the field of testing and assessment, it has also brought many legal and ethical challenges (see Section 14.4). Consequently, the American Psychological Association (APA) published the first set of guidelines for computer-based testing and test interpretations in 1986. Various other guidelines have been published since then, with the *Guidelines for Computer-based and Internet-delivered Testing* of the International Test Commission (ITC) (2006) being the most recent.

14.2.2 **In South Africa**

14.2.2.1 **Early history**

The earliest work in automated testing in South Africa was done at the National Institute for Personnel Research (NIPR), then part of the Council for Scientific and Industrial Research (CSIR), when they developed tests for selecting airline (military) pilots. Other developments at the NIPR included the tilting-room-tilting-chair apparatus as well as a number of mechanical-electrical apparatus tests and driving simulation tasks during the early 1970s. These projects can logically be regarded as the forerunners of computerized testing at the NIPR.

In the late 1970s to early 1980s, a computerized testing system was developed by Malcolm Coulter at the NIPR on a VARIAN minicomputer. Initially the VARIAN had only a printer terminal and no operating system. Malcolm Coulter wrote the operating system and the drivers for the visual display units that were later acquired, as well as the testing software. The system was later adapted for a research project on basic cognitive abilities.

In the second half of 1979, the Psychometrics Group of the NIPR undertook a contract project to computerize tests for selection purposes for Eskom. The information technology platform was the Control Data PLATO system, which was initially developed for computer-based education in the 1970s by the University of Illinois, but was adapted at the NIPR for psychological testing.

Not only was almost the full range of NIPR tests computerized in this project, but a sophisticated test management system was developed, enabling assessment practitioners at remote locations to request an assessment battery to be set up by sending their requirements via the wide area network to the psychologist at the head office. The psychologist set up the battery, and the battery travelled back via the network to the testing site. Encrypted results were sent back and the battery file was disabled. Security was extensive in order to keep unauthorised people from gaining access to the tests and the results.

Technically, the NIPR's PLATO-based testing system was very sophisticated even by today's standards. The 'Viking' terminals that were used had touch screens as well as sophisticated graphics capabilities (monochrome) which were used in the test administration programmes. The system had programmes for item analysis, basic statistics, regression, and factor analysis. Of critical importance was what was termed 'crash proofing' – if testing was interrupted due to a technical problem, it was possible to resume exactly where you left off without any loss of information. Also critical was the inclusion of mini tests after the instruction sequences. Test-takers who did not answer the examples correctly were routed back to repeat the instructions and practice examples; after a few failures, they were not allowed to continue with that particular test. The system supported the compilation of test batteries and provided a choice of norm groups. It was also possible to update norms for local contexts based on the people who had been tested by a particular assessment practitioner.

The PLATO-based test system was used at a few universities, the South African Airways, Eskom, and the NIPR. The NIPR operated a computerized test room which initially had 14 terminals, and tested many of its vocational guidance clients using a computer. Due to sanctions that were imposed by overseas countries in an effort to force South Africa to dismantle apartheid, further developments were not possible and maintenance of the hardware became too expensive. Undoubtedly, the next wave of computerized test development that followed in South Africa was an attempt at overcoming the problems caused by sanctions.

Eskom as well as the NIPR still required a computerized testing system. At that time personal computers (PCs) became available. In 1986 the Computerized Testing Unit of the NIPR developed a new PC-based test system, commissioned by the United Building Society (now ABSA). The new system, called PsiTest, developed by Malcolm Coulter and Nanette Tredoux, eventually contained almost all the psychological and occupational tests in the NIPR and the Human Sciences Research Council (HSRC) catalogues. Eskom and ABSA used the system countrywide, as did a large number of private clients, and several universities used it in their counselling centres. Despite its relative simplicity by today's standards, the system was extremely secure, stable and reliable, and was used by major organisations well into the 1990s.

Also interesting, was the fact that the computerized PsiTest tests soon had more up-to-date norms than the paper-based versions of the tests. This information was never incorporated into the HSRC's paper-based test catalogue. In PsiTest, it was possible to collect response latency data, keep a record of the number of errors made and the number of corrections per item, as well as the number of response changes per item and per scale for multi-scale tests. This data provided important information – for example, one could see if test-takers were confused by particular items, or if they started rushing and answered questions carelessly towards the middle of the questionnaire. Help and on-screen instructions were interactive and context-sensitive (particularly for graphic tests). Reporting, however was primitive by today's standards and consisted largely of standard score profiles and item response statistics given in tabular form. Only one test, the Jung Personality

Questionnaire, had a narrative report, which was rather limited.

About a year into the development of PsiTest, the HSRC commissioned the SIEGMUND system through its Education group. The SIEGMUND system incorporated the tests developed by the HSRC's group Education. It administered and scored the tests but did not collect the detailed information on particular responses, and the security on the system was more basic. It was marketed differently, mainly to educational institutions and private practitioners.

One of the first Windows-based tests developed in South Africa was an in-basket type interactive work simulation developed for Liberty Life during 1993–1994 by Nanette Tredoux. Called PsiSim, this was separate from the PsiTest system, and operated in Windows. The 1990s also saw the development of computerized report-writing systems for existing tests. These were done by private entrepreneurs and of particular note was the report-writing system developed for the 16-PF questionnaire by Prof. Dan de Wet.

The early history of computer-based testing in South Africa was particularly impressive as the innovative South African test developers kept pace with, and sometimes set the pace in, the international arena in the drive to move assessment into the technological era. However, due to the political climate of the day, this promising start was not sustained to the same extent from the 1990s up to the present time.

14.2.2.2 Current perspective

In South Africa, as was the case elsewhere in the world, many of the available initial computer-based tests started off as **paper-based tests** (often also referred to as pencil-and-paper tests), which were computerized when appropriate technology became available (as outlined in Section 14.2.2.1). In most instances at present, both the paper-based and computer-based versions of commonly used international measures are available to assessment practitioners. Examples of such tests include the following: the Occupational Personality Questionnaire (OPQ), 15FQ+ Questionnaire, Myers-Briggs Type Indicator (MBTI), Jung Type Indicator (JTI), Customer Contact Styles Questionnaire (CCSQ), Occupational Interest Profile (OIP), Occupational Personality Profile (OPP), Graduate and General Reasoning Tests, and the Critical Reasoning Test Battery.

The first computer-based test battery developed in South Africa which dealt with ability measurement in an **adaptive** manner (see Section 13.3.1) was the Computerized Adaptive General Scholastic Aptitude Test (GSAT-Senior). This was created using all the items of the paper-based GSAT Senior (form A and B). It has been standardized for English- and-Afrikaans-speaking South Africans between the ages of 13 years 6 months and 18 years, although it can be used for adults as well (Claassen, De Beer, Ferndale, Kotze, Van Niekerk, Viljoen, and Vosloo, 1991; Pickworth, Von Mollendorf and Owen, 1996).

The Learning Potential Computerized Adaptive Test (LPCAT) is a further computer-adaptive measure that has been developed. It is a dynamic computerized adaptive test for the measurement of learning potential in the nonverbal figural reasoning domain (De Beer, 2005). The LPCAT was developed not only to assess the present level of general nonverbal reasoning performance, but also the projected future level of performance that the individual could attain if relevant training opportunities were provided. The information provided by the LPCAT scores therefore allows the assessment practitioner to assess the level to which a person could potentially be developed in terms of training and developmental opportunities (De Beer, 2000a,b; De Beer and Marais, 2002).

Within the career testing field, a new computerised interest inventory is being developed in South Africa and is due to be released in 2009. The Career Preference Computerised Adaptive Test (CPCAT) (de Beer, Marais, Maree and Skrzypczak, 2008) uses an adaptive three-dimensional model of career-related preferences based on career fields, activities and environments. The CPCAT can be used for career counselling in individual assessment, for screening and selection purposes and for development purposes. An innovative feature of the CPCAT is that it provides polar charts that indicate the match of the individual's against any selected profile to provide comparative information on the eight highest rated dimensions of the particular selected profile (current profession or applied for profession).

According to Kriek and Whitford (2006), about 300,000 Internet-delivered tests (IDT) are administered per month across the world, and there is a 40% increase in IDT in South Africa over the past two years. Currently most CBTs and IDTs used in South Africa are used in the personnel selection and training fields. The other field in which CBTs are being used with increased frequency is in neuropsychological assessment, but many of the measures have not been researched and adapted for the multicultural South African context yet.

In a survey conducted by the Human Sciences Research Council (HSRC), South African assessment practitioners expressed ambivalent feelings towards computer-based testing (Foxcroft, Paterson, Le Roux, and Herbst, 2004). On the one hand, some practitioners felt threatened by computer-based tests and expressed concern about how low levels of computer familiarity among test-takers would impact on the test scores. On the other hand, practitioners who have experienced the benefits of computer-based testing first hand, especially for large scale testing, complained about the fact that there are too few computerized tests available in South Africa. In this regard, it should be noted that the HSRC survey revealed that only 25% of the 25 most frequently used measures are computer-based or have a computer-based version. Furthermore, some of the unease among practitioners when it comes to using CBTs and IDTs could be linked to the fact that very few training programmes introduce trainee assessment practitioners to computer-based and Internet-delivered tests and testing. For example, Foxcroft (2007) reports that only 25% of the tests that Registered Counsellors and Psychometrists are exposed to during their training are CBTs, which appears to be far too low a percentage in the modern testing era. This led Foxcroft (2007) to query whether psychometric and psychological assessment training in South Africa is stuck in the classical tradition of testing, possibly because the lecturers were not exposed to CBT and IDT and thus continue to teach the paper-based measures they were exposed to in their training.

As computerized tests are being used more widely in South Africa, issues are arising in practice regarding the fairness of applying computer-based tests with technologically unsophisticated test-takers and the control of computer-and Internet-based tests (Fisher and Broom, 2006; Foxcroft, Seymour, Watson, and Davies, 2002). We will discuss these issues in Sections 14.3 and 14.4.

14.3 Evaluation of computer-based and Internet-delivered testing

14.3.1 Advantages and disadvantages of computer-based and Internet-delivered testing

14.3.1.1 Advantages of computer-based testing

Research evidence suggests that test-takers find computer-based assessment more enjoyable than traditional paper-based assessment (Eyde and Kowla, 1987; Foxcroft, Paterson, Le Roux, and Herbst, 2004; Foxcroft, Seymour, Watson, and Davies, 2002; Foxcroft, Watson, Greyling, and Streicher, 2001).

The advantages of administering tests by means of computers are established and well known and include the following:
- ultimate levels of standardization of assessment instructions are achieved;
- the potential biasing effect of the assessment practitioner is eliminated as the computer administers and scores the measure in an objective way;
- there is a reduction in the amount of time needed for the assessment;
- it provides the opportunity to obtain more information about test-takers (such as precisely recording and storing their response time to items), as well as providing instant scoring that allows for prompt feedback to both the assessment practitioners and test-takers;
- given the graphic capabilities of computers, it has become possible to measure spatial and perceptual abilities to a far greater extent than is possible with paper-based tests;
- computerized assessment is particularly suitable

for test-takers who have physical and neurological disabilities in that voice-activated and touch screen responses are possible;

- assessment can be individually tailored – this is particularly useful when groups of people are being assessed as the effects of cheating can be minimized;

- it provides the assessment practitioner with a greater element of control; if, for example, you want to limit the response time for any single item, the computer can easily be programmed to flash the item on the screen for a specific duration of time;

- fewer assessment practitioners and assessment assistants are needed during the administration of a computerized measure; this is cost-effective and less labour-intensive, and means that some assessment practitioners can be released for other activities;

- the errors that arise from inaccurate scoring by assessment practitioners are decreased when scoring is done by the computer; and

- computerized testing increases test security as test materials cannot be removed from the test room easily.

Another advantage of computerized assessment is that it creates the possibility for tailored or **adaptive assessment**. With **computerized adaptive (CAT)** assessment measures, the items are ordered according to level of difficulty. If the test-taker answers several items correctly at a certain level of difficulty, the test-taker is presented with items of greater difficulty, and *vice versa*. Through this process, the computer programme can determine the ability level of the test-taker in a short space of time. Adaptive testing therefore individualizes a test by adapting the level of item difficulty depending on the individual's response, which, in turn, reduces total testing time (Kaplan and Saccuzzo, 1997). This tailoring was made possible with the introduction of **Item Response Theory (IRT)** (Murphy and Davidshofer, 1994). You can turn to Chapters 6 and 7 (sections 7.4.2.2 and 7.4.2.3) for a discussion of IRT.

Clarke, Madaus, Horn and Ramos (2000) highlight that computer adaptive testing takes advantage of computer technology by adapting the test to suit the knowledge level or ability of the test-taker. Gregory (2007) argues that the advantages of computerized adaptive testing (CAT) are twofold, namely, that each test-take is assessed with the same level of precision as testing continues until the criterion has been met and that CAT is efficient as fewer items are needed than in conventional tests.

14.3.2 **Disadvantages of computer-based testing**

Although all of the testing environment problems associated with paper-based testing are relevant to computer-based testing as well (e.g. noise, temperature), it also includes a host of new ones. These include power conditions, machine availability hardware/software compatibility and capability, screen size and clarity, font characteristics, and line length and spacing (Leeson, 2006). Screen clarity is of particular interest as studies have suggested that computer screens take longer to read than printed materials (Kruk and Muter, 1984) although reading performance under high screen resolution conditions has been found to match reading performance on paper copies (Leeson, 2006). Furthermore, socio-cultural and linguistic factors influence the test-takers' ability to interact with the computer. Evers and Day (1997), for example, cite research indicating that the cultural environment in which people live influences the way in which they experience computer interfaces. Given the diversity of cultures in South Africa, the role of the cultural background of test-takers is particularly pertinent. Greyling (2000) notes that programmes that are developed for users from different cultural backgrounds and with different levels of computer expertise, create especially unique challenges for the interface designers of systems. Some of the design issues that are affected by culture are, for example, format conventions for numbers, dates, time, and currency, as well as the use of icons, symbols, and colours.

Bugbee and Bernt (1990) argue that computer equipment and performance is perhaps the greatest potential problem in this mode of testing. A unique yet serious problem with large-scale computerized testing is system failure, where the computers crash and testing is brought to a standstill. The equivalent problem in paper-based testing would be losing all the answer sheets before they were scored or recorded – something which is less likely to happen than a computer crash.

Further concerns and disadvantages of computerized assessment can be summarized as follows:

- concerns about copyright violation when measures are made available on the Internet;
- lack of security when measures are available on the Internet;
- problems of confidentiality, which could arise when unauthorized people gain access to large amounts of information stored on computers;
- computer-generated assessment reports still require skilled clinical judgement as far as interpretation is concerned – something which is often ignored by inexperienced assessment practitioners;
- computerized scoring routines may have errors or may be poorly validated; such problems are often difficult to detect within the software;
- computerized testing involves high costs in item development as a much larger item pool is required in order to address the issue of security and over-exposure of items, as well as technical issues associated with computerized adaptive testing;
- computerized assessment packages are sometimes unnecessarily costly and the psychometric properties of the computerized measures have not always been researched adequately as failuring to have the product on the market quickly places a financial burden on the test development company;
- vital qualitative information about test-taking behaviour and problem-solving strategies cannot be accessed readily during computerized assessment;
- human-computer interface issues arise in that test-takers, especially older adults, may have a phobia about using computers; this could raise their anxiety levels and, in turn, have a negative impact on their test performance;
- lack of computer sophistication (literacy) on the part of some of the test-takers could impact negatively on their performance; in this regard, there is a need to expose test-takers

to a practice session and a practice measure to provide them with sufficient time to familiarize themselves with the keyboard and using a computer, before the assessment takes place.

There is a wealth of literature which suggests that if test-takers are thoroughly prepared for the testing and familiarized with the computer beforehand, a lack of computer literacy has less impact on test performance (Powers and O'Neill, 1993; Taylor, Jamieson, Eignor, and Kirsch, 1998). However, within the South African context, where exposure to technology in general has been uneven and is greater for people from advantaged backgrounds than disadvantaged backgrounds, familiarizing test-takers with the computer and the requirements of the test may not necessarily remove all the potential adverse impact of a lack of computer literacy on test performance. Indeed, there are some indications that the level of technological sophistication impacts on test performance, with the performance of technologically less sophisticated test-takers being the most adversely affected (Fisher and Broom, 2006; Foxcroft, Watson, and Seymour, 2004).

Nonetheless, given the more widespread use of computers and information technology in the workplace, the increased access to computers in schools, and the widespread use of sophisticated cellular phones, exposure to technology is increasing in the South African society and the adverse impact on computer-based test performance is probably diminishing (Foxcroft, Watson, and Seymour, 2004). For example, Figure 14.1 highlights findings from Foxcroft (2004b) in which the performance of incoming student cohorts on a computer-based test battery was tracked over a three-year period. Two groups of students were identified each time, namely, those who were using a computer for the first time and those who were more familiar with using a computer. The various groups were matched according to culture, home language, gender, and school performance. You should note that all test-takers were provided with a practice session prior to testing in order to familiarize them with the computer requirements of the test. Furthermore, test-takers needed to use only the enter key and space bar to answer the multiple-choice questions.

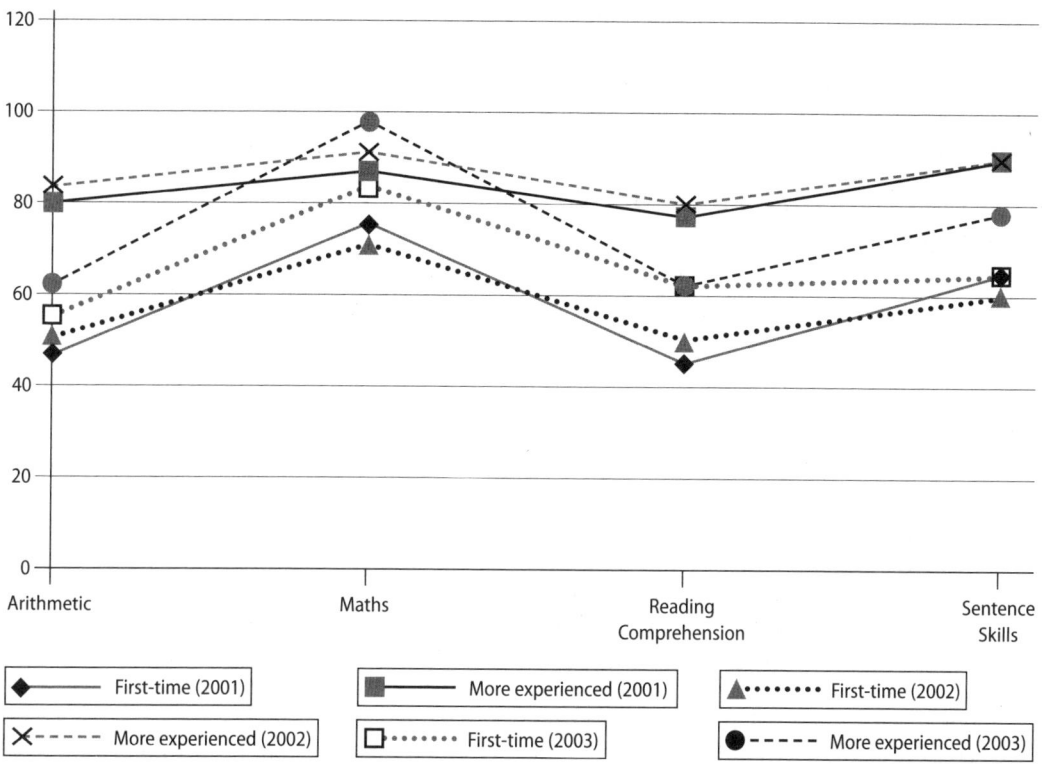

Figure 14.1 Comparison of performance of first-time and more experienced test-takers on computer-based tests

As you can see from the figure, while first-time computer-users performed significantly worse on the tests than the more experienced users in the 2001 and 2002 samples, the difference in the performances of the two groups was reduced and was no longer significant for the 2003 comparison, although the trend remained the same.

Conflicting results have been found in the literature regarding the influence of past computer experience on performance in computerized tests (Powers and O'Neill, 1993). Lee (1986) found, for example, that previous computer experience significantly affects performance on computerized tests, while Wise, Barnes, Harvey, and Plake (1989) and Gallagher, Bridgeman, and Cahalan (2000) found no direct relationship between computer familiarity and computerized test performance. However, it has been found consistently that familiarizing test-takers with computers and the requirements of taking a specific CBT reduces the disadvantage that test-takers who are less

familiar with computers may have (Lee, 1986; Powers and O'Neill, 1993; Taylor et al., 1998). Of interest is that Schaeffer (1995) remarks that, although research indicates that test-takers with little or no computer familiarity can learn to use a testing system effectively, not enough research has been conducted on test-takers who are not familiar with technology in general. Clearly, the findings of Foxcroft (2004b) support this view and in developing countries such as South Africa this line of research should be pursued. Furthermore, the findings concur with international findings (e.g. Leeson, 2006), where it has been reported that as computer technology becomes more accessible in a society, the impact of computer familiarity (or lack thereof) decreases.

It is also interesting to note that computer familiarity and literacy is not only an issue for test-takers in South Africa but also for assessment practitioners. In an HSRC survey about test use patterns, as mentioned earlier, some practitioners indicated that they feel threatened by computers due to their own low levels of computer literacy and that they consequently refrain from using computer-based tests (Foxcroft, Paterson, Le Roux, and Herbst, 2004).

14.3.2 Challenges of Internet-delivered testing

Bartram (2002) asserts that, in view of the fact that the Internet has become an integral part of the everyday lives of many people, Internet-delivered testing will increasingly become the medium of choice. He highlights the following challenges related to Internet-delivered testing:

- *Performance:* Although the Internet allows for the rapid delivery of tests, disrupted connections to the Internet sometimes result in testing being interrupted. In addition, timed testing cannot always be done in a reliable way via the Internet. Furthermore, given that there is not a standard web browser, available browsers display information in slightly different ways. Consequently, an Internet-delivered test will not have a consistent appearance on the screen as the appearance will vary depending on the browser used. Bartram (2002) argues that performance issues such as these can be overcome by downloading the test materials, although this might cause the assessment practitioner some frustration if the Internet connection is slow.

- *Security:* Internet-delivered testing has brought with it concerns regarding the security of the test, the test-taker's identity (both in terms of authenticating the test-taker's identity as well as preserving his/her identity), and test results.

- Bartram (2002) argues that in Internet-delivered testing test security is not a major concern as one of the advantages of using the Internet is that the test remains on the server of the test distributor and not on the computer of the assessment practitioner or the test-taker. The test distributor is also in a better position to exercise control over who is allowed access to the test (i.e. qualified and appropriately registered assessment practitioners) and to provide assessment practitioners with the most up-to-date version of the test.

- Authenticating the identity of the test-taker,

however, is a very real problem in Internet-delivered testing and has no easy solution. Although it is possible to limit access to the test by requiring a username and password and although there have been advances in identification technology (e.g. fingerprint recognition and retinal eye pattern recognition), such control is still not sufficient to confirm the identity of the test-taker and to check that cheating does not take place in high-stakes assessment in particular (e.g. job selection). Consequently, the presence of an assessment practitioner is still required, which poses some limitations on where the Internet-delivered testing can occur. While remote closed-circuit television (CCTV) monitoring may provide a solution, it will require dedicated, technologically well-equipped test centres where the authentication of the test-taker and the monitoring of the session can be controlled. Such test centres could minimize the number of assessment practitioners needed to supervise Internet-delivered test sessions.

- Before stepping off the point of test-taker authentication, it is important to realize that CBT and IDT have raised questions about whether a supervisor always needs to be present. In the classical testing tradition, test administration was either reasonably closely supervised in large scale group testing (known as the **supervised mode**), or highly supervised and controlled (**managed mode**) in individual and high stakes testing. CBT and IDT have introduced two other modes, namely, the **controlled mode** where there is no supervision but access to the tests taken is controlled via logon names and passwords, and the **open mode** where anyone can access and complete the test without supervision and there is no logon identification. While the open mode is not advocated, there is a growing body of research related to the controlled mode in terms of unproctored (unsupervised) Internet testing (UIT). While Tippins, Beaty, Drasgow, Gibson, Pearlman, Segall, and Shepherd (2006) conclude that the jury is still out on the widespread use of controlled UIT, they nonetheless conclude that while UIT is not appropriate for high stakes testing, it shows promise in employment selection when used to screen out applicants from a large pool but thereafter corroborating evidence *inter alia* in the form of test information gathered under supervised and highly supervised and controlled conditions is necessary before a decision is made to employ someone. In addition, there is a need for stringent research into the validity and reliability of a test administered in a controlled, unsupervised way over the Internet. The research to date has been promising. For example, in a South African study, Holtzhausen (2004) found that scale reliabilities and inter-correlations were not compromised by controlled UIT, and that the pattern of test performance and mean scores were essentially similar for the online unsupervised and the paper-based supervised versions of a measure.

- The data generated from an Internet-delivered test are stored on a central server, which allows for greater levels of security compared to data stored in filing cabinets by the various assessment practitioners. The centralised storage of data makes it easier to manage the data and to make it available for research and development purposes. The test-taker should agree to all arrangements related to where the data will be stored and who will have access to it before the test session commences.

- *Fairness:* Concern has been expressed about the so-called 'digital divide' between those with access to computer technology and those without it. Test-takers who have not had access to computer technology and the Internet are likely to be disadvantaged by this, which could impact on their test performance and thus raise issues of fairness and bias. Consequently, test distributors and assessment practitioners should try to obtain up-to-date information about the equality of access for the various client groups that they serve. Where equality of access is an issue, alternative assessment measures need to be used. While the latter is the fairest way of dealing with the problem as seen from the test-taker's perspective, it complicates matters for assessment practitioners in the recruitment and selection field in particular as it will re-

duce the speed at which the test-taker can be assessed.

14.3.3 **Computer-based test interpretation and reporting**

Since the beginning of the twenty-first century, computer-based test interpretation (CBTI) systems have been commercially available for most tests. The CBTI programmes are generally developed following either a clinical or a statistical approach (Aiken, 2002). In the clinical approach, the programme attempts to mirror the clinical and psychodiagnostic judgement of experienced clinicians. In the statistical approach, interpretations are based on research findings related to differences between two contrasting groups of people. Sometimes a combination of the two approaches is used.

Some CBTI systems provide the practitioner with the ability to choose the norm group to be used in generating the report, and even to create and update their own norms. This has considerable advantages. One of the positive aspects of CBTI reports is that these can sometimes alert the assessment practitioner to certain implications of test scores that they might not have noticed. However, over the years, queries have been raised regarding the validity of CBTI systems and reports. The main concern relates to the fact that these have not been comprehensively validated and that they are based on inadequate norms and research findings. Reliability is sometimes also problematic with CBTI systems. Consequently, assessment practitioners should ensure that the supporting documentation provided with the CBTI system contains adequate validity, reliability, and normative information. In this regard, the test evaluation system developed by the European Federation of Psychologists Associations (EFPA) highlights the nature and standard of validity and reliability information required for CBTI systems (http://www.efpa.be/).

Furthermore, assessment practitioners should not attach so much value to CBTI reports that they use them as a substitute for their clinical judgement. Instead, practitioners should supplement and complement the CBTI report with information from other sources as well as their own observation, before using their clinical judgement to formulate their own understanding or opinion of the client's functioning. In addition, the assessment practitioner should sign the modified report on the test as this indicates that he/she takes personal responsibility for the contents of the report.

›› CRITICAL THINKING CHALLENGE 14.1

As part of a skills development initiative, the CEO of a large company wanted to start a career development programme for employees. He wanted his employees to have access to career measures that would help them to understand themselves and map their career path. As all his employees had a computer linked to a network with the necessary in-built security (e.g., password protected), he decided to load the Myers-Briggs Type Indicator (MBTI) onto the network. Employees could access the MBTI on their computer by using a unique password given to each one by the Human Resources Department. The computer programme explained the test to the employees after which the employees then completed the test items. The answers were sent to a counsellor in the Human Resources Department. She ran the scoring programme and generated the test interpretation report. This report was then e-mailed to the employee, with the offer that he/she could make an appointment to discuss the results with the counsellor if needs be.

- What are the advantages and disadvantages of using computer-based testing in this example?
- What are the advantages and disadvantages of computer-based test interpretation (CBTI) in this example?
- What other information besides test information could have helped these employees to gain insight into their career development? (Hint: You should be able to get some ideas from Chapter 13).

14.4 Good practices in using computer-based and Internet-delivered testing

As is the case with traditional paper-based tests, the use of computer-based and Internet-delivered testing is subject to the same ethical, professional, and legal standards that govern psychological as-

sessment in general. We discussed these standards in Chapter 8 in detail. However, computer-based and Internet-delivered testing have highlighted a number of unique ethical, professional, and legal issues. This has resulted in the development of separate sets of guidelines to assist assessment practitioners in addressing these issues.

In this section we will focus on some of the ethical issues related to computer-based and Internet-delivered testing as well as guidelines for addressing them in practice.

14.4.1 Who can administer and use computer-based and Internet-delivered psychological tests in South Africa?

Although computer-based and Internet-delivered psychological tests are highly structured and are administered and scored in an automated way, they must be used (administered, interpreted, and reported on) by appropriately registered psychology professionals. Why? Think back to the discussion in Chapter 8 in which we pointed out that psychological tests are under statutory control in South Africa. This implies that only an appropriately registered psychology professional may use psychological tests. The ethical code for psychology specifies that assessment must always be done within the context of a clearly defined professional relationship. Administering a psychological test via the computer or Internet does not change the fact that all the conditions that apply regarding who may use psychological tests also apply to computer-based tests. It can be argued that computer-based psychological tests need to be used by appropriate psychology professionals for the following reasons:

- Not all test-takers are sufficiently familiar with computers; the assessment practitioner should recognize this and offer an alternative mode of testing where necessary.
- The professional in control of the test session needs to be able to manage contingencies as they arise in a professional manner (e.g. managing test-taker anxiety or power failures).
- Computer-based test interpretation reports contain highly sensitive and professional information that needs to be handled by a professional.

- Observation of test behaviour is a valuable source of information. Such observation is best done by a trained professional as opposed to a mere test administrator.

Nonetheless, we need to be mindful of the fact that in the modern testing era, the availability of online testing has contributed to the internationalization of assessment in that measures can be delivered from almost anywhere in the world to almost anywhere in the world. This has posed challenges related to the different regulations in place for controlling and using tests in different countries. Consequently, this has:

> raised the need for there to be some international agreement on standards of best practice related to testing over the Internet. Individual countries and their professional associations are no longer closed systems that can set regulations about testing independent of what is happening in the world around them. (Bartram, 2006, 121-122)

Consequently, although the Health Professions Act currently requires that only appropriate psychology professions can use computer-based and Internet-delivered psychological measures, as research into unsupervised Internet testing (UIT) and test-taker authentication produces a more consistent body of findings, it might be necessary in time to critically evaluate whether our current regulations are still appropriate for the modern testing era.

14.4.2 **Good practice guidelines for computer-based and Internet-delivered testing**

Various guidelines have been produced internationally by psychological associations over the years (e.g. the American Psychological Association, the British Psychological Association). The International Test Commission (ITC) has synthesized the various guidelines in existence and expanded them so as to produce a truly international set of guidelines. The ITC's *Guidelines for Computer-based and Internet-delivered Testing* were released in

2006 and are available at http://www.intestcom. org. According to the ITC guidelines, assessment practitioners who use computer-based and Internet-delivered testing need to do the following:
- give due regard to technological issues in computer-based (CBT) and Internet testing;
- attend to quality issues in CBT and Internet testing;
- provide appropriate levels of control over the test conditions; and
- make appropriate provision for security and safeguard privacy in CBT and Internet testing.

Specific competencies associated with each of these four aspects are explained in the ITC guidelines for test developers, test publishers, and assessment practitioners.

While the South African adaptation of the ITC's guidelines on computer-based and Internet-delivered testing (2006) is still in draft form, the following good practice guidelines represent the minimum professional and ethical standards that South African assessment practitioners should adhere to when using computer-based and Internet-delivered tests:
- Ensure that the practitioners themselves have the competence to use computer-based and Internet-delivered tests.
- Establish the potential utility of the computer-based test.
- Choose a technically (psychometrically) sound computer-based test that has been evaluated and classified by the Psychometrics Committee of the Professional Board for Psychology.
- Check for equivalence of paper- and computer-based versions, especially if the two versions are to be used interchangeably.
- Give consideration to human factors and issues of fairness when using a computer-based test. Where test-takers have low levels of computer familiarity or have certain neurological or physical problems that make computer-administered testing unsuitable, assessment practitioners should offer them an alternative, paper-based option.
- Prepare test-takers appropriately through practice tutorials or tests.
- Verify the identity of test-takers. This is especially

important for Internet-delivered testing.

- Closely supervise the administration of the computer-based test so as to provide appropriate support to the test-taker during the session.
- Psychology professionals in South Africa are not permitted to allow test-takers to complete unsupervised psychological tests via the Internet. A professional needs to be in attendance at all times, even for Internet-delivered testing, as it is illegal for a paper-based, computer-based, or Internet-delivered psychological test to be administered by anyone other than a psychology professional registered with the HPCSA.
- Ensure that contingency plans are in place if technology fails. For example, switch to a paper-based test if is equivalent to the computer-based version.
- Ensure that the computer-based test is securely stored.
- Check the computer scoring system and the accuracy of the classification system used to generate reports.
- Interpret results appropriately and be aware of the limitations of computer-based test interpretation (CBTI) systems. Modify the report where necessary and complement it with additional information before signing (and thus professionally owning) it.
- Ensure that the results are securely stored.
- Debrief test-takers. This is especially important if test-takers became anxious as a result of having to use computer technology to complete the test.

The South African guidelines, once finalised, will be available at the following web site: http://www.hpcsa.org.za.

The use of computer-based and Internet-delivered testing poses challenges for professional training programmes in South Africa. To date, as was pointed out in 14.2.2.2, very few training programmes cover such testing in a comprehensive way. If the next generation of psychology professionals are to enhance their assessment practice with the innovations offered by computer-based and Internet-delivered testing, they would require appropriate training in, among others, the following aspects:

- information literacy;
- the development, advantages and disadvantages of, and issues in computer-based and Internet-delivered testing;
- the professional practice standards that need to be adhered to in computer-based and Internet-delivered testing; and
- experience in using computer-based and Internet-delivered tests and computer-based test interpretation (CBTI) systems.

In the test use survey conducted by the HSRC, participants indicated that, other than skilling new professionals by means of training in computer-based and Internet-delivered testing, experienced assessment practitioners also had a need for such re-skilling (Foxcroft, Paterson, Le Roux, and Herbst, 2004). This could be done through offering continuing professional development workshops on computer-based and Internet-delivered testing.

You should note that test publishers also need to adhere to certain guidelines to ensure that only people who are legally and professionally permitted to use psychological tests gain access to computer-based and Internet-delivered tests. Among other things, test distributors should ensure that computer-based and Internet-delivered tests may only be marketed on the Internet to psychology professionals who are allowed to use them. A mechanism which can verify whether the prospective user is legally permitted to use the test therefore needs to be available and a signature must be obtained from the user.

14.5 New horizons (including multimedia)

As the rapid advancement in and expansion of computer technology is likely to continue, further innovations in assessment measures are likely to come to the fore. In this regard, Parshall, Spray, Kalohn, and Davey (2002) have developed a five-dimension framework for understanding and driving innovation in computer-based assessment. Their innovation framework includes:

- *Innovations in item format*: This relates specifically to the type of responses made by the test-taker. For example, whether the test-taker must select a response (e.g. in a multiple-choice item) or construct a response (e.g. in an essay or when completing a spreadsheet).

- *Innovations in response action:* This relates to the way in which the test-taker must respond to an item, for example, by using a mouse to click on a bubble or by making use of a drag-and-drop function.
- *Innovations in media inclusion:* This entails the increasing use of non-text stimuli such as colour photographs, audio and video clips, and virtual reality simulations.
- *Innovations in extent of interactivity:* This refers to the extent to which the test architecture 'reacts' to the response of the test-taker, as is done, for example, in the case of computerized adaptive testing.
- *Innovations in scoring methods:* There are increasing ways in which the test-taker's responses can be converted into quantitative scores. For example, the number of correct answers can be added up, item response theory can be used to score computerized adaptive tests, and sophisticated algorithms can be used to score essays.

In addition to these five innovations, Drasgow (2002) adds a further one, namely:

- *Authenticity:* Innovative item types try to emulate real-world tasks, which make them more authentic in the eyes of the test-taker. The following are some examples of innovative items types: constructed response item types in which the test-takers enter formulae as their answers in a mathematics test; drag-and-connect item types in which objects are dropped and connected in a flowchart or where the test-taker drags a phrase or sentence and drops it into a passage or paragraph; items that involve editing text; the use of small simulations (or simettes) that simulate client interactions or computer-based case simulations where the test-taker can request case history information, suggest treatments, and evaluate their effectiveness, and so on; and the use of video clips of a social situation to assess interpersonal skills.

The innovations highlighted above as well as many others that will appear in the next decade have the potential to not only make assessment more authentic, or real-world in nature, but will also enable practitioners to measure aspects that have been difficult to assess via paper-based measures to date (e.g. interpersonal skills).

In closing, Messick (1988), when considering the profound impact that computers and audiovisual technology could have on our conceptualization of assessment over subsequent decades, concluded that

… although the modes and methods of measurement may change, the basic maxims of measurement, and especially of validity, will retain their essential character. The key validity issues are the interpretability, relevance, and utility of scores, the import or value implications of scores as a basis for action, and the functional worth of scores in terms of social consequences of their use. (p. 33)

Despite the many advantages of computer-based and Internet-delivered testing, assessment practitioners need to be careful not to be so dazzled by the technology that they forget that the value of any test, whether it is paper- or computer-based, lies in its appropriateness for the intended purpose, its suitability in relation to the characteristics of the intended test-takers, and its psychometric soundness.

This was the last stop in the *Types-of-Measures Zone*. Here are a few web sites where you can obtain additional information on, and evaluations of, assessment measures – http://www.unl.edu/buros (Buros Institute of Mental Measurement), http://www.cua.edu/www/eric.ae (ERIC Clearinghouse on Assessment and Evaluation), and http://www.cse.ucla.edu (National Center for Research on Evaluation, Standards, and Student Testing).

As you look back over this zone, there are a number of critical concepts that you should have grasped. By answering the following questions you will be able to assess whether you have mastered the critical concepts.

CHECKING YOUR PROGRESS **14.1**

14.1 What is intelligence?

14.2 How can cognitive functioning be assessed? Provide some examples of both individual and group measures of general cognitive functioning and specific cognitive functions.

14.3 How can affect, adjustment, and coping be assessed? Give some examples of measures.

14.4 What is personality and how can its various dimensions be assessed? Give some examples of different types of personality measures.

14.5 What is career assessment? Give some examples of the measures used in career assessment.

14.6 Explain what is meant by the terms 'computer-based tests', 'Internet-delivered testing', and 'computerized adaptive tests', and highlight some of the advantages and disadvantages of such testing.

14.7 Discuss some of the professional practice guidelines that South African practitioners should follow when using computer-based and Internet-delivered tests.

The final stretch of the journey lies ahead. You will be travelling in the *Assessment Practice Zone* again, where you will learn to apply what you have learnt to the everyday practice of assessment.

Assessment
Practice Zone (2)

We are now in Part 2 of the Assessment Practice Zone and you are now entering the final section of your journey! There is still quite a lot to be seen and digested at the remaining stops.

Part

4

15 You will explore how the different types of measures to which you have been introduced are applied in a variety of contexts.

16 You will explore issues related to interpreting measures and reporting on assessment results.

17 You will investigate the factors that influence the outcome of an assessment.

18 And finally ... you will be able to take a peak at some of the future perspectives in assessment. Enjoy the rest of the journey!

The use of assessment measures in various applied contexts

GERT ROODT, LOUISE STROUD, CHERYL FOXCROFT, AND DIANE ELKONIN

Chapter

15

CHAPTER OUTCOMES

In this chapter, you will be required to draw on your knowledge of fair and ethical assessment practices (covered in Chapters 1, 7, 8, 9 and 14) and the cognitive, affective, personality, interest, and career measures that were covered in Chapters 10 to 13 of the Types-of-Measures Zone. In this chapter, we will discuss how these and other measures are applied in certain contexts. At the end of this chapter you will be able to:

> explain how psychological assessment is applied in industry;
> explain what developmental assessment is, what functions are assessed, and the different types of measures used;
> explain how assessment measures are used in education contexts; and
> understand how psychological assessment is used for psychodiagnostic purposes in a variety of contexts.

15.1 Assessment in industry

Assessment in industry can be divided into three broad areas. The first area is concerned with the psychological measurement of attributes of individuals in the workplace. Most assessment measures used for this purpose can be classified as psychological measures or techniques. The second and the third areas are respectively concerned with the assessment of groups and organizations. In the latter two cases, the measures used are not necessarily classified as psychological measures, although the principles of test construction (psychometric theory) are used in their development.

15.1.1 Assessment of individuals

Individuals in the workplace are assessed for various reasons. The goals of individual assessment are the following:

- firstly, to assess individual differences for selection and employment purposes; and
- secondly, to assess inter- and intra-individual differences for placement, training, and development as well as compensation and reward purposes.

Psychological measures or other assessment instruments that comply with the reliability and validity requirements are used in personnel selection, performance appraisal, situational tests, and assessment centres. We will discuss each of these contexts briefly.

15.1.1.1 Personnel selection

Perhaps the most widely used function of psychological measures in industry is to assist in screening, selection and employment decisions. Psychological assessment measures generate useful data that supplement other sources of personal information about a candidate, such as biographic information, work history, personal references and interview information. Other initial screening devices listed by Cascio and Aguinis (2005) are honesty (integrity) tests (see Chapter 17); Weighted Application Blanks or Biographical Information Blanks; drug tests and even polygraph tests.

Basically, two approaches are used in the application of psychological measures for selection purposes. In the first instance, individuals are compared with the job specifications in terms of their personal characteristics or personality traits. This approach is called an **input-based approach** because individuals are matched with what is required from a job. This approach is also referred to as the psychometric evaluation or testing approach. For instance, a fisherman must have tenacity, patience, and the ability to resist boredom. What do you think the requirements are for a driver of a passenger bus? Several psychological assessment measures can be used to assess these characteristics or traits. Personality, aptitude and ability tests come to mind that can assess these characteristics, traits or job requirements in a reliable and valid manner. Other measures listed by Cascio and Aguinis (2005) in this regard are projective techniques, personal history data and peer assessments. We will not discuss these measures in detail here since they have already been discussed in more depth in other chapters of this book.

The second approach is an **output-based approach** where individuals are compared in relation to the required output standards of a job. In this instance, the aim is to determine whether the individual has the necessary competencies to perform a particular task or job. This approach is also referred to as the **competency assessment** approach. The ability to read fluently, to write, to operate a lathe, or to drive a vehicle skilfully are all examples of competencies that might be required to perform a particular job. What competencies do you think are required to lead a specialist police reaction team that deals with abductions and hostages? Measures that are used to assess a person's competencies reliably and validly are not normally classified as psychological measures, although they should nonetheless be reliable and valid competency assessments.

The basic assumptions underlying these two assessment approaches are fundamentally different. In the first approach, a predictive approach is followed where personal characteristics are matched with job requirements or specifications. In the latter approach a person's competencies are assessed in order to determine whether they meet minimum performance criteria or standards. The challenge in both these approaches, however, remains to address the issues around bias and adverse impact. All assessment measures have to demonstrate that they are neither biased or showing any adverse impact when applied in a multi-cultural or in a diversity context.

Some categories of these measures will be discussed in the next sections.

15.1.1.2 **Performance ratings or assessment**

Psychometric theory is also applied in the assessment or rating of a person's job performance. Again, we have input- and output-based approaches. The **input-approach** refers to the evaluation of a person's input, such as personality traits, personal attributes, or characteristics that are important for achieving high performance standards in a job. In the **output-approach** only those job competencies as specified by the job requirements are assessed.

When performance appraisals are conducted, they should be reliable and valid. For this reason, the performance assessment measures are based on psychometric principles and are evaluated for reliability and validity. It has been found that the use of multiple assessors in performance reviews normally results in more reliable and valid assessments. Lately, the use of the so-called **360-degree competency** assessments (Theron and Roodt, 1999, 2000), as opposed to the traditional, single performance appraisal where a ratee's performance is only rated by a single rater, is gaining ground.

15.1.1.3 **Situational tests**

There is a wide range of different situational techniques and measures that can be used for making employment decisions. Most of these situational tests are also used in the **Assessment Centre** or **Situational Judgement Test** context. Both Assessment Centres and Situational Judgement Tests (Lievens, 2006) have gained popularity in the recent past for making selection and employment decisions. The face validity of these assessment techniques plays a major role in this state of affairs. We will discuss some of these techniques briefly below:

Simulations (role play)

Simulations attempt to recreate an everyday work situation. Participants are then requested to play a particular role and to deal with a specific problem. Other role players are instructed to play certain fixed roles in order to create consistency in different simulations. Trained observers observe the candidate to assess specified behavioural dimensions. Reliability and validity of simulations can vary according to the training and experience of observers, knowledge of the behaviours that need to be observed, and the consistency of the other role players.

Vignettes

Vignettes are similar to simulations but are based on a video or film presentation in which the candidate is requested to play the role of a particular person (such as the supervisor or manager) and to deal with the problem. Vignettes are more consistent in terms of the presentation of the scenario than simulations, but are open to many possible solutions from which a candidate may choose.

Leaderless group exercises

In this instance, a group of candidates is requested to perform a particular task or to deal with a specific problem while being observed. Trained observers rate the leadership qualities and other behavioural dimensions that the candidates display during their interactions.

In-basket tests

The **in-basket** test typically consists of a number of typical letters, memos, and reports that the average manager or supervisor confronts in his/her in-basket or these days in their e-mail inbox. The candidate is requested to deal with the correspondence in an optimal way. The responses of the candidate are then evaluated by a trained observer.

Interviews

Interviews can either be classified as structured or unstructured. In the **structured interview**, there is a clearly defined interview schedule which specifies the content and the order of questions during the interview. The responses to specific questions may also be closed or fixed, meaning that the respondent has to choose between a limited number of provided options. Questions are normally structured in such a way that they elicit specific reactions or responses from the candidate which are then evaluated for appropriateness. Such structured interviews may still yield highly reliable results as was found with the use of structured, competency rating interviews (Cronbach Alpha = 0,94) (Roodt, 2007).

Unstructured interviews do not have any particular schedule and lack the structure and order of the structured interview. Responses to questions may in this instance be totally open. Trained interviewers (such as experienced psychologists) can still elicit valuable information from such unstructured interviews.

A word of caution should be raised against the use of unstructured interviews (conducted by unqualified and/or inexperienced persons) for screening, selection and employment decision purposes. In many organizations the dominant (or even unlawful) practice of conducting employment interviews and to solely base employment decisions on the outcomes of such interviews, still remains. Can the people who are conducting such interviews provide you with evidence on such interviews' reliability and validity? The function of employment interviews therefore is to supplement other assessment data and to verify other outstanding or contradicting information.

All the above-mentioned situational tests should still comply with the requirements of reliability and validity as specified in the Employment Equity Act. This can be achieved by the training of raters, the selection of content valid exercises or simulations, standardized assessment procedures, and standardized stimuli (settings). Ultimately, assessment practitioners also have to conduct reliability and validity analyses on their assessment data in order to provide validation evidence.

15.1.1.4 Assessment centres

Assessment centres (ACs) are best described as a combination of the above-mentioned exercises (role plays, simulations, in-basket tests, and leaderless group exercises) where candidates are observed by a number of trained observers for specified behavioural dimensions applicable in a specific job (e.g. that of a manager or a supervisor). The International Guidelines (2000, p. 2) define ACs as consisting of:

A standardized evaluation of behaviour based on multiple inputs. Several trained observers and techniques are used. Judgements about behaviour are made, in major part, from specifically developed assessment simulations. These judgements are pooled in a meeting among the assessors or by a statistical integration process. In an integration discussion, comprehensive accounts of behaviour, and often ratings of it, are pooled. The discussion results in evaluations of the performance of the assessees on the dimensions/competencies or other variables that the assessment center is designed to measure. Statistical combination methods should be validated in accordance with professionally accepted standards.

Schlebusch and Roodt (2008, p. 2) again define ACs as a simulation-based process employing multiple assessment techniques and multiple assessors to produce judgements regarding the extent to which a participant displays selected competencies required to perform a job effectively. ACs are usually employed for development or selection purposes. Several variations exist within these two broad categories. Schlebusch and Roodt argue that a more structured and systematic approach towards AC design, development, implementation, and evaluation could enhance their reliability and validity.

ACs have gained in popularity in recent times because of their high face validity. Candidates can relate to the exercises and simulations because they perceive them as relevant and appropriate in the work context. A word of caution, however, needs to be expressed. ACs must be evaluated in terms of their content validity, the training and experience of observers, the selection of exercises, and the predictive validity of these centres. Schlebusch and Roodt (2008) provided a number of practical suggestions on improving the reliability and validity of ACs. These suggestions relate to improving the consistency of:

1. the context in which ACs are conducted;
2. the presentation of the simulations;
3. the administration and observation processes; and
4. the role plays and performance of the role players.

The more consistent ACs are conducted, the less the error variance that will occur across different applications.

Pietersen (1992), some years ago, cautioned users and supporters of ACs and called for a moratorium on the use of ACs. His plea was based on the relatively poor predictive validity of ACs at the point in time. However, recent developments in more sophisticated research methods (such as structural equation modelling and meta analyses) have led to more conclusive evidence that AC scores validly predict (Thornton and Rupp, 2006) and explain a substantial amount of variance in job performance (Ones, 2008).

15.1.2 **Assessment of workgroups or work teams**

As indicated earlier, the second broad category of assessment is focused on the assessment of workgroups or work teams (or sub-groups such as dyads and triads) in terms of their unique processes, characteristics and structures (also refer to Van Tonder and Roodt (2008) in this regard). These types of assessments are mainly used for diagnostic and development purposes and are not classified as psychological measures, but would most probably yield more valuable results in the hands of an experienced industrial psychologist.

Let us first explain what is meant by the terms processes, characteristics and structures in a group context:

- **Group Processes:** Aspects such as leadership, conflict-handling (Rahim, 1989), negotiation, communication, group dynamics, and decision-making are some of the group processes that can be assessed. Other relevant group behavioural processes that can be assessed are group think or group shift, power in groups and conformity to group norms.
- **Group Characteristics:** Groups can be assessed and categorized in terms of their own unique characteristics, such as their level of cohesion, group development stages, dominant leadership style, conflict handling and negotiation styles, level of trust or group effectiveness criteria.
- **Group Structure:** Groups can also be assessed in terms of their structure, such as the status of members in terms of their primary reference group (in-group or out-group), their respec-

tive team roles in the group, their sociometry (social networks or interaction patterns) (Hart and Nath, 1979) and their different status levels within the group or within sub-groups.

The results obtained from group assessments are used for inter-group or even intra-group comparisons. Although groups are the targets for assessment, the assessment data are still obtained at an individual level. In other words, subjective individual assessments are collated to describe group processes, characteristics or structures. Measures used to assess group processes, characteristics and structures have to be based on sound psychometric principles in order to be reliable and valid.

15.1.3 **Assessment of organizations**

As indicated before, the third broad category of assessment focuses on the assessment of organizations (or organizational sub-units such as sections or divisions) in terms of their unique processes, characteristics and structures (also refer to Van Tonder and Roodt (2008) in this respect). This group of assessments is also largely used for diagnostic and development purposes and are also not classified as psychological measures. But these measures would also yield more valuable results in the hands of an experienced industrial psychologist.

We need to explain first what is meant by the terms organizational processes, characteristics, and structures in an organizational context:

- **Processes:** Processes such as organizational communication, corporate climate and culture (e.g. Van der Post, De Coning and Smit, 1997; Dannhauser and Roodt, 2001), and organizational socialization (e.g. Storm and Roodt, 2002) and mentoring (e.g. Janse van Rensburg and Roodt, 2005), as well as organizational change processes (e.g. Kinnear and Roodt, 1998; Coetzee, Fourie and Roodt, 2002) are some of the organizational processes that can be assessed.
- Other behavioural processes such as work alienation, employee engagement, job involvement, burn-out, work stress, organizational commitment as well as stereotyping and prejudice are relevant behavioural processes in

the organizational context. A host of local and international measures exist (too many to list) that can assess these processes.

- **Characteristics** Organizations can also be evaluated in terms of their identity, strategic style, the organizational effectiveness criteria they choose to use, their organizational policies, practices and procedures as well as other similar characteristics.
- **Structure** Organizations can be evaluated in terms of the different design options and their different structural configurations, as well as the operating model or value discipline they wish to adhere to (Potgieter and Roodt, 2004).

The results obtained from organizational assessments are used for inter-organizational comparisons or even intra-organizational comparisons.

Although organizations are the targets for assessment in this instance, the assessment data are still obtained at an individual level. In other words, subjective individual assessments are collated to describe an organizational process, characteristic or structure. Measures used to assess organizational processes, characteristics, and structures also have to be based on sound psychometric principles in order to be reliable and valid.

15.1.4 **Organizational research opportunities**

Knowledge of psychometric theory is useful in industry as far as the application and refinement of psychological assessment measures for assessing individual (and intra-individual) differences, are concerned. Furthermore, knowledge related to psychological measurement can also be applied to the assessment of group and organizational characteristics, processes, and structures in a valid and reliable way. In this regard, many research opportunities present themselves as there is a lack of research into measures that tap group and organizational processes, characteristics, and structures.

>> CRITICAL THINKING CHALLENGE **15.1**

You work in the human resources section of a large motor manufacturing company. You are asked to assess a team of engineers who design new cars to as-
certain how they handle conflict. Using your knowledge of different types of assessment measures as well as your knowledge about the basic principles of psychological measurement, how would you set about this assessment? What measures and techniques, both psychological and other, would you use and what would you do to ensure the validity and reliability of your assessment findings?

15.2 **Infant and pre-school developmental assessment**

Imagine a one-week-old baby. What do you think such a small infant can and cannot do? Perhaps, at this age, you would expect the baby to be able to suck from a bottle, or the mother's breast; to grasp your finger; and to turn its head towards you when you touch its cheek. You would certainly not expect a one-week-old infant to sit up and talk to you or walk over to you and, when hungry, ask you for a sandwich. You would, however, expect such behaviour of a three-year-old child. These observed changes in behaviour that take place over time are referred to as developmental changes, and provide us with guidelines to judge whether a child's behaviour is age-appropriate or not.

Just as you have observed developmental changes in children, many others have also done so and some of them have become well known for their theories of human development. Undoubtedly, one of the most prominent of these was Charles Darwin (1809–1882) who is hailed by many as the scientific father of child development. Although the long-term impact of Darwin's contribution has been seriously questioned by critics (e.g. Charlesworth, 1992), there is, however, sufficient evidence to support the fact that his work provided a catalyst for a number of renowned developmental psychologists (e.g. Stanley Hall, Arnold Gesell, Jean Piaget, and Sigmund Freud), whose theories form the basis of measures designed to assess the age-appropriateness of an infant or child's development.

15.2.1 **Why do we assess development?**

Long before scientific studies of children were carried out, it was an accepted fact that the early years are critical in the child's development. This was expressed in the old Chinese proverb, 'As the twig is bent, so the tree's inclined'. In a more poetic way, Milton expressed the same fact when he wrote, 'childhood shows the man, as morning shows the day' (Hurlock, 1978, p. 25). The growth and development that occurs during these early years of childhood has a significant impact on later development (Luiz, 1997). Since the early 1970s it has been internationally recognized that the identification of children with difficulties should take place as early as possible. These difficulties cover a vast spectrum and range, from difficulties of movement to difficulties of speech. Thus, the rationale for assessing a child's development at an early age is simple: the sooner a child's difficulties can be identified, the sooner an intervention can be implemented and, hence, the sooner a child can be assisted. Considering the South African history and current context, there are many children who do not have access to adequate resources and learning opportunities and thus fall within the disadvantaged bracket. Without some form of assessment, these children may go unnoticed and their developmental difficulties only be detected when they fail to master the developmental milestones. It may prove more challenging to intervene in the older child's life and sadly the window of opportunity may be missed. Therefore, the goal of early childhood assessment within the South African context should be to 'acquire information and understanding that will facilitate the child's development and functional abilities within the family and community' (Shonkoff and Meisels, 2000, p. 232). Greenspan and Meisels (1996) define developmental assessment as 'a process designed to deepen the understanding of a child's competencies and resources, and of the care-giving and learning environments most likely to help a child make fullest use of his or her developmental potential' (p. 11).

15.2.2 **What functions do we assess?**

Brooks-Gunn (1990), in her book entitled *Improving the Life Chances of Children at Risk*, stressed that the measurement of the well-being of a child includes the assessment of physical, cognitive, social, and emotional development. Thus, a compre-

hensive developmental assessment should include these four aspects of functioning, which are not mutually exclusive. A problem in one area may have an effect on another area. For example, a socially and emotionally deprived child may present with delayed cognitive development as a result of the lack of social and emotional stimulation. However, if this problem is detected at an early age and the child is provided with intensive stimulation, the cognitive deficit may disappear after a period of time. The holistic view of child development cannot be emphasized enough, and by implication a holistic perspective to the developmental assessment of South African children is vital in view of the poor social conditions the majority of South African children are experiencing (Luiz, 1994).

15.2.3 **How do we assess?**

Developmental measures can be categorized as either **screening** or **diagnostic** measures. **Developmental screening** involves 'a brief, formal evaluation of developmental skills' (Squires, Nickel, and Eisert, 1996), which attempts to identify children who may be potentially at risk for developmental difficulties. Some screening measures can be administered by non-specialists (e.g. parents, educators, clinic nurses) who have been trained to use them. In comparison to screening measures, **diagnostic measures** can be described as in-depth, comprehensive, individual, holistic measures used by trained professionals. The aim of diagnostic measures is to identify the existence, nature, and severity of the problem.

As with diagnostic measures, **screening measures** often assess a child holistically. Typically, they examine areas such as fine and gross motor coordination, memory of visual sequences, verbal expression, language comprehension, social-emotional status, and so on. Screening measures are cost effective as children can be effectively assessed in a short space of time. The results from screening measures are generally qualitative in nature, in that they categorize the child's performance, rather than provide a numerical score (Foxcroft, 1997). Furthermore, screening measures usually provide an overall view of the child's development, rather than information relating to specific areas. **Comprehensive diagnostic measures**, on the other hand, provide numerical scores and/or age equivalents for overall performance as well as for each specific area assessed. As both types of measures have advantages and disadvantages, any comprehensive plan of developmental assessment should incorporate both screening and diagnostic instruments (Brooks-Gunn, 1990).

15.2.4 What developmental measures are available for South African children?

What is the state of developmental assessment in South Africa? During the last decade, researchers have made a concerted effort to address the need for more reliable and valid developmental measures for South African children. The focus of this research has been twofold, namely the construction of new culture-reduced tests (e.g. Grover-Counter Scale (HSRC, 1994)) and adapting, refining, and norming appropriate tests that have been constructed and proven to be valid and reliable in other countries (e.g. the Bayley, McCarthy, and Griffiths Scales). We will briefly describe the developmental measures currently in frequent use with South African children. It must, however, be emphasized that the authors do not claim that these are the only measures in use.

15.2.4.1 Global developmental screening measures

Denver II

The Denver Developmental Screening Test (DDST) was first published in 1967 and revised in 1990 as the Denver II (Frankenburg and Dodds, 1990; Frankenburg et al., 1990). The Denver II can be administered to children from 0 to 72 months (six years). The domains tapped are personal-social development, language development, gross- and fine-motor development. The results obtained from the Denver II categorize the child's current development into one of three categories namely, Abnormal, Questionable or Normal development (Nuttall, Romero, and Kalesnik, 1992). The Denver II was developed in the United States and, although research on the applicability of the scales is under way in South Africa (Luiz, Foxcroft, Kotras,

and Jamieson, 1998), there are, as yet, no norms available for South African children.

Vineland Adaptive Behaviour Scales, Second Edition (Vineland-II)

The Vineland-II (Sparrow, Cicchetti, and Balla, 2005) is a revision of the Vineland Social Maturity Scale and Vineland Adaptive Behaviour Scale (Doll, 1965). The scales assess personal and social competence of individuals from birth to adulthood. The scales measure adaptive behaviour in four domains: Communication, Daily Living Skills, Socialization, and Motor Skills (Nuttall, Romero, and Kalesnik, 1992). They do not require the direct administration of tasks to an individual, but instead require a respondent who is familiar with the individual's abilities and general behaviour. This makes the scales attractive to use with individuals with special needs (e.g. a child with hearing or motor difficulties).

Goodenough-Harris Drawing Test (the Draw-a-Person test)

This test (Harris, 1963) is utilized with children between the ages of five and sixteen years. It involves the drawing of a person, which is scored against seventy-three characteristics specified in the manual. Alternatively, drawings can be compared with twelve ranked drawings (Quality Scale Cards) for each of the two scales. The results provide a non-verbal measure of mental ability (Nuttall, Romero, and Kalesnik, 1992).

The Draw-A-Person Intellectual Ability Test for Children, Adolescents, and Adults (DAP:IQ) by Reynolds and Hickman (2004) allows for the estimation of cognitive ability of an individual. This is achieved through the provision of a common set of scoring criteria against which intellectual ability can be estimated from a human figure drawing (HFD).

Miller Assessment for Preschoolers (MAP)

The MAP (Miller, 1988) is a short, yet comprehensive, assessment tool that aids the identification of developmental delays in a number of domains, namely neural foundations, coordination, verbal, non-verbal, and complex tasks (Nuttall, Romero, and Kalesnik, 1992).

Other tests

Other internationally used measures include the following: Battelle Developmental Inventory Screening Test (BDIST) (Newborg, Stock, Wnek, Guidubaldi, and Svinicki, 1984); Developmental Profile II (DP-II) (Alpern, Boll, and Shearer, 1980); and the Preschool Development Inventory (PDI) (Ireton, 1988). However, research relating to their applicability, reliability, and validity with South African children is lacking. Therefore, the results obtained by South African children on these scales should be interpreted with caution.

15.2.4.2 **Educationally focused screening measures**

It is important to assess the extent to which young children are developing the necessary underpinning skills that are the essential building blocks for being able to successfully progress in the early school years. Research has shown that the sooner children at risk for scholastic difficulties are identified and the earlier that appropriate intervention and educational instruction are instituted, the better the chances are that these children will develop to their full potential (Nuttall, Romero, and Kalesnik, 1992).

Educationally focused screening measures tend to tap important underpinning skills related to school learning tasks that are predictive of early school success. These skills include the following: cognitive skills, language, motor skills, copying shapes, concept development, memory, perceptual processes, lateral preference, and lateral (left-right) discrimination. If you compare these skills with the ones tapped by the measures that we considered in Section 15.2.4.1, you will notice that there is a considerable overlap in the skills assessed by more educationally focused screening measures and measures designed to assess global developmental progress and delays (Gredler, 1997). In this section, we will look at some of the measures that are used to assess whether a pre-school or Grade 1 child is at risk for developing scholastic difficulties. The spotlight will mainly fall on measures that have been developed in South Africa.

School-readiness Evaluation by Trained Testers (SETT)

The SETT (Joubert, 1984) is an individual measure that aims to determine whether a child is ready for

school or not. The SETT is administered in such a way that a learning situation, similar to that in the classroom, is created. The SETT provides an evaluation of a child's developmental level in the following areas: language and general (or intellectual) development, physical and motor development, and emotional and social development.

Aptitude Test for School Beginners (ASB)

The ASB (HSRC, 1974) can be administered on a group or individual basis. It aims to obtain a comprehensive picture of specific aptitudes of the school beginner and evaluates the cognitive aspects of school readiness. The ASB comprises eight tests: Perception, Spatial, Reasoning, Numerical, Gestalt, Coordination, Memory, and Verbal Comprehension. The instructions are available in the seven most commonly spoken African languages and norms are available for a variety of different groups of children.

School-entry Group Screening Measure (SGSM)

The SGSM (Foxcroft, Shillington and Turk, 1990) is a non-verbal cognitive group screening measure developed in South Africa for five- to nine-year-old children. The SGSM measures the following cognitive abilities: simultaneous visual-motor functioning, visual sequential processing, cognitive flexibility, attention, and incidental memory. These abilities are measured over four separate subtests namely, Visual-motor, Reasoning, Incidental Memory, and Visual-spatial. The SGSM has been found to be a fairly accurate predictor of whether or not a child is at risk for later scholastic difficulties. Test instructions are available in English, Afrikaans, Xhosa, Zulu, and Southern Sotho.

Other tests

Other batteries designed elsewhere in the world that are used in South Africa include Developmental Indicators for Assessment of Learning – Third Edition (DIAL-3) (Mardell-Czudnowski and Goldenberg, 1990) and Screening Children for Related Early Educational Needs (SCREEN) (Hresko, Hammill, Herbert, and Baroody, 1988).

While the measures discussed above are largely standardized assessment batteries, a number of individual measures can be grouped together to form a battery which assesses school readiness abilities. Individual measures often used include the following: Revised Motor Activity Scale (MAS) (in Roth, McCaul, and Barnes, 1993); Peabody Picture Vocabulary Test-Third Edition (PPVT-III) (Dunn and Dunn, 1981); Developmental Test of Visual-Motor Integration – Fifth Edition (VMI) (Beery, Buktenica, and Beery, 2005); Teacher Temperament Questionnaire (TTQ); Stress Response Scale (SRS); and the Personality Inventory for Children – Second Edition (PIC-2).

15.2.4.3 Diagnostic measures

In this section we will focus on measures that provide a more comprehensive assessment of development, which enables the results to be used for diagnostic purposes. We will focus on international measures that have been adapted for use in South Africa. Among these measures are the Griffiths Scales of Mental Development – Extended Revised and the McCarthy Scales of Mental Abilities, which were described in Chapter 10 (section 10.3.1) and will thus not be repeated here. Another developmental measure not discussed in Chapter 10 is the Bayley Scales of Infant Development.

Bayley Scales of Infant Development – Second Edition (BSID-II or Bayley II)

The Bayley II (Bayley, 1969) is used to identify children between the ages of one to forty-two months (three-and-a-half years) with developmental delays or those suspected of being 'at risk'. The Bayley II is divided into three scales: the Mental Scale, the Motor Scale, and the Behaviour Rating Scale. The use of all three scales provides a comprehensive assessment. Norms for interpreting the performance of black South African children on the original Bayley Scales published in 1969 are available (Richter and Griesel, 1988). However, no South African norms are available for the revised scales.

15.2.4.4 Shortcomings of developmental assessment

Among the shortcomings of developmental assessment in South Africa identified by Luiz (1994) are that:

- specific measures are standardized for specific cultural, socio-economic, and language groups to the exclusion of others and there are limited standardized measures that assess the development of black pre-school children;
- specific measures are standardized for specific age groups to the exclusion of others;
- due to the specificity of measures regarding age ranges and cultural groups, related research is fragmentary in nature, resulting in limited generalizability of research findings; and
- measures do not always provide a holistic picture of development as socio-emotional functioning is not always assessed.

The need to adapt, refine and norm appropriate tests that have been constructed and proven valid and reliable in other countries for use in the South African context has been emphasized and identified as a priority. Through adapting assessment measures such as the Wechsler Intelligence Scale for Children – Fourth Edition (WISC-IV) and the Wechsler Pre-School and Primary Scale of Intelligence-Revised (WPPSI-R), other diagnostic developmental measures used widely in the international arena become more accessible to the South African context.

15.2.4.5 Information from other sources and observations

Everyone involved with the care and education of children will have observed mental development in the practicalities of day-to-day situations. Such observations combined with established common knowledge are the basis for our every day understanding of where a particular child is in his or her development (Preston, 2005). Other than objective psychological assessment information, valuable developmental information can be obtained from a variety of sources (e.g. the parent(s)/caregiver, crèche-mother, pre-school teacher). Indeed, the use of multi-disciplinary teams to assess development is spreading (Preston, 2005). Naturalistic observation of a child's play can also provide the assessment practitioner with valuable information as to whether the child is capable of cooperative play, whether the child can initiate activities on his/her own, and so on. The emphasis is on the

>> **CRITICAL THINKING CHALLENGE 15.2**

Case Study

John is four years eleven months old. He is the first-born child in the family and his mother has little experience of what a child of John's age should be able to do. She is concerned as she has noticed that his drawings do not seem as advanced as those of her neighbour's child who is of similar age to John. She is advised to have John assessed by a psychologist. A developmental assessment using the Griffiths Scales of Mental Development is completed and the following results are obtained. When interpreting the results, a quotient (score) below 90 is considered to be below average, a quotient between 90 and 109 is considered to be average, a quotient between 110 and 119 is above average, and a quotient of 120 and above is considered to be superior.

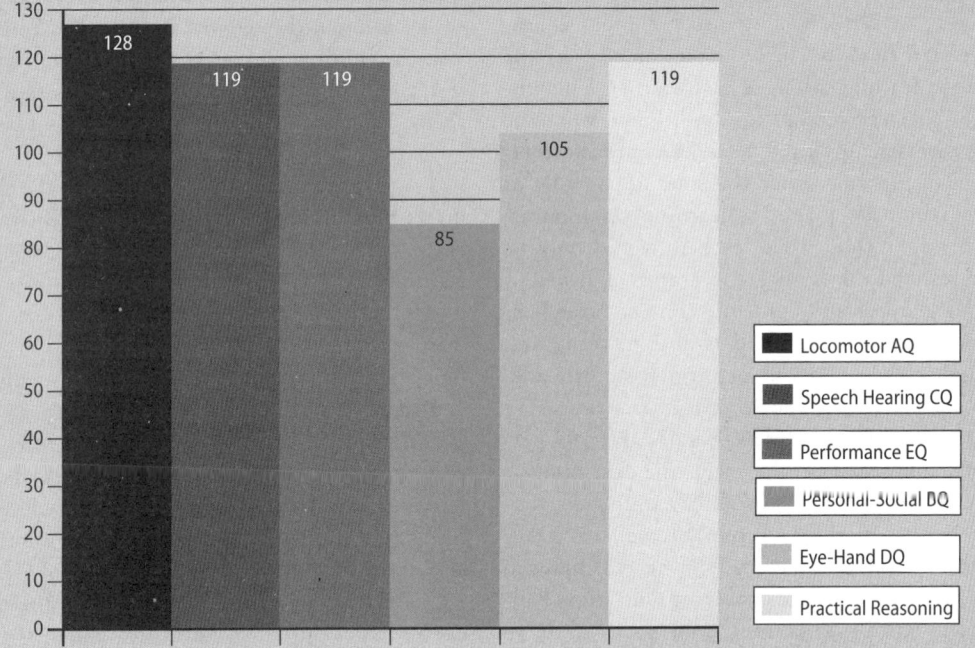

Figure 15.1 Profile of John's performance on the Griffiths Scales

Questions regarding John's assessment:
1. Why do you think the psychologist used a diagnostic, as opposed to a screening measure?
2. Summarize John's level of development and indicate what his strengths and weaknesses are.
3. South African children tend to perform at a lower level than British children on the Eye and Hand Coordination Subscale. Hypothesize possible reasons for this trend.
4. South African children also tend to perform at a higher level than British children on the Locomotor Subscale. Hypothesize possible reasons for this trend.

observation of the whole child within the child's total environment at a point in time (Preston, 2005). This information can be integrated with the assessment results and the observations of the assessment practitioner to form a holistic picture of the young child's development.

15.3 The role of psychological assessment in education

15.3.1 The uses of psychological measures in educational settings

15.3.1.1 Uses for school-age learners

Much has been written about the introduction of outcomes-based education (OBE) in South Africa. In OBE, among other things, educators need to tailor their instruction to meet the unique learning needs of each learner. This implies that the teacher needs to know what the learners' strengths and weaknesses are and their level of functioning at the start of a grade, or new education phase, or learning programme. You might think that teachers would only be interested in knowing the status of development of a learner's academic competencies (e.g. how many words a child is able to recognize, whether the child can perform basic arithmetic computations, and so on). In fact, knowing something about a child's overall cognitive, personal, and social development, the development of critical skills (e.g. the ability to listen attentively or to work in a group), as well as certain attitudes and behaviours (e.g. an eagerness to learn, attitude towards studying, and study habits), is equally important. It is particularly in this regard that psychological measures can be used along with measures of academic achievement to identify learners' strengths and weaknesses. The information gained about learners from such an assessment will assist educators in planning their instructions more effectively and referring learners with special needs for appropriate intervention and help.

We will use a practical example to illustrate some of the uses of psychological measures in educational settings as outlined above, as well as to alert you to some ethical considerations. Foxcroft and Shillington (1996) reported on a study in which they were approached by a group of Grade 1 teachers to assist them in identifying children with special education needs prior to the start of Grade 1, so that the educational input could be tailored to the learners' needs. As a large number of children had to be assessed, a measure that could be administered in a group context was necessary. Furthermore, as the children were from diverse linguistic backgrounds, the measure needed to be administered in their home language. Many of the children came from disadvantaged backgrounds and had not had the opportunity to participate in formal early childhood development programmes. Consequently, to ensure that there was no discrimination against these children, the selected measure had to provide the children with an opportunity to practise test tasks before they were actually assessed on them. For the assessment to provide useful information, Foxcroft and Shillington (1996) also had to ensure that appropriate aspects of the children's functioning were assessed. They therefore chose to use the School-entry Group Screening Measure (SGSM) (see Section 15.2) as it assesses underpinning abilities that are critical for academic progress in the early grades, namely visual-motor ability, reasoning, attention and memory, and visual-spatial ability.

The SGSM is, furthermore, a group test, the administration instructions are available in different South African languages, and each subtest starts with practice items. The reason for assessing the children before the start of Grade 1 was explained to the parents and informed consent was obtained from them. Parents were very positive about the fact the teachers were going to such efforts to identify whether their children had specific needs that required specific intervention. Based on the SGSM results, observations made by the teachers made about the children's test behaviour, and information obtained from an interview with the parents (conducted by the teachers), children who were at risk academically were identified. The instructional programme for these high-risk children was tailored to enrich their development specifically in the areas in which they had difficulty. When all the Grade 1 learners were re-assessed on the SGSM in June of the Grade 1 year, what do you think was found? Figure 15.2 shows the average developmental gains made by the high- and low-risk children.

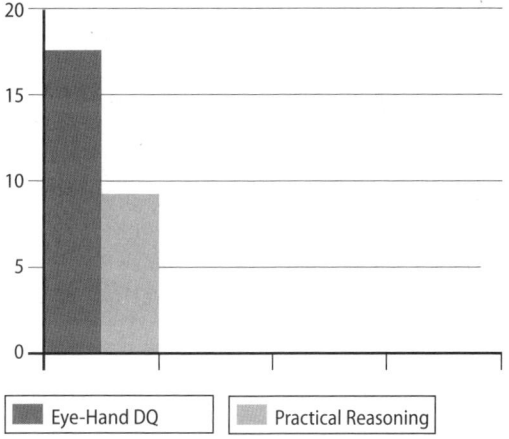

Figure 15.2 Developmental Gains

The developmental gains made by high-risk children were almost twice as great as those made by their low-risk peers. Providing high-risk children with enriched input enhanced their development. Furthermore, by the end of the year, 68 per cent of the high-risk children were found to be ready to tackle Grade 2. Thus, although these children entered Grade 1 at a developmentally disadvantaged level in relation to their low-risk peers, the instruction that they received helped them not only to catch up developmentally, but also to cope successfully with the academic demands of Grade 1. The remaining 32 per cent of the high-risk children who were not able to successfully master the academic demands of Grade 1 were referred to a psychologist for more comprehensive, **psychodiagnostic assessment** (see Section 15.4 to discover more about diagnostic assessment). Some of these children were found to have specific learning problems that required remedial intervention, while others were found to be cognitively challenged and thus needed to be placed in a special school where the academic demands were less intense. A few of the high-risk children were found to have behavioural disorders (e.g. Attention Deficit Hyperactivity Disorder). These children required therapeutic intervention from a psychologist and referral to a paediatrician for possible prescription of medication.

The above example illustrates a number of important aspects of the use of psychological assessment in educational contexts. Before you read any further,

go through the material again and try to list what you have learned about psychological assessment.

Using the example cited above, some of the critical aspects of the use of psychological assessment in educational contexts are that:

- it is important to clearly match what needs to be assessed with educational or curricula objectives and learning outcomes. This implies that psychological measures that are widely used in educational settings should be researched in terms of their predictive validity and might have to be adapted so that they are aligned more closely with the learning outcomes of the various grades;
- care needs to be taken to cater for the linguistic and other special needs of learners during the assessment so that learners are not unfairly disadvantaged by the assessment;
- it is important that assessment practitioners and educators inform parents regarding the purpose of the assessment and obtain their informed consent;
- the results of an appropriately performed psychological assessment can be of invaluable benefit to the teacher to assist him/her in planning how best to facilitate learning and development in his/her learners;
- psychologists and teachers can work together to gather assessment data that can inform appropriate educational intervention and programme development;
- assessment assists in identifying learners with special educational needs and talents who may need to be given specialized educational, accelerated, or academic development programmes and who might benefit from psychological intervention. Children with special education needs include those with learning problems, those who are mentally challenged, those who are physically challenged, those who are gifted (highly talented), and those who have behavioural disorders which make it difficult for them to progress scholastically.

15.3.1.2 **Uses in higher education contexts**

Entrance to universities and universities of technology is usually dependent on meeting certain entrance requirements. Traditionally, matriculation results have been used when determining admission to higher education programmes. However, there is a growing body of research which points to the unreliability of matriculation results in predicting academic success in higher education, especially for learners from disadvantaged educational backgrounds (e.g. Foxcroft, 2004a; Skuy, Zolezzi, Mentis, Fridjhon, and Cockroft 1996). Furthermore, there is a need to broaden access to higher education, especially for historically disadvantaged South Africans. In addition, national and international research findings suggest that the combination of entrance assessment results with high school performance leads to significantly better predictions of academic performance (Anastasi and Urbina, 1997; Foxcroft, 2004a; Griesel, 2001; McClaran, 2003). Consequently, as happens elsewhere in the world, a number of universities and universities of technology in South Africa have instituted assessment programmes to supplement matriculation information. Such an assessment needs to tap generic or basic academic competencies such as verbal, numerical, or reasoning abilities, which are seen as the foundation for success in higher education programmes. In addition to these generic competencies, subject specific content (e.g. Chemistry or Accountancy) may also be assessed. However, it is not sufficient to simply tap academic competencies, as research has indicated that there are personal attributes and behaviours that are equally important for academic success. Fields of interest, motivation, study skills, having career goals, academic self-belief, and leadership ability have *inter alia* been found to be related to academic success.

Apart from assisting in admissions decisions, another advantage of assessing learners on entry to higher education programmes is that the resultant information can be used to guide programme planning and the development of student support initiatives. Furthermore, assessment results can be used to counsel students regarding the most appropriate programme placement for them as well as specific aspects of their functioning that require more development. Assessment at entry to higher education thus has the potential to go beyond simply trying to select learners with the potential to succeed. It can, in fact, serve a more developmental purpose, which ultimately benefits the learner.

Currently, an important drawback of the admissions testing conducted at various higher education institutions relates to the fact that there is not a nationally developed and standardized battery of tests that can be used by all institutions. This means that if an applicant applies to three different institutions he/she will probably be asked to write three different, but also somewhat similar admissions tests. Furthermore, if one test battery was used by all institutions, more systematic research could be conducted about incoming learners which could be of value to the high school, further education, and higher education sectors. In order to address this situation, there is an initiative underway currently to develop **national benchmark tests** in academic literacy, quantitative literacy, and mathematics (Foxcroft, 2005). These tests will be **criterion-referenced** in nature to facilitate the setting of **benchmarks** for entry into different programmes (e.g. certificates, diplomas, degrees). You can follow the development of these tests by consulting www.he-enrol.ac.za.

15.3.2 Types of measures used in educational settings

15.3.2.1 Achievement measures

These can be defined as measures that tap the effects of relatively standardized instructional input. **Achievement measures** are often summative or provide a final/terminal evaluation of a learner's status on completion of a programme or grade. Evaluations administered at the end of a specific course or time span are examples of achievement measures.

Some achievement measures have been developed for certain learning domains, such as reading and mathematics for various grade levels, and are usually **normed** across the entire country. However, this is not currently the case with achievement measures in South Africa. This is due to the fact that during the apartheid years, there were many different education systems and curricula, and during the past few years outcomes-based education has been introduced. Consequently, there are currently very few standardized achievement measures available in South Africa that are appropriately aligned with the new curriculum. Furthermore, there are no standardized achievement measures available that have been appropriately normed for all South Africans. **Criterion-referenced achievement tests** are gradually becoming more popular than norm-referenced tests. This is due to the fact that criterion-referenced achievement tests allow for a learner's performance to be pegged on a continuum of learning outcomes of increasing complexity. This provides a rich description of what a learner knows and is able to do and indicates which aspects need to be developed in order to reach the next step of the continuum. You can consult Foxcroft (2005) for a more complete discussion on criterion-referenced achievement tests.

Teacher-developed measures are used more commonly in South Africa, as teachers need to find a means of validly assessing learning performance in the classroom. Ideally, the teacher would select a variety of assessment measures or tasks to best evaluate the learners' ability or proficiency. The choice of measure should be based on the nature of the information that the teacher wants to obtain, or the purpose of the assessment. For example, if the teacher wants to assess knowledge acquisition, it would be better to use a **multiple-choice type question**, which taps that specific knowledge domain. However, if the teacher needs to discover the levels of analysis, integration, critical thinking capacity, and the ability of the learner to synthesize diverse information, it would be more appropriate to use an **essay-type question**.

An additional form of achievement assessment is that of **portfolio assessment**. This is a collection or portfolio of examples of a learner's work over a period of time and allows for documentation of the learner's work. The decision regarding which material should be included in the portfolio is often a collaborative effort between the learner and teacher, who together gather examples of the learner's work. This has the additional advantage of allowing the learner the opportunity for self-assessment.

15.3.2.2 **Aptitude measures**

Aptitude measures are used to assess and predict the specific ability that a person has to attain success in an area where that specific ability

is required (see Chapter 10). For example, if an aptitude assessment reveals that a person has an aptitude for art, the assumption is that he/she has many of the characteristics and capabilities to become a successful artist. There are different types of aptitude measures. For example, a numerical aptitude test may predict the learner's future performance in mathematics, while a test of two- or three-dimensional perception may assist in the selection of a learner for an architecture course.

15.3.2.3 **General and specific cognitive measures**

Measures of **general intelligence** (see Chapter 10 for examples) are used in educational settings for a number of reasons. A child's intelligence quotient or IQ serves as a guideline regarding the child's accumulated learning in a variety of learning environments. The IQ scores obtained will indicate the child's intellectual functioning, which may, in turn, assist the psychologist or teacher to make decisions regarding the child's potential. Individual analysis and interpretation of subtest scores, called a scatter analysis, provide indications regarding a child's vocabulary, comprehension, short- and long-term memory for both words and numbers, problem-solving ability, and visual spatial ability. This will assist the psychologist to provide guidance to the child's teacher about possible remediation. A difference in scores on verbal and performance abilities may indicate specific learning problems, while the manner in which the child has approached the test situation as well as the level of concentration and attention span shown by the child provide valuable qualitative information.

Measures of **cognitive ability** should never be administered in isolation, and interpretation of the results should take the entire child into account. This means that the child's emotional state, family background, physical health, or specific trauma will all have some influence on test scores. The use of a single test score to make decisions regarding the child should be seen as an unethical assessment practice.

Measures of **specific cognitive functions** refer to such functions as visual and auditory sequential memory or specific learning tasks (see Chapter 10). The selection of specific cognitive measures is usually dictated by the specific problems experienced by the child in the classroom. A child who is experiencing problems, for example, with phonics will be assessed on specific language-related measures so that the nature of the problem can be diagnosed. The accurate diagnosis of a problem enables appropriate remedial intervention to be instituted.

15.3.2.4 **Personality-related measures**

'**Personality-related**' measures include *inter alia* personality measures and measures of temperament, motivation, task orientation, and interpersonal styles. Chapters 11, 12, and 13 provided you with information about these types of measures. Here, we will focus on the use of such measures in educational contexts.

Different personality types and different temperaments may impact on academic performance. By assessing personality and temperament, the teacher can be assisted in gaining insight into the child's personality characteristics and how best to handle the child. For example, the child whose natural temperament is relaxed and confident will cope better with the demands of the classroom than one who is naturally more anxious and fearful. If both children have a specific learning problem, the confident child may respond well to remediation, while the more anxious child may withdraw into further emotional problems. The teacher would need to tailor her teaching to suit the nature of the child by offering more challenges to the first and more nurturing to the second.

15.3.2.5 **Dynamic assessment**

Dynamic or guided **assessment** is adaptable and is closely aligned with the approaches used in tests of potential where learning opportunities are provided as part of the testing process (see Chapters 10 and 17). The potential of a learner is assessed by observing how well he/she can learn in a situation where the assessment practitioner is the assessor, instructor, and clinician (Anastasi and Urbina, 1997). In dynamic assessment, there is a deliberate departure from standardized assessment procedures so as to elicit additional qualitative information about the learner. Murphy and Maree (2006) argue that conventional assessment is a product-based approach while dynamic assessment is a process-oriented approach that focuses on the learning that takes place during an assessment session. As dynamic assessment focuses on future potential rather than current ability, an advantage of this assessment approach is that it can overcome some of the cultural and educational biases associated with assessment outcomes of conventional tests (Murphy and Maree, 2006).

Dynamic assessment is often employed as a useful adjunct during remedial intervention. The learner may be assessed before the intervention (pre-test) to establish a baseline functioning and to provide a clear idea of what learning experiences should be facilitated. After guided instruction, an assessment (post-test) will reveal the nature of the learning outcomes achieved (and the gain in scores from pre- to post-test) and will indicate those which still need attention. Further instruction followed by a re-assessment will guide further interventions until the goals have been attained (this is often referred to as the **test-teach-test approach**). Readers should consult Murphy and Maree (2006) for an overview of research in the field of dynamic assessment in South Africa.

> **» CRITICAL THINKING CHALLENGE 15.3**
>
> You have been asked to address teachers at a primary school about the use of psychological assessment in schools. Prepare the talk that you will give.

15.4 **Psychodiagnostic assessment**

15.4.1 **What is psychodiagnostic assessment?**

Consider the following case scenarios:

- A person commits a murder but claims that he is innocent as a voice 'inside his head' told him to do this.
- An eight-year-old child just cannot sit still in class and is constantly fidgeting. She constantly daydreams and cannot focus her attention on her schoolwork. She disrupts the other children, makes insensitive remarks, has aggressive outbursts, and has very few friends

as a result. Her teacher wonders if she lacks discipline and structure at home, or whether she has a more serious behavioural disorder.

- A Grade 2 pupil is not making sufficient progress at school, despite the fact that he seems to be intelligent. The teacher needs to know whether this child has a specific learning problem which will require remedial intervention, or whether the child needs to be placed in a special class or school.
- A sixty-year-old man has a stroke and the neurologist and family want to know which cognitive functions are still intact and how best to plan a rehabilitation programme that will address his cognitive and emotional well-being.
- During a custody hearing, information needs to be provided in order to decide which parent should be granted legal custody of a minor child. The court needs guidance regarding which parent would be the better option.
- Following a motor vehicle accident in which an individual sustained a serious head injury, the family wishes to submit an insurance claim as they argue that the individual has changed completely since the accident and will never be able to independently care for herself again. The insurance company needs to know whether these claims are valid before they will settle the claim.

For each of the above scenarios, **psychodiagnostic assessment** can provide valuable information to aid in answering the questions being asked. As you will discover in this section, psychodiagnostic assessment does not refer to a specific assessment context. Rather, it refers to particular purposes for which psychological assessment is used. Psychologists often find themselves in a position where they have to conduct an in-depth assessment of an individual's cognitive, emotional, behavioural, and personality functioning. The purpose of such an in-depth assessment is to obtain a comprehensive picture of an individual's functioning so as to determine the extent to which an individual might, for example, be:

- intellectually challenged,
- diagnosed as having a specific learning problem, which is impeding his/her progress at school,

- diagnosed as suffering from a behavioural disorder such as Attention Deficit Disorder or a dependency disorder (in the case of drug and alcohol abuse),
- suffering from a major psychiatric disorder (e.g. schizophrenia, bipolar disorder, depression), or
- suffering from a neuropsychological disorder (i.e. he/she might be experiencing cognitive, emotional, and personality disturbances as a result of impaired brain functioning).

Psychodiagnostic information can be employed, for example, to make a psychiatric diagnosis and guide the nature of the intervention required. Additionally, psychodiagnostic information can be used in a **psycholegal** context to guide the court in reaching complex decisions (e.g. in custody and child abuse cases, for a motor vehicle accident claim). The nature of the referral question will determine the purpose(s) that the psychodiagnostic assessment must serve and how such an assessment process will be structured. Generally speaking, the process followed in psychodiagnostic assessment is as follows:

- Comprehensively evaluate an individual (or family) using multiple assessment measures and multiple sources (collateral information).
- Establish the presence or absence of certain psychological (e.g. hallucinations, personality disturbances), neuropsychological (e.g. reversals, neglect of one side of the body), or physical symptoms (e.g. fatigue, loss of appetite).
- Compare the symptoms identified with standard psychiatric and neuropsychological disorders to determine in which category of disorders the individual best fits.
- Make a prognosis regarding the future course of the disorder and a prediction regarding the extent to which the person will benefit from psychotherapeutic intervention, as well as the need for other types of intervention (e.g. psycho-pharmacological treatment, occupational therapy).
- Prepare an oral or written report on the outcomes of the assessment, the resultant recommendations, and, in the case of a psycholegal (forensic) assessment, express an expert opinion on the matter being considered by the court.

Psychodiagnostic assessment, like all other forms of psychological assessment, is a dynamic and flexible process. There is no single assessment measure or procedure that will be able to provide a comprehensive picture of the intellectual, emotional, and psychological functioning of a client. The psychologist, therefore, has to develop a **battery of assessment measures** and procedures applicable to the needs of the specific client and in response to the specific referral question. The term battery is understood in this context as a particularly selected group of measures and procedures that will provide the required information to the psychologist, and by implication therefore, different assessment batteries are selected for different clients or patients (see also Chapter 9). We will briefly discuss some of the psychological measures and procedures that are often used.

15.4.2 Assessment measures and procedures

15.4.2.1 Interviews

An initial, detailed interview is usually the first step in the assessment process. The initial interview may be seen as a **semi-structured** form of assessment, as opposed to structured, standardized, and more formal assessment measures, such as intellectual or personality measures, for example. The initial interview is conducted either with the client or, as in the case of under-age children, the parent or guardian of the client, or some other involved and appropriate caregiver. The information gained from this type of assessment is varied and the specific goal of the interview will depend on the nature of the information that the psychologist is attempting to discover. This implies that the psychologist will tailor the nature of the **open and closed questions** asked, in order to elicit different varieties of information. For example, the initial interview aimed at obtaining information about a school age child with a suspected learning problem, will differ from the questioning used when the psychologist attempts to obtain information from a psychiatric client to determine the best therapy.

The initial interview, therefore, is a dynamic and flexible process that relies heavily on the knowledge and expertise of the psychologist. The information gained may be **factual** in nature (e.g. the duration of a particular symptom), or **inferred** information, such as the interpretation of particular non-verbal behaviour or even the avoidance by the client of an area of information. The verbal information offered by the client may be either confirmed or contradicted by the non-verbal and behavioural information expressed either consciously or unconsciously by a client.

Details of the client's family and cultural background, birth and developmental history, educational history, psychosocial development, work history, marital status, significant illnesses (physical and mental), and so on, are obtained during the initial interview. It is also important to gain information about the history of the present problem and the factors that seemed to precipitate and perpetuate it. The initial interview information is often cross-validated by interviewing significant others in the person's family or place of employment.

Apart from serving a history-taking function, the initial interview provides the psychologist with an opportunity to gain first-hand insight into the client's mental and emotional state. A mental status examination is thus often conducted as part of the initial interview. A mental status examination usually consists of providing a client with certain activities or stimuli and observing his/her response. For example, to see how well a person is orientated to time, the psychologist will ask the client what day of the week it is, what the date is, of what month, and of what year? A mental status examination usually covers the client's physical appearance; sleeping and eating habits; whether the client is orientated for time, place, and person; psychomotor functioning (e.g. does the client's hand shake when he/she picks up something); an analysis of the fluency and nature of the client's speech; screening of the client's higher-order intellectual functioning (e.g. attention, memory, social judgement); and screening of the client's emotional status. Patrick (2000) provides a brief record form for a mental status examination that practitioners can use as a guide. You can access this form from www.nev.dgp.org.au/files/programsupport/mentalhealth/Mental%20Exam%20-%20

form.pdf? Furthermore, the Mini-Mental State (Folstein, Folstein and McHugh, 1975) is an example of a formalized mental status exam which is widely used as a brief cognitive screening measure in neuropsychological assessment, especially for dementia. Administration and scoring are standardized and cut-off scores are provided to identify abnormal performance that could be indicative of dementia.

The information gained from the mental status examination can provide the psychologist with clues regarding aspects of functioning that need to be explored further and verified by using more structured assessment measures. In addition, the initial interview together with the mental status examination provide the psychologist with the opportunity to establish whether the client can be formally, and comprehensively, assessed and whether the assessment will need to be tailored in any way.

When interviewing significant others in the client's life to verify and elaborate on the information obtained in the initial interview, the psychologist must always keep in mind the fact that the various stakeholders in the assessment process have **competing values** (see Chapter 8). When conflicting information is obtained, the reason for this can often be traced back to the differing vested interests of the parties involved. For example, in view of the financial compensation that an individual may receive for the cognitive impairment or emotional trauma suffered as a result of a head injury sustained in a motor vehicle accident, family members might not always be totally truthful and may exaggerate difficulties that the individual has in an attempt to secure the compensation.

15.4.2.2 **Psychological assessment measures**

From the information obtained from the initial interview as well as collateral information, the psychologist is able to **hypothesize** the nature and origin of the problem that the client may be experiencing. The psychologist will then develop an **assessment battery** that will specifically assist him or her to explore and investigate all these hypotheses. In view of the comprehensive nature of the assessment required, all the following areas (or domains) of functioning need to be covered in an assessment battery:

- arousal, attention and modulation (regulation) of behaviour;
- motor and sensory functions;
- general cognitive abilities;
- language-related abilities;
- non-verbal abilities and visual perception;
- memory and the ability to learn new information;
- concept formation, planning, and reasoning;
- emotional status and personality; and
- academic skills (reading, writing, and basic calculations).

Although there might be more attention paid to some of the above aspects, depending on the picture of the client's functioning that emerges and the hypotheses being pursued, information needs to be gathered on all the aspects. The full spectrum of psychological measures covered in this book could potentially be included as part of an assessment battery. Some measures, such as an intelligence test battery, are quite cost effective as the various subtests tap a number of the important aspects that need to be assessed. In other instances, specialized measures may be used. For example, when a person who has sustained a head injury is being assessed, it might be useful to use measures that have been specifically developed to tap neuropsychological functions, or measures that have been researched in relation to how people with head injuries or other neuropsychological disorders perform on them.

The value of comprehensive psychodiagnostic assessment can be considerably enhanced if the psychologist forms part of a multidisciplinary team. Psychodiagnostic information obtained from a psychologist can be collated and integrated with information from other professionals, such as social workers, occupational therapists, paediatricians, and speech therapists, to obtain a very comprehensive picture of the person's functioning.

15.4.3 **Psychological knowledge and expertise**

A wealth of information about the functioning of the client is thus obtained from a variety of measures and sources during the psychodiagnostic assessment process. The task of the psychologist is to integrate all this complex and diverse information in order to develop an understanding of the present status and functioning of the client. From this understanding, the psychologist is able to draw conclusions and make judgements regarding the most appropriate form of intervention that will best benefit the needs of the client.

The ability to ask pertinent questions in an initial interview, pick up on non-verbal cues, plan an appropriate assessment battery, and integrate the diverse information to form a detailed understanding of the person's behaviour and problem requires considerable skill, expertise, and knowledge on the part of the psychologist. It is for this reason that psychologists tend to choose to focus on only one type of psychodiagnostic assessment. Some focus more on psychiatric assessment, where knowledge of psychiatric disorders as described in the *Diagnostic and Statistical Manual of Mental Disorders* (DSM-IVR) or the ICD 10 is of prime importance if a sound psychiatric diagnosis is to be made. Others focus on the child custody and access assessment. In this instance, the psychologist needs to be intimately familiar with the various laws pertaining to custody, access, and the rights of minor children, the research literature related to child-rearing practices and custody outcomes, and the commonly used assessment measures. Certain psychologists choose to focus mainly on neuropsychological assessment. Not only is a thorough knowledge of brain organization and functioning required, as well as knowledge of common neuropsychological disorders (e.g. head trauma, epilepsy, cerebrovascular accidents, tumours), but also knowledge and expertise related to specialized neuropsychological assessment measures. Then there are psychologists who focus on the assessment of children and adults who have been sexually abused or raped, and so on. Due to choice or certain emphases during training, psychologists tend to develop specific expertise regarding one or some of the applications of psychodiagnostic assessment discussed in this section. It is due to the specialist knowledge and expertise in psychodiagnostic assessment that they often find themselves working and testifying in legal or forensic settings. This is the topic of the next section.

15.4.4 Psycholegal or forensic assessment

The term **psycholegal assessment** is used to indicate broadly the use of psychological assessment information for legal purposes. Forensic assessment is more narrowly focused and concerns itself primarily with the determination of the capacity of a person to testify, sanity, criminal responsibility, and the extent to which the defendant is dangerous and may repeat the same criminal behaviour.

The fact that psychologists operate within a scientific paradigm and assess human behaviour using rigorous methods and measures enables them to fulfil a unique function in legal settings (Louw and Allan, 1998). It is important to keep in mind, however, that when psychologists testify in legal settings they do so as **expert witnesses**. Merely being a psychologist does not make the person an expert. To be considered an expert, the psychologist must have built up specialist knowledge and expertise in a particular area of psychology and must be recognized as an expert by his/her professional peers. By virtue of this specialist knowledge and expertise, the psychologist will be able to testify before the court and to express an informed opinion regarding the matter at hand.

When a psychologist undertakes a psycholegal assessment and provides expert testimony in court cases, he/she must do so in an ethically responsible way. This is especially important as the psychologist should never take sides or be biased. At all times, the psychologist needs to express an unbiased professional opinion, irrespective of any pressure placed on him/her by lawyers, attorneys, and so on. To adhere to good conduct practices in psycholegal assessment and testimony, the psychologist should:

- ensure that psychological assessment findings are used as the basis for generating conclusions, as this provides the court with verifiable information;
- ensure that all the information in the report, as well as the recommendations made, can be substantiated;
- testify truthfully, honestly, candidly, and in an unbiased manner;

- acknowledge the limitations of the information that was gathered and the conclusions that were reached; and
- avoid performing multiple and potentially conflicting roles (e.g. being a witness and a consultant for the defence). It is very important that the psychologist clarifies his/her role as expert from the outset.

It might interest you to know in which areas South African psychologists tend to do the most psycholegal work. Louw and Allan (1998) found that child custody cases together with personal injury cases (e.g. assault cases, assessment of the symptoms following a head injury in a motor vehicle accident) comprised 53 per cent of the psycholegal activities undertaken by South African psychologists. In a test use survey, Foxcroft, Paterson, le Roux and Herbst (2004) found that 5,6% of psychologists surveyed indicated that they frequently undertake child custody assessment, while 8,3% indicated that they frequently perform other types of psycholegal assessments.

Custody evaluations, in particular, pose many challenges to psychologists as the different parties who have a stake in the assessment are in an adversarial position to each other. The ethical practice standards required for child custody assessments entail the following:

- independent interviews and assessment sessions with both parents; parents need to be reminded that, while they need to respond honestly and truthfully, the outcome of the assessment will be used to make a custody decision, which may or may not be perceived by them as being favourable;
- several interviews and assessment sessions with each child alone; children need to be informed about the purpose of the assessment;
- an assessment session with the parent and children together; ideally, both parents should have an opportunity to be observed interacting with their children;
- interviews with or obtaining written information from neighbours, general practitioners, social workers, teachers, baby-sitters, grandparents, friends, and so on.

15.4.5 **Limitations of psychodiagnostic assessment**

We stressed that the ability to reach an accurate psychodiagnostic conclusion requires extensive training and experience. Even then, the potential to formulate incorrect opinions is ever present. As we pointed out in Chapter 1, psychological assessment culminates in the forming of an **informed opinion**, which, since it is an opinion, always leaves the possibility that the wrong opinion was reached. Psychologists might inadvertently err on the side of selectively attending to only certain bits of information, or selectively remembering certain aspects of an interview, or not following up on a critical piece of information, or employing faulty logic. All of these can lead to incorrect conclusions. Psychologists thus need to guard against becoming overconfident and need to keep the possibility that they might be wrong uppermost in their minds.

» CRITICAL THINKING CHALLENGE 15.4

Forty-eight-year-old Robert has recently been retrenched. Since then, he struggles to sleep at night, has lost his appetite, sits at home staring into space and sighing, and he complains of feeling very down in the dumps. His wife becomes increasingly concerned about his lack of drive and energy and his depressed mood. Robert is referred to you (as a psychologist) by his general practitioner to find out what his problem is, as there is no physical cause for his symptoms. What type of questions would you ask Robert in the initial interview? What aspects of functioning would you want to tap when you plan an assessment battery?

CHECKING YOUR PROGRESS 15.1

15.1 Describe some of the purposes for which individuals, groups, and organizations are assessed in industry.

15.2 Distinguish between a structured, an unstructured, and a semi-structured interview.

15.3 Explain what is meant by the term 'developmental assessment' and provide some examples of development measures.

15.4 Distinguish between achievement and aptitude tests used in educational settings.

15.5 Define the concept 'assessment battery'.

15.6 What is 'psycholegal assessment'?

By now you should have quite a few snapshots of the way in which assessment measures are used in different contexts. At our next stop in the *Assessment Practice Zone*, you will have an opportunity to explore issues related to the interpretation of measures, as well as how to report on the results of an assessment.

Interpreting and reporting assessment results

KATE W GRIEVE AND CHERYL FOXCROFT

Chapter

16

CHAPTER OUTCOMES

What does a test score mean?
Do assessment results tell you everything?
Why do test scores have to be interpreted?
What does validity have to do with the interpretation of assessment results?
Can you combine mechanical and non-mechanical ways of interpreting test scores?
How does the interpretation of norm-referenced and criterion-referenced measures differ?
Do you need special skills for conveying assessment results?
Who has access to assessment results?
How can I avoid misinterpretation of assessment results in written reports?

This chapter deals with the different ways of interpreting assessment results and reporting or conveying these to the people concerned. By the end of this chapter you will be able to:

> explain different methods of interpreting assessment results;
> explain the ethical considerations that need to be adhered to when conveying assessment results;
> explain the basic methods that can be used to convey assessment results; and
> understand the purpose and nature of an assessment report.

Assessment measures are used for two main purposes: research and applied practice. In the **research** situation, tests are used in a variety of ways, depending on the purpose of the research. When you are faced with tests that measure a similar domain, your choice of test will be determined by the research problem. For example, if you were interested in assessing the home environments of malnourished children, you might decide to use the Home Screening Questionnaire (Coons, Frankenburg, Gay, Fandal, Lefly, and Ker, 1982), because it takes all aspects of a young child's environment into account, rather than another measure, such as the Family Environment Scale (Moos and Moos, 1986) that focuses on relationships between family members.

In **practical applications**, assessment measures are used to help professionals to gain more information about a person and to facilitate therapeutic intervention. For example, assessment measures may be used for child and adult guidance, to evaluate scholastic achievement, to investigate pathology or determine individual strengths and weaknesses, and for selection, placement and training of people in industrial or commercial organizations (see Chapter 15). Assessment measures are generally used to answer specific questions about a person. For example, if a child is not performing well at school, you may wonder if this is due to limited intellectual ability, emotional problems, or environmental difficulties. Assessment measures can help us understand people's functioning and indicate where intervention is required.

16.1 **Interpretation**

Once you have administered a measure and obtained a score, you have to decide what that result means for the specific person who was assessed. In order to reach the best possible decision, detailed information is required about the person concerned. Why is this so? A test score on its own is meaningless (and you will learn more about this in Chapter 17). A test score only becomes meaningful when it is viewed in the light of information about the particular measure used, as well as all aspects of the particular person and the specific purpose of the assessment. The assessment practitioner therefore has to interpret a test score in order for it to be meaningful.

16.1.1 **The relation between interpretation and validity**

In order to use assessment results in a meaningful way, there must be some relation between the results and what is being interpreted on the basis of those results. For example, if we interpret a verbal intelligence quotient of 79 as meaning that a child has below average verbal ability (because the average is 100 and the standard deviation is 15), we must know that the child does indeed have poor verbal skills. We can look at another example in a different context. You have many applicants for a job and can only appoint forty, so you decide to give them all an aptitude measure and accept only those applicants who obtain scores above a certain **cut-off score**. You need to know beforehand that there is a relation between the cut-off score and job success, otherwise you may appoint applicants who perform above the cut-off score but cannot do the work (see Chapter 3).

This brings us to the question of **validity** (see Chapter 5). Interpretations of test scores depend on the validity of the measure or the information used. There are different forms of interpretation that, to a greater or lesser extent, are related to the different types of validity discussed in Chapter 5.

16.1.1.1 **Descriptive interpretation**

Descriptive interpretations try to describe the test-takers as they are and in terms of the way they behave at the time of testing. Descriptive interpretations are based on currently available information. For example, a descriptive interpretation of an IQ score of 100 would be that the test-taker is average. Descriptive interpretations do not include attempts to interpret a score in terms of prior ability or disadvantage or in terms of future predicted behaviour.

Descriptive interpretations are dependent on construct, content, and concurrent validity. For example, on completing an interest inventory, Lebo has a higher score for scientific than practical interests. The descriptive interpretation that Lebo is better at research-related activities than mechanical ones can only be made if sufficient information is available about the validity of the measure. Firstly, there has to be proof that the assessment measure does in fact measure research and mechanical abilities (**construct validity**). After all, scientific interests could include other things besides research, and practical interests could include abilities other than mechanical. Secondly, the items in the measure should be suitable for the standardization population. For example, the content of the items should actually reflect scientific or practical interests (**content validity**). Thirdly, the test scores should correlate with scores on other measures of the same characteristic (**concurrent validity**). If these conditions are not met, the interpretation will not be valid.

16.1.1.2 **Causal interpretation**

Causal interpretation refers to the kind of interpretation that is made about conditions or events in a test-taker's background, based on assessment results. For example, the decision may have to be made as to whether a child has the ability to do well in an academic course or would do better in a technical school. If the child has worked hard and, despite a supportive environment, still struggles with academic tasks, the interpretation could be made that there is some condition (perhaps a learning disability) that makes academic study difficult. A possible explanation for current behaviour is found by interpreting the test score in the light of the child's past development. In this case, validity can be determined by examining information on the children in the standardization sample to establish whether certain past events (such as a neurological condition) have any bearing on current assessment scores. This type of interpretation can also help, for example, to determine the effect of a head injury on the basis of assessment results (see Chapter 15).

Causal interpretations can also be made for scores on a personality measure. For example, in the case of the Children's Personality Questionnaire (see Chapter 11), the appendix to the manual contains a summary of the background and biographic correlates available for each factor. There is empirical evidence that a low score on the emotional stability factor is associated with parental divorce or separation, or conflict among children in the family (Madge and Du Toit, 1967).

16.1.1.3 **Predictive interpretation**

Look at the following example: Andrea obtains high scores for numerical ability, three-dimensional reasoning, and mechanical insight on an aptitude measure. The counsellor interprets these scores as meaning that Andrea has the ability to follow a career in the field of engineering. This is an example of **predictive interpretation**. The counsellor knows that there is a relation between current aptitude in these fields and a future criterion, in this case a successful career in engineering. This type of interpretation rests heavily on the predictive validity of the aptitude measure.

16.1.1.4 **Evaluative interpretation**

The fourth form is that of **evaluative interpretation**, which combines an interpretation of a test score with a value judgement based on available information about the test-taker. This is generally what happens in a counselling situation. Evaluative interpretations lead to a recommendation, which can only be justified if the validity of the other information is known. Let's look at the following example: A young woman who has a specific reading disability does well on an intelligence measure and wants to know whether she should study law. She also has an interest in accounting and business. The counsellor makes the following evaluative interpretation: despite her above average intellectual ability, it is recommended that she does not study law at university due to her reading difficulty, but should rather pursue her interest in the business field. This recommendation implies that a reading disability will have a negative effect on the ability to study law and presumes that a reading disability predicts performance in law (predictive validity). On the other hand, the assumption is made that a reading disability will not affect performance in the business world. This type of recommendation, based on evaluative interpretations of assessment results, can only be made when supported by validity data.

You can see that, as you shift from a descriptive approach to an evaluative approach, you move away from objective data towards more subjective assessment (Madge and Van der Walt, 1997). The descriptive approach relies on an assessment result to describe the individual, while the others rely on increasingly more subjective input, until interpretation is combined with professional evaluation in the last form of interpretation.

16.1.2 **Methods of interpretation**

In general, there are two broad approaches to the interpretation of assessment results, mechanical and non-mechanical.

16.1.2.1 **Mechanical interpretation of assessment results**

The **mechanical** approach is the psychometric or statistical way of looking at assessment results. Cronbach (1970) has also called it an actuarial approach. What this means is that an assessment result is interpreted purely as a statistic. Those who support this method of interpreting assessment results do so on the basis that it is objective, reliable, scientific, mathematically founded, and verifiable (Madge and Van der Walt, 1997). In other words, it fits in with the logical positivistic or empirical approach to understanding behaviour, which rests on the assumption that all behaviour is observable and measurable. An example of this method of interpretation can be found in computerized interpretation of assessment scores (see Chapter 14). For example, users of the MMPI-2 (see Chapter 11) may obtain a computer printout of numerical scores on each of the subscales, as well as diagnostic and interpretive statements about the test-taker's personality and emotional functioning.

Mechanical interpretation includes the use of **profile analysis** and comparison of standard scores as well as techniques such as regression and discriminant analysis. In this way, scores are used like a recipe. That is, in the same way that ingredients are combined according to a recipe to make a cake, certain combinations of scores can be interpreted to mean something specific. In this way, mechanical methods are better suited to prediction purposes than to descriptive or evaluative interpretations.

Profile analysis

'A profile is defined as a graphical representation of a client's test scores which provides the test user with an overall picture of the testee's performance and his [or her] relative strong and weak points' (Owen and Taljaard, 1996, p. 133).

A **profile** can be compiled from scores using different measures (such as several cognitive measures), or scores from subtests of the same measure (such as the 16PF). When using scores from different measures, it is important that:

- the norm groups for the different measures are comparable;
- the scores are expressed in the same units (e.g. standard scores); and
- errors of measurement are taken into account.

However, it is important to note that a profile that describes a particular population may not hold for an individual. That is, not all subjects with a specific disorder necessarily manifest a specific cognitive profile associated with the group having that disorder and in addition, there may be others who manifest the pattern or profile but do not have the disorder. In addition to test results, information on other areas of functioning should also be considered when identifying or describing specific disorders and conditions.

16.1.2.2 **Non-mechanical interpretation of assessment results**

Most assessment measures are developed to meet rigorous psychometric criteria such as validity and reliability. In an ideal world, assessment scores would give a perfect indication of a person's attributes or abilities. In the real world, scores are seldom perfect indicators and the person administering the measure has to interpret the scores in the light of other information about the test-taker. This is referred to as **non-mechanical** interpretation. In other words, assessment scores are not regarded as statistics but meaning is inferred from assessment results. This is what happens in clinical practice and this approach is described as impressionistic or dynamic, because it is more sensitive and encompasses a more holistic view of the test-taker. The assessment practitioner uses background information, information gained from interviews, as well as test results, to form an image of impression of the test-taker (see Chapters 1 and 15). One of the main advantages is that test data can be used together with information that can be obtained from facts and inferences obtained through clinical methods (Anastasi and Urbina, 1997).

Of course, there are always dangers in non-mechanical interpretation, the greatest danger being the possibility that the assessment practitioner could over-interpret the available data. The assessment practitioner has to guard against the tendency to overemphasize background information and under-emphasize test scores and individual attitudes and behaviours of the test-taker. The non-mechanical approach is more difficult and demanding than the mechanical approach due to the element of subjectivity. This approach requires greater responsibility from the assessment practitioner to understand the theoretical basis of the measure, its statistical properties, as well as the assessment practitioner's own orientation and subjective input. Responsibility can be gained through thorough academic training, keeping up to date with developments in the field, as well as extensive training and experience with the assessment measures.

16.1.2.3 Combining mechanical and non-mechanical approaches

Both the mechanical and non-mechanical approaches have been criticized (Madge and Van der Walt, 1996). Supporters of the non-mechanical approach criticize the mechanical approach for being artificial, incomplete, oversimplified, pseudo-scientific, and even blind. On the other hand, the non-mechanical approach is criticized for being unscientific, subjective, unreliable, and vague.

In fact, the two approaches should not be seen as mutually exclusive. They can be integrated and used to complement each other. Matarazzo (1990) has suggested that the most effective procedure in our present state of knowledge is to combine clinical and statistical approaches. The mechanical approach may be used to obtain a score on an intelligence measure, but the non-mechanical approach can be used to consider that score in the light of what is known about the test-taker's particular context. For example, a score of 40 on a motor proficiency test would be below average for

most children, but, for a child who has sustained a severe head injury and has some residual paralysis, this score may mean that considerable progress has been made. It is important that any measure used should have sound statistical properties and that the assessment results should be viewed within the context of an evaluation of the test-taker, in order for these to be interpreted meaningfully.

Behavioural cluster analysis is a particular method of interpreting and synthesizing diverse results from a test battery to identify congruent patterns of behaviour/competencies linked to disorders (e.g., a mild head injury, a learning problem) or a particular job competency profile by combining mechanical and non-mechanical approaches. The first step in behavioural cluster analysis is to list all the measures used that tapped a certain behaviour/competency. For example, to assess the verbal reasoning ability of an applicant a Reading Comprehension test and the Similarities and Vocabulary subtests of an intelligence test were used and an interview was conducted. The second step is to interpret each of the test scores obtained mechanically. The third step is to combine all the test information obtained together with behavioural observations and collateral information to arrive at an **integrated descriptive narrative** of the verbal reasoning ability of the applicant (using the non-mechanical interpretation method). For example, as the applicant obtained an average score for the Vocabulary subtest, could express herself clearly when answering questions during the interview, and obtained below average scores for Similarities and Reading Comprehension, the integrative descriptive narrative could be as follows: While the applicant has a good vocabulary and expresses herself clearly, she has some difficulty to think systematically and logically when she needs to analyze, evaluate and understand complex written material and verbal arguments. Behavioural cluster analysis would be conducted for each of the behaviours/competencies assessed to determine whether the pattern of performance across the behaviours/competencies is congruent with a certain disorder or job competency profile. For example, lawyers need to have good verbal reasoning ability. So, if a school-leaver wishes to pursue a career in law, but has some verbal reasoning difficulties, a career counsellor might either suggest that the person pursues another career or that certain verbal reasoning skills (e.g., identifying and developing an argument) need to be developed.

16.1.3 Interpretation of norm-referenced tests

In Chapters 1 and 6 you were introduced to the idea that there are two types of measures, norm-referenced and criterion-referenced. You will no doubt remember that in a **norm-referenced** measure each test-taker's performance is interpreted with reference to a relevant standardization sample (Gregory, 2007). Let us look at a practical example. On the SSAIS-R (see Chapter 10), the mean scaled score for each subtest is 10. This means that a child who obtains a scaled score of 10 is considered average *in comparison to the performance of all the children in the normative sample*. Therefore, it is important to establish that the particular child you are assessing matches or is relatively similar to the characteristics of the normative sample. If they do not match, you do not have a basis for comparison and your interpretation of the test score will not be meaningful. The results of norm-referenced measures are often reported as scores, such as **percentile ranks** or **standard scores** (see Chapter 3), which are calculated on the basis of the performance of the group on whom the measure was normed.

In practice, it often happens that the test-taker does not exactly match the normative sample. For example, in South Africa we often have to use measures that were normed in other countries. This factor must be taken into account when interpreting assessment results. In this instance, the score cannot be considered an accurate reflection of the test-taker's ability but should be seen as merely an approximate indication. **Clinical interpretation** then becomes particularly important. For example, many of the neuropsychological measures currently used to determine the presence or severity of brain damage were developed overseas and local alternatives do not exist. However, due to commonalities in brain-behaviour relationships and the cognitive processes associated with them, there is sufficient evidence that certain patterns of scores are applicable cross-culturally (Shuttleworth-Jordan, 1996). These measures can be used

in a multicultural society such as South Africa, provided that the scores are interpreted qualitatively and not in a recipe fashion.

16.1.4 Interpretation of criterion-referenced measures

Whereas norm-referenced measures are interpreted within the framework of a representative sample, **criterion-referenced** measures *compare the test-taker's performance to the attainment of a defined skill or content* (Gregory, 2007). In other words, the focus is on what the test-taker can do rather than on a comparison with the performance of others (norm-referenced). An example of a criterion-referenced measure with which we are all familiar is a school or university examination. The test-taker is required to master specific subject content and examinations are marked accordingly, irrespective of how well or badly other students perform. In this way, criterion-referenced measures can be meaningfully interpreted without reference to norms. What matters is whether the test-taker has met the criterion, which reflects mastery of the content domain required (in the case of academic examinations, the criterion is usually a mark of 50 per cent).

16.2 Principles for conveying test results

The importance of how feedback on the outcome of assessment is conveyed is often not clearly understood by an assessment practitioner. There are certain practical and ethical considerations to be taken into account when conveying assessment results to test-takers and other interested people. Not only the content but also the way in which assessment results are conveyed can have a considerable impact on people's lives. Assessment should not be seen as an isolated event. It is part of the process of evaluating and taking action in the interests of the test-taker (see Chapter 1). In the case of psychological assessment, the assessment process (that includes conveying results) should be seen as a form of psychological intervention. Decisions that are made on the basis of assessment results can change the course of someone's life.

16.2.1 Ethical considerations

Certain professional ethical values guide the use

and interpretation of results as well as the way in which these results are conveyed (see Chapter 8). The discussion that follows pertains to psychological measures in particular but, in general, should be taken into account with any kind of measure.

Irrespective of whether psychological measures or other procedures are used, all behavioural assessment involves the possible invasion of privacy (Anastasi and Urbina, 1997). This principle sometimes conflicts with psychologists' (and other professionals') commitment to the goal of advancing knowledge about human behaviour. The deciding factor is usually the purpose of the assessment. However, whatever the purpose, the protection of privacy is of greatest importance.

16.2.1.1 **Confidentiality**

By law, psychological services are confidential. This means that a psychologist may not discuss any aspect relating to clients (or test-takers) without their consent. Assessment practitioners must respect the test-taker's right to confidentiality at all times.

The right to confidentiality raises the question: Who should have access to assessment results? Assessment results may not be divulged to anyone without the knowledge and consent (preferably written) of the test-taker. However, in some instances, a psychologist may be compelled by law to provide assessment results. When required to do so, the psychologist should make it clear that he/she is doing this under protest. Ethical dilemmas do arise regarding the issue of confidentiality (see Box 16.1) and the professional has to take responsibility for whatever action is taken, always remembering that serving the best interests of the test-taker is paramount.

BOX 16.1 DILEMMAS OF CONFIDENTIALITY

While you are administering a test to Thabo (who is ten years old), he confides in you that he is a victim of sexual abuse and that the perpetrator is a well respected member of the family. What should you do? The situation in South Africa dictates that if you suspect abuse of any kind, you are required by law to report it. In matters of sexual abuse, it is generally best to encourage the person concerned to report the problem themselves. In the case of a

child, this is more difficult. If you decide to report the matter yourself, make sure to have all the facts first, to take steps to protect the child (this requires simultaneous multidisciplinary intervention) and to ensure that professional services are available to the family to deal with reactions to the matter. If adequate steps are not taken, serious complications may arise. Gregory (2007) cites the example of a young woman who unexpectedly told the psychologist that her brother, who lived at home with their mother, was a paedophile. The psychologist informed the police who raided the home. The mother was traumatized by the event and became very angry at her daughter, resulting in their estrangement. The daughter then sued the psychologist for breach of confidentiality.

It is not considered a breach of confidentiality when psychologists provide information to other professionals who are consulting members of a professional team. For example, in psycho-legal (forensic) cases, a psychologist may discuss an individual with other members of a multidisciplinary team (see Chapter 15). The guiding principle should be that the psychologist shares information to the extent that it is in the best interests of the individual concerned.

The situation is made a little more difficult in the work context where the interests of the organization generally predominate over those of the individual (see Chapter 8). The psychologist has to ensure that the data is used for the purpose for which the person was assessed only. For example, if a psychologist administers a measure to determine a person's clerical skills, the results should not be used to give an indication of that person's intellectual ability.

16.2.1.2 **Accountability**

The psychologist should remember that he/she is, at all times, accountable for the way in which assessment measures are used and the interpretations that are made, as well as for protecting the security of test results. Proper training, an up to date knowledge base, and sensitivity to the needs of the test-taker are essential components of the assessment procedure. You can consult Chapters 8 and 18 for more information in this regard.

It is important to remember that test-takers have rights as well (see Box 16.2).

Accountability also includes taking steps for the safe and secure storage of assessment results and disposal of obsolete data. Assessment data should be stored securely so that no unauthorized person has access to it. Psychologists are required to keep records of client data, but when assessment information is obsolete and may be detrimental to the person concerned, the data should be destroyed.

16.2.2 **Methods of conveying assessment results**

Assessment results should always be conveyed within the context of an interpersonal situation or relationship. This means that the assessment practitioner should be prepared to be supportive of the test-taker's emotional reactions to the results. The assessment practitioner also needs to show respect for the test-taker's rights and welfare. Assessment results should be conveyed with sensitivity and directed at the level on which the test-taker is functioning. The psychologist should be aware of the person's ability to take in the information and may need to convey results at different times, as and when the person is ready.

It is often helpful to ask the test-taker about his/her own knowledge or feelings about the aspect of behaviour that was assessed. This may serve as a starting point for further elaboration. Discussing the test-taker's experience of the measures can provide information that can confirm the validity of the results or throw light on ambiguous findings. The test-taker should also be given the opportunity to express feelings about the assessment procedure and to ask for further information.

Assessment results should be conveyed in a way that will best serve the original purpose for which the test was administered. If, for example, you collect test data with the aim of revising a school curriculum, the test results should be interpreted and conveyed with that purpose in mind.

As far as possible, assessment results should be conveyed in general terms, in descriptive form rather than as numerical scores. Test scores such as those obtained on intelligence measures, are often misunderstood and may lead to labelling which can stigmatize a person. This is particularly important when the test-taker differs from the members of the norm group, in which case the score obtained may not be an adequate reflection of the test-taker's capabilities or characteristics. In addi-

---

BOX 16.2 A TEST-TAKER'S BILL OF RIGHTS

When someone is referred for assessment, it is easy for the assessment practitioner to adopt a position of authority and lose sight of the individual concerned. Part of professional accountability is to consider the rights of test-takers (Rogers, 1997).

Test-taker's Bill of Rights

Respect and dignity	Always, not negotiable
Fairness	Unbiased measures and use of test data
Informed consent	Agreement to assessment with clear knowledge of what will happen; right to refuse
Explanation of test results	Clear and understandable explanation
Confidentiality	Guarantee that assessment results will not be available to others without your express permission
Professional competence	Assessment practitioners well trained
Labels	Category descriptions should not be negative or offensive
Linguistic minorities	Language ability should not compromise assessment results
Persons with a disability	Disability should not compromise assessment results

tion, the assessment practitioner should use language that is understandable and avoid technical terminology or jargon.

Probably the most important point is that communicating assessment results should always occur in a context that includes consideration of all relevant information about the individual who takes the measure. We will discuss the importance of this point in Chapter 17. Contextual information provides a framework that makes any test result richer and more meaningful.

16.2.3 **Conveying children's assessment results**

Children are usually assessed not at their own request but because they are referred by parents, the school, or other interested parties. It is, therefore, important to involve children in understanding the reasons for being assessed and in conveying assessment results.

Children may misinterpret the reasons for assessment. For example, a fourteen-year-old girl living in a children's home was referred for psychological assessment to assist with guidance and future planning. The girl was very resistant to assessment because she thought it meant she was going to be sent to an industrial school. Explaining the purpose of assessment and how it would serve her best interests ensured her cooperation and enhanced her performance. Similarly, involving her in the feedback of assessment results made the process more meaningful and helped her feel part of the decisions being made about her life.

When children are to be assessed, the assessment practitioner has the obligation to explain to parents the nature of the measures to be used, the conclusions that can be reached, and the limitations of the assessment data.

Parents are often mystified by psychological measures and subsequent intervention is made more meaningful by involving them in the process. The reason for assessing the child determines the information that is conveyed to parents. The psychologist needs to be honest with parents, but also sensitive to the possibility of upsetting them. The results of the assessment can be conveyed in the form of a description of the child's functioning, indicating what action needs to be taken, rather than merely providing scores or labels. For example, it may be more helpful to explain to parents that a child is distractible and needs more structure and routine, than saying that the child has an attention deficit disorder, a label that can lead to stigmatization and negative perceptions. The psychologist should emphasize the child's strengths and encourage the parents to do the same. Parents sometimes have unrealistic expectations about their children, which can be damaging in itself. The psychologist can help parents to gain a more realistic perception of their children's abilities without resorting to scores and diagnoses.

The psychologist also needs to take the parents' characteristics and situation into account when conveying information about assessment results. On one hand, this applies to their education or knowledge of assessment, for example, the terms that the psychologist uses should fit in with the parents' life experience. In addition, it also applies to the anticipated emotional responses to the information as they will not always receive the results with calm and rational acceptance. Many parents come away from an information session feeling bewildered or angry, because they have not fully understood what has been said or the implications of the findings and may have been too self-conscious to say so. The psychologist should be sensitive to them and allow opportunities for expressing feelings and asking questions that concern them.

It is not always preferable for the child who was assessed to be present when the results are discussed. When the focus is on abilities and aptitudes, the results can be discussed with child and parents together. When emotional or behavioural issues are the focus, separate discussions can be followed up by joint sessions as required for therapeutic reasons.

You can consult texts on counselling skills for more in-depth treatment of this topic.

16.3 **Reporting assessment results in written form**

Communicating assessment results usually includes the preparation of a written report that is often followed by discussion and consultation with the test-taker and other interested parties. Parents, educational institutions, and other organizations often request written reports on assessment results. Even if a report is not requested, it is useful to prepare one not only as a record for future use, but also because it helps to organize and clarify thoughts about the test results. It serves a synthesizing function for the person who administers the measures.

There is no one standard way in which reports should be written. In terms of style, reports should be written clearly and simply, avoiding professional jargon, with the main aim of avoiding misinterpretation of results. The following are general guidelines for effective report writing:

- provide identifying information, including the date of the assessment;
- focus on the purpose for which the individual was tested;
- provide relevant facts only; if some background information is required, provide only the detail relevant to the assessment process;
- write the report with the nature of the audience in mind; if the report is for parents it may be more personal or informal but if it is directed at an organization, different information may be required;
- comment on the reliability and validity of the assessment. For example, the extent that the client cooperated and was motivated to perform optimally can be used to reflect on the accuracy/validity of the test results obtained;
- list the assessment measures and other information-gathering techniques (e.g., an interview) that were used. Some practitioners prefer to write their report by presenting the results for each measure separately, while others prefer to organize the report according to the behavioural domains/competencies assessed and provide an integrative descriptive narrative per behavioural domain/competency;
- concentrate on the test-taker's strengths and weaknesses that constitute differentiating characteristics; the measure of an effective report is whether it is unique to the individual or could apply equally well to someone else;
- use general, understandable terms to describe behaviour;

- focus on interpretations and conclusions; test scores are not included in reports but may be divulged on special request and with the consent of the test-taker;
- where recommendations are made, it must be evident to the reader why or how these flow from the assessment results;
- uphold ethical standards and values;
- remember that the quality of technical presentation says a great deal about you as a professional;
- as the report writer is ultimately accountable for what is contained in the report, ask yourself whether you can substantiate everything that you have written;
- remember to authenticate your report. That is, sign it and include your credentials (e.g., 'registered clinical psychologist'). Where the assessment practitioner is not yet registered for independent practice (e.g., an intern, a psychometrist – supervised practice), the report must be developed and co-signed by a registered psychologist.

In the past, confidential reports could be withheld, even from the person who took the measures. In terms of South Africa's new constitution, individuals have a right to any information about themselves. This means that reports cannot be withheld as confidential. However, apart from this consideration, the main aim of the report should be to provide meaningful information that will be useful to test-takers for the purpose for which they were assessed.

16.4 **Conclusion**

In this chapter, you have learnt that there are different ways of interpreting and conveying assessment results, according to the purpose of assessment, the individual being assessed, and the context in which that individual functions. Interpretation of assessment results relies on the validity of the particular measures used and methods of interpretation vary according to the type of measures applied. In the face of all this variation, it is the human element that is the most important. The trained professional makes assessment results meaningful by interpreting them in an ethically acceptable and personally accountable way, based on training and expert knowledge. In this way, numbers (test scores) can be transformed into valuable information that serves the best interest of the individual.

›› CRITICAL THINKING CHALLENGE 16.1

Page back to Critical thinking challenge 15.2 in Chapter 15. A case study was presented of a four-year-old, John, who was assessed as his mother thought that his drawings were immature. The assessment findings on the Griffiths Scales are provided in Critical thinking challenge 15.2. Write a report for the mother on the assessment results using the principles outlined above. Do not use psychological jargon, focus on his strengths, and make practical suggestions regarding aspects of John's development that need to be stimulated.

CHECKING YOUR PROGRESS 16.1

16.1   Briefly describe the role of test validity in descriptive and evaluative interpretation of test scores.

16.2   Distinguish between descriptive and predictive interpretation of test results.

16.3   What are the three criteria for profile analysis based on scores from different measures?

16.4   Discuss the main advantages and disadvantages of non-mechanical interpretation of assessment results.

16.5   Discuss the use of a behavioural cluster approach to interpreting and integrating assessment results.

16.6   In the context of guidelines for report writing, provide a critical discussion of the statement that test scores should not be included in the report on the results of the assessment.

16.7   John's parents have requested psychological assessment for him because he is not doing well at school and is starting to display acting out behaviour. His parents are very disappointed because they have made sacrifices for him and expect great things of him. The assessment results suggest that John is of low average intellectual ability, he is not coping at school, and feels unsure of himself. As a result, he engages in behaviour that helps him feel in control. What guidelines should you use when you convey the test results?

By now, you are well aware of the complexities of assessment practice. Our next stop will further highlight the many factors that impact on the assessment process.

Factors affecting assessment results

KATE W GRIEVE AND CHERYL FOXCROFT

Chapter

17

CHAPTER OUTCOMES

What does a test score mean?
Is a test score a true reflection of my ability?
Are test scores genetically determined?
Does depression affect test performance?
Do socio-cultural experiences make a difference to test performance?
Are there equivalent measures for different language and cultural groups?
How do differing environments affect test performance?
Are city children smarter than children living in rural areas?
What is test wiseness?
What does variation in subtest scores of a measure tell you?
Can the person administering the measure influence assessment results?
Is any single measure suitable for South Africa's heterogeneous population?
A score is a score is a score ...

Psychological assessment is based on the notion that people have inherent abilities and characteristics that can be measured. These broad traits or abilities are partly inherited but are not static, because the way they are manifest can vary according to different contexts and conditions. It is because we assume that traits permeate behaviour in many contexts that we undertake psychological measurement and make assumptions about behaviour as it is manifest in varying situations. However, it is important to remember that a test score is just a number. It is not equivalent to the ability that is being measured. When we measure two kilograms of potatoes we know exactly what we are measuring; with psychological measures, however, we cannot measure an attribute or ability directly and we therefore have to infer it from a person's test performance. In so doing, we give the person a score (or number) on the basis of the response given. A score is therefore an inferred or indirect measure of the strength of that attribute or ability. You learned about measurement error in Chapter 3, and will therefore know that there are factors in addition to a person's inherent ability that can influence scores and the meaning of those scores. In this chapter, we will look at some important factors that should be considered when interpreting performance on psychological measures.

Imagine that you have selected a suitable measure, administered it carefully, and scored the protocol. You have probably also worked out a scaled score with reference to a normative group (see Chapter 3). But what does that score actually mean? You may be puzzled by this question so let us look at some examples.

The first case study concerns John, a man of thirty-four years of age, who is the managing director of an international company and a consultant for several other business concerns. He has a pilot's license and plays chess on a national level. He was head boy of his school, obtained distinctions in all his subjects, and was voted the boy most likely to succeed by his class. John was referred for assessment because he recently had difficulties coping with his business commitments. The second case study involves Thandi, who is twenty years old and a prospective university student. Her father is a manual labourer, she comes from a disadvantaged environment and the quality of her high school education was poor. Thandi requested help in deciding whether she would be capable of doing a science degree. John and Thandi are assessed with a standardized intelligence scale and both obtain an IQ of 105. Does this score mean the same for both individuals? We will return to discuss these examples later, but they serve as an introduction to this chapter in which we discuss some of the important factors that have to be taken into account when interpreting a test score. By the end of this chapter you will be able to:

> understand how the individual's context impacts on assessment results;
> understand how variations in administering a measure impacts on assessment performance;
> understand the factors to consider when interpreting variations in test scores;
> explain how characteristics of the assessment practitioner can impact on assessment performance;
> explain how characteristics of the test-taker impact on assessment performance;
> understand the impact of cheating on test performance and how to detect and combat it; and
> understand how bias impacts on the validity of the assessment results.

17.1 Viewing assessment results in context

As we pointed out right from Chapter 1, a test score is only **one piece of information** about how a person performs or behaves. Therefore, if we look at an individual in terms of a test score only, we will have a very limited understanding of that person. This is why Claassen (1997) wrote: 'Never can a test score be interpreted without taking note of and understanding the context in which the score was obtained' (p. 306).

In addition to the test score, the information in which we are interested can be obtained by examining the **context** in which a person lives. When you think about it, you will realize that people actually function in several different contexts concurrently. At the lowest level, there is the **biological context**, referring to physical bodily structures and functions, which are the substrata for human behaviour and experiences (see Section 17.1.1). Then there is the **intrapsychic context**, which comprises abilities, emotions, and personal dispositions (see Section 17.1.2). Biological and intrapsychic processes are regarded as interdependent components of the individual as a psycho-biological entity. In addition, because people do not live in a vacuum, we need to consider a third and very important context, which is the **social context** (see Section 17.1.3). The social context refers to aspects of the environments in which we live, such as our homes and communities, people with whom we interact, work experiences, as well as cultural and socio-political considerations.

In addition to looking at the effects of the different contexts within which people function, we also need to examine **methodological** considerations such as test administration, which may also influence test performance and therefore have a bearing on the interpretation of a test score (see Section 17.2).

17.1.1 **The biological context**

17.1.1.1 **Age-related changes**

One of the most obvious factors that affect test performance is chronological age. This is why measures are developed for certain age groups based on the skills and interests characteristic of that particular age group. A good illustration of this point can be found in infant and pre-school measures (see Chapters 10 and 15), which differ in content according to the age range they cover. Traditionally, measures for infants (i.e. young children from birth to approximately two years of age) include items that largely measure sensory and motor development and in this way differ from measures for older children. Measures for older children (from about two-and-a-half to six years) focus more on the child's verbal and conceptual abilities, because development at this stage is highly verbal and symbolic. If you wonder why this is so, you can look at well-known theories of development, such as that of Piaget. You will note that early infant development proceeds through the medium of sensory and motor skills, such as

hearing and producing sounds, manipulating objects or gaining increasing muscular and postural control. In fact, Piaget (Piaget and Inhelder, 1971) describes cognitive development during the first two years of the infant's life as the sensorimotor period. After the age of two, children use their verbal and cognitive skills to start reasoning about the world around them. The content of tests for pre-school children reflects their changing abilities. However, there is not necessarily continuity in development from infancy to childhood and the meaning of an infant's test score rests on certain assumptions that we have about the nature of early development (see Box 17.1).

BOX 17.1 PREDICTABILITY OF INFANT MEASURES OF MENTAL ABILITY

Infant intelligence as assessed by traditional measures is a very poor predictor of later intelligence. Studies have indicated that there is a low correlation between traditional psychometric test scores in the first year of life and later IQ. Between eighteen months and four years of age, the ability of mental tests to predict later IQ increases gradually and, by five years, the correlations can be as high as 0.80 to 0.90 (Gibbs, 1990). There are several possible explanations for the poor predictability of infant measures. Firstly, the nature of the developmental process may not be as continuous as we think. Children may develop at different rates at different times. Secondly, infant tests are strongly influenced by fine motor coordination and sociability, whereas the contents of intelligence measures for slightly older children are more closely related to abilities required for successful school performance. These abilities are typically acquired by approximately eighteen months of age in some rudimentary form, the time at which infant measures start to increase in predictive ability. In addition, early development is 'plastic' or malleable, and environmental events, over which infants have little control, may alter their genetically determined developmental course. Socio-economic status and the quality of the home environment have a strong influence on children's intellectual functioning (Richter and Grieve, 1991).

In cases where infants are neurologically impaired and function considerably below average, there is a greater degree of continuity (and therefore greater predictability) between functioning in infancy and childhood, due to the biological constraints on development. Although the severity of the disability can also be influenced by the quality of the child's caring environment, the range of outcomes is restricted, compared to that of a non-impaired child.

The degree of predictability also seems to depend on the type of test that is used. For example, the new infant intelligence measures that are based on information processing techniques, such as recognition, memory and attentiveness to the environment, have much greater predictive validity than the more traditional measures (Gibbs, 1990).

As children grow older, their intelligence increases with respect to their ability to perform intellectual tasks of increasing difficulty and to perform them faster (this is referred to as their **mental age**). For this reason, **standardized measures** of intellectual ability have **norms** for different age groups. The ratio between mental age and chronological age is fairly constant up to a certain age and, therefore, IQ scores also remain fairly constant. Mental age starts levelling off after the age of sixteen and it is generally found that performance on most intelligence tests shows no further noticeable improvement. Adults' scores may vary a little as a result of life experience and subsequent accumulated knowledge, but ability level remains mostly the same. Scores on intelligence measures therefore stabilize during early adulthood and then start declining after the age of approximately fifty years, as older persons react more slowly and are less able to cope with new situations. It is essential to have knowledge about the normal pattern of cognitive changes in the elderly so that abnormal changes, such as those associated with dementia, can be detected and the elderly and their families can receive the necessary assistance.

It is important to note that an **IQ score** in no way fully expresses a person's intelligence (see also Chapter 10). The score is an indication of performance on a sample of tasks used to assess aspects of intellectual ability in a particular assessment situation. There are many non-intellectual (non-cognitive) factors that influence performance on a measure of intellectual ability – this is the focus of this chapter.

17.1.1.2 Physical impairments

There is a wide variety of physical conditions that can have an effect on test performance. Consider the following example: While you are testing Mrs Garies who is sixty-eight years old, you find that you have to keep repeating questions and providing explanations and you wonder if her understanding is poor. When you calculate her score, you note that it is low for her age, and, based on her difficulties in understanding, you conclude that she is mentally impaired. Would you be correct? If you had discovered in the course of your interview that Mrs Garies has a hearing problem (but is too proud to admit it), you would realize that her low test score is a function of her hearing impairment and that she may not have limited mental ability. As you saw in Chapter 9, by using specific measures designed for people with disabilities or by adapting measures and administration procedures, a better indication can be obtained of their true level of functioning.

As you saw in Chapter 15, an important part of the assessment process involves taking a thorough medical history. Previous trauma, such as a stroke or head injury (see Box 17.2) can have a permanent effect on intellectual ability. In general, poor scores are obtained on intelligence measures where there is radiological evidence of neurological impairment.

BOX 17.2 THE EFFECTS OF TRAUMATIC BRAIN INJURY

South Africa has one of the highest rates of traumatic brain injury in the world. There are different types of brain injury and the consequences of the injuries vary as a result of individual differences in physiological make-up, personal temperament and ability factors, as well as social circumstances. When there is a focal injury (a blow to one particular part of the brain), the impairment is usually limited to those functions served by the specific area of the brain that is injured. When injury is widespread, there may be diffuse axonal injury that results in microscopic damage throughout the brain. This type of injury is frequently sustained in car accidents due to abrupt acceleration-deceleration and rotational forces and is often more debilitating than focal injuries, because a larger area of the brain is involved. People who have sustained diffuse brain injury, particularly if it is a severe injury, usually have residual cognitive difficulties in the areas of attention and concentration, verbal functioning and memory, as well as motor slowing (Lezak, 1995). There are often behavioural difficulties, such as increased irritability and aggression, decreased motivation and emotional disorders, such as depression. There is no one pattern of symptoms and the effects of brain injury vary with age, the location and severity of the injury, and the personal and social circumstances of the person concerned. However, the effects of brain injury are generally seen in poor performance on intelligence tests and neuropsychological measures designed to assess different functions and abilities. An intelligence measure alone is often not sufficient to identify brain impairment, because a previously intelligent person may be able to rely on previously well-learned and established patterns of behaviour and abilities and still be able to perform adequately while, at the same time, being unable to cope with new situations and the demands of daily living.

Deficits in cognitive functioning often also accompany serious illnesses, such as cerebral malaria (Holding et al., 2004), meningitis, chronic fatigue syndrome (Busichio, Tiersky, Deluca, and Natelson, 2004), or HIV/Aids infection (Reger, Welsh, Razani, Martin, and Boone, 2002).

Speech impairments present another type of problem. If the assessment practitioner cannot understand the verbal responses of a speech impaired client, lower scores may be awarded than would be the case if the responses were understood. There is an example of a young man with cerebral palsy who was sent to an institution for the severely mentally retarded because his speech was almost incomprehensible and he had very little motor control. The young man befriended another patient who slowly began to understand the sounds he was making and typed out what he was saying on computer. It was subsequently discovered that the young man had a great deal of ability and he was helped to

write a book on his experiences. Even if they can speak well, patients with cerebral palsy or other motor impairments may be penalized by timed tests, and a proper indication of their ability can only be obtained by using alternative measures or adapting standard measures.

In addition to permanent disabilities, there are also transient physical conditions that can depress test scores. An example of such a condition is chronic pain, which has a negative effect on the deployment of existing abilities. Even things that sound trivial, such as disturbed sleep, can interfere with a person's functioning and lead to lowered test scores (Aloia, Arnedt, Davis, Riggs, and Byrd, 2004). In addition, it is important to note whether the person is taking any medication. For example, excessive intake of painkillers can affect performance on psychological measures and some drugs have side effects like attention difficulties or motor slowing. In some cases, medication may improve intellectual functioning, for example antiretroviral therapy improves cognitive functioning in people with HIV/Aids (Richardson et al., 2002). Chronic alcohol abuse can also have a negative effect on cognitive functioning and test performance (Lezak, 2004).

17.1.2 **The intrapsychic context**

When we consider the **intrapsychic context**, we look at people's experiences and feelings about themselves. It is difficult to separate the biological and intrapsychic factors because one's experiences, interpretations, feelings, and personality depend on biologically based processes such as perception, cognition, emotion, and motivation, as well as the genetic and experiential contributions to these processes.

17.1.2.1 **Transient conditions**

Transient conditions refer to everyday events that unexpectedly crop up and upset us sufficiently so that we are 'not ourselves' and cannot perform as well as we normally do. Imagine that you are on your way to write an examination. A car jumps a red robot and collides with yours. Fortunately there is relatively minor damage, you are unhurt, and you go on your way, concentrating on getting to the exam hall in time. However, when you get your exam paper, you have difficulty understanding the questions, your concentration wanders, you find it hard to express yourself properly, and after an hour you give up and go home. What has happened? Stress and anxiety in any form can interfere with normal functioning, such as the ability to think clearly, to concentrate, and to act on plans and intentions. This is particularly apparent where psychological assessment is concerned. The person may be anxious because he/she does not know what psychological measures are, or may be afraid that the measures might reveal or confirm some weakness or something unpleasant. The person then cannot think clearly and this results in poor performance. A similar situation can arise when a person is upset about a bereavement in the family, or worried about a sick child. On a more severe level, post traumatic stress experienced by people who have been involved in violent and often horrifying events, can significantly impair functioning (Beckham, Crawford, and Feldman, 1998).

17.1.2.2 **Psychopathology**

When psychopathological conditions are present, these usually impair the person's assessment performance (Moritz, Ferahli, and Naber, 2004). For example, cognitive functioning is negatively affected by disorders like anorexia and bulimia nervosa (Tchanturia et al., 2004), anxiety, or depression (Popp, Ellison, and Reeves, 1994). Depression is frequently manifested in problems with memory and psychomotor slowing, as well as difficulty with effortful cognitive tasks (Bostwick, 1994). These conditions may then mask the person's true level of functioning on psychological measures.

17.1.3 **The social context**

We now come to what is probably the most difficult, yet most important, set of factors that have to be considered when interpreting assessment performance. At the beginning of this chapter, we said that a test score has no meaning unless it is viewed in context. Let us look at some of these aspects relating to the social contexts in which people live.

17.1.3.1 **Schooling**

Most intelligence measures are an indirect measure of what the individual has learned during the lifespan and, as such, are strongly influenced by schooling experiences (Nell, 2000). This is because formal education provides us with the problem-solving strategies, cognitive skills, and knowledge that we need to acquire information and deal with new problems, which is what is required by traditional intelligence measures.

It follows that there is a strong relation between scores on intelligence measures and scholastic and academic achievement (Holding et al., 2004). One would expect that an adult who has no more than a Grade 5-level education might obtain a fairly low score on an intelligence measure, but it would be surprising if a person of the same age who passed Grade 12 obtained the same low score. Schooling experiences influence how people think or the reasoning strategies they use, how they approach problems, their ability to deal with issues in an independent way, as well as their ability to work accurately and quickly (see the discussion on **test wiseness** in Section 17.1.3.5).

However, the situation in South Africa is complicated by the fact that attainment of a particular grade is not necessarily the best indicator of what a person is able to achieve. There is evidence that it is not only the grade that counts but the quality of schooling as well. Poorer quality schooling makes it difficult for students to compete on an equal footing with those from more advantaged educational backgrounds. For example, Grade 12 learners with poorer quality schooling in the previously disadvantaged areas of South Africa may not have the same knowledge base or skills as a learner with a Grade 12 from a school in a privileged area (Shuttleworth-Edwards et al., 2004). Similarly, the number of years of formal education a person has does not mean the same for everyone. Six years of quality schooling is obviously not the same as six years of poor schooling. The students with poorer quality schooling are less likely to have acquired the same level of cognitive skills (which are necessary for successful test performance) as the advantaged students. For this reason, users of the WAIS-III standardized for use in South Africa are cautioned to take adequate account of all the factors impinging on test performance when interpreting scores (Claassen, Krynauw, Paterson and wa ga Mathe, 2001)

What does this mean in practice? If a pupil from

a large, poorly run school in Soweto and a pupil from a well run school in one of the better areas in Johannesburg both achieve the same score on a traditional measure of intelligence, this does not necessarily mean that they both have the same level of intellectual ability. The student from Soweto may have a great deal of potential ability, but, because the schooling experience did not equip the student with the kinds of information and skills needed for good performance on the measure, the score obtained may be an underestimation of that pupil's potential ability. For this reason, newer intelligence measures are designed to measure potential ability, rather than relying heavily on knowledge and skills obtained from formal schooling (see Box 17.3) and also Chapter 10.

BOX 17.3 THE ASSESSMENT OF LEARNING POTENTIAL

Taylor (1994) has developed an assessment approach that assesses learning potential, evaluating the person on future developmental capacity rather than on prior knowledge and skills. Learning potential measures appear to measure the construct of fluid intelligence. Traditional measures tend to incorporate questions that require the individual to draw on knowledge or skills acquired in the formal educational system, or on other enriching experiences (such as those derived from reading extensively). The main purpose of learning potential measures is to incorporate learning exercises in the material and to assess how effectively the individual copes with and masters strange tasks. New competencies are developed in the test room itself, where all individuals have the same opportunity to acquire the new knowledge and skill. Learning potential measures evaluate individual differences in terms of learning variables rather than knowledge variables. Such learning requires the individual to cope with and attempt to master new cognitive challenges. This approach to assessment appears to offer a great deal of promise in terms of avoiding the influence of prior knowledge and skills or the lack thereof. However, the claimed differences between learning potential measures and existing measures have yet to be unequivocally demonstrated and the validity of learning potential measures proven. In terms of the latter, Murphy and Maree (2006) re-

viewed the use of measures of learning potential at Higher Education institutions in South Africa. They reported both positive and negative findings with respect to learning potential measures being able to predict academic success. In addition, they concluded that when learning potential measures were used in combination with conventional measures, the assessment results provided information of a higher quality that either of the two types of measures on their own.

17.1.3.2 **Language**

Language is generally regarded as the most important single moderator of performance on assessment measures (Nell, 2000). This is because performance on assessment measures could be the product of language difficulties and not ability factors if a measure is administered in a language other than the test-taker's home language. At some time in our lives, we have probably all had to read or study something written in a language different to our own and, even though we may have a working knowledge of that language, we experience the feeling that it takes longer to process the material in another language. We can think and discuss so much better in our own language. By the same token, we would probably therefore perform better in a test that is written and administered in our home language than in a test in a second language. In this way, language becomes a potential source of bias (see Chapters 6, 7 and 9). When a test is written in a different language, it may present a range of concepts that are not accessible in our home language.

You may think that the problem can be solved by translating the measure. Although this is the solution in some instances, this is not always the case because there are other difficulties (see Chapter 7). Some languages do not have the concepts and expressions required by measures and an equivalent form of the measure cannot be translated. Measures of verbal functioning pose a particular problem. For example, you cannot merely translate a vocabulary test into another language because the words may not be of the same level of difficulty in the two languages.

There is also the problem of what is the most

suitable language to use (see Chapter 9). Let us consider an example. Itumeleng speaks Northern Sotho at home, together with a little bit of English and some Zulu he has learned from his friends. From Grade 4 his lessons at school have been presented in English and he is currently studying through the medium of English at university. He has acquired most of his knowledge and experience in English and he has a working knowledge of concepts in English. Would it be better to assess Itumeleng's level of ability in English or in his home language? There is no simple answer to this question. Many students prefer to be assessed in English but do not have the advantages of people whose home language is English; they are therefore not comparable. It is unfortunate that this situation often results in a double disadvantage in that their competence in both languages is compromised. For example, students may have some knowledge of English but it may not be very good and, at the same time, having to study in English can detract from further development of their home language. This would have an influence on assessment performance and may mask the actual ability that the measure is designed to assess.

An additional problem arises from the fact that a combination of languages, referred to as a 'township patois', is commonly used in the residential areas surrounding cities and a pure version of one language is seldom spoken. A child who grows up speaking the patois would be at a disadvantage if assessed with a formally translated measure. The solution may lie in bilingual or multilingual assessment and this remains a challenge for the field of psychometrics in South Africa (see Chapters 6, 7, and 9).

17.1.3.3 Culture

Our culture has a pervasive influence on the way we learn, think about things, and behave. In fact, culture cannot be considered as a separate factor, exerting an influence apart from other factors in the person's environment. It is an integral part of that environment. Although there may be cultural differences in test scores, there is no decisive evidence that culture influences competence rather than performance. In other words, although socio-cultural factors may affect manifestations of underlying cognitive and emotional processes, it is unlikely that cultural differences exist in the basic component cognitive processes (Miller, 1987). For example, empirical studies have shown that the pattern and sequence of acquisition according to the Piagetian stages of cognitive development is universal, although the rate of acquisition may vary amongst different cultures (Mwamwenda, 1995). This is why it is important to take cultural differences into account when interpreting test performance.

The content of any measure will reflect the culture of the people who designed the measure and the country in which it is to be used (see Chapters 1, 6, and 7). Clearly, people who do not share the culture of the test developers will be at a disadvantage when taking that particular measure. For example, a child's performance on a memory task is likely to vary according to the way in which the task is constructed – the more familiar the nature of the task, the better the performance (Mistry and Rogoff, 1994). Despite several attempts, there is no such thing as a culture-free measure but assessment practitioners can be sensitive to culture fairness in assessment. For example, items should be examined for cultural bias (see Chapters 6 and 7). When a measure is administered to a person who does not share the culture of the people who developed it and the country in which it was standardized, the assessment practitioner should always consider that the test score obtained may not be a good reflection of the person's true level of functioning due to the influence of cultural factors. An additional consideration is that measures and their resultant scores cannot be assumed to have **equivalent meaning** for different cultures and countries (see Chapter 7). For example, a Spanish version of the Wechsler Adult Intelligence Scales has been developed, but there is doubt about its suitability for Spanish-speaking people living in the United States. When considering adopting a measure developed elsewhere, **validation studies** have to be undertaken first (see Chapter 7).

According to the belief that behaviour is shaped by prescriptions of the culture, its values and guiding ideals, it is accepted that cultural experience influences the meaning of events for an individual and, therefore, responses will differ among cultures. This is particularly important in a projective measure, such as the Thematic Apperception Test, that rests on the assumption that the stories an individual tells based on the pictorial stimulus material will reveal something of the person's personality disposition. For example, a card showing a picture of a man working on a farm may elicit different responses according to the culture of the person being tested. One person may say that the man is poor because he is working the land himself and has no labourers to help him, while another may say the man is rich because he has his own land that he can farm. A different response should not be seen as a deficient (poorer or abnormal) one but should be viewed as a function of the person's culture.

In addition to the number of different cultures in South Africa, we also have the problem of variations in acculturation. **Acculturation** refers to the process by which people become assimilated into a culture. This process occurs at different speeds and is not the same for all facets of behaviour. We see, for example, that many people who move from rural areas into cities generally let go of values associated with a more traditional way of life and adopt a more Western way of living. But not everything changes at the same pace. There might be quite a quick change in the way the person dresses or in habits such as watching television, but the person might still adhere to more traditional beliefs such as consulting a faith healer rather than a psychologist when there are problems. There are wide interpersonal differences in the degree and pace of acculturation. We cannot, for example, presume that someone who has lived in a city for five years has adopted Western values. Differences in acculturation have important implications for performance on assessment measures due to the impact of the familiarity with the culture on which the measure is based (see for example Kennepohl, Shore, Nabors, and Hanks, 2004). The closer the person's personal values and practices are to the culture, the more appropriate the measure. In turn, if the measure is appropriate, the person's test performance is more likely to be an accurate indication of his/her actual level of functioning. The effects of acculturation can be seen in the closing of the gap in intelligence test scores of black and white South African students

who have benefitted from good quality education (Shuttleworth-Edwards et al., 2004).

In some cases, it becomes very difficult to know which measure is most appropriate to use. Let us consider the following example. Nomsa is twelve years old and her home language is Xhosa. She attends a school in a middle class suburb, speaks English at school, and has friends from different cultural groups. Should she be assessed with the Individual Scale for Xhosa-speaking Pupils because of her home language or with the SSAIS-R (see Chapter 10) because of her situation? There is no easy answer to this question. Each person's situation has to be considered individually, according to his/her familiarity with the predominant language and culture.

The most important point to remember is that without measures with culturally relevant content and appropriate norms, fair testing practices may be compromised. The use of potentially culturally biased measures may have enormous implications for making important decisions in people's lives. For example, people may be denied educational and occupational opportunities due to a test score that is not a valid indicator of their ability. However, to add points to a score to compensate for cultural differences (so-called 'affirmative assessment') does not provide the answer. For instance, if a psychologist used a particular test in an attempt to determine a specific deficit, adding points may mask the presence of a deficit and this would not be responsible practice. The potential contribution of cultural influences to assessment performance should always be kept in mind.

17.1.3.4 **Environmental factors**

Performance on measures of ability is influenced by variation of environmental factors. We need to consider **distal factors**, or those relating to the wider environment, such as socio-economic status and the degree of exposure to an enriching social environment, as well as **proximal factors**, or those relating to the individual's immediate environment, such as socialization experiences in the home. Why is this important? Environmental factors determine the types of learning experiences and opportunities to which we are exposed and this, in turn, affects our level of ability and the extent to which we are able to use that ability. This, of course, plays a role in test performance.

The home environment

There are certain child rearing practices that have been shown to promote the development of competence and cognitive abilities that are tapped by traditional measures of development. The kinds of child rearing practices shown to promote children's development are parental responsivity (including fathers' involvement) and the provision of home stimulation in the form of the mother's active efforts to facilitate cognitive and language skills, allowing the child to explore the possibilities of the environment, encouraging interaction with the environment, and supporting the development of new skills (Grieve and Richter, 1990). However, there are also indications that universal assumptions about development do not apply equally to the process of development in all cultures. Certain culturally sanctioned child rearing practices may appear to be contradictory to mainstream western practices but should not necessarily be seen as deviant or detrimental (Garcia Coll and Magnuson, 2000). Therefore, in assessing children, it is important to understand children and their families in relation to both the immediate and larger socio-cultural environment and the ways in which cultural factors operate in the child's environment. Individual differences within cultures should also be taken into account. Consider, for example, the view that traditional mothers in Africa tend to be more authoritarian, directive, and conforming in comparison to Western mothers (Kendall, Verster, and Von Mollendorf, 1988). These attitudes are believed to constrain the deployment of cognitive skills required by frequently used ability tests. However, this view does not necessarily apply to all mothers, and does not mean that there is no variation within any cultural group. Most parents act in ways which they perceive to be in the best interests of their children, irrespective of culture (Garcia Coll and Magnuson, 2000). For example, despite living in disadvantaged communities in South Africa, there are mothers who are able to structure their children's environments in order to promote their children's mental development,

irrespective of cultural practices and impoverished environments (Richter and Grieve, 1991).

There are certain characteristics of household structure that can also influence children's abilities. Overcrowding, for example, has generally been found to have an adverse affect on cognitive development as well as on the educational performance of young children. A study of South African children from previously disadvantaged communities has suggested that overcrowding negatively influences children's cognitive milieus by, for example, limiting and interrupting exploratory behaviour, decreasing the number of intimate child-caretaker exchanges, and increasing noise levels (Richter, 1989). Overcrowding does not only have a negative effect on children's development but has been shown to have a detrimental effect on adults as well. However, overcrowding does not necessarily have a negative impact; it all depends on whether the person interprets the situation as stressful. People who have grown up in crowded homes and are used to crowded places generally find them less unpleasant than people who are used to a greater degree of privacy. Overcrowded homes may even offer an advantage to young children, as a result of the possibility of multiple caretakers to provide affection and see to their needs, particularly in cases where their mothers work away from home.

Socio-economic status

Socio-economic status (SES) refers to the broader indices of a person or family's social standing. The major indicators of SES are education, occupation, and income. You may wonder why this would affect performance on psychological measures. A person's SES is important because it determines the type of facilities that are available (such as schools, libraries, clinics, and other social services), the opportunities that present themselves, and the attitudes generally exercised by others in the same socio-economic group. The socio-economic aspects of the environment thus have a significant influence on the experiences that moderate abilities, attitudes, and behaviour. It has been found, for example, that mothers with relatively high levels of education are more likely to provide stimulating home environments than mothers who are less educated. The educated mothers are more likely to read magazines and newspapers (and therefore are more informed about issues), play actively with their children, help them learn rhymes and songs, and take them on outings (Richter and Grieve, 1991). These types of activities help to promote children's development and well-being. Similarly, talking about current issues and having books at home help to promote a culture of learning.

Some of the socio-economic factors that are associated with educational disadvantage are poverty (see Box 17.4), poor health, malnutrition, inadequate school facilities, poor social adjustment, absence of cultural stimulation, lack of books and the other aspects of modern civilization that contribute to the development of Western ways of thinking, which is what is measured in traditional psychological measures. People from disadvantaged environments often do not perform well on psychological measures because the tasks are unfamiliar and may be regarded as unimportant. Achievement in many cognitive measures is a function of the ability to develop strategies to solve problems in the test situation, as well as of being motivated to do well.

BOX 17.4 GROWING UP IN POVERTY

There are indications that of all the continents, sub-Saharan Africa has the highest share of the population living in absolute poverty. For a child, being poor means being at risk for developing both physical and psychological problems. What are these risks? In comparison with children from higher socio-economic backgrounds, children from impoverished backgrounds experience, amongst other things, a greater number of perinatal complications, higher incidence of disabilities, greater likelihood of being in foster care or suffering child abuse, greater risk for conduct disorders, and arrest for infringements of the law. One of the major reasons for developmental risk is believed to be associated with the fact that poverty increases the risk of inattentive or erratic parental care, abuse, or neglect because a significant proportion of parents living in poverty lack the personal and social resources to meet their children's needs (Halpern, 2000). Many young adults living in impoverished inner-city communities have personal experi-

ences of parental rejection or inadequate nurturance, disrupted family environments, parental substance abuse, family violence and difficulties at school. These adverse conditions have a negative effect on their own abilities as parents as well as their ability to form adult relationships, the capacity to complete schooling, to obtain and keep jobs, and to manage their households. In addition, overstressed parents can adversely influence their children in an indirect way by communicating their despondency and despair. This does not mean that all parents in impoverished circumstances are unable to fulfill parenting roles successfully. However, it suggests that consideration should be given to the fact that the stress of poverty can play a major role in directly undermining the efforts of even the most resourceful parents and can therefore detract from the quality of child care.

Urbanization

It is generally found that urban children show superiority over rural children in terms of cognitive performance (Mwamwenda, 1995). The reason for this may be that the enriched and invigorating urban environment stimulates those aspects of cognition usually assessed by formal psychological measures. It is also more likely that provision is made for formal schooling in urban rather than rural environments and access to education at an early age is considered to be the single most powerful factor facilitating cognitive development. Urbanization is also associated with higher parental levels of education and we pointed out earlier that better educated mothers are more likely to provide the kind of home environments that are believed to be beneficial for children's cognitive development.

The effects of urbanization on the changes in people's ability as measured by psychological measures can be seen in South African studies that enable the comparison of test performances of children over a period of thirty years. When the New South African Group Test (NSAGT) was standardized in 1954, it was found that English-speaking pupils were better than Afrikaans-speaking pupils at all age and education levels by an average of 10 IQ points. When the successor of the NSAGT, the

General Scholastic Aptitude Test (GSAT) was administered in 1984, a difference of 5 IQ points in favour of English-speaking children aged twelve, thirteen, and fourteen years was reported. The reduction of the difference between the groups is ascribed to the fact that, during the period between 1954 and 1984, Afrikaans-speaking whites went through a period of rapid urbanization during which their level of education and income increased significantly. The gradual convergence of the scores corresponded with the more general process of cultural and economical convergence between the populations, facilitated by the process of urbanization.

Urbanization must, however, be considered as a global variable that cannot offer a complete explanation for the psychological mechanisms which account for differences in ability.

17.1.3.5 **Test wiseness**

All the factors that we have discussed here contribute to a state of **test wiseness** or test-taking skills (Nell, 2000) (see Chapters 8 and 9). Such skills include assuming that you need to work as fast and as accurately as you can, and that items get progressively more difficult (van Ommen, 2005). Many illiterate adults, those with little schooling, or those who live in isolated communities are not 'test wise'. This means that they do not have the skills for and understanding of the requirements for successful test performance. Often they do not understand the motivation for doing the assessment measure and are unfamiliar with the ethic of working quickly and accurately.

Clearly, socio-cultural experiences can affect the quality of responses to a psychological measure. Assessment techniques developed for Western children do not always have the same applicability to non-Western children, depending on the ability that one is assessing. Culture can determine the availability or priority of access to the repertoire of responses that the person has, irrespective of the responses that the examiner requires. Not only language differences, but also demands posed by test requirements create problems, because they relate to social skills, the development and expression of which are encouraged in Western society. Experiences within particular socio-cultural contexts can

significantly influence a person's understanding of the meaning of a task, and may place greater emphasis on competencies and cognitive processes that differ from those expected in the assessment situation. It must be noted, however, that, while culture plays a contributory role, it cannot be isolated from the social and personal contexts in which people live.

Case studies

Before we consider methodological aspects of assessment, this seems to be a good point to return to our case studies. Go back to the beginning of the chapter and read the paragraph describing John and Thandi again. Initially you may have thought that an IQ score of 105 is average and therefore did not consider it further. But you probably had some interesting thoughts about these case studies as you worked through the sections on the different contexts that need to be taken into account when interpreting test performance.

Let us look at John first. His IQ score was 105, which is a very average score. Given John's scholastic and occupational history, one would expect him to obtain a much higher IQ score. After all, he had good quality schooling and has remarkable scholastic and occupational achievements, he does not appear to be socio-economically disadvantaged, and he seems to be well motivated to perform in many different spheres of life. The complaint that John has recently not coped well at work, together with the lower than expected IQ score, should lead you to look for other factors that may influence his test performance. You discover that John sustained a concussive head injury six months ago. He was hospitalized for a few days but, because he did not sustain any orthopaedic injuries, he thought he was fine and was back at work within a few weeks. You decide to refer John for further neuropsychological assessment, which confirms functioning symptomatic of a closed head injury and John is referred for treatment.

Thandi's situation is somewhat different. Once again, an IQ score of 105 is very average and you may think that Thandi may not be able to cope with the demands of a science degree. Let us think again. Thandi and John were assessed with the same measure. Look at the difference between Thandi and John's backgrounds. In comparison with Thandi's situation, John's background is clearly far more conducive to the development of the skills necessary for doing well on psychological measures in terms of schooling, SES, and socio-cultural factors. In addition, the measure may not have been developed or normed for people of Thandi's background. Importantly, the measure was probably administered in a language other than Thandi's home language. It is, therefore, quite possible that this test score is an underestimation of Thandi's true level of ability. It would be preferable to work together with the student counsellor to suggest a subject choice that will allow Thandi to demonstrate her capabilities before a final study direction is chosen. If you do not consider the possible effects of Thandi's background on her test performance, you may prevent her from finding out whether or not she can realize her dreams.

These case studies should serve as an illustration that a test score is not always what it seems to be. Each individual has to be viewed within the parameters of their own situation and background, and all possible contributory factors need to be considered.

17.2 Methodological considerations

The process of psychological assessment is dynamic and can be influenced by many factors. Most assessment practitioners try to ensure that the test results provide the most accurate reflection of the abilities or characteristics being measured but, in this process, there are many factors that can influence the outcome of the measure. This is why we need to pay attention to the important role of test administration, the influence of the assessment practitioner, the status of the person taking the measure, standardized procedures, test bias, and construct validity.

17.2.1 Test administration and standardized procedures

In Chapter 9, we discussed the issue of the importance of adhering to standardized instructions

regarding the administration of psychological measures in detail and will not repeat it here. However, each assessment situation is unique and assessment practitioners may, for a variety of reasons, have to adjust the standardized procedures slightly. Flexibility and minor adjustments to test procedures are often desirable or even necessary. However, changes should not be random but should be done deliberately and for a reason, according to the needs of the person being tested.

The need to adjust standardized procedures is often required when assessing children, people with physical and mental disabilities, and brain-injured individuals, for example (see Chapters 9 and 15). Any changes in standardized procedures should be noted in written form, so that they can be taken into consideration when interpreting test performance.

17.2.2 Interpreting patterns in test scores

At the beginning of this chapter, we pointed out that a test score is just a number. It is, therefore, important that one should not place too much emphasis on a specific score that a test-taker obtains in a single assessment session (see Chapter 1). You know that there are many potential sources of error and these have to be explored before you can decide whether the test score really represents the person's level of ability. A person's profile of scores should be interpreted only **after investigating all available personal information**, including biographical and clinical history, evaluation by other professionals, as well as test results (see Chapter 1).

The most important reason why a score, such as an IQ, cannot be interpreted as constituting an exact quantification of an attribute of an individual is that we have to take measurement error into account. The **standard error of measurement** indicates the band of error around each obtained score, and examiners should be aware of the SEM for each subtest before interpreting the test-taker's score (see Chapter 3). The possibility of errors in measurement also has to be taken into account when examining the differences between subtest scores on a composite scale, such as an intelligence scale. The observed differences between scores could be due to chance and may not be a reflection of real differences. We need to examine this situation further.

Some psychologists place a great deal of importance on the differences in an individual's scores on the various subtests of an intelligence scale, for example, or between verbal and performance intelligence quotients. You must remember that there can be a wide variation in subtest performance in normal individuals and that this variation or scatter does not necessarily indicate pathology. Scatter amongst subtests on an intelligence scale is in itself not an indicator of brain dysfunction, but is, rather, a characteristic of the cognitive functioning of the individual and can indicate strengths and weaknesses. For example, a child who obtains much lower scores on non-verbal subtests, in comparison to verbal subtest scores, may have a perceptual problem.

The best way to examine and interpret differences in subtest scores is to examine the incidence of subtest differences in the standardization sample for a particular measure. In the United States, for example, one study (Matarazzo, 1990) revealed an average subtest scatter (difference between highest and lowest subtest scaled scores) of six points on the Wechsler Adult Intelligence Scale. In this situation, a difference of six points is average but the difference can range from one to sixteen points in normal individuals. However, there are times when a difference of a few scaled points between two subtest scores can be clinically meaningful and should be explored further. For example, if an English teacher obtains scaled scores of 12 for an Arithmetic subtest and 9 for Vocabulary, this would be suspicious as one would expect an equally high score on Vocabulary due to the teacher's language ability. Again, it is important to integrate test scores with personal and social history, as well as relevant medical and clinical findings, before a meaningful interpretation can be made.

The same applies to differences between verbal and performance intelligence quotients. Previously it was thought that a marked discrepancy between verbal and performance quotients was an indication of pathology. However, this is not necessarily the case, particularly when it is the only indicator of possible impairment. This was confirmed in a South African study (Hay and Pieterse, 1994) that investigated large differences between verbal and performance intelligence quotients using the SSAIS-R in a psychiatric population. There was a mean difference of 23 points between verbal and non-verbal intelligence quotients, but there was no relation between the size of the discrepancy and the presence or absence of brain damage. This implies that a pattern of scores on its own is not definitive. The scores have to be considered together with results from other measures and information from other sources. Again, the important point is to interpret scores in context.

17.2.3 Influence of the assessment practitioner

The most important requirement for good assessment procedure is that the assessment practitioner should be well prepared in advance (see Chapter 9). Assessment is a psychological intervention, not a mechanical process. For this reason, it is important for the assessment practitioner to establish rapport with the test-taker (see Chapter 9). The establishment of rapport is particularly important when assessing children (see Chapter 9). It is difficult to establish rapport when the assessment practitioner's energy is being taken up with finding the right test or page, reading the instructions, and trying to work out what to do next. The assessment practitioner needs to be familiar with the procedure and at ease in the situation. Failure to establish rapport can have a negative impact on test performance in that the test-taker's ability may be underestimated or distorted.

Through experience, assessment practitioners learn that they have to respond differently to different people, according to their needs and problems, and react accordingly. The assessment practitioner also has to be aware of the possible effect of his/her own expectations on the test-taker's responses. This is a special instance of the self-fulfilling prophecy (Terre'Blanche and Durrheim, 1999). Through subtle postural and facial cues, for example, assessment practitioners can convey their expectations and thereby limit or encourage the test-taker's responses. The assessment practitioner may also fail to assess a test-taker properly due to certain expectations. For example, if the examiner is of the opinion that the test-taker is low functioning, the examiner may not explore the limits of the test-taker's ability. By expecting a low level of performance, the examiner may fail to determine the test-taker's potential.

17.2.4 **Status of the test-taker**

17.2.4.1 **Anxiety and motivation**

Do you remember how you felt when you last took a test? The majority of people will have to take a psychological measure at some stage in their lives, either at school or at work. Most people who have to take psychological measures experience a certain amount of anxiety at the idea of being tested. Although a certain amount of anxiety is beneficial because it increases arousal, a large amount of anxiety has a detrimental effect on test performance. Anxiety can be reduced by the assessment practitioner's own manner of interacting with the test-taker, establishing **rapport**, and seeing to a well-organized, smoothly running assessment procedure (see Chapter 9).

If the person is not motivated to take a measure, his/her performance will be lower than the level of actual functioning. It is important that test-takers should know why they are taking a measure and what the benefit will be. The person may be suspicious regarding the purpose of the measure and may lack motivation to perform well.

17.2.4.2 **Faking bad, malingering and faking good**

A person may deliberately perform badly on measures if it is in his/her interests to do so. This is referred to as **malingering** or **faking bad** (see Chapter 12). It has been suggested that individuals who seek monetary compensation for injuries or those who are on trial for criminal offenses may malinger or consciously do badly on measures. Although it is not possible to detect malingering in every case, there are techniques that can help to identify malingering (see for example Ross, Krukowski, Putnam, and Adams, 2003).

> ### **BOX 17.5** MALINGERING
>
> Malingering, also referred to as sick role enactment, may occur when people respond, deliberately or unconsciously, in ways that they think will indicate the presence of an impairment, such as a brain injury or memory impairment. Tests for malingering have been put forward but these have not been unequivocally successful (Lezak, 2004). It is difficult to detect malingering from one measure, but the experienced psychologist can usually identify a problem by considering all sources of information, such as comparing different assessment results and examining test performance in relation to interview data. The psychologist can be guided by two general considerations. One is whether the individual has some motivation to fake test performance and the second is whether the overall pattern of assessment results is suspicious in the light of other information that is known about the person (Gregory, 2007). For example, consider the situation of a person who is claiming compensation after a motor vehicle accident. He complains about a memory problem and does poorly on a memory test, yet in an interview demonstrates considerably intact memory. This would warrant further investigation.

Another form of faking is seen in the tendency for people to respond to test items in a socially desirable way. For example, most people would respond true to the statement 'I would help a blind person who asks for assistance to cross the street' because it supports a socially desirable attribute. The socially desirable response may not be accurate because many people do not really enjoy helping others. To counter this problem, the construction of tests may include relatively subtle or socially neutral items to reduce the possibility that test-takers will fake or give socially desirable responses. Another approach is to construct special scales for the purpose of measuring faking or socially desirable responses, which can be embedded in an inventory or administered in a battery of measures (see Chapter 12).

There are ways of controlling for faking in the construction of psychological measures, but the assessment practitioner has to be aware of the possibility that responses will not always be a true reflection of the test-taker's attitudes or characteristics.

17.2.4.3 **Cheating**

A major challenge facing the validity of assessment

results in large scale testing used for pre-selection or selection purpose in industry and for admissions purposes in higher education is to identify the number of test-takers that cheat (which is an extreme form of faking) and to introduce mechanisms to reduce cheating (or test fraud). Caveon test security, which is the leader internationally in data forensics and test security services have found that in the fields of educational and skills testing 5% to 20% of test-takers are likely to cheat in some form or another (www.caveon.com). What can be done about this? Assessment practitioners and organizations could conduct regular security audits to ensure that their on no security breaches which could results in test materials being 'leaked' to test-takers. For computer-based and Internet-delivered tests, data forensic audits could be undertaken to analyse the extent of aberrant or unusual patterns of scores which could flag possible cheating. You can read more about data forensics by accessing http://www.caveon.com/articles/tao.htm.

Part of obtaining **informed consent** is to not only spell out the purpose of the assessment, the confidentiality of the results, what feedback will be provided, but to also address the matter of what the consequences will be of **cheating** or test fraud. To underline the latter, test-takers can be requested to sign an **honesty contract** (Burke, 2006) which could include:

- the expectation that the test-taker will respond honestly and without help from anyone else;
- the expectation that the test-taker will respect the honesty of the assessment and not share the content of the measures administered with anyone; and
- that the candidate accepts that verification of the assessment results will be undertaken and that the test-taker might be required to take a verification assessment.

Lastly, some organizations use various methods (e.g. polygraphs, reference checks, interviews and integrity tests) to assess how honestly applicants have responded, especially in pre-employment screening asssessment, 'as most employers want to minimize dishonest and counterproductive behavior among their employees' (Coyne and Bartram (2002, p. 15). Coyne and Bartram (2002) assert that the most controversial of these methods is the use of **integrity tests** to predict dishonest behaviour. While integrity tests have been found to be valid, reliable and fair in general, the main concern with such tests is whether it is possible for an employer to judge an applicant's honesty on the basis of a self-report measure.

17.2.4.4 **Practice effects**

Given the widespread use of tests for selection purposes and the competency-based approach that most organizations use, some applicants are likely to be asked to take the same test each time they apply for a job. A similar situation arises when learners apply to study at higher education institutions as most admissions tests cover the same competencies or constructs. What effect does taking a test a number of times have on the performance of the test-taker? That is, are there 'practice effects'? Reeve and Lam (2007) assert that practice effects can be sizeable but that there has been insufficient research to explore the reasons for the gains made due to re-taking the same test. For example, they argue that test scores could increase when re-taking the test due to cognitive affective and motivational factors. Reeve and Lam further conclude that in 'the context of predicting individual differences in score gains across repeated administrations, it is likely that those with higher self efficacy (perhaps because of successful past performances) are more likely to gain more from practice than those without such efficacious beliefs' (p. 229). In view of the fact that practice (through having taken the test previously), can impact on test performance, practitioners should be aware of this and organizations should re-think retesting policies.

17.2.5 **Bias and construct validity**

In earlier chapters you were introduced to the notion of **validity** (Chapter 5) and **test bias** (Chapters 6 and 7). It is important to remember that a measure is only valid for the particular purpose for which it was designed. When a measure is used in a different way, the validity must be determined for the context in which it is to be used. For example, several short forms of the Wechsler Adult Intelligence Scale (WAIS) have been developed and these have been found to correlate highly with the full battery. However, one short form of the WAIS may be useful in assessing patients with Parkinson's disease but may overestimate IQ scores in patients with brain tumours. This is because different combinations of subtests are often used for specific populations. When interpreting assessment results, it is important to establish the construct validity of the measure for your particular purpose, otherwise your results may be invalid.

An additional consideration in interpreting assessment results is that of the age of the measure. Both test content and norms need to be updated regularly, due to technological developments and naturally occurring social changes (see Chapter 6). The use of outdated norms and outdated test content can lead to inaccurate and invalid assessment results. Furthermore, the items should not function in different ways for different cultures (see Chapters 6 and 7). If there is evidence of test and item bias for a particular measure for a particular group of people, the assessment results will not provide an accurate reflection of their functioning.

17.3 **Conclusion**

What have we learned from all this? In this chapter, you have been introduced to several ideas about test scores and assessment results. Perhaps the most important is that a test score on its own is limited in what it can tell us about a person's behaviour. The test score represents a person's performance. The person's ability or trait is inferred from the score. In order for scores to be meaningful, we need to look at the scores in context and in terms of the psychometric properties of the measure. Many problems and tricky issues have been raised, particularly with regard to applying psychological measures in a heterogeneous society such as South Africa. Given these difficulties, you may be wondering whether psychological assessment is desirable, or even whether it is worth using psychological measures at all. The answer,

a qualified 'Yes', lies in the ability of the person administering and interpreting the measures to do so competently and responsibly. Psychological assessment is a necessary condition for equity and efficient management of personal development. By not using measures, you could be denying many individuals access to resources or opportunities. By not using measures responsibly, you could be denying individuals their rights.

>> **CRITICAL THINKING CHALLENGE 17.1**

Write a short press release in which you motivate the continued use of psychological measures against the backdrop of the numerous factors that affect the accuracy and reliability of the assessment results.

CHECKING YOUR PROGRESS 17.1

17.1 Why do standardized measures of intellectual ability have norms for different age groups?

17.2 Provide examples of transient conditions that can affect test performance.

17.3 Case study: Becky is a nine-year-old girl whose home language is Afrikaans. Her father worked as a labourer on the railways but has been unemployed for ten years. Her mother is a housewife but has a history of psychiatric illness. Becky is having difficulties at school and has been referred for assessment because her teacher wants more information about her intellectual ability. What steps should you take to ensure that you obtain the best possible picture of her ability?

17.4 Critically discuss the statement that the number of years of schooling completed relates to performance on intelligence tests.

17.5 What evidence do we have that acculturation affects test performance?

17.6 What is the effect of using a test with outdated norms?

What the future holds for psychological assessment

CHERYL FOXCROFT AND GERT ROODT

CHAPTER OUTCOMES

By the end of this chapter you will be able to:
> list the key themes that recur in the field of psychological assessment;
> understand that psychological assessment continues to be a core competency of psychology professionals;
> understand the rights and responsibilities of test developers, publishers, and distributors;
> list some of the ways to encourage assessment practitioners to take personal responsibility for ethical assessment practices;
> understand how the quality of assessment training and the teaching of assessment can be improved;
> understand that measures need to attain minimum quality standards and that capacity building is needed to nurture test development expertise;
> describe the challenges and opportunities faced by assessment in relation to technological advances; and
> explain why it is important that assessment practitioners dialogue with politicians and policy-makers.

And so, to the final stop of the journey through psychological assessment territory.

18.1 Themes that recur in psychological assessment

Critical Thinking Challenge 2.1 in Chapter 2 asked you to track the key themes that emerge when one looks at the historical development of assessment both locally and internationally. Maybe you should look back at what you wrote down before you read any further. Also, in view of the fact that you have broadened your understanding of assessment in Chapters 3 to 17, you might want to add some more themes that you have become aware of.

Here are some of the key themes that tend to recur in the field of psychological assessment:

- The centrality of psychological assessment to the professional practice and the discipline of psychology.
- Conceptualizing the scope and nature of psychological assessment.
- Question marks around the usefulness of psychological assessment.
- Misuse of assessment measures and results.
- Multicultural and multilingual assessment challenges.
- Professional practice standards.
- Guidelines for and gaps in the training of assessment practitioners.
- Understanding and interpreting assessment information against the total context of the person being assessed.
- The rights and responsibilities of test-takers.
- The need to inform the various stakeholders who use assessment information regarding the value of assessment and the ethical use of assessment information.
- What constitutes a good measure?
- The development and use of measures are shaped by the needs and politics of the day.
- Statistical and technological advances have impacted on the development and use of measures.

As we look into our crystal ball and try to predict future trends and issues in the field of psychological assessment, it is reasonable to assume that the themes that have recurred in the past will make their appearance in the future as well. In this chapter, we will contemplate what the future may hold as regards the professional practice and development of psychological assessment measures.

18.2 The centrality of psychological assessment to the profession of psychology

You will remember from Chapter 2 that, early on in the history of psychological measurement, psychological assessment was delineated as being the domain of the profession of psychology. Is psychological assessment still seen as being the domain of psychology and will it continue to be so? Let us consider this issue from both an international and a South African perspective.

18.2.1 International perspectives

'Psychological testing has been a defining function for psychologists since the field's inception' (Hull, Howerton, and Bolin, 2005. p. 357). To substantiate this assertion, Hull, Howerton and Bolin (2005) argue that assessment services have been one of the most important contributions of psychology to society and that some even regard psychological testing as the highest technical achievement of psychology (e.g. Swenson, 1997).

The International Test Commission (ITC) and the European Federation of Professional Psychology Associations (EFPPA) conducted a worldwide survey about testing and the use of assessment (Bartram and Coyne, 1998). One of the questions concerned whether 'The use of psychological tests should be restricted to qualified psychologists'. Respondents had to indicate on a five-point scale whether they strongly disagreed (1), disagreed (2), were neutral (3), agreed (4), or strongly agreed (5) with this statement. The mean response was 4.45 and the standard deviation was small (SD = 0.75). Respondents were thus in close agreement that the use of psychological measures should be restricted to the profession of psychology. Furthermore, while respondents tended to agree that certain measures could be administered and scored by non-psychologists, they felt that the interpretation and feedback should be restricted to psychologists.

The strong perception that psychological

assessment belongs to the domain of psychology thus persists across the world. Surprisingly then, another important finding of the ITC/EFPPA survey was that psychologists need to become more involved in assessment, as only 14 per cent of those who practice educational, clinical, occupational, and forensic assessment were found to be psychologists (Bartram and Coyne, 1998). There is thus a gap between the perception that psychological assessment should be restricted to psychologists and the reality of who performs such assessments. Why? There are many reasons. For example, there are certain schools of psychologists who, for ideological, moral, or political reasons, perceive that the use of psychological measures perpetuates social inequalities, and leads to the inappropriate and sometimes discriminatory labelling of people. In certain countries in Europe (e.g. France and Sweden), there was such a strong anti-test lobby during the 1970s and 1980s that psychological assessment suffered a severe knock. Training programmes included very little if any psychometric training, very little psychometric research was undertaken, and very few new measures were developed (Grégoire, 1999). In the ensuing vacuum that arose, other professionals (e.g. HR practitioners and teachers) started using measures, some of which could be labelled as psychological measures. The problem that many European countries face in the first decade of the twenty-first century is how to regain control over who is permitted to use psychological measures (Grégoire, 1999; Muniz et al., 1999), especially since the 1990s saw a surge in interest in psychological assessment in Europe.

The use of testing technicians in the United States in particular is also becoming a contested terrain. Testing technicians usually hold a bachelor's degree in psychology, are not licensed or certified by a professional body to practice and are trained and supervised by licensed psychologists to administer selected psychological measures, especially in the field of neuropsychology. The 're-stricted tests' include the Minnesota Multiphasic Personality Inventory, the Wechsler Intelligences Scales and neuropsychological batteries such as the Halstead-Reitan test battery. The major concern expressed by psychologists and professional associations in the United States is that these measures require a high level of psychological and testing knowledge and experience to be administered and scored appropriately, and testing technicians do not have such knowledge and experience. Having reviewed the literature, professional guidelines and legal requirements, Hull, Howerton, and Bolin (2005) conclude that as 'findings obtained from psychological tests have a long-term impact on people's lives, using testing technicians appears to be ethically questionable' (p. 371).

18.2.2 Issues around psychological assessment measures being part of the domain of psychology in South Africa

We pointed out in Chapter 2 that, despite the negative criticism that has rightfully been levelled at psychological assessment in South Africa, academics, clinicians, and assessment practitioners in industry are still optimistic about the valuable contribution that psychological assessment can make in our rapidly transforming society. For example, in an article that was published in the Sunday Times on 24 May 1998, Kasthuri Nainaar, the chairman of the Society for Industrial Psychology at the time, was quoted as follows:

> When used appropriately, psychometrics can offer an objective, fair and productive method of assessment in organizations. Furthermore, it can play an important role in the affirmative action process (p. 5).

The findings from an HSRC test use survey (Foxcroft, Paterson, Le Roux, and Herbst (2004) lend further support to the notion that despite certain shortcomings, assessment practitioners and key stakeholders in industry still perceive psychological assessment to be of value. Among the reasons given for this were that assessment measures were perceived to be objective and better than alternative methods such as interviews, and that 'psychological testing was central to the work of psychologists, provided structure in sessions with clients, provided a framework for feedback and reporting, and assisted in gathering baseline information' (Foxcroft, Paterson, Le Roux, and Herbst, 2004, p. 134). Furthermore, Petersen (2004) argues that among the key primary level health care services that registered counsellors in particular can provide is that of assessment.

Not only do psychology professionals perceive psychological assessment as being central to their work, but it is listed as a core competency of psychologists, registered counsellors and psychometrists in the professional practice framework developed by the Professional Board for Psychology. Furthermore, in Chapter 8, it was pointed out that, according to the Health Professions Act, Act 56 of 1974, the use of psychological measures constitutes a psychological act that is restricted to the domain of the psychology profession. From the perspective of the profession and also in terms of the Act, there seems to be little doubt that psychological assessment is one of the core activities of psychology professionals.

However, this does not detract from the fact that there are important issues concerning delineating psychological assessment as falling in the domain of psychology, which need to be resolved. For example, while the Act clarifies that psychological assessment falls in the domain of psychology, the practical development and implementation of the Act has presented many challenges. Strictly speaking, only psychologists may purchase psychological measures. However, as you saw in Chapter 8, the label of 'psychological test' is only attached to a measure after it has been put through a classification process. If test developers and publishers market their measures without submitting these for classification, there is a strong possibility that potential psychological measures could be purchased and consequently used by non-psychologists. The 1990s witnessed an influx of foreign test publishing companies into the assessment market in South Africa. If there are no legal restrictions on the use and purchase of measures in the country where the test publishing company has its headquarters, it is difficult for these companies to understand that their measures may be restricted for use in South Africa.

How can we find a way of getting test developers and publishers to submit their measures for classification in future? Through press releases, written communications, and road shows, the Professional Board for Psychology has alerted assessment practitioners, test developers and publishers, employers, organized labour, the education sector, and the general public that only classified measures should be used if sound assessment practices are to be achieved.

Another mechanism is in place to assist in encouraging test developers and publishers to submit their measures for classification. Test developers and publishers are required to display a classification certificate issued by the Psychometrics Committee of the Professional Board in the test manual. This is making it increasingly difficult for test developers and publishers to ignore the need to have their measures classified, and it also assists assessment practitioners in determining whether a measure has been classified.

Our discussion thus far has focused on the fact that the Act restricts the use of psychological measures to psychology professionals. However, a pressure group has developed that believes that it is unnecessary to restrict the use of all psychological measures to psychologists. This is especially true in the case of computerized measures, where the administration, scoring, and sometimes interpretation are all done on computer. A strong case is being made that suitably trained people should be allowed to use such measures. However, as we pointed out in Chapter 14, there are sound professional and legal reasons why a psychology professional should be present during the administration of a computer-based or Internet-delivered test. Furthermore, as far as computer-based test interpretation is concerned, the computer-generated report and feedback of the results, as well as the expertise and facilitative, empathic skills of a psychologist are needed. The debate that has ensued around this has led to many questions being asked regarding whether and under what circumstances it would be possible, desirable and ethical to have non-psychologists administer and score psychological measures. What training and status would such assessment practitioners need to have? Who would employ such practitioners? Is this a desirable option given that some Registered Counsellors and psychometrists struggle to find employment? Page back to 18.2.1 for the debate around the use of testing technicians in the United States, where similar questions have been grappled with.

18.3 **Demystifying, re-conceptualizing, and rediscovering the usefulness and scope of psychological assessment**

As we pointed out in Chapter 2, the popularity of psychological assessment has waxed and waned over the years, both in South Africa and on the international front. During periods when the value and usefulness of psychological assessment has been strongly questioned, introspection on the part of assessment practitioners, professional bodies, and test developers tended to result in a re-affirmation of the value of assessment, re-conceptualization of the scope of assessment, and innovations in the development of measures. As psychological assessment in South Africa is currently on the upsurge but is also the subject of much professional, government, and public scrutiny, we need to discuss some of the challenges that need to be confronted directly. After all, we aim to underline rather than draw a line through the value of psychological assessment in this country.

18.3.1 **Demystifying psychological measures and their use**

Generally speaking, psychological assessment often appears to take on mystical proportions for the lay person. The notion that a psychologist, by asking a few questions and getting a client to do a few things like making a pattern with blocks, can deduce the intelligence of the client or aspects of his/her personality is intriguing and may fill the lay person with awe. However, a large segment of the South African population has no or very little formal training. For this section of the population, psychological assessment is not only mystifying, but it is a totally foreign concept.

Not only is psychological assessment a bit of a mystery to the ordinary person in the street, but the misuse of assessment has left many South Africans with a negative perception of psychological assessment and its use. Many people, for example, hold the view that the use of psychological assessment measures is probably a 'clever' way of pre-

venting people from deprived and disadvantaged backgrounds from entering the labour market or gaining access to appropriate education or other opportunities. As we discussed in Chapter 2, the origin of this perception can be traced back to South Africa's apartheid past. We also pointed out in Chapter 2 that the anti-test lobby has succeeded in mobilizing psychologists to critically examine the usefulness of psychological assessment measures. Instead of becoming disillusioned, there is in fact a growing band of practitioners who have rediscovered the value of psychological assessment.

Whether people think that assessment measures are mystical or whether they have negative perceptions about their use, the issue that needs to be addressed is how do we debunk the myths and negative perceptions that people hold about psychological assessment?

One way of debunking the myths and changing perceptions would be to launch a large-scale **information dissemination** campaign to inform South Africans from all walks of life and of all ages about psychological assessment and its benefits. Assessment practitioners, test developers, distributers and publishers, and professional associations need to accept the challenge of informing the broader South African community about psychological assessment and its usefulness. Every possible opportunity to disseminate information should be utilized. For example, staff or union meetings, parent-teacher evenings, community meetings, television and radio interviews, press releases, and posting information on web sites can be used to explain the value and ethical use of psychological assessment measures. The **personal benefits** of psychological assessment, such as greater self-insight and a better understanding of oneself, as well as the ability to identify aspects that need development or to inform career decisions, need to be highlighted. Opportunities should also be created for the general public to express their fears so that these fears can be dispelled and myths can be replaced with facts.

Information regarding the value of psychological assessment, the ethical use of assessment, and the psychometric standards that assessment measures need to meet should also be disseminated to company directors and managers, human resource practitioners, educators, policy-makers, and so forth.

In the same way as individuals need to be informed about the personal benefits of assessment, companies and educational institutions need to be informed about the **corporate** or **educational benefits** of psychological assessment. Assessment practitioners should therefore develop the capacity to assess the cost-benefit of any assessment to a company or educational institution if they are to use assessment measures. **Cost-benefit assessment** should also take into consideration the time-saving and the cost-saving potential of psychological assessment measures, as opposed to other assessment alternatives.

18.3.2 Widening the use of assessment measures and assessment technology

Traditionally, psychological assessment has been limited to the assessment of individual attributes. This provides the field of psychological assessment with a very specific psychometric or testing flavour. Very few truly South African measures exist that can be used for assessing group or team processes and also group or team attributes. In a similar vein, measures that can assess organizational processes, functioning, and attributes are much needed. Furthermore, very little is known about the preferences of customers and consumers with regard to specific products or services. Measures that can tap these aspects could be very valuable to the marketers and developers of products.

On the educational front, with the advent of outcomes-based education (OBE) in South Africa, there are no South African measures that are adequately aligned with the critical and specific outcomes at the various exit levels of the National Qualifications Framework (NQF). Much work has been done by the Council for Educational Research (ACER) in Australia in developing measures that are aligned with the educational and personal outcomes that the Australian outcomes-based system sets out to achieve. The approach that has been used has been interesting in that developmentally based progress maps have been devised and

empirically verified for key learning outcomes (e.g. reading, mathematics, social development). Thick, performance-based descriptions are provided at each point on the progress map. Specific measures and portfolio procedures have been devised to assist teachers to peg a child at a specific point on a progress map. South African test developers need to investigate how the advent of OBE has shaped the development of appropriate measures that can be used in educational contexts in other countries, and then either adapt them or develop similar measures locally.

Any attempt to widen the application of assessment technology to other applications (for instance, benchmarking, progress maps, audits, impact evaluations, monitoring, etc.) and to other target-groups should be welcomed with great enthusiasm. The appropriate development and verification of such applications should be encouraged and supported, particularly by those who are knowledgeable about the development and validation of psychological measures. This will, no doubt, provide a great challenge to young researchers and test developers and will lead to new innovations in assessment and the development of measures.

Exploring innovative ways in which item response theory (IRT), which we discussed in Chapters 6, 7, and 14, can be employed for item and test development and refinement purposes is likely to be one of the main growth points of psychological assessment in the twenty-first century. In this regard, Chan, Drasgow, and Sawin (1999) undertook an innovative study in which they used IRT to highlight the fact that item and test characteristics change over time. Furthermore, they suggested how IRT methods could be used to dynamically evolve and refine measures over time by asserting that:

> Compared with the classical test theory framework where a person's ability is measured by a number-correct score that is specific to a given set of items, the IRT person ability parameter is independent of the specific set of items administered. This suggests that IRT can be used to update tests, with items being dropped over time if they

are found to exhibit DIFF (Chan, Drasgow, and Sawin, 1999, p. 618).

Lastly, as we discussed in Chapter 14, innovative new item-types are coming to the fore in computer-based tests. Such innovations will lead to more authentic tests that tap constructs that could not be meaningfully measured before.

18.4 **Assessment misuse and ways of addressing this problem**

As the misuse of assessment measures is a worldwide concern (Bartram and Coyne, 1998), ways of addressing this problem need to be found. Both in South Africa and internationally, there is a strong perception that while legal regulations need to be in place for purposes of gross or severe abuse, the introduction of more regulations will not stamp out abuse in the long run. As we pointed out in Chapter 8, the onus needs to be placed on the assessment practitioner to ensure that ethical assessment practices become the norm. How can this be achieved? Let us explore a few possibilities in this regard.

18.4.1 **Developing an awareness and appropriate training materials**

An interesting way of raising consciousness about the misuse of measures, as well as creating an awareness of good, ethical assessment practices, has been highlighted by Robertson and Eyde (1993). They reported on a project undertaken by the Test User Training Work Group (TUTWoG) in the United States to improve the quality of assessment. The aim of the project was to 'develop appropriate training materials to reduce the incidence of test misuse among practitioners using standardized educational and psychological tests' (Robertson and Eyde, 1993, p. 137). The work group was interdisciplinary in nature and included representation from test publishers and professional associations. To aid the work group in deciding what type of training materials should be developed, a survey was conducted among 218 experts in the assessment field. The findings revealed

that what was required 'was an interdisciplinary casebook containing case studies that represented actual instances of good and poor test use' (Robertson and Eyde, 1993, p. 137), which could supplement textbooks.

A casebook containing seventy-eight case studies of real-life incidents of good and poor use of assessment measures was thus prepared. The book was entitled *Responsible Test Use: Case Studies for Assessing Human Behavior*. The seventy-eight case studies covered seven settings, namely counselling and training; education; employment; mental health; neuropsychology; speech, language, and hearing; and general. The case studies were presented and organized in such a way that they reflected the natural sequence of events in the assessment process, namely test selection; test administration and scoring; communication of results to clients; and administrative and organizational policy issues. Professional training and responsibility issues were also covered in the case studies. A worksheet was also developed to facilitate the cross-referencing of cases in the casebook with textbooks used in training programmes. The core domains into which cases were divided for this purpose were test selection, administration and scoring; psychometrics (reliability, validity, norms); types of tests; special applications (e.g. disabilities, minorities, translations, legal or ethical considerations); and miscellaneous topics.

Perhaps the profession of psychology in South Africa should take a leaf out of the book of their colleagues in the United States. It would appear to be a very good idea to compile a book of case studies related to real-life incidents of good and poor assessment practices in South Africa. An interdisciplinary, collaborative work group of all relevant stakeholders in psychological assessment should be established to compile such a book, as this will contribute to the richness of the spectrum of case studies included, as well as to the spectrum of target groups to whom the book will appeal. Not only will such a casebook raise awareness of professional and ethical issues in assessment practice for all stakeholders, but it can also serve a valuable purpose in training new assessment practitioners.

A further leaf that South Africa can take out of the books of the British Psychological Society

(BPS) (www.psychtesting.org.uk) and the American Psychological Association (http://www.apa.org/topics/topictesting06b.html) is that they have dedicated web sites where information about psychological measures, issues in assessment, and best practices can be found. This not only provides practitioners with information, but the Psychological Testing Centre of the BPS even provides the public with information (e.g. What are the main features of a psychological test?).

18.4.2 **Guidelines and responsibilities for all stakeholders**

The International Test Commission's International Guidelines for Test Use (Version 2000), the ITC's Guidelines for Computer-based and Internet-delivered Testing (2006), the Code of Practice for Psychological and Other Similar Assessment in the Workplace (Society for Industrial and Organisational Psychology in South Africa, 2006a) and the Guidelines for the Validation of Assessment Procedures (Society for Industrial and Organisational Psychology in South Africa, 2006b) are examples of guidelines that are available to guide practice standards for assessment practitioners and other stakeholders in South Africa. However, these guidelines are mainly directed at assessment practitioners in order to ensure the ethical and professional use of assessment measures. There is a need for guidelines to be developed that cover the rights and responsibilities of all the stakeholders in the field of psychological assessment in South Africa.

First and foremost, the interests of the test-takers, as the most vulnerable party in the assessment process, should be protected. As we pointed out previously (see Chapters 8 and 16), test-takers should be properly informed regarding the nature of the assessment and the use to which the assessment results will be put prior to being assessed, and they should also receive appropriate feedback on the assessment results. As a matter of some urgency, a set of South African guidelines that clearly spell out the rights and responsibilities of test-takers should be developed by a working group comprised of the major stakeholders in the field of psychological assessment. This working group could use the guidelines on test-taker roles and responsibilities that the American Psychological Association has devel-

oped as a point of departure (see http://www.apa.org/science/ttrr.html). It might also be necessary to develop separate guidelines regarding rights and responsibilities for special groups such as children, disabled people, and so on.

A strong feeling is also developing in international and local circles, that test developers, publishers, and distributors should develop a professional code of conduct, which can address ethical issues and set professional practice standards related to test development, adaptation, and refinement, as well as the marketing and purchasing of measures. In this regard, the *Code of Fair Testing Practices in Education* (1988), developed in the United States as well as the ITC's *Guidelines for Computer-based and Internet-delivered Testing* (2006), can provide some pointers regarding what should be included in a code for developers, publishers, and distributors. Aspects that the code should cover are that test developers, publishers, and distributors should:

- provide the information that assessment practitioners require to select appropriate measures (e.g. the purpose of the measure; validity and reliability evidence; the appropriateness of the measure for people from different racial, ethnic, cultural, or linguistic backgrounds; the equivalence of different language versions of a test or paper- and computer-based versions; plus any specialized skills required to administer the measure or interpret the result);
- provide information to assist assessment practitioners to interpret scores (e.g. explain the meaning and limitations of scores, describe the normative population clearly);
- strive to develop and adapt measures that are as fair as possible for test-takers of different cultural or gender groups or with disabilities; and
- warn assessment practitioners about the dangers of applying the measure inappropriately or misusing the information obtained from the measure or the computer-based test interpretation system (CBTI).

Ideally, test developers, publishers, and distributors in South Africa should organize themselves into a professional association and take the lead in developing a code of practice for test development, adaptation, and distribution. While attempts have been made to establish an association of test publishers here, a code of conduct has not yet been developed.

The role of the Departments of Labour, Education, and Health and Welfare in regulating the different role-players in the field of psychological assessment also needs to be clarified. Some people argue that government departments are ideally placed to fulfil a regulatory role. However, the different government departments also use psychological assessment measures and the question arises whether the government can be both player and referee on the same field.

As was pointed out in Chapters 1 and 8, not all measures are psychological measures and not all people who use measures are psychologists. In Section 18.2.2, we pointed out that there is a lobby group developing, especially in industry, that questions whether all psychological measures need to be restricted to use by psychologists. Furthermore, these lobbyists also believe that practice and training standards should be developed for all assessment practitioners, and not just for psychological assessment practitioners. While many people believe that this is necessary, it is not immediately obvious which role player should initiate a working group to tackle this issue. The Professional Board for Psychology has been given a specific mandate as regards training and practice standards for psychological assessment. They would thus be operating outside the scope of their mandate if they initiated such a working group. Maybe the initiative needs to be taken by appropriate parties in the labour and educational sectors of the government?

18.4.3 **Assessment policies**

The ITC's *International Guidelines for Test Use* (version 2000) and the *Code of Practice for Psychological Assessment for the Workplace in South Africa* (1998) suggest that individual assessment practitioners and organizations should develop an assessment policy and make this policy known to those who are assessed. The value of such a policy lies in the fact that, by developing an assessment policy, practitioners and organizations must clearly articulate what they perceive to be fair and ethical assessment practices. Furthermore, by capturing the policy in

print and working through it with those being assessed, assessment practitioners and organizations unequivocally bind themselves to abiding by the practices stated in their policy. By developing an assessment policy, therefore, individual assessment practitioners and organizations will soon find themselves accepting personal responsibility for fair, ethical, and professional assessment practices, and, ultimately, the public will benefit. In Chapter 8, we provided some pointers for developing an assessment policy. Training programmes should also assist trainee assessment practitioners to develop the necessary skills to formulate an appropriate assessment policy.

> **» CRITICAL THINKING CHALLENGE 18.1**
>
> Write down the key aspects that you think that your assessment policy should cover. Select a target group whom you want to inform about your assessment policy (e.g. clients, management, teachers). Then develop a pamphlet that spells out your assessment policy. Always keep your target group in mind as this will determine what you need to include. Remember not to include psychological assessment jargon that will be unfamiliar to most people.

18.5 **Training in psychological assessment**

In a general sense, training programmes need to expose assessment practitioners to both the science as well as the 'art' of assessment. While the use of assessment measures represents the more quantitative component of assessment, the broad gathering of relevant information and the synthesis and integration of all assessment information to describe and understand human functioning represents the 'art' of assessment. It is probably true to say that most training programmes err on the quantitative side, as it is easier to train practitioners in the use of measures than it is to skill them in synthesis and integration. Herein lies one of the foremost challenges for assessment training programmes. Let us consider some challenges which training programmes are either currently facing or will face in the very near future.

18.5.1 Gaining clarity about what should be focused on in training

From what you have read in this book, you have probably inferred that psychological assessment measures are only as good as the practitioners who use them. Therefore, assessment practitioners (at all levels) need sound training in the administration and scoring of psychological assessment measures, in the interpretation of the data generated by specific measures, and in how to synthesize, integrate, and cluster assessment information from a variety of sources to arrive at a description and understanding of a person's functioning.

Assessment practitioners should also be trained in how to properly inform test-takers, how to motivate them to participate in the assessment, and how to establish rapport with the test-taker and put them at ease. Furthermore, test-takers should receive understandable feedback on their assessment results. There is an art to providing oral feedback, especially if it is 'bad news' feedback. Practitioners thus need to be thoroughly trained in providing oral feedback in a variety of different contexts. It is equally true that there is an art to producing written feedback in the form of reports. Assessment practitioners need to be trained in the purpose that reports serve and how to write reports for different target audiences in different applied settings.

Assessment practitioners also need to make informed choices with regard to the purchase of appropriate assessment measures. In order to do this, they should be able to evaluate measures on a wide range of properties, for instance, the different dimensions of validity, all aspects of reliability, and the underlying theoretical constructs that are being assessed. The selection of validation samples and the statistical procedures that were used for validation purposes should also be clearly understood. Thus, during their training, assessment practitioners need to receive a thorough grounding in psychometrics and in gathering validity data on the measures that they use.

18.5.2 A competency-based approach to training

It could be argued that all the points that were raised in Section 18.5.1 concerning training have prob-ably always been aspired to in psychological assessment training programmes. However, not only do training programmes have to continue to aspire to the competencies mentioned, but more uniformity also needs to be achieved in training programmes, so that all psychological assessment practitioners in the country will have the same, minimum, discernible competencies as regards assessment.

As we have pointed out before (see Chapter 8), all education and training qualifications in South Africa have to meet the requirements of the South African Qualifications Authority (SAQA) to be nationally recognized and registered on the National Qualifications Framework (NQF). The basic underlying philosophy of the NQF is an outcomes-based one. In line with this philosophy, the professional practice framework developed by the Professional Board for Psychology spells out core competencies, among which are assessment-related competencies, for Psychologists, Psychometrists and Registered Counsellors. The face of professional psychology training programmes thus stands at the threshold of a radically different, **competency-based** approach to training, which will pose many challenges. Among the challenges related to training in psychological assessment will be the following:

- the identification of the specific competencies that need to be developed to attain the core assessment competencies;
- how to developmentally align the development of specific competencies for the different levels of assessment practitioners;
- how to achieve a balance between developing knowledge competencies, applied (skill) competencies, and attitudinal competencies (e.g. to value sound assessment practices) in psychological assessment. In this regard, Ahmed and Pillay (2004) caution that care will need to be taken to train clinical counselling and educational psychology students to be clinicians rather than technicians. Consequently, sufficient emphasis needs to be placed on history taking, background information and observation with testing being but one of the tools available for diagnostic purposes;
- how to decide on the scope of measures to which assessment practitioners should be exposed as

well as the variety of assessment situations in which they should gain practical experience; and

• how to appropriately assess and monitor the development of the desired knowledge, skills, and attitudinal competencies. Written examinations might be effective to assess knowledge competencies and some applied competencies, but will not be effective with regards to assessing a practitioner's assessment skills.

One of the main advantages of a competency-based approach to training is that all assessment practitioners will enter professional practice with the same baseline competencies, irrespective of where they received their training. This is definitely in the best interest of the public and it can uplift the standard of professional practice in general. Furthermore, we pointed out in Chapter 8 that a national Professional Board examination needs to be passed by practitioners prior to their being licensed to practice professionally. Clear communication regarding the nature and scope of the examination will have to be forthcoming from the Professional Board, so that those being evaluated can adequately prepare themselves. Furthermore, the Professional Board has set a high standard in developing appropriate evaluations, as well as in conducting and assessing (marking) the evaluations. The Professional Board has set the standard at a minimum of 70 per cent to pass the evaluation, which is considerably higher than the usual passing benchmark of 50 per cent.

Other than developing competency-based programmes, the time has come to set standards for those involved in assessment training. Assessment courses are difficult to present as the basic measurement concepts are difficult to convey in an easily understandable way. Furthermore, given that assessment is both an 'art' and a science, the lecturer/trainer needs to be conversant with the theoretical and psychometric underpinnings of assessment, as well as being a practitioner who can use real-life examples and experiences to highlight professional practice aspects. Thus, those who teach assessment modules in professional training programmes need to be experienced practitioners themselves with a broad assessment knowledge base. In this regard, Eyde and Childs (1998) sur-

veyed the qualifications of those who teach assessment courses in the United States, and found that senior faculty members tended to teach assessment courses and that 76 per cent of them had doctoral degrees. A similar study should be conducted in the South African context, and minimum qualification levels, experience, and assessment practice expertise should be established for those who train the different levels of assessment practitioners.

As you have gathered throughout this book, the field of psychological assessment is dynamic and ever-evolving. Not only is the shelf life of measures short, but new measures are being developed all the time and new professional practice issues and policies constantly come to the fore. It is thus important that assessment practitioners keep abreast of developments in the assessment field. Until recently, the onus was on the assessment practitioner to do so. It has now become mandatory for psychology professionals to participate in continued professional development (CPD) through attending CPD-approved workshops, conferences, home study programmes, peer supervision groups, and so on. Failure to do so can have dire consequences, the most serious being that the registered person's name can be erased from the register. The introduction of CPD in South Africa has been welcomed by those in the psychological assessment field as assessment practitioners will now not only be obliged to upgrade and update their assessment knowledge and skills, but CPD-providers will create learning and training opportunities to make this possible.

18.6 Setting quality standards for measures and capacity building for test developers

In Section 18.5.1 the point was made that psychological assessment measures are only as good as the assessment practitioners who use them. In this section, we are going to contemplate the corollary of this, namely that the quality of the assessment that is performed is also determined by how good the measures are.

18.6.1 **Setting quality standards for assessment measures**

In other countries, for example, the Netherlands, the United Kingdom, Sweden and the United States, comprehensive guidelines have been developed to specify the standards that psychological assessment measures need to meet. Test developers and distributors thus have a clear idea of the standards that their measures need to meet. In addition, assessment practitioners can hold a particular measure up to these standards, to judge whether or not it is a good measure for them.

In South Africa, there are two important resources that can be consulted. In the Society for Industrial and Organisational Psychology's *Guidelines for the Validation of Assessment Procedures* (2006b), assessment practitioners are alerted to the most important aspects to consider when evaluating a measure for use. Practitioners are also provided with the technical know-how to undertake their own validation studies in the SIP guidelines.

Furthermore, the Psychometrics Committee has produced guidelines for classifying psychological measures, as well as guidelines for reviewers to use when commenting on the technical and psychometric quality of a measure that they are reviewing for classification purposes (Psychometrics, Professional Board for Psychology, 1999a, 1999b). As these guidelines have benchmarked the standards for psychological assessment measures, South African test developers and distributors have the task of ensuring that their measures meet these standards.

Assessment practitioners should use available guidelines as well as the information provided in Chapter 6 on evaluating a measure to draw up their own evaluation guidelines.

18.6.2 **Facing up to the challenge of developing and adapting culturally appropriate measures**

Some of the assessment measures that were developed during the apartheid era can be criticized for not having paid adequate attention to the cultural appropriateness of the constructs being tapped, as well as the item content. Of all the measures currently being used in industry, clinical, and counselling practice, and in educational and psycholegal contexts, most have not been thoroughly researched for bias, few cross-cultural studies have been published on their use here, and very few are available in a variety of South African languages (Foxcroft, Paterson, Le Roux, and Herbst, 2004). The establishment of cross-cultural research databases on commonly used South African measures should therefore be strongly encouraged, and web sites should be developed to assist researchers to gain access to these databases easily. Likewise, the publication of research into the cultural appropriateness of measures in scientific journals and via the electronic media should be seen as being of prime importance. Furthermore, new measures that are developed should be more broadly applicable and sensitive to the multicultural South African context using some of the methods described in Chapters 6 and 7.

As we pointed out in Chapter 7, developing and adapting measures that are cross-culturally appropriate in a linguistically diverse society such as South Africa poses certain challenges and dilemmas. In the years that lie ahead, South African test developers are going to have to face these challenges head on. Among other things:

- Decisions will have to be made regarding how best to develop culturally common measures. Claassen (1995) and Taylor and Boeyens' (1991) proposal that members of all the cultures concerned should be actively involved in all stages of the development of culturally common measures is a sound one. Suggestions regarding how this could be achieved in practice are provided in Chapters 6 and 7.
- Rather than discarding internationally recognized measures, a balance will need to be achieved between developing culturally relevant, home grown or indigenous, South African measures and adapting and norming certain international measures. It is feared, on the one hand, that, if only culturally relevant measures are developed, this will be a slow and costly process (Shuttleworth-Jordan, 1996). On the other hand, international measures must be empirically researched on our multicultural population, culturally loaded items

must be identified and revised, and local norms must be developed, otherwise assessment practitioners will not know whether the measure is fair and unbiased and can thus be used with confidence.

- The best way or ways to delineate and compile norm groups must be found (Grieve and Van Eeden, 1997; Huysamen, 1986; Nell, 1997; Schepers, 1999). Grieve and Van Eeden (1997) suggest that the factors that moderate test performance in a heterogeneous society provide a useful starting point when trying to identify homogenous norm groups. Factors such as language proficiency, cultural background, extent of urbanization, socio-economic level, extent and quality of formal education, as well as 'test wiseness' have been found to be important moderator variables in South Africa (Nell, 1997). Huysamen (1986) furthermore argues that, other than developing separate norms for different target groups, which is fairly costly, the other route would be to select only those items that do not unfairly discriminate between the different groups and to then use only one (common) norm group. In this instance, the more unique aspects of a particular group may be discarded in favour of what they have in common with other groups.

While the challenges related to developing tests that will be appropriate for the multicultural and multilingual South African population are enormous, there is some concern at the lack of vision and leadership from within the ranks of psychology on this issue. The fact that we do not have sufficient culturally appropriate measures available in a variety of languages has been identified repeatedly as a need for the past two decades at the very least. However, very little has been done to address this need. In the HSRC survey into test use patterns (Foxcroft, Paterson, Le Roux, and Herbst, 2004) attempts were made to integrate the findings and develop a test development and adaptation **agenda** for South Africa. Among the key elements of the agenda in this regard are:

- the need to establish a test review system and to undertake a systematic review of all the tests used here;

- the list of frequently used tests generated by the survey provide pointers for the tests that should be earmarked for review, updating, and possible adaptation from a cross-cultural and linguistic perspective;

- new culturally and linguistically sensitive measures need to be developed using appropriate cross-cultural methodologies; the possibility of developing more computer-based tests needs to be explored; and

- a strategy needs to be developed to identify those who should drive and coordinate the test development and adaptation process in South Africa as well as those who should actually develop the tests.

Foxcroft, Paterson, Le Roux, and Herbst (2004) suggest that the Psychometrics Committee of the Professional Board for Psychology should initially take responsibility for establishing a task force to fine-tune the agenda, set timeframes, and to then oversee its implementation.

18.6.3 **Capacity-building in test development**

There are currently only a few expert test developers in South Africa. Why? When the National Institute of Personnel Research (NIPR) and the Centre for Edumetric Research were incorporated into the Human Sciences Research Council (HSRC), the HSRC, which received government funding, became the largest test development agency in South Africa. Following the political changes in South Africa, the HSRC was privatized and reviewed its position in relation to new national research priorities and needs. Test development has remained a focus area of the HSRC, but to a much lesser extent, and personnel have been severely rationalized. Where, you might ask, have all the test developers gone who have left the HSRC? Some have moved into other spheres of psychology, some have moved to academic institutions where their academic teaching load often has to take precedence over assessment research, some have moved to other test development and distribution agencies, and others have left the country and have found test development jobs in countries such as Australia and the United States. In the process, the science and technology of developing assessment measures in South Africa have been dealt a serious blow.

Given the contribution that psychological assessment can potentially make towards the effective utilization of human resources in South African companies (against the background of South Africa's poor rating in the World Competitiveness Report), South Africa needs more test development and measurement experts. The science of psychological assessment (psychometric theory) can be applied beyond the psychometric assessment of individual attributes in the narrow traditional sense. Psychometric theory can also be applied to the assessment of work-groups, business organizations, and the outcomes of training and education programmes. A concerted effort should be made by all departments of psychology (general, clinical, counselling, industrial, educational, and research) at our local universities to develop and establish expertise in test development. Furthermore, in view of the fact that computerized measures are going to dominate the field in the near future, interdisciplinary training programmes offered by psychology departments, in collaboration with computer science and information technology departments, will become a necessity if we want to develop expertise in computerized test development.

18.7 The challenge of technology

Everson (1997) asserts that there is the exciting possibility that new theories of measurement, along with advances in technology, will lead to substantial advances in assessment measures and approaches to assessment. For example, have you ever heard of **virtual assisted testing** (VAT)? Well, it has to do with stretching the frontiers of psychological assessment even further by using virtual reality technology. By means of virtual reality technology, a work environment can, for example, be realistically created and a person's potential performance in such a real life situation can be assessed. One of the advantages of VAT is that it can assess complex patterns of cognitions (e.g. atten-

tion, memory, quick reaction time) and personality traits (e.g. control of emotions, stress, coping). Such patterns are difficult to assess in an interrelated way using traditional assessment methods. VAT also lends itself to being used as both a selection tool and for training purposes. In case you think that this is a rather far-fetched idea, a multidisciplinary consortium of European organizations has already produced three prototype VAT measures, which were introduced to psychologists who attended the VI European Congress of Psychology in Rome in 1999. The use of virtual reality technology to change the face and expand the frontiers of psychological assessment has the potential to become one of the most exciting developments in the assessment field during the twenty-first century. As we pointed out in Chapter 14, the increased use of computer technology in assessment is leading to more authentic, real-world assessment but is also raising additional professional and ethical concerns which need to be negotiated.

18.8 Dialoguing about psychological assessment

When we considered the historical development of psychological assessment in Chapter 2, we saw that psychological assessment measures were often developed to address certain societal needs. It is very important that the field of psychological assessment is not only reactive, but also proactive.

18.8.1 Dialoguing about assessment in the political arena

In Chapter 2, we pointed out that past and present political dispensations have shaped the field of psychological assessment in South Africa. The present government has placed psychological assessment firmly in the spotlight. The passing of the Employment Equity Act has clearly revealed the government's intolerance with the misuse of assessment in the workplace. What we have not mentioned before is that, had psychologists from the Professional Board, the Psychological Society of South Africa, the People Assessment Initiative, and those working in industry, not provided written and verbal submissions regarding the wording and essential implications of the Employment Equity Act, psychological assessment would have been banned in industry. A valuable lesson was learned in the process. It is vitally important that psychology professionals do not distance themselves from debates in which they are well able to express an informed, scientifically grounded opinion. When legislation and policies are being drafted that could affect the practice of assessment, psychology professionals need to make sure that they make use of all opportunities afforded to them to engage in dialogue with relevant and key stakeholders. In this way, they will be able to inform the legislative or policy-making process, rather than merely reacting to it.

18.8.2 **Academic and scientific debates to resolve issues and problems that arise in practice**

No technology can ever be fully developed – neither can the field of psychological assessment. Scientists and academics should thus be encouraged to engage in scientific and academic debates around any unresolved assessment issue or any emerging issue. Such engagement can be facilitated and guided by sound research and publications in scientific journals. Furthermore, assessment practitioners need to anticipate issues and identify unresolved problems that arise in practice and try to find solutions to them. The establishment of a psychological assessment interest group within a professional society or an organization could provide assessment practitioners with opportunities to air their views and brainstorm solutions to practical problems.

18.9 **Concluding remarks**

For the moment, we have reached the end of our journey into the world of psychological assessment. We hope that you have enjoyed the journey and that you share our enthusiasm for the valuable role that psychological assessment can play in assisting individuals, organizations, educational and training institutions, and the broader South African society. However, given the sensitive nature of psychological assessment and the potential for misuse, we hope that this book has provided you with some of the more important signposts regarding fair and ethical assessment practices. When you begin, or continue, your real life journey as an assessment practitioner, we hope that the lessons that you have learned will transcend 'book knowledge' and will make a difference to the way in which you practise psychological assessment.

References

Abrahams, F. & Mauer, K.F. (1999a). The Comparability of the constructs of the 16PF in the South African Context. *South African Journal of Industrial Psychology*, 25(1), pp. 53–59.

Abrahams, F. & Mauer, K.F. (1999b). Qualitative and statistical impacts of home language on responses to the items of the Sixteen Personality Factor Questionnaire (16PF) in South Africa. *South African Journal of Psychology*, 29, pp. 76–86.

Ahmed, R. & Pillay, A.L. (2004). Reviewing clinical psychology training in the post-apartheid period: Have we made any progress? *South African Journal of Psychology*, 34(4), pp. 630–656.

Aiken, L.R. (2002). *Psychological testing and assessment.* (11th edition). Massachusetts: Allyn and Bacon, Inc.

Adler, D.A., McLaughlin, T.J. & Rogers, W.H. (2006). Job performance deficits due to depression. *The American Journal of Psychiatry*, 163(9), pp. 1569–1576.

Allan, M.M. (1992). The performance of South African normal preschool children on the Griffiths Scales of Mental Development: A comparative study. Unpublished Doctoral Dissertation, University of Port Elizabeth.

Allen, M.J. & Yen, W.M. (1979). *Introduction to measurement theory.* Brooks/Cole Publishing Company; Monterey, California.

Aloia, M., Arnedt, J., Davis, J., Riggs, L., & Byrd, D. (2004). Neuropsychological sequelae of obstructive sleep apnea-hypopnea syndrome: A critical review. *Journal of the International Neuropsychological Society*, 10(5), pp. 772–785.

Alpern, G.D., Boll, T.J., & Shearer, M. (1980). *The Developmental Profile II.* Aspen, CO: Psychological Development Publications.

American Association on Mental Retardation (1992). *Mental retardation: Definition, classification, and system of supports* (9th ed.). Washington, DC: American Association on Mental Retardation.

Anastasi, A. (1986). Evolving concepts of test validation. *Annual Review of Psychology*, 37, pp. 1–15.

Anastasi, A. & Urbina, S. (1997). *Psychological testing* (7th edition). Upper Saddle River, NJ: Prenctice-Hall.

Antonovsky, A. (1979). *Health, stress and coping.* San Francisco: Jossey-Bass.

Antonovsky, A. (1987). Unravelling the mystery of health: How people manage stress and stay well. San Francisco: Jossey-Bass.

Antonovsky, A. (1996). The salutogenic model as a theory to guide health promotion. *Health Promotion International*, 11(1), pp. 11–18.

Argyle & Crossland, (1987). Dimensions of positive emotions. *British Journal of Social Psychology*, 26, pp. 127–137

Badenhorst, F.H. (1986). Die bruikbaarheid van die Senior Suid-Afrikaanse Indivduale Skaal vir die evaluering van Blanke Afrikaanssprekende, hardhorende kinders (The suitability of the Senior South African Indivdual Scale for evaluating white Afrikaans-speaking children who are hard of hearing). Unpublished master's dissertation, University of Stellenbosch.

Bagnato, S.J. & Neisworth, J.T. (1991). *Assessment for early intervention: Best practices for professionals.* New York: The Guilford Press.

Bakker, A., & Demerouti, E. (2008). Towards a model of work engagement. *Career Development Journal*, 13, pp. 209–223.

Baran, S. (1972). *Projective Personality Test/Projektiewe Persoonlikheidstoets.* Johannesburg: National Institute for Personnel Research.

Bar-on, R. (1997). *BarOn Emotional Quotient Inventory Technical Manual.* Toronto: Multi-Health Systems Inc.

Bartram, D. (2002). *The impact of the Internet on testing: Issues that need to be addressed by a code of good practice.* Key note address delivered at the International Test Commission's conference on Computer-based testing and the Internet: Building guidelines for best practice, Winchester, 13–15 June 2002.

Bartram, D. (2003). Policy on the design of test-related products for Executive users (Version 1.0). London: SHL.

Bartram, D. (2006). The internationalization of testing and new models of test delivery on the Internet. *International Journal of Testing*, 6(2), pp. 121–131.

Bartram, D. (2008a). *Global versus local personality norms: Logical and methodological issues.* Paper presented at the 6th Conference of the International Test Commission, Liverpool, UK, 14–16 July 2008. (Can be accessed online at www.intestcom.org).

Bartram, D. (2008b). An ISO standard for assessment in work and organizational settings. In J. Bogg (Ed.), *Testing International, 20, December 2008*, p. 9–10. (Can be accessed online at www.intestcom.org).

Bartram, D. & Coyne, I. (1998). *The ITC/EFPPA survey of testing and test use in countries world-wide: Narrative report.* Unpublished manuscript, University of Hull, United Kingdom.

Bayley, N. (1969). *Manual for the Bayley Scales of Infant*

Development. New York: The Psychological Corporation.

Beck, A.T., Steer, R.A. & Brown, G.K. (1996). *BDI II Manual.* Boston: The Psychological Corporation.

Beckham, J., Crawford, A., & Feldman, M. (1998). Trail Making Test performance in Vietnam combat veterans with and without post traumatic stress disorder. *Journal of Traumatic Stress,* 11(4), pp. 811–820.

Beery, K.M., Buktenica, N.A., & Beery, N.A. (2005). *Beery™-Buktenica Developmental Test of Visual-Motor Integration (Beery™-VMI)* (5th edition). Florida: Psychological Assessment Resources.

Bekhet, A.K., Zauszniewski, J.A. & Nakhla, W.E. (2008). Happiness: theoretical and empirical considerations. *Nursing Forum,* 43(1), pp. 12–24.

Beller, M., Gafni, N. & Hanani, P. (1999). *Constructing, adapting, and validating admissions tests in multiple languages.* Invited paper presented at the conference of the International Test Commission on Adapting Tests for Use in Multiple Languages and Cultures, Washington, DC, United States of America.

Betz, N.E. (2007). Career self-efficacy: Exemplary recent research and emerging directions. *Journal of Career Assessment,* 15, pp. 403–422.

Biesheuvel, S. (1943). *African intelligence.* Johannesburg: South African Institute of Race Relations.

Biesheuvel, S. (1949). Psychological tests and their application to Non-European peoples. In *The year book of education,* pp. 87–126. London: Evans.

Biesheuvel, S. (1952). Personnel selection tests for Africans. *South African Journal of Science,* 49, pp. 3–12.

Blanchflower, D.G. & Oswald, A.J. (2002). Well-being over time in Britain and the USA. *Journal of Public Economics,* 88, pp. 1359–1386.

Bloom, S. (2008, August). Employee Wellness Programs, *Professional Safety,* pp. 41–42.

Bollwark, J. (1992). *Using item response models in test translation studies: A look at anchor test length.* Paper presented at the meeting of the National Council on Measurement in Education, San Francisco, CA.

Borgen, F.H. & Betz, N.E. (2008). Career self-efficacy and personality: linking career confidence and the healthy personality. *Journal of Career Assessment,* 16, pp. 22–43.

Bostwick, J. (1994). Neuropsychiatry of depression. In J. Ellison, C. Weinstein, & T. Hodel-Malinofsky (Eds), *The psychotherapist's guide to neuropsychiatry,* pp. 409–432. Washington, DC: American Psychiatric Press.

Botha, C. & Pienaar, J. (2006). South African correctional occupational stress: The role of psychological strengths. *Journal of Criminal Justice,* 34, pp. 73–84.

Bracken, B.A. & Barona, A. (1991). State of the art procedures for translating, validating and using psychoeducational tests in cross-cultural assessment. *School Psychology International,* 12, pp. 119–132.

Brescia, W. & Fortune, J.C. (1989). Standardized testing of American Indian students. *College Student Journal,* 23, pp. 98–104.

Brislin, R.W. (1986). The wording and translation of research instruments. In W. J. Lonner & J. W. Berry (Eds), *Field methods in cross-cultural psychology,* pp. 137–164. Newbury Park, CA: Sage Publishers.

Brody, N. (2003a). Construct validation of the Sternberg Triarchic Abilities Test: comment and reanalysis. *Intelligence,* 31, pp. 319–329.

Brody, N. (2003b). What Sternberg should have concluded. *Intelligence,* 31, pp. 339–342.

Brooks-Gunn, J. (1990). Identifying the vulnerable young children. In D. E. Rogers and E. Ginsberg (Eds), *Improving the life chances of children at risk,* pp. 104–124. Boulder, CO: Westview Press.

Brown, O. (2002). *The biopsychosocial coping and adjustment of medical professional women.* Unpublished master's treatise, University of Port Elizabeth.

Budoff, M. (1987). Measures for assessing learning potential. In C.S. Lidz (Ed.). *Dynamic assessment: An interactional approach to evaluating learning potential,* pp. 173–195. New York: Guilford Press.

Bugbee, Jr., A.C., & Bernt, F.M. (1990). Testing on computer: findings in six years of use 1982–1988. *Journal of Research on Computing in Education,* 23(1), pp. 87–101.

Bunderson, C.B., Inouye, D.K., & Olsen, J.B. (1989). The four generations of computerized educational measurement. In R.L. Linn (Ed.). *Educational measurement* (3rd edition). New York: Macmillan.

Burke, E. (2006). *Better practice for unsupervised online assessment.* SHL White Paper. London: SHL Group. (www.shl.com)

Busbin, J.W. & Campbell, D.P. (1990). Employee wellness programs: A strategy for increasing participation. *Journal of Health Care Marketing,* 10(4), pp. 22–30.

Busichio, K., Tiersky, L., DeLuca, J., & Natelson, B. (2004). Neuropsychological deficits in patients with chronic fatigue syndrome. *Journal of the International Neuropsychological Society,* 10(2), pp. 278–285.

Busseri, M.A., Sadavan, S.W. & DeCourville, N. (2007). A hybrid model for research on subjective well-being: Examining common – and component-specific sources of variance in life satisfaction, positive affect and negative affect. *Social Indicators Research,* 83(3), pp. 413–445.

Campbell, D.P. & Fiske, D.W. (1959). Convergent and discriminant validation by the multitrait-multimethod matrix. *Psychological Bulletin*, **56**, pp. 81–105.

Campione, J.C. & Brown, A.L. (1987). Linking dynamic assessment with school achievement. In C.S. Lidz (Ed.). *Dynamic assessment: An interactional approach to evaluating learning potential*, pp. 82–115. New York: Guilford Press.

Carroll, J.B. (1997). Psychometrics, intelligence and public perception. *Intelligence*, **24**(1), pp. 25–52.

Cartwright, S., & Cooper, C.L. (2002). ASSET: An Organisational Stress Screening Tool – The Management Guide. Manchester: RCL Ltd.

Carvalho, A. 2005. *Meaning of work and life role salience in a South African context: A cross-cultural comparison*. Unpublished Masters dissertation, University of Johannesburg, Johannesburg.

Cascio, W.F. (2006). Safety, health and employee assistance programs. (7th Ed.), In *Managing Human Resources: Productivity, quality of work life, profits* (pp.584–623). Boston: McGraw-Hill.

Cascio, W.F. & Aguinis, H. (2005). *Applied Psychology in Human Resource Management*. Upper Saddle River, New Jersey: Pearson.

Casillas, A. & Robbins, S.B. (2005). Test adaptation and cross-cultural assessment from a business perspective: Issues and recommendations. *International Journal of Testing*, **5**(1)pp. 5–21.

Cattell, H.B. (1989). *The 16PF: Personality in depth*. Champaign, IL: Institute for Personality and Ability Testing.

Cattell, R.B. & Cattell, M.D. (1969). *The High School Personality Questionnaire*. Champaign, IL: Institute for Personality and Ability Testing.

Cattell, R.B., Cattell, A.K., & Cattell, H.E. (1993). *The Sixteen Personality Factor Questionnaire, Fifth Edition*. Champaign, IL: Institute for Personality and Ability Testing, Inc.

Cattell, R.B., Eber, H.W., & Tatsuoka, M.M. (1970). *Handbook for the Sixteen Personality Factor Questionnaire*. Champaign, IL: Institute for Personality and Ability Testing.

Cattell, R.B. & Scheier, I.H. (1961). *The meaning and measurement of neuroticism and anxiety*. New York: Ronald Press.

Cattell, R.B., Scheier, I.H., & Madge, E.M. (1968). *Manual for the IPAT Anxiety Scale*. Pretoria: Human Sciences Research Council.

Chambers, L.W. (1993). The McMasters Health Index Questionnaire: An Update. In S.R. Walker & R.M. Rosen (Eds), *Quality of life assessment: Key issues of the 1990s*. Lancaster, England: Kluwer Academic Publishers.

Chan, K-Y, Drasgow, F., & Sawin, L.L. (1999). What is the shelf life of a test? The effect of time on the psychometrics of a cognitive ability test battery. *Journal of Applied Psychology*, **84**(4), pp. 610–619.

Charlesworth, W.R. (1992). Darwin and Developmental Psychology: Past and Present. *Developmental Psychology*, **28**(1), pp. 5–6.

Cheung, F. M., Leung, K., Fan, R., Song, W. Z., Zhang, J. X., & Zhang, J. P. (1996).

Development of the Chinese Personality Assessment Inventory (CPAI). *Journal of Cross-Cultural Psychology*, 27, pp. 181–199.

Claassen, N.C.W. (1990). The comparability of General Scholastic Aptitude Test scores across different population groups. *South African Journal of Psychology*, **20**, pp. 80–92.

Claassen, N.C.W. (1995). *Cross-cultural assessment in the human sciences*. Paper presented at a work session on the meaningful use of psychological and educational tests, Human Sciences Research Council, 24 October 1995.

Claassen, N.C.W. (1996). *Paper and Pencil Games (PPG): Manual*. Pretoria: Human Sciences Research Council.

Claassen, N.C.W. (1997). Cultural differences, politics and test bias in South Africa. *European Review of Applied Psychology*, **47**(4), pp. 297–307.

Claassen, N.C.W., De Beer, M., Ferndale, U., Kotzé, M., Van Niekerk, H.A., Viljoen, M., & Vosloo, H.N. (1991). *General Scholastic Aptitude Test (GSAT) Senior Series*. Pretoria: Human Sciences Research Council.

Claassen, N.C.W., De Beer, M., Hugo, H.L.E., & Meyer, H.M. (1991). *Manual for the General Scholastic Aptitude Test (GSAT)*. Pretoria: Human Sciences Research Council.

Claassen, N.C.W. & Hugo, H.L.E. (1993). The relevance of the general Scholastic Aptitude Test (GSAT) for pupils who do not have English as their mother tongue (Report ED-21). Pretoria: Human Sciences Research Council.

Claassen, N.C.W., Krynauw, A., Paterson, H., & wa ga Mathe, M. (2001). *A standardisation of the WAIS-III for English-speaking South Africans*. Pretoria: Human Sciences Research Council.

Claassen, N.C.W. & Schepers, J.M. (1990). Groepverskille in akademiese intelligensie verklaar op grond van verskille in sosio-ekonomiese status (Group differences in academic intelligence that can be explained by differences in socio-economic status).

South African Journal of Psychology, **20**, pp. 294–302.

Claassen, N.C.W., Van Heerden, J.S., Vosloo, H.N., & Wheeler, J.J. (2000). *Manual for the Differential Aptitude Tests Form R (DAT-R)*. Pretoria: Human Sciences Research Council.

Claassen, L., Schepers, J.M. & Roodt, G. (2004). Werkwaardes van akademici [Work values of academics]. *SA Journal of Industrial Psychology,* **30**(4), pp. 82–92.

Clarke, M.M., Maduas, G.F., Horne, C.L., & Ramos, M.A. (2000). Retrospective on educational testing and assessment in the 20th century. *Journal of Curriculum Studies*, **32**(2), pp. 159–181.

Coetzee, C.J.H., Fourie, L. & Roodt, G. (2002). The development and validation of the communication-for-change questionnaire. *SA Journal of Industrial Psychology,* **28** (3), pp. 16–25.

Coetzee, N. & Vosloo, H.N. (2000). *Manual for the Differential Aptitude Tests Form K (DAT-K)*. Pretoria: Human Sciences Research Council.

Coetzer, W. J., & Rothmann, S. (2004, August). *A model of work wellness of employees in an insurance company*. Poster presented at 28th International Congress of Psychology, Beijing, China.

Conn, S.R., & Rieke, M.L. (1998). *The 16PF Fifth Edition Technical Manual* (2nd ed.). Champaign, IL: Institute for Personality and Ability Testing, Inc.

Coons, C.E., Frankenburg, W.K., Gay, E. C., Fandal, A.W., Lefly, D.L. & Ker, C. (1982). Preliminary results of a combined developmental/environmental screening project. In N.J. Anastasiow, W.K. Frankenburg & A. Fandal (Eds), *Identifying the developmentally delayed child*, pp. 101–110. Baltimore: University Park Press.

Cooper, C. L., & Dewe, P. J. (2004). *Stress: A brief history*. Oxford: Blackwell Publishing.

Cotton, G, (2004). Health in the workplace. *Occupational Health*, **56**(12), pp. 2–6.

Coyne, I. & Bartram, D. (2002). Assessing the effectiveness of integrity tests: A review. *International Journal of Testing*, **2**(1), pp. 15–34.

Crites, J.O. (1981). Career counselling: Models, methods and materials. New York: McGraw Hill.

Cronbach, L. (1970). *Psychological testing* (3rd edition). New York: Harper & Row.

Dannhauser, Z. & Roodt, G. (2001). Value disciplines: Measuring customer preferences. *Journal of Industrial Psychology*, **27**(1), pp. 8–16.

Das, J.P., Naglieri, J.A., & Kirby, J.R. (1994). *Assessment of cognitive process: The PASS theory of intelligence*. Boston: Allyn and Bacon.

Davey, D.M. (1989). *How to be a good judge of character*.

London: Kogan Page.

Dawis, R.V., & Lofquist, L.H. (1984). *A psychological theory of work adjustment*. Minneapolis, MN: University of Minnesota Press.

De Beer, M. (2000a). Learning potential computerized adaptive test (LPCAT): User's manual. Pretoria: Unisa Press

De Beer, M. (2000b). The construction and evaluation of a dynamic, computerised adaptive test for the measurement of learning potential. Unpublished D. Litt et Phil dissertation, University of South Africa.

De Beer, M. (2004). Use of differential item functioning (DIF) analysis for bias analysis in test construction. *SA Journal of Industrial Psychology,* **30**(4), pp. 52–58.

De Beer, M. (2005). Development of the Learning Potential Computerized Adaptive Test (LPCAT). *South African Journal of Psychology,* **35**(4), pp. 717–747.

De Beer, M. (2006). Dynamic testing: Practical solutions to some concerns. *South African Journal of Industrial Psychology*, **32**(4), pp. 8–14.

De Beer, M. & Marais, C. (2002). *Follow-up case studies of learning potential assessment*. Paper presented at the 8th South African Psychology Congress (PsySSA), University of the Western Cape, Cape Town, 24–27 September 2002.

de Beer, M., Marais, C., Maree, D. & Skrzypczak, F. (2008). *The Career Preference Computerized Adaptive Test (CPCAT): Development and main features*. Paper presented at the 6th conference of the International Test Commission, Liverpool, July 2008.

De Bruin, G.P. (1996). *An item factor analysis of the Myers-Briggs Type Indicator (Form G Self-scorable)*. Paper presented at the International Type User's Conference. Sandton, Johannesburg.

De Bruin, G.P. (2002). The relationship between personality traits and vocational interests. *Journal of Industrial Psychology,* **28**(1), pp. 49–52.

De Bruin, G.P. & Nel, Z.J. (1996). 'n Geïntegreerde oorsig van empiriese navorsing oor loopbaanvoorligting in Suid-Afrika: 1980–1990 (An integrated overview of empirical research concerning career counselling in South Africa: 1980–1990). *South African Journal of Psychology*, **26**, pp. 248–251.

De Bruin, K., De Bruin, G.P., Dercksen, S., & Hartslief-Cilliers, M. (2005). Can measures of personality and intelligence predict performance in an adult basic education training programme? *South African Journal of Psychology,* **35**, pp. 46–57.

De Bruin, G.P. & Taylor, N. (2005). Development of the Sources of Work Stress Inventory. *South African Journal of Psychology,* **35**(4), pp. 748–765.

Deci, E.L. & Ryan, R.M. (2008). Hedonia, eudemonia, and well-being: an introduction. *Journal of Happiness Studies*, 9, pp. 1–11.

Department of Education (2001). Education White Paper 6. Special needs education: Building an inclusive education and training system. Pretoria: Department of Education.

Department of Education. (2004). *Summary outline of the draft national strategy for screening, identification, assessment and support*. July 2004. Pretoria: Department of Education. Available at http://education. pwv.gov.za.

Department of Education (2005). Conceptual and operational guidelines for the implementation of inclusive education: District-based support teams. Pretoria: Department of Education.

De Ridder, J.C. (1961). *The personality of the urban African in South Africa*. New York: Humanities Press.

Dewa, C.S., McDaid, D. & Ettner, S.L. (2007). An international perspective on worker mental health problems: Who bears the burden and how are the costs addressed? *Canadian Journal of Psychiatry*, 52(6), pp. 346–357.

Dickman, B.J. (1994). An evaluation of the Grover-Counter Test for use in the assessment of black South African township children with mental handicaps. Unpublished Doctoral dissertation, University of Cape Town.

Diener, E. & Emmons, R.A. (1984). The independence of positive and negative effect. *Journal of Personality and Social Psychology*. 47(5), pp. 1105–1117.

Diener, E., Emmons, R. A., Larsen, R. J., & Griffin, S. (1985). The Satisfaction With Life Scale. *Journal of Personality Assessment*, 49, pp. 71–75.

Diener, E., Kesebir, P. & Lucas, R. (2008). Benefits of accounts of well-being – for societies and for psychological science. *Applied psychology: An international review*, 57, pp. 37–53.

Diener, E., Sapyta, J.J. & Suh, E. (1998). Subjective well-being is essential to well-being. *Psychological Inquiry*, 9(1), pp. 33–38.

Dierendonck, D., Diaz, D., Rodriguez-Carvajal, R., Blanco, A. & Moreno-Jiménez, B. (2008). Ryff's six-factor model of psychological well-being. *Social Indicators Research*, 87(3), pp. 473–479.

Doll, E.A. (1965). *Vineland Social Maturity Scale*. Minnesota: American Guidance Service.

Drasgow, F. (2002). *New items and new tests: Opportunities and issues*. Key note address delivered at the International Test Commission's conference on Computer-based testing and the Internet: Building guidelines for best practice, Winchester, 13–15 June 2002.

Dunn, L.M. & Dunn, L.M. (1981). *Peabody Picture Vocabulary Test – Revised*. Circle Pines, MN: American Guidance Service.

Du Toit, H.A. (1986). *'n Voorlopige standaardisering van die SAIS (Nie-verbaal) vir gehoorgestremdes* (A preliminary standardization of the SSAIS (Non-verbal) for the hearing disabled). Unpublished master's disertation, University of Stellenbosch.

Du Toit, L.B.H. (1983). *Manual for the Jung Personality Questionnaire*. Pretoria: Human Sciences Research Council.

Du Toit, R. & De Bruin, G.P. (2002). The structural validity of Holland's R-I-A-S-E-C model of vocational personality types for young black South African men and women. *Journal of Career Assessment*, 10, pp. 62–77.

Du Toit, R. & Gevers, J. (1990). *Die Self-ondersoekvraelys ten opsigte van beroepsbelangstelling (SOV): Handleiding* (The self-examination questionnaire regarding career interest: Handbook). Pretoria: Raad vir Geesteswetenskaplike Navorsing (HSRC).

Du Toit, W. & Roodt, G. (2003). The discriminant validity of the Culture Assessment Instrument: A comparison of company cultures. *SA Journal of Human Resource Management*, 1(1), pp. 77–84.

Ellis, B.B. (1989). Differential item functioning: Implications for test translation. *Journal of Applied Psychology*, 74, pp. 912–921.

Ellis, B.B. (1991). Item response theory: A tool for assessing the equivalence of translated tests. *Bulletin of the International Test Commission*, 18, pp. 33–51.

Employment Equity Act, number 55 (1998).

Encouraging corporate wellness maintenance (29 August 2007). Retrieved July 15, 2008, from http://www.bizcommunity.com/Article/196/141/17623.html

England, J. & Zietsman, G. (1995). *The HSRC stakeholder survey on assessment*. Internal report prepared for Human Resources: Assessment and Information Technology, Human Sciences Research Council, Pretoria, South Africa.

Erasmus, P.F. (1975). *TAT-Z Catalogue No. 1676*. Pretoria: Human Sciences Research Council.

Evers, V. & Day, D. (1997). *The role of culture in interface*. Proceedings of *INTERACT '97*, pp. 260–267, Sydney, Australia, 14–18 July.

Everson, H.E. (1997). A theory-based framework for future college admissions tests. In S. Messick (Ed.), *Assessment in higher education*, Hillsdale, New Jersey: Erlbaum.

Eyde, L.D. & Childs, R.A. (1998). *Developing emerging*

professional competencies: Are US doctoral programs in measurement and assessment sufficiently proactive? Paper presented at a symposium on Test Use and Test User Qualifications: An international perspective at the 24th International Congress of Applied Psychology, San Francisco, United States of America, 11 August 1998.

Eyde, L.D., & Kowla, D. M. (1987). Computerized psychological testing: An introduction. *Applied Psychology: An International Review*, 36(3/4), pp. 223–235.

Eysenck, H.J. (1986). Inspection time and intelligence: A historical introduction. Personality and Individual Differences, 7(5), pp. 603–607.

Eysenck, H.J. (1988). The concept of 'Intelligence': Useful or useless. *Intelligence*, 12, pp. 1–16.

Eysenck, H.J. & Eysenck, M.W. (1958). *Personality and individual differences*. New York: Plenum Publishers.

Feuerstein, R., Rand, Y., Jensen, M.R., Kaniel, S., & Tzuriel, D. (1987). Prerequisites for assessment of learning potential: The LPAD model. In C.S. Lidz (Ed.). *Dynamic assessment: An interactive approach to evaluating learning potential*, pp. 35–51. New York: Guilford Press.

Fick, M.L. (1929). Intelligence test results of poor white, native (Zulu), coloured and Indian school children and the educational and social implications. *South African Journal of Science*, 26, pp. 904–920.

Fisher, K.N. & Broom, Y.M. (2006). *Computerised neuropsychological testing in South Africa.* Paper presented at the 10th national conference of the South African Clinical Neuropsychological Association. Cape Town,

Folstein, M.F., Folstein, S.E. and McHugh, P.R. (1975). Mini-mental state. *Journal of Psychiatric Research,* 12, pp. 189–195.

Foster, W.H. & Vaughan, R.D. (2005). Absenteeism and business costs: (does), substance abuse matter? *Journal of Substance Abuse Treatment*, 28(1), pp. 27.

Fouché, F.A. & Grobbelaar, P.E. (1971). *Manual for the PHSF Relationships Questionnaire.* Pretoria: Human Sciences Research Council.

Foulke, J. & Sherman, B. (2005). Comprehensive workforce health management – not a cost, but a strategic advantage. *Employment Relations Today*, 32(2), pp. 17–29.

Fourie, L., Rothmann, S., & Van de Vijver, F.J.R. (2008). A model of work-related well-being for non-professional counsellors in South Africa. *Stress & Health*, 24, pp. 35–47.

Foxcroft, C.D. (1997a). Updated policy document on psychological assessment: the challenges facing us in the new South Africa. Unpublished manuscript, University of Port Elizabeth.

Foxcroft, C.D. (1997b). Psychological testing in South Africa: Perspectives regarding ethical and fair practices. *European Journal of Psychological Assessment*, 13(3), pp. 229–235.

Foxcroft, C.D. (2004a). Evaluating the school-leaving examination against measurement principles and methods: From the Matriculation examination to the FETC. Paper presented at the Matric Colloquium of the Human Sciences Research Council, Pretoria, November 2004.

Foxcroft, C.D. (2004b). *Computer-based testing: Assessment advances and good practice guidelines for practitioners.* Workshop presented at the 10th national congress of the Psychological Society of South Africa, Durban, September 2005.

Foxcroft, C.D. (2004c). Planning a Psychological Test in the Multicultural South African Context. *South African Journal of Industrial Psychology.*

Foxcroft, C.D. (2005). *Benchmark tests: What, why and how.* Pretoria: SAUVCA.

Foxcroft, C.D. (2007). *Teaching Psychological Assessment: What? How? Who?* Paper presented at the 1st Teaching of Psychology in South Africa conference, Bloemfontein, 22–23 March 2007.

Foxcroft, C.D. (2008). *NMMU access testing: Philosophy, principles, and process.* Paper presented at a symposium on admissions testing at the University of Johannesburg, April 2008.

Foxcroft, C.D. & Aston, S. (2006). Critically examining language bias in the South African adaptation of the WAIS-III. *South African Journal of Industrial Psychology,* 32(4), pp. 97–102.

Foxcroft, C.D. & Davies, C. (2008). Historical perspectives on psychometric testing in South Africa. In van Ommen, C. and Painter, D. (Eds.), *Interiors: A history of psychology in South Africa* (pp. 152-181). Pretoria: University of South Africa Press.

Foxcroft, C.D. & de Bruin, G.P. (2008). *Facing the challenge of the language of assessment and test adaptation.* Paper presented at the XXIX International Congress of Psychology, Berlin, Germany, July 2008.

Foxcroft, C.D., Paterson, H., Le Roux, N., & Herbst, D. (2004). *Psychological assessment in South Africa: a needs analysis.* Pretoria: Human Sciences Research Council.

Foxcroft, C.D., Shillington, S.J., & Turk, M. (1990). *The development of a "culture-fair" Group Reasoning Test: the play is staged.* Paper presented at the 8th national Congress of Psychological Association of South Africa, Port Elizabeth.

Foxcroft, C.D. & Shillington, S.J. (1996). *Sharing psychology with teachers: A South African perspective*. Paper presented at the 26th International Congress of Psychology, Montreal, Canada, 16–21 August 1996.

Foxcroft, C.D., Seymour, B.B., Watson, A.S.R., & Davies, C. (2002). *Towards building best practice guidelines for computer-based and Internet testing*. Paper presented at the 8th National Congress of the Psychological Society of South Africa, University of the Western Cape, Cape Town, 24–27 September 2002.

Foxcroft, C., Watson, M.B., de Jager, A., & Dobson, Y. (1994). *Construct validity of the Life Role Inventory for a sample of university students*. Paper presented at the National Conference of the Student Counsellors Society of South Africa. Cape Town.

Foxcroft, C.D., Watson, A.S.R., Greyling, J., and Streicher, M. (2001). *CBT challenges relating to technologically unsophisticated test-takers in multilingual contexts*. Paper presented at the European Congress of Psychology, London, July 2001.

Foxcroft, C.D., Watson, A.S.R., and Seymour, B.B. (2004). *Personal and situational factors impacting on CBT practices in developing countries*. Paper presented at the 28th International Congress of Psychology, Beijing, China, 8–13 August 2004.

Frankenburg, W.K. & Dodds, J.B. (1990). *Denver II: Screening Manual*. Denver, Colorado: Denver Developmental Materials.

Frankenburg, W.K., Dodds, J.B., Archer, P., Bresnick, B., Maschka, P., Edelman, N., & Shapiro, H. (1990). *Denver II: Technical Manual*. Denver, Colorado: Denver Developmental Materials.

Fremer, J. (1997). *Test-taker rights and responsibilities*. Paper presented at the Michigan School Testing Conference, Ann Arbor, Michigan, USA, February 1997.

Frey, D., Jonas, E., & Greitemeyer, T. (2003). Intervention as a major tool of a psychology of human strengths: Examples from organizational change and innovation. In L.G. Aspinwall, & U.M. Staudinger (Eds), *A psychology of human strengths: Fundamental questions and future directions for positive psychology* (pp. 149–164). Washington, DC: American Psychological Association.

Frydenburg, E. & Lewis, R. (1993). *Administrator's manual: The ACS*. Melbourne: The Australian Council for Educational Research.

Gallagher, A., Bridgeman, B., & Cahalan, C. (2000). *The effect of computer-based tests on racial/ethnic, gender and language groups*. GRE Board Professional Report No. 96–21P. Princeton, NJ: Educational Testing Service.

Garcia Coll, C. & Magnuson, K. (2000). Cultural differences as sources of developmental vulnerabilities and resources. In J. Shonkoff & S. Meisels (Eds), *Handbook of Early Childhood Intervention* (2nd edition), pp. 94–114. Cambridge: Cambridge University Press.

Gardner, H. (1983). Frames of mind: The theory of multiple intelligence. New York: Basic Books.

Gelman, D., Hager, M., Doherty, S., Gosnell, S., Raine, G. & Shapito, D. (4 May 1987). Depression. *Newsweek*, pp. 42–48.

Gibbs, E. (1990). Assessment of infant mental ability. In E.D. Gibbs and D. M. Teti (Eds), *Interdisciplinary assessment of infants: A guide for early intervention professionals*, pp. 7–89. Baltimore, MD: Paul H Brookes.

Gintiliene, G. & Girdzijauskiene, S. (2008) Test Development and Use in Lithuania. In J. Bogg (Ed.), *Testing International, 20, December 2008*, p. 7–8. (can be accessed at www.intestcom.org).

Gottfredson, L.S. (2003). Dissecting practical intelligence theory: Its claims and evidence. *Intelligence, 31*, pp. 343–397.

Golden, J.W. (1979). Clinical interpretation of objective psychological tests. New York: Grune & Stratton.

Goleman, D. (1995). Emotional intelligence – why it can matter more than IQ. London: Bloomsbury.

Gordon, L.V. & Alf, E.F. (1960). Acclimatization and aptitude test performance. *Educational and Psychological Measurement, 20*, pp. 333–337.

Gorsuch, R.L. (1983). *Factor analysis*. Hillsdale, NJ: Lawrence Erlbaum.

Gould, S.J. (1981). *The mismeasure of man*. London: The Penguin Group.

Gredler, G.R. (1997). Issues in early childhood screening and assessment. *Psychology in the Schools, 34*(2), pp. 98–106.

Greenspan, S.I., & Meisels, S.J. (1996). Toward a new vision for the developmental assessment of infants and young children. In S.J. Meisels & E Fenichel (Eds.), *New Visions for the developmental assessment of infants and young children*, pp. 11–26. Washington, DC: Zero to Three: National Center for Infants, Toddlers, and Families.

Grégoire, J. (1999). Emerging standards for test applications in the French-speaking countries of Europe. *European Journal of Psychological Assessment, 15*(2), pp. 158–164.

Gregory, R.J. (2000). *Psychological testing. History, principals, and applications* (3rd edition). Boston: Allyn and Bacon.

Gregory, R.J. (2007). *Psychological testing: History, principles and applications*. (5th edition). Boston: Pearson Education.

Greyling, J.H. (2000). The compilation and validation of a computerised selection battery for computer science and information systems students. Unpublished doctoral dissertation, University of Port Elizabeth.

Griesel, H. (2001). Institutional views and practices: Access, admissions, selection and placement. In SAUVCA (2001), *The challenges of access and admissions*. Pretoria: South African Universities Vice-Chancellors Association.

Grieve, K.W. & Richter, L.M. (1990). A factor analytic study of the Home Screening Questionnaire for infants. *South African Journal of Psychology*, 20(4), pp. 277–281.

Grieve, K.W., & van Eeden, R. (1997). The use of the Wechsler Intelligence Scales for Adults and the implications for research and practical application in South Africa. Paper presented at a national symposium on the future of intelligence testing in South Africa. Human Sciences Research Council, Pretoria, South Africa, 6 March 1997.

Griffiths, R. (1954). *The abilities of babies*. London: Child Development Research Centre.

Griffiths, R. (1970). *The abilities of young children*. London: Child Development Research Centre.

Grigorenko, E.L. & Sternberg, R.J. (1998). Dynamic testing. *Psychological Bulletin*, 124(1), pp. 75–111.

Guilford, J.P. (1936). *Psychometric methods*. New York: McGraw-Hill Book Company.

Hagtvet, K.A. & Johnsen, T.B. (Eds). (1992). *Advances in test anxiety research* (Vol. 7). Amsterdam: Swets & Zeitlinger.

Halpern, R. (2000). Early intervention for low income children and families. In J. Shonkoff & S. Meisels (Eds), *Handbook of Early Childhood Intervention* (2nd edition), pp. 361–386. Cambridge: Cambridge University Press.

Hambleton, R.K. (1993). Translating achievement tests for use in cross-national studies. *European Journal of Psychological Assessment*, 9, pp. 54–65.

Hambleton, R.K. (1994). Guidelines for adapting educational and psychological tests: a progress report. *Bulletin of the International Test Commission in the European Journal for Psychological Assessment*, 10(3), pp. 229–244.

Hambleton, R.K. (2001). The next generation of ITC test translation and adaptation guidelines. *European Journal for Psychological Assessment*, 17, pp. 164–172.

Hambleton, R.K. (2004). Adapting achievement tests in multiple languages for international assessments. In A.C. Porter and A Gamoran (Eds), *Methodological advances in cross-national surveys of educational achievement*, pp. 3–23. Washington, D.C.: Board of International Comparative Studies in Education, National Academy Press.

Hambleton, R.K. & Bollwark, J. (1991). Adapting tests for use in different cultures: Technical issues and methods. *Bulletin of the International Test Commission*, 18, pp. 3–32.

Hambleton, R.K. & De Jong, J.H.A.L. (2003). Advances in translating and adapting educational and psychological tests. *Language Testing*, 20(2), pp. 127–134.

Hambleton, R.K. & Kanjee, A. (1995). Increasing the validity of cross-cultural assessments: Use of improved methods for test adaptations. *European Journal of Psychological Assessment*, 11, pp. 147–157.

Hambleton, R.K., Merenda, P.F., & Spielberger, C.D. (Eds.) (2005). *Adapting Educational and psychological Tests for Cross-Cultural Assessment*. Mahwah, NJ: Lawrence Erlbaum Associates, Inc.

Hambleton, R.K. & Swaminathan, H. (1985). *Item response theory: Principles and applications*. Boston: Kluwer-Nijhof.

Hambleton, R.K., Swaminathan, H., & Rogers, H. J. (1991). *Fundamentals of item response theory*. Newbury, CA: Sage Publishers.

Hammer, A.L. & Marting, M.S. (1988). *Manual for the Coping Resources Inventory: Research edition*. Palo Alto, CA: Consulting Psychologists Press.

Hanekom, N. & Visser, D. (1998). Instemmingsgeneigdheid en verskillende item en responsformate in 'n gesommeerde selfbeoordelingskaal [Response acquiescence and different item and response formats in summated self-completion scales]. *Tydskrif vir Bedryfsielkunde*, 24(3), pp. 39–47.

Harris, Đ.B. (1963). Children's drawings as measures of intellectual maturity: A revision and extension of the Goodenough Draw-a-Man test. New York: Harcourt, Brace and World.

Hart, J.W. & Nath, R. (1979). Sociometry in Business and Industry: New Developments in Historical Perspective. *Group Psychotherapy, Psychodrama and Sociometry*, 32, pp. 128–149.

Harter, J. K., Schmidt, F. L., & Hayes, T. L. (2002). Business-unit-level relationship between employee satisfaction, employee engagement, and business outcomes: A meta-analysis. *Journal of Applied Psychology*, 87, pp. 268–279.

Hathaway, S.R. & McKinley, J.C. (1989). *MMPI-2*. Minneapolis: University of Minnesota Press.

Hatuell, C. (2004). The subjective well-being and coping resources of overweight adults at Port Elizabeth fitness centres. Unpublished master's treatise, University of Port Elizabeth.

Hay, J.F. & Pieters, H.C. (1994). The interpretation of large differences in a psychiatric population between verbal IQ (VIQ) and non-verbal IQ (NVIQ) when using the Senior South African Individual Scale (SSAIS). In R. van Eeden, M. Robinson, & A. Posthuma (Eds), *Studies on South African Individual Intelligence Scales*, pp. 123–138. Pretoria: Human Sciences Research Council.

Health Professions Act, Act 56 of 1974. Health Professions Council of South Africa.

Helms-Lorenz, M., van de Vijver, F.J.R., & Poortinga, Y.H. (2003). Cross-cultural differences in cognitive performance and Spearman's hypothesis: g or c? *Intelligence*, 31, pp. 9–29.

Heuchert, J.W.P., Parker, W.P., Stumpf, H. & Myburgh, C.P.H. (2000). The five-factor model of personality in South African college students. *The American Behavioural Scientist*, 44, pp. 112–129.

Heyns, P. M., Venter, J. H., Esterhuyse, K. G., Bam, R. H., Odendaal, D. C. (2003). Nurses caring for patients with Alzheimer's disease: Their strengths and risk of burnout. *South African Journal of Psychology*, 33, pp. 80–85.

Hill, K. & Sarason, S.B. (1966). The relation of test anxiety and defensiveness to test and school performance over the elementary school years. *Monographs of the Society for Research in Child Development*, 31, (2, Serial No. 104).

Hirschfeld, R.R. (2000). Validity studies: Does revising the intrinsic and extrinsic subscales of the Minnesota Satisfaction Questionnaire Short Form make a difference?' *Educational Psychological Measurement*, 60, 255–270.

Holding, P., Taylor, H., Kazungu, S., Mkala, T., Gona, J., Mwamuye, B., Mbonani, L., & Stevenson, J. (2004). Assessing cognitive outcomes in a rural African population. *Journal of the International Neuropsychological Society*, 10(2), pp. 261–270.

Holland, J.L. (1985). Making vocational choices: A theory of vocational personalities and work environments (2nd edition). Englewood Cliffs, NJ: Prentice-Hall.

Holland, J.L. (1997). Making vocational choices: A theory of vocational personalities and work environments (3rd edition). Odessa, FL: Psychological Assessment Resources.

Holland, P.W. & Thayer, D.T. (1988). Differential item performance and the Mantel Haenszel procedure. In H. Wainer & H.I. Braun (Eds), *Test validity*, pp. 129–145. Hillsdale, NJ: Lawrence Erlbaum Associates, Inc.

Holburn, P.T. (1992). Test bias in the Intermediate Mental Alertness, Mechanical Comprehension, Blox and High Level Figure Classification Tests (Contract Report C/Pers 453). Pretoria: Human Sciences Research Council.

Holtzhausen, G. (2004). Mode of administration and the stability of the OPQ32n: Comparing Internet (controlled) and paper-and-pencil (supervised) administration. Unpublished master's dissertation, University of Pretoria.

Horn, B.S. (2000). *A Xhosa translation of the revised NEO Personality Inventory*. Unpublished master's dissertation, University of Port Elizabeth, South Africa.

Howell, D.C. (1995). *Fundamental statistics for the behavioral sciences*. Belmont, CA: Wadsworth Publishing.

Hresko, W.P., Hammill, D.D., Herbert, P.G. and Baroody, A.J. (1988). *Screening children for related early educational needs*. Austin.

HSRC (1974). Manual for the Aptitude Test for School Beginners. Pretoria: HSRC.

HSRC (1994). Manual for the Grover-Counter Scale of Cognitive Development. Pretoria: HSRC.

HSRC (1999/2000). *HSRC Test Catalogue: Psychological and proficiency tests*. Pretoria: Human Sciences Research Council.

Hugo, H.L.E. & Claassen, N.C.W. (1991). The functioning of the GSAT Senior for students of the Department of Education and Training (Report ED–13). Pretoria: Human Sciences Research Council.

Hulin, C.L., Drasgow, F., & Parsons, C.K. (1983). *Item response theory: Application to psychological measurement*. Home-wood, Illinois: Dow Jones-Irwin.

Hull, J.D., Howerton, D.L., & Bolin, A.U. (2005). The use of testing technicians: Critical issues for professional psychology. *International Journal of Testing*, 5(4), pp. 357–375.

Hurlock, E.B. (1978). *Child Development: International Student Edition* (6th ed.). Tokyo: McGraw-Hill.

Huysamen, G.K. (1986). *Sielkundige meting – 'n Inleiding* (Psychological measurement: An Introduction). Pretoria: Academica.

Huysamen, G.K. (1996a). Psychological measurement: An introduction with South African examples (3rd revised edition). Pretoria: Van Schaik.

Huysamen, G.K. (1996b). Matriculation marks and aptitude test scores as predictors of tertiary educational success in South Africa. *South African Journal of Higher Education*, 10(2), pp. 199–207.

Huysamen, G.K. (2002). The relevance of the new APA standards for educational and psychological testing for employment testing in South Africa. *South African Journal of Psychology*, 32(2), pp. 26–33.

Huysamen, G.K. (2006). Coefficient Alpha: Unnecessarily ambiguous; unduly ubiquitous. *SA Journal of Industrial Psychology*, 32(4), pp. 34–40.

Institute for Personality and Ability Testing. (2006). *16PF5 Users Manual: South African version*. Champaign, IL: Author.

International Guidelines (2000). *Guidelines and ethical considerations for assessment center operations*. International Task Force on Assessment Center Guidelines. San Francisco, CA: International Congress on Assessment Center Methods.

International Test Commission (1999). *International guidelines for test-use* (Version 2000). Prepared by D. Bartram. Available at http://www.intestcom.org

International Test Commission (ITC) (2006). International guidelines on computer-based and Internet-delivered testing. *International Journal of Testing*, 6(2), pp. 143–171. Can also be accessed from www.intestcom.org

Ireton, H. (1988). *Preschool Development Inventory*. Minneapolis: Behavior Science Systems.

Isaacson, L.E. & Brown, D. (1997). *Career information, career counselling and career development*. Boston, MA: Allyn and Bacon.

Jackson, D.N. & Messick, S. (Eds.) (1978). *Problems in Human Assessment*, Huntington, NY: Robert E. Krieger Publishing Company.

Jansen, P. & Greenop, K. (2008). Factor analyses of the Kaufman assessment Battery for Children assessed longitudinally at 5 and 10 years. *South African Journal of Psychology*, 38(2), pp. 355–365.

Janse van Rensburg, K. & Roodt, G. (2005). A normative instrument for assessing the mentoring role. *SA Journal of Human Resource Management*, 3(3), pp. 10–19.

Johnson, W., Bouchard, T.J., Krueger, R.F., McGue, M., & Gottesman, I.I. (2004). Just one g: Consistent results from three test batteries. *Intelligence*, 32, 95–107.

Jopie van Rooyen & Partners (2007). *Catalogue*. Johannesburg: Jopie van Rooyen & Partners, SA.

Joseph, L. & van Lill, B. (2008). Investigating subscale differences among race and language groups on the Occupational Personality Profile. *South African Journal of Psychology*, 38(3), pp. 501–514.

Joubert, M. (1981). *Manual for the Interpersonal Relations Questionnaire*. Pretoria: Human Sciences Research Council.

Kammann, R. & Flett, R. (1983). Affectometer 2: A scale to measure current level of general happiness.

American Journal of Psychology, 35(2), pp. 259–265.

Kanjee, A. (1992). *Differential item functioning: Description and detection*. (Laboratory for Psychometric and Evaluative Research Report No. 257). Amherst, MA: University of Massachusetts.

Kanjee, A, (2007). Using logistic regression to detect bias when multiple groups are tested. *South African Journal of Psychology*, 37(1), pp. 47–61.

Kaplan, R.M. & Saccuzzo, D.P. (1997). *Psychological testing: Principles, applications, and issues* (4th edition). Pacific Grove, California, USA: Brooks/Cole Publishing Company.

Karson, S. & O' Dell, J.W. (1976). *A guide to the clinical use of the 16PF*. Champaign, IL: Institute for Personality and Ability Testing.

Kaufman, A.S. (1979). *Intelligent testing with the WISC–R*. New York: John Wiley & Sons.

Kendall, I.M., Verster, M.A., & Von Mollendorf, J. W. (1988). Test performance of blacks in Southern Africa. In S.H. Irvine & J.W. Berry (Eds), *Human abilities in cultural context*, pp. 299–339. New York: Cambridge University Press.

Kennepohl, S., Shore, D., Nabors, N., & Hanks, R. (2004). African American acculturation and neuropsychological test performance following traumatic brain injury. *Journal of the International Neuropsychological Society*, 10(4), pp. 566–577.

Kennet-Cohen, T., Bronner, S. & Cohen, Y. (2003). *Improving the predictive validity of a test: A time-efficient perspective*. Paper presented at the annual meeting of the National Council on measurement in Education, Chicago, 2003.

Kern, R.S., Nuechterlein, K.H., Green, M.F., Baade, L.E., Fenton, W.S., Gold, J.M. et al. (2008). The MATRICS Consensus Cognitive Battery, Part 2: Co-Norming and Standardization. *The American Journal of Psychiatry*, 165, pp. 214–220.

Keyes, C.L.M. & Haidt, J. (2003). Introduction: human flourishing-the study of that which makes life worthwhile. In C.L.M. Keyes & J. Haidt. *Flourishing Postive Psychology and the life well-lived*. Washington: American Psychological Association.

Keyes, C. L. M., Wissing, M., Potgieter, J. P., Temane, M., Kruger, A., Van Rooy, S. (2008). Evaluation of the mental continuum-short form (MHF-SF) in Setswana-speaking South Africans. Clinical Psychology & Psychotherapy, 15, pp. 181–192.

Kinnear, C. & Roodt, G. (1998). The development of an instrument for measuring organisational inertia. *Journal of Industrial Psychology*, 24(2), pp. 44–54.

Kline, P. (1994). *An easy guide to factor analysis*. London: Routledge.

Knoetze, J., Bass, N. & Steele, G. (2005). The Raven's Coloured progressive Matrices: Pilot norms for isiXhosa-speaking primary school learners in peri-urban Eastern Cape. *South African Journal of Psychology,* 35(2), pp. 175–194.

Koch, S.E. (2005). *Evaluating the equivalence, across language groups, of a reading comprehension test used for admissions purposes.* Unpublished doctoral thesis, Nelson Mandela Metropolitan University, Port Elizabeth, South Africa.

Koch, S.E., Foxcroft, C.D., & Watson, A.S.R. (2001). A developmental focus to student access at UPE: Process and preliminary insights into placement assessment. *South African Journal for Higher Education,* 15(2), pp. 126–131.

Koller, P.S. & Kaplan, R.M. (1978). A two-process theory of learned helplessness. *Journal of Personality and Social Psychology,* 36, pp. 1077–1083.

Kriek, H. & Whitford, C. (2006). Unproctored Internet testing (UIT) in employment settings: Opportunities, dilemmas, and "Better practice". Paper presented at the SIOPSA conference, Pretoria, 7 June 2006.

Kroukamp, T.R. (1991). The use of personality-related and cognitive factors as predictors of scholastic achievement in Grade One: A multivariate approach. Unpublished doctoral dissertation, University of Port Elizabeth.

Krug, S.E. (1981). *Interpreting 16PF personality patterns.* Champaign, IL: Institute for Personality and Ability Testing.

Krug, S.E. & Johns, E.F. (1986). A large scale cross-validation of second-order personality structure defined by the 16PF. *Psychological Reports,* 59, pp. 683–693.

Kruk, R.S. & Muter, P. (1984). Reading continuous text on video screens. *Human Factors,* 26, pp. 339–345.

Kuncel, N.R., Hezlett, S.A., & Ones, D.S. (2004). Academic Performance, Career Potential, Creativity, and Job Performance: Can One Construct Predict Them All? Journal of Personality and Social Psychology, 86, pp. 148–161.

Landman, J. (1988). Appendix to the manual of the Junior South African Individual Scales (JSAIS): Technical details and tables of norms with regard to 6- to 8-year-old Indian pupils. Pretoria: Human Sciences Research Council.

Landman, J. (1989). *Die ontwikkeling en standaardisering van 'n individuele intelligensieskaal vir Xhosasprekende leerlinge* (The development and standardization of an individual intelligence scale for Xhosa-speaking pupils). Unpublished doctoral thesis, Potchefstroom

University for Christian Higher Education.

Langley, P.R. (1989). *Gerekenariseerde loopbaanvoorligting: 'n Evaluering van die DISCOVER-stelsel* (Computerized career counselling: An evaluation of the Discover system). Unpublished doctoral thesis. Rand Afrikaans University.

Langley, R. (1993). Manual for use of the Life Role Inventory. Pretoria: Human Sciences Research Council.

Langley, R. (1995). The South African work importance study. In D.E. Super, B. Sverko & C.E. Super (Eds) *Life roles, values, and careers,* pp. 188–203. San Francisco, CA: Jossey-Bass.

Langley, R., Du Toit, R., & Herbst, D.L. (1992a). *Manual for the Career Development Questionnaire.* Pretoria: Human Sciences Research Council.

Langley, R., Du Toit, R., & Herbst, D.L. (1992b). Manual for the Values Scale. Pretoria: Human Sciences Research Council.

Lanyon, R.I. & Goodstein, L.D. (1997). *Personality assessment* (3rd edition). New York: Wiley.

Larsen, R.J. & Buss, D.M. (2002). Personality psychology: Domains of knowledge about human nature. Boston, MA: McGraw-Hill.

Lee, J.A. (1986). The effects of past computer experience on computerized aptitude test performance. *Educational and Psychological Measurement,* 46, pp. 727–733.

Leeson, H.V. (2006). The mode effect: A literature review of human and technological issues in computerized testing. *International Journal of Testing,* 6(1), pp. 1–24.

Lewandowski, D.G. & Saccuzzo, D.P. (1976). The decline of psychological testing: Have traditional procedures been fairly evaluated? *Professional Psychology,* 7, pp. 177–184.

Lezak, M.D. (1987). *Neuropsychological assessment* (2nd edition). New York: Oxford University Press.

Lezak, M.D. (1995). *Neuropsychological Assessment* (3rd edition). New York: Oxford University Press.

Lezak, M., Howieson, D., & Loring, D. (2004) *Neuropsychological assessment* (4th edition). New York: Oxford University Press.

Lidz, C.S. (Ed.). (1987). Dynamic assessment: An interactive approach to evaluating learning potential. New York: Guilford Press.

Lievens, F. (2006). *The use of Situational Judgment Tests (STJ) in high stakes selection settings.* Keynote address presented at the 26th Annual Conference of the AC study Group, 23–24 March, Protea Hotel, Stellenbosch.

Likert, R. (1932). A technique for the measurement of attitudes. *Archives of Psychology,* no 140.

Lilford, N. (10 September 2008). Absenteeism reaches new heights in South Africa. *HR Future.* Available from http://www.hrfuture.net/display_web_article.php?article_id=144&category_id=5

Linn, R.L. (1989). Current perspectives and future directions. In R.L. Linn (Ed.), *Educational measurement* (3rd edition). New York: Macmillan.

Linn, R.L. & Gronlund, N.E. (2000). *Measurement and assessment in teaching* (8th edition). Upper Saddle River, New Jersey: Prentice-Hall, Inc.

Locurto, C. (1991). Sense and nonsense about IQ – the case for uniqueness. New York: Praeger.

Loeppke, R. (2008). The value of health and the power of prevention. *International Journal of Workplace Health Management*, 1(23), pp. 95–108.

Lopes, A., Roodt, G., & Mauer, R. (2001). The predictive validity of the APIL-B in a financial institution. *Journal of Industrial Psychology*, 27(1), pp. 61–69.

Lord, F.M. (1980). Applications of item response theory to practical testing problems. Hillsdale, NJ: Erlbaum.

Louw, D.A. & Allan, A. (1998). A profile of forensic psychologists in South Africa. *South African Journal of Psychology*, 28(4), pp. 234–241.

Luiz, D.M. (1994). *Children of South Africa. In search of a developmental profile.* Inaugural and Emeritus Address D34. Port Elizabeth: University of Port Elizabeth.

Luiz, D.M. (1997). *Griffiths Scales of Mental Development: South Africa studies.* Port Elizabeth: University of Port Elizabeth.

Luiz, D.M., Barnard, A., Knoesen, N., Kotras, N., Horrocks, S., McAlinden, P., Challis, D., & O'Connell, R. (2006). *Griffiths Mental Development Scales – Extended Revised. Administration Manual.* Oxford: Hogrefe – The Test Agency Ltd.

Luiz, D.M., Foxcroft, C.D., & Stewart, R. (1999). *The construct validity of the Griffiths Scales of Mental Development.* Child: Care, Health and Development. London.

Luiz, D.M., Foxcroft, C.D., & Povey, J. (2006). The Griffiths Scales of mental development: A factorial validity study. *South African Journal of Psychology*, 36(1), 192–214.

Luiz, D.M., Foxcroft, C.D., Worsfold, L., Kotras, N., & Kotras, H. (2001). The Griffiths Scales of Mental Development: An evaluation prediction of scholastic achievement. *South African Journal of Education*, 2(2), pp. 81–83.

Luiz, D.M., & Heimes, L. (1988). The Junior South African Intelligence Scales and the Griffiths Scales of Mental Development: A correlative study. In D.M. Luiz (Ed.), *Griffiths Scales of Mental Development: South African studies*, pp. 1–15. Port Elizabeth: University of Port Elizabeth.

Lundy, A. (1985). The reliability of the Thematic Apperception Test. *Journal of Personality Assessment*, 49, pp. 141–145.

MacAleese, R. (1984). Use of tests. In H.D. Burck & R.C. Reardon (Eds), *Career development interventions.* Springfield, IL: Charles C. Thomas.

Madge, E.M. (1981). Manual for the Junior South African Indivdual Scales (JSAIS). Part I: Development and standardization. Pretoria: Human Sciences Research Council.

Madge, E.M. & du Toit, L.B.H. (1967) 'n Samevatting van die bestaande kennis in verband met die primêre persoonlikheids-faktore wat deur die Persoonlikheids-vraelys vir Kinders (PVL), die Hoërskool-persoonlikheidsvraelys (PSPV) en die Sestienpersoonlikheidsfaktorvraelys (16PF) gemeet word. (Byvoegsel tot die handleiding vir die PVK, HSPV en 16PF) (A conclusion to the existing knowledge regarding the primary personality factors that are measured by the Personality Questionnaire for Children, the High School Personality Questionnaire and the Sixteen Personality Factors Questionnaire (Addition to the guide for the PVK, HSPV and 16PF)). Pretoria: Human Sciences Research Council.

Madge, E. & van der Walt, H.S. (1996) Interpretation and use of psychological tests. In K. Owen & J.J. Taljaard, *Handbook for the use of Psychological and Scholastic tests of the HSRC* (revised edition), pp. 121–137. Pretoria: Human Sciences Research Council.

Madhoo, K. (1999). *The coping orientation and coping resources of patients in cardiac rehabilitation.* Unpublished master's treatise, University of Port Elizabeth.

Mardell-Czudnowski, C.D. & Goldenberg, D.S. (1990). *Developmental Indicators for the Assessment of Learning – Revised.* Circle Pines, MN: American Guidance Service.

Marquez, J. (2008). Study: Wellness plans failing to engage workers. *Workforce Management,* 87(9), p. 15.

Maslach, C., Jackson, S.E & Leiter, M.P. (1996). *Maslach Burnout Inventory: Manual* (3rd ed.). Palo Alto, CA: Consulting Pshychologists Press.

Mason, J.C. (1992, July). Healthy equals happy plus productive. *Management Review,* pp. 33–37.

Mason, J.C. (1994, July). The cost of wellness. *Management Review*, pp. 29–32.

Matarazzo, J. (1990). Psychological assessment versus psychological testing: Validation from Binet to the school, clinic and courtroom. *American Psychologist*, 45(9), pp. 999–1017.

Matthews, G., Zeidner, M., & Roberts, R.D. (2002). *Emotional Intelligence: Science and Myth*. Cambridge, MA: MIT Press.

Mauno, S., Kinnunen, U. & Ruokolainen, M. (2006). Exploring work- and organisation-based resources as moderators between work-family conflict and job attitudes. *Work & Stress*, 20, pp. 210–233.

May, D. R., Gilson, R. L., & Harter, L. M. (2004). The psychological conditions of meaningfulness, safety, and availability and the engagement of the human spirit at work. *Journal of Occupational and Organizational Psychology*, 77, pp. 11–37.

Mayer, J.D. & Salovey, P. (1997). What is emotional intelligence? In P. Salovey & D. Sluyter (Eds), *Emotional development and emotional intelligence: Implications for educators*, pp. 3–31. New York: Basic Books.

McAdams, D.P. (1980). A thematic coding system for the intimacy motive. *Journal of Research in Personality*, 14, pp. 414–432.

McAdams, D.P. (1982). Intimacy motivation. In A.J. Stewart (Ed.), *Motivation and society*, pp. 133–171. San Francisco, CA: Jossey-Bass.

McAdams, D.P. (1994). *The person: An introduction to personality psychology*. Fort Worth, TX: Harcourt Brace.

McAdams, D.P. (1995). What do we know when we know a person? *Journal of Personality*, 63, pp. 365–396.

McCarthy, D. (1944). A study of the reliability of the Goodenough drawing test of intelligence. *Journal of Psychology*, 18, pp. 201–216.

McCarthy, D. (1972). *Manual for the McCarthy Scales of Children's Abilities*. New York: Psychological Corporation.

McCaulley, M.H. (2000). The Myers-Briggs Type Indicator in counseling. In C.E. Watkins, Jr. & V.L. Campbell (Eds), *Testing and assessment in counseling practice* (2nd edition), pp. 111–173. Mahwah, NJ: Lawrence Erlbaum Publishers.

McClaran, A. (2003). From "admissions" to "recruitment": The professionalisation of higher education admissions. *Tertiary Education and Management*, 9, pp. 159–167.

McClelland, D.C. (1985). *Human motivation*. Glenview, IL: Scott, Foresman.

McClelland, D.C., Atkinson, T.W., Clark, R.A., & Lowell, E.L. (1953). *The achievement motive*. New York, NY: Appleton-Century-Crofts.

McClelland, D.C. & Boyatzis, R.E. (1982). The leadership motive pattern and long term success in management. *Journal of Applied Psychology*, 67, pp. 737–743.

McClelland, D.C., Koestner, R. & Weinberger, J. (1989). How do self-attributed and implicit motives differ? *Psychological review*, 96, pp. 690–702.

McIntire, S.A. & Miller, L. (2000). *Foundations of Psychological testing*. Boston: McGraw-Hill Higher Education.

McCrae, R.R., Costa, P.T., Jr., Martin, T.A., Oryol, V.E., Rukavishnikov, A.A., Senin, I.G., Hrebícková, M., Urbánek, T. (2004). Consensual validation of personality traits across cultures. *Journal of Research in Personality*, 38, pp. 179–201.

McMahon, M., Patton, W. & Watson, M.B. (2003). Developing qualitative career assessment processes. *Career Development Quarterly*, 51, pp. 194–202.

McMahon, M. & Watson, M.B. (2008). Systemic influences on career development: Assisting clients to tell their career stories. *The Career Development Quarterly*, 56, pp. 280–288.

McMahon, M., Watson, M. & Patton, W. (2005). Qualitative career assessment: Developing the My System of Career Influences Reflection Activity. *Journal of Career Assessment*, 13, pp. 476–490.

McReynolds, P. (1986). History of Assessment in Clinical and Educational Settings. In Nelson, R.O. and Hayes, S.C. (Eds), *Conceptual Foundations of Behavioral Assessment*. New York: The Guilford Press.

Meiring, D. (2006). *SAPI project*. http://www.meiringd.co.za/sapi project.htm.

Meiring, D. (2007), *Bias and equivalence of psychological measures in South Africa*. Ridderkerk, Netherlands: Ridderprint B.V.

Meiring, D., van de Vijver, F.J.R. & Rothmann, S. (2006). Bias in an adapted version of the 15FQ+ in South Africa. *South African Journal of Psychology*, 36(2), pp. 340–356.

Meiring, D., van de Viyver, F.J.R., Rothmann, S. & Barrick, M.R. (2005). Construct, item and method bias of cognitive and personality measures in South Africa. *South African Journal of Industrial Psychology*, 31, pp. 1–8

Meiring, D., van de Vijver, F.J.R., Rothmann, S. & Sackett, P.R. (2006). Internal and external bias of cognitive and personality measures in South Africa. In Meiring, D. (2007), *Bias and equivalence of psychological measures in South Africa*, pp. 67–102. Ridderkerk, Netherlands: Ridderprint B.V.

Mershon, B. & Gorsuch, R.L. (1988). Number of factors in the personality sphere. *Journal of Personality and Social Psychology*, 55, pp. 675–680.

Messick, S. (1988). The once and future issues of validity. In Wainer, H. & Braun, H. (Eds), *Test validity*, pp. 33–45. Hillsdale, NJ.: Lawrence Erlbaum.

Meyer, J.C. (1980). *Die ontwikkeling, standaardisering en validering van die Kodus-belangstellingsvraelys* (The development, standardization and validation of the Kodus-interest Questionnaire). Unpublished doctoral thesis, University of Stellenbosch.

Meyer, J.C. (1998). The development and standardisation of a new interest questionnaire. *South African Journal of Psychology*, 28, pp. 36–40.

Mfusi, S.K. & Mahabeer, M. (2000). Psychosocial adjustment of pregnant women infected with HIV/AIDS in South Africa. *Journal of Psychology in Africa, South of the Sahara, the Caribbean and Afro-Latin America*, 10(2), pp. 122–145.

Miller, L.J. (1988). *Miller Assessment for Preschoolers*. San Antonio, TX: The Psychological Corporation.

Miller, R. (1987) Methodology: A focus for change. In K.F. Mauer & A.I. Retief (Eds), *Psychology in context: Cross-cultural research trends in South Africa*. Pretoria: Human Sciences Research Council.

Mistry, J. & Rogoff, B. (1994). Remembering in cultural context. In W. Lonner & R. Malpass (Eds), *Psychology and culture*, pp. 139–144. MA: Allyn & Bacon.

Moodley, N. (2005, February 9). Absenteeism cost R12 bn a year, with up to R2.2bn due to Aids. *Business Report*. Retrieved September 10, 2008, from http://www.busrep.co.za/index.php?fSectionId=611&fArticleId=2403031

Moos, R. & Moos, B. (1986). *Family Environment Scale manual* (2nd edition). Palo Alto, California: Consulting Psychology Press.

Morgan, C.D. & Murray, H.A. (1935). A method for investigating fantasies: The Thematic Apperception Test. *Archives of Neurology and Psychiatry*, 34, pp. 289–306.

Moritz, S., Ferahli, S., & Naber, D. (2004). Memory and attention performance in psychiatric patients. *Journal of the International Neuropsychological Society*, 10(4), pp. 623–633.

Muniz, J., Prieto, G., Almeida, L., & Bartram, D. (1999). Test use in Spain, Portugal and Latin American countries. *European Journal of Psychological Assessment*, 15(2), pp. 151–157.

Murphy, K.R. & Davidshofer, C.O. (1998). *Psychological testing: principles and applications* (4th edition). New Jersey: Prentice-Hall International, Inc.

Murphy, K.R. & Davidshofer, C.O. (2001). *Psychological testing: principles and applications* (5th edition). New Jersey: Prentice-Hall International, Inc.

Murphy, R., & Maree, D.J.F. (2006). A review of South African research in the field of dynamic assessment. *South African Journal of Psychology*, 36(1), pp. 168–191.

Mwamwenda, T.S. (1995). *Educational Psychology: An African perspective* (2nd edition). Durban: Butterworths.

Myers, I.B. & McCaulley, M.H. (1985). *Manual: A guide to the development and use of the Myers-Briggs Type Indicator*. Palo Alto, CA: Consulting Psychologists Press.

Naglieri, J.A. (1997). Planning, attention, simultaneous, and successive theory and the cognitive assessment system: A new theory-based measure of intelligence. In P. Flanagan, J.L. Genshaft & P.L. Harrison (Eds), *Contemporary Intellectual Assessment – Theories, tests and issues*, pp. 247–267. New York: Guilford Press.

Naicker, A. (1994). The psycho-social context of career counselling in South African schools. *South African Journal of Psychology*, 24, pp. 27–34.

Naude, J. L. P., & Rothmann, S. (2004). The validation of the Maslach Burnout Inventory – Human services survey for emergency medical technicians in Gauteng. *South African Journal of Industrial Psychology*, 30, pp. 21–28.

Nell, V. (1994). Interpretation and misinterpretation of the South African Wechsler-Bellevue Adult Intelligence Scale: a history and a prospectus. *South African Journal for Psychology*, 24(2), pp. 100–109.

Nell, V. (1997). Science and politics meet at last: The insurance industry and neuropsychological norms. *South African Journal of Psychology*, 27, pp. 43–49.

Nell, V. (1999a). Cross-cultural neuropsychological assessment: Theory and practice. New Jersey: Lawrence Erlbaum.

Nell, V. (1999b). Standardising the WAIS-III and the WMS-III for South Africa: legislative, psychometric, and policy issues. *South African Journal of Psychology*, 29(3), pp. 128–137.

Nell, V. (2000). Cross-cultural neuropsychological assessment: Theory and practice. New Jersey: Erlbaum.

Nell, R.D. (2005). *Sress, coping resources and adjustment of married mothers in the teaching profession*. Unpublished master's treatise, Nelson Mandela Metropolitan University.

Nevill, D.D. & Super, D.E. (1986). *The Role Salience Inventory: Theory, application and research*. Palo Alto, CA: Consulting Psychologists Press.

Newborg, J., Stock, J.R., Wnek, L., Guidubaldi, J., & Svinicki, J. (1984). *The Battelle Developmental Inventory*. Allen, TX: DLM Teaching Resources.

Nikolaou, I. (2003). The development and validation of a measure of generic work competencies. *International Journal of Testing*, 3(4), pp. 309–319.

Nuttall, E.V., Romero, I., & Kalesnik, J. (Eds) (1992). *Assessing and Screening Preschoolers: Psychological and Educational Dimensions.* United States of America: Allyn and Bacon.

Nzimande, B. (1995). *Culture fair testing? To test or not to test?* Paper delivered at the Congress on Psychometrics for Psychologists and Personnel Practitioners, Pretoria, 5–6 June 1995.

Olivier, N.M. & Swart, D.J. (1974). *Manual for the Aptitude Tests for School Beginners (ASB).* Pretoria: Human Sciences Research Council.

Ones, D. (2008). *Recent Assessment Centre research: A recap.* Keynote address presented at the 28th Annual Conference of the AC study Group, 12–14 March, Protea Hotel, Stellenbosch.

Owen, K. (1989a). Test and item bias: The suitability of the Junior Aptitude tests as a common test battery for white, Indian and black pupils in Standard 7. Pretoria: Human Sciences Research Council.

Owen, K. (1989b). The suitability of Raven's Progressive Matrices for various groups in South Africa. *Personality and Individual Differences,* 13, pp. 149–159.

Owen, K. (1991). Test bias: the validity of the Junior Aptitude Tests (JAT) for various population groups in South Africa regarding the constructs measured. *South African Journal of Psychology,* 21(2), pp. 112–118.

Owen, K. (1992a). *Test-item bias: Methods, findings and recommendations.* Pretoria: Human Sciences Research Council.

Owen, K. (1992b). The suitability of Raven's Standard Progressive Matrices for various groups in South Africa. *Personality and Individual Differences,* 13, pp. 149–159.

Owen, K. (1996). Aptitude tests. In K. Owen & J.J. Taljaard (Eds). *Handbook for the use of psychological and scholastic tests of the HSRC,* pp. 191–270. Pretoria: Human Sciences Research Council.

Owen, K. (1998). The role of psychological tests in education in South Africa: Issues, controversies and benefits. Pretoria: Human Sciences Research Council.

Owen, K. & Taljaard, J.J. (1995) *Handleiding vir die gebruik van sielkundige en skolastiese toetse van die RGN.* Pretoria: Human Sciences Research Council.

Owen, K. & Taljaard, J.J. (Eds) (1996). *Handbook for the use of psychological and scholastic tests of the HSRC* (revised edition). Pretoria: Human Sciences Research Council.

Parshall, C.G., Spray, J.A., Kalohn, J.C., and Davey, T.

(2002). *Practical considerations in computer-based testing.* New York, NY: Springer-Verlag.

Parsons, F. (1909). *Choosing a vocation.* New York: Houghton Mifflin.

Patrick, J. (2000). *Mental status examination rapid record form.* Accessed on 20 January 2009 from www.nev.dgp.org.au/files/programsupport/mentalhealth/Mental%20Exam%20-%20form.pdf?

Patton, W. & McMahon, M. (1999). *Career development and systems theory: A new relationship.* Pacific Grove, CA: Brooks/Cole.

Paunonen, S.V. & Ashton, M.C. (1998). The structured assessment of personality across cultures. *Journal of Cross-Cultural Psychology,* 29, pp. 150–170.

Petersen, I. (2004). Primary level psychological services in South Africa: can a new psychological professional fill the gap? *Health Policy and Planning,* 19(1), pp. 33–40.

Peterson, C. (2006). *A primer in positive psychology.* New York: Oxford University Press.

Petkoon, L. & Roodt, G. (2004). The discriminant validity of the culture assessment instrument: A comparison of company sub-cultures. *SA Journal of Industrial Psychology,* 30(1), pp. 74–82.

Petrill, S.A., Pike, A., Price, T. & Plomin, R. (2004). Chaos in the home and socioeconomic statuse are associated with cognitive development in early childhood: Environmental mediators identified in a genetic design. *Intelligence,* 32, 445–460.

Piaget, J. & Inhelder, B. (1971). *Mental imagery in the child* (Trans. P. A. Chilton). London: Routledge & Kegan Paul.

Pickworth, G., Von Mollendorf, J.W., & Owen, K. (1996). The use of the computer in career counselling and test administration. In K. Owen and J.J. Taljaard (Eds) (1996), *Handbook for the use of psychological and scholastic tests of the HSRC,* pp. 439–443. Pretoria: HSRC.

Piedmont, R.L. Bain, E. McCrae, R.R. & Costa, P.T. (2002). The applicability of the five-factor model in a sub-Saharan culture: The NEO-PI-R in Shona. In R.R. McCrae & J. Allik (Eds.), *The five-factor model of personality across cultures,* pp. 155–173. New York: Kluwer Academic/Plenum.

Pietersen, H.J. (1992). Die waarde van die takseersentrum: 'n repliek (The value of the taxation centre: A reply). *Tydskrif vir Bedryfsielkunde,* 18(1), pp. 20–22.

Potgieter, A. & Roodt, G. (2004). Measuring a customer intimacy culture in a value discipline context. *SA Journal of Resource Management,* 2(3), pp. 25–31.

Plomin, R., & Petrill, S.A. (1997). Genetics and intelligence: What's new? *Intelligence,* 24(1), pp. 53–77.

Plug, C. (1996). An evaluation of psychometric test construction and psychological services supported by the HSRC. Unpublished manuscript, University of South Africa.

Popp, S, Ellison, J., & Reeves, P. (1994). Neuropsychiatry of the anxiety disorders. In J. Ellison, C. Weinstein & T. Hodel-Malinofsky (Eds), *The psycho-therapist's guide to neuropsychiatry*, pp. 369–408. Washington, DC: American Psychiatric Press.

Powers, D.E. & O'Neill, K. (1993). Inexperienced and anxious computer users: Coping with a computer administered test of academic skills. *Educational Assessment*, 1(2), pp. 153–173.

Preamble to the Constitution of the World Health Organization as adopted by the International Health Conference, New York, 19–22 June, 1946; signed on 22 July 1946 by the representatives of 61 States (Official Records of the World Health Organization, no. 2, p. 100) and entered into force on 7 April 1948.

Prediger, D.J. (1974). The role of assessment in career guidance. In E.L. Herr (Ed.), *Vocational guidance and human development*. Boston: Houghton Mifflin.

Preston, P. (2005). Testing Children: A Practitioner's Guide to the Assessment of Mental Development in Infants and Young Children. Germany: Hogrefe & Huber Publishers

Prinsloo, C.H. (1992). Manual for the use of the Sixteen Personality Factor Questionnaire, Form E (16PF, Form E). Pretoria: Human Sciences Research Council.

Professional Affairs Board Steering Committee on Test Standards, British Psychological Society (2002). *Guidelines for the development and use of computer-based assessments.* Psychological Testing Centre, British Psychological Society: London. (Available at www.psychtesting.org.uk)

Psychometrics, Professional Board for Psychology (November 1999). *Training and examination guidelines for psychometrists and registered counsellors (psychometry).* Pretoria: Health Professions Council of South Africa.

Psychometrics, Professional Board for Psychology (1999a). *Policy on the classification of psychometric measuring devices, instruments, methods and techniques.* Pretoria: Health Professions Council of South Africa.

Psychometrics, Professional Board for Psychology (1999b). Guidelines for reviewers for the classification of psychometric tests, measuring devices, instruments, methods and techniques in South Africa. Pretoria: Health Professions Council of South Africa.

Psytech (2007). *Catalogue.* Johannesburg: Psytech SA.

Quinn, R.E. & Rohrbauch, J. (1981). A Competing Values Approach to Organisational Effectiveness. *Public Productivity Review*, 5, pp. 122–140.

Rahim, M.A. (Ed.) (1989). *Managing conflict: An integrative approach.* New York: Praeger.

Ramsay, L. J., Taylor, N., De Bruin, G. P., & Meiring, D. (2008). The Big Five personality factors at work: A South African validation study. In J. Deller (Ed.), *Research contributions to personality at work.* Munich and Mering, Germany: Rainer Hampp Verlag.

Raven, J.C. (1965). *Progressive Matrices.* London: H.K. Lewis.

Reckase, M.D. (1988). *Computerized adaptive testing: a good idea waiting for the right technology.* Paper presented at the meeting of the American Educational Research Association, New Orleans.

Ree, M.J. & Earles, J.A. (1996). Predicting occupational criteria: Not much more than g. In I. Dennis & P. Tapsfield (Eds), *Human abilities: Their nature and measurement*, pp. 151–166. Mahwah, NJ: Lawrence Erlbaum.

Reed, J. (2003). Diseases have an impact on the shop floor: THE BUSINESS CASE: SOUTH AFRICA. *Financial Times.* Retrieved September, 10, 2008, from ProQuest database.

Reeve, C.L. & Lam, H. (2007). The relation between practice effects, test-taker characteristics and degree of g-saturation. *International Journal of Testing,* 7(2), pp. 225–242

Reger, M., Welsh, R., Razani, J., Martin, D., & Boone, K. (2002). A meta-analysis of the neuropsychological sequelae in HIV infection. *Journal of the International Neuropsychological Society,* 8(3), pp. 410–424.

Reis, H.T., Sheldon, K.M., Gable, S,L., Roscoe, J. & Ryan, R.M. (2000). Daily well-being: the role of autonomy, competence, and relatedness. *Personality and Social Psychology Bulletin,* 26(4), pp. 419–435.

Retief, A.I. (1987). Thematic apperception testing across cultures: Tests of selection versus tests of inclusion. *South African Journal of Psychology,* 17, pp. 47–55.

Retief, A. (1992). The cross-cultural utility of the SAPQ: Bias or fruitful difference? *South African Journal of Psychology,* 22, pp. 202–207.

Reynolds, C.R. & Hickman, J.A. (2004). Draw-a-Person Intellectual Ability Test for Children, Adolescents, and Adults (DAP: IQ). Los Angeles: Western Psychological Services.

Richardson, J., Martin, N., Danley, K., Cohen, M., Carson, V., Sinclair, B., Racenstein, J., Reed, R., & Levine, A. (2002). Neuropsychological functioning in a cohort of HIV infected women: Importance of antiretroviral therapy. *Journal of the International Neuropsychological Society,* 8(6), pp. 781–793.

Richter, L.M. (1989). Household density, family size and the growth and development of black children: a cross-sectional study from infancy to middle childhood. *South African Journal of Psychology,* 19 (4), pp. 191–198.

Richter, L.M. & Griesel, R.D. (1988). Bayley Scales of Infant Development: Norms for Interpreting the Performance of Black South African Infants. Pretoria: Institute of Behavioural Sciences.

Richter, L.M. & Griesel, R.D. (1991). The McCarthy Scales of Children's Abilities – Adaptation and norms for use amongst Black South African children. Pretoria: University of South Africa.

Richter, L.M. & Grieve, K.W. (1991). Cognitive development in young children from impoverished African families. *Infant Mental Health Journal,* 12(2), pp. 88–102.

Ring, L., Hofer, S., McGee, H., Hickey, A. & O'Boyle, C.A. (2007). Individual quality of life: can it be accounted for by psychological or subjective well-being? *Social Indicator Researcher,* 86, pp. 443–461.

Robertson, G.J. & Eyde, L.D. (1993). Improving test use in the United States: The development of an interdisciplinary casebook. *European Journal of Psychological Assessment,* 9(2), pp. 137–146.

Robinson, M. (1989). Bylae tot die Hand-leiding vir die Junior Suid-Afrikaanse Individuale Skale (JSAIS): Tegniese besonderhede en normtabelle vir 6- tot 8-jarige leerlinge (Appendix to the Manual for the Junior South African Individual Scales (JSAIS): Technical details and tables of norms for the 6- to 8-year-old pupils). Pretoria: Human Sciences Research Council.

Robinson, M. (1994). Manual for the Individual Scale for General Scholastic Aptitude (ISGSA). Part III: Norm tables. Pretoria: Human Sciences Research Council.

Robinson, M. (1996). Manual for the Individual Scale for General Scholastic Aptitude (ISGSA). Part I: Background and standardization. Pretoria: Human Sciences Research Council.

Robinson, M. & Hanekom, J.M.D. (1991). *Die JSAIS en ASB as hulpmiddels by die evaluaring van skoolgereedheid* (The use of the JSAIS and ASB for the evaluation of school readiness). Pretoria: Human Sciences Research Council.

Roe, R.A. (2008). *The impact of testing on people and society.* Paper presented at the 6ᵗʰ Conference of the International Test Commission, Liverpool, UK,

14–16 July 2008. (Can be accessed online at www. intestcom.org).

Roger, E.A.S. (1989). The Number and Quantity Concepts subtest of the Junior South African Individual Scale as predictor of early mathematical achievement. Unpublished master's dissertation, University of Port Elizabeth.

Rogers, T.B. (1997). Teaching ethics and test standards in a psychological course: A Test Taker's Bill of Rights. *Teaching of Psychology,* 24(1), pp. 41–46.

Roodt, G. (1991). *Die graad van werkbetrokkenheid as voorspeller van persoonlike welsyn: 'n studie van bestuurders* (The degree of job involvement as predictor of personal well-being: A study of managers). Unpublished doctoral dissertation, University of the Free State.

Roodt, G. (2007). *The reliability of structured interviews: Competency rating interviews as a case in point.* Paper presented at the 27th Annual Conference of the AC study Group, 14–16 March, Protea Hotel, Stellenbosch.

Rosen, S., Simon, J.L., Thea, D.M. & Vincent, J.R. (2000). Care and treatment to extend the working lives of HIV-positive employees: Calculating the benefits to business. *South African Journal of Science,* 96(6), pp. 300–304.

Rosen, S., Vincent, J.R., MacLeod, W., Fox, M., Thea, D.M. & Simon, J.L. (2004). The cost of HIV/AIDS to businesses in southern Africa. *Official Journal of the International AIDS Society,* 18(2), pp. 317–324.

Rosenthal, R. & Rosnow, R.L. (1991). *Essentials of behavioral research: Method and data analysis* (2nd edition). New York: McGraw-Hill.

Ross, S., Krukowski, R., Putnam, S., & Adams, K. (2003). *Memory assessment scales in detecting probable malingering in mild head injury.* Paper presented at the 26th Annual International Neuropsychological Society Mid-year Conference, Berlin, Germany.

Roth, M., McCaul, E., & Barnes, K. (1993). Who becomes an 'at-risk' student? The predictive value of a kindergarten screening battery. *Exceptional Children,* 59(4), pp. 348–358.

Rounds, J.B. & Tracey, T.J. (1996). Cross-cultural structural equivalence of RIASEC models and measures. *Journal of Counseling Psychology,* 43, pp. 310–329.

Runyon, R.P. & Haber, A. (1980). *Fundamentals of behavioral statistics.* Reading, MA: Addison-Wesley Publishing Company.

Ryff, C.D. & Keys, C.L.M. (1995). The structure of psychological well-being revisited. *Journal of Personality and Social Psychology,* 69(4), pp. 719–727.

Ryff, C.D. & Singer, B. (2003). Flourishing under fire:

resilience as a prototype of challenged thriving. In C.L.M. Keyes & J. Haidt. *Flourishing Positive Psychology and the life well-lived.* Washington: American Psychological Association.

SA: 1 in 3 mentally ill. (2007, October). Retrieved September 27, 2008, from http://www.health24.com/mind/Mental_health_in_SA/1284-1031,42638.asp

Salovey, P. & Mayer, J.D. (1990). Emotional Intelligence. *Imagination, Cognition and Personality,* 9(3), pp. 185–211.

Samelson, F. (1979). Putting psychology on the map: Ideology and intelligence testing. In A. R. Buss (Ed.), *Psychology in social context.* New York: Irvington.

Sanderson, K. & Andrews, G. (2006). Common mental disorders in the workforce: recent findings from descriptive and social epidemiology. *Canadian Journal of Psychiatry,* 51(2), pp. 63–76.

Sarason, I.G. (Ed.). (1961). Test anxiety and the intellectual performance of college students. *Journal of Educational Psychology,* 52, pp. 201–206.

Sattler, J.M. (1988). *Assessment of children.* (3rd edition). San Diego, CA: Author.

Saunders, E. (2002). Assessing human competence: Practical guidelines for South African managers. Randburg, South Africa: Knowledge Resources.

Schaufeli, W. B., & Bakker, A. (2003). *Utrecht Work Engagement Scale. Preliminary manual.* Occupational Health Psychology Unit, Utrecht University.

Schaufeli, W. B., & Bakker, A. B. (2004). Job demands, job resources, and their relationship with burnout and engagement: A multi-sample study. *Journal of Organizational Behavior,* 25, pp. 293–315.

Schaap, P. (2003). The construct comparability of the PIB/SPEEX stress index for job applicants from diverse cultural groups in South Africa. *South African Journal of Psychology,* 33(2), pp. 95–102.

Schaeffer, G.A. (1995). The introduction and comparability of the computer adaptive GRE General Test. *ETS Research Report 95-20.*

Schaap, P. & Basson, J.S. (2003). The construct equivalence of the PIB/SPEEX motivation index for job applicants from diverse cultural backgrounds. *South African Journal of Industrial Psychology,* 29(2), pp. 49–59.

Scheier, M. F., Carver, C. S., & Bridges, M. W. (1994). Distinguishing optimism from neuroticism (and trait anxiety, self-mastery, and self-esteem): A reevaluation of the Life Orientation Test. *Journal of Personality and Social Psychology,* 67, pp. 1063–1078.

Schlebusch, S. & Roodt, G. (Eds.) (2008). *Assessment Centres: Unlocking potential for growth.* Johannesburg: KnowRes Publishing.

Schepers, J.M. (1992). *Toetskonstruksie: Teorie en Praktyk* [Test Construction: Theory and Practice]. Johannesburg: RAU Drukpers.

Schepers, J.M. (1999). The Bell-curve revisited: a South African perspective. *Journal of Industrial Psychology,* 25(2), pp. 52–63.

Schepers, J.M. (2005). *Technical manual: Locus of control inventory (Revised edition 2003).* Johannesburg: Jopie van Rooyen & Partners.

Schepers, J.M., & Hassett, C.F. (2006). The relationship between the fourth edition (2003) of the Locus of Control Inventory and the Sixteen Personality Factor Questionnaire (version 5). *South African Journal of Industrial Psychology,* 32, pp. 9–18.

Schmidt, F.E. & Hunter, J.E. (1998). The validity and utility of selection methods in personnel psychology: Practical and theoretical implications of 85 years of research findings. *Psychological Bulletin,* 124, pp. 262–274.

Schnetler, J. (Ed.) (1989). *Opnamemetodes en -praktyk* [Survey methods and practice]. Pretoria: Raad vir Geesteswetenskaplike Navorsing.

Schnetler, J. (1989). Beginsels van vraag- en vraelyskonstruksie [Principles of question and questionnaire construction]. In J. Schnetler (Ed.) *Opnamemetodes en -praktyk* [Survey methods and practice]. Pretoria: Raad vir Geesteswetenskaplike Navorsing.

Schuerger, J.M. (2002). The Sixteen Personality Factor Questionnaire (16PF). In C.E. Watkins, Jr. & V.L. Campbell (Eds), *Testing and assessment in counseling practice* (2nd ed.), pp. 73–110. Mahwah, NJ: Lawrence Erlbaum Publishers.

Schuhfried (1999). Vienna Test System: Computer-aided psychological diagnosis. Randburg: Dover Institute.

Sears, S. (1982). A definition of career guidance terms. A National Vocational Guidance Association perspective. *The Vocational Guidance Quarterly,* 31, pp. 137–143.

Sechrest, L. (1978). Incremental validity. In D.N. Jackson and S. Messick (Eds) *Problems in Human Assessment,* Huntington, NY: Robert E. Krieger Publishing Company.

Seligman, M.E.P (2003). Foreword: The past and future of positive psychology. In C.L.M. Keyes & J. Haidt. *Flourishing Positive Psychology and the life well-lived.* Washington: American Psychological Association.

Sharf, R.S. (2006). Applying career development theory to counselling. London: Thomson.

Sherwood, E.T. (1957). On the designing of TAT pictures, with special reference to a set for an African people assimilating western culture. *Journal of Social Psychology,* 45, pp. 161–190.

Shillington, S.J. (1988). An Afrikaans MMPI: Some variables which affect the responses of a normal Afrikaans population. Unpublished doctoral dissertation, University of Port Elizabeth.

Shisana, O. (2002). *The current situation of HIV/AIDS in South Africa*. Retrieved August 28, 2004, from http://www.hsrcpublishers.ac.za

SHL (2007). Product and training catalogue. Pretoria: SHL.

Shonkoff, J.P., & Meisels, S.J. (2000). *Handbook of early Childhood Interventio* (2nd ed.). Cambridge: Cambridge University Press.

Shuttleworth-Edwards, A., Kemp, R., Rust, A., Muirhead, J., Hartman, N., & Radloff, S. (2004) Vanishing ethnic differences in the wake of acculturation: A review and preliminary indications on WAIS-III test performance in South Africa. *Journal of Clinical and Experimental Neuropsychology*, 26(7), pp. 903–920.

Shuttleworth-Jordan, A.B. (1996). On not reinventing the wheel: a clinical perspective on culturally relevant test usage. *South African Journal of Psychology*, 26(2), pp. 96–102.

Simner, M.L. & Goffin, R.D. (2003). A position statement by the International Graphonomics Society on the use of graphology in personnel selection testing. *International Journal of Testing*, 3(4), pp. 353–364.

Simon, B. (1999, September). Employers slow to grasp the reality: BUSINESS AND AIDS. *Financial Times*. Retrieved September 10, 2008, from Proquest database.

Skuy, M., Zolezzi, S., Mentis, M., Fridjhon, P., & Cockcroft, K. (1996). Selection of advantaged and disadvantaged South African students for university admission. *South African Journal of Higher Education*, 10(1), pp. 110–117.

Smit, G.J. (1971). *Die verband tussen bepaalde nie-intellektuele faktore en akademiese sukses* (The relationship between specific non-intellectual factors and academic success). Unpublished doctoral dissertation, University of Pretoria.

Smit, G.J. (1991) *Psigometrika* (2nd edition). Pretoria: HAUM.

Smit, G.J. (1996). *Psychometrics: Aspects of measurement*. Pretoria: Kagiso.

Smith, S.A. (2002). *An evaluation of response scale formats of the Culture Assessment Instrument*. Unpublished D Phil thesis, Johannesburg: Rand Afrikaans University.

Smith, S.A. & Roodt, G. (2003). An evaluation of response scale formats of the Culture Assessment Instrument. *SA Journal of Human Resource Management*, 1(2), pp. 60–75.

Society for Industrial and Organisational Psychology in South Africa (2006a). *Code of Practice for Psychological and Other Similar Assessment in the Workplace*. Pretoria: Author (in association with the People Assessment Initiative (PAI)).

Society for Industrial and Organisational Psychology in South Africa (2006b). *Guidelines for the Validation of Assessment Procedures*. Pretoria: Author (in association with the People Assessment Initiative (PAI)).

Solano-Flores, G., Turnbull, E. & Nelson-Barber, S. (2002). Concurrent development of dual language assessments: An alternative to translating tests for linguistic minorities. *International Journal of testing*, 2(2), pp. 107–129.

Spangler, W.D. (1992). Validity of questionnaire and TAT measures of need for achievement. Two meta-analyses. *Psychological Bulletin*, 112, pp. 140–154.

Sparrow, S.S., Cicchetti, D.V., & Balla, D.A. (2005). *Vineland-II Adaptive Behavior Scales* (2nd edition). Minnesota: AGS Publishing.

Spector, P.E. (1988). Development of the work locus of control scale. *Journal of Occupational Psychology*, 61, pp. 335-340.

Spielberger, C.D., Gorsuch, R.L. & Lushene, R.E. (1970). *The State-Trait Anxiety Inventory: Test Manual for Form X*. Palo Alto: Consulting Psychologists Press.

Squires, J., Nickel, R.E., & Eisert, D. (1996). Early detection of developmental problems: Strategies for monitoring young children in the practice setting. *Developmental and behavioural paediatrics*, 17(6), pp. 420–427.

Stead, G.B. & Watson, M.B. (1998). The appropriateness of Super's career theory among black South Africans. *South African Journal of Psychology*, 28, pp. 40–43.

Steele, G. & Edwards, D. (2002). The development and validation of the Xhosa translations of the Beck Depression Inventory, the Beck Anxiety Inventory, and the Beck Hopelessness Scale. Paper presented at the 8th annual congress of the Psychological Society of South Africa (PsySSA), Cape Town, South Africa, 24–27 September 2002.

Sternberg, R.J. (1984). A contextualist view of the nature of intelligence. *International Journal of Psychology*, 19, pp. 307–334.

Sternberg, R.J. (2003). Issues in the theory and measurement of successful intelligence: A reply to Brody. *Intelligence*, 31, pp. 331–337.

Sternberg, R.J. & Grigorenko, E.L. (2002). *Dynamic testing: The nature and measurement of learning potential*.

Cambridge: Cambridge University Press.

Storm, L. & Roodt, G. (2002). Die verband tussen organisasiesosialisering and organisasieverbondenheid [The relationship between organisation socialisation and organisational commitment]. *SA Tydskrif vir Bedryfsielkunde,* 28(1), pp. 14–21.

Strong, E.K. (1927). *Vocational Interest Blank.* Stanford, CA: Stanford University Press.

Strümpfer, D.J.W. & Wissing, M.P. (1998). *Review of the South African data on the Sense of Coherence Scale as a measure of fortigenesis and salutogenesis.* Paper presented at the 4th Annual Congress of the Psychological Society of South Africa (PsySSA), 9–11 September 1998, Cape Town, South Africa.

Super, D.E. (1983). Assessment in career guidance: Toward truly developmental counseling. *Personnel and Guidance Journal,* 61, pp. 555–562.

Super, D.E. (1990). A life-span, life-space approach to career development. In D. Brown & L. Brooks (Eds), *Career choice and development,* pp. 197–261. San Francisco, CA: Jossey-Bass.

Super, D.E. (1994). A life span, life space perspective on convergence. In M.L. Savickas & R.L. Lent (Eds), Convergence in career development theories: Implications for science and practice, pp. 63-74. Palo Alto, CA: CPP Books.

Super, D.E. (1995). Values: Their nature, assessment and practical use. In D.E. Super, B. Sverko & C.E. Super (Eds) *Life roles, values, and careers,* pp. 54–61. San Francisco, CA: Jossey-Bass.

Super, B. Sverko & C.E. Super (Eds). (1995). *Life roles, values, and careers.* San Francisco, CA: Jossey-Bass.

Swanson, J.L. (1996). The theory is the practice: Trait-and-factor/person-environment fit counselling. In M.L. Savicks & W.B. Walsh (Eds), *Handbook of career counselling theory and practice,* pp. 93–108. Palo Alto, CA: Davies-Black.

Swart, C., Roodt, G. & Schepers, J.M. (1999). Itemformaat, differensiële itemskeefheid en die faktorstruktuur van 'n selfvoltooiingsvraelys [Item format, differential item skewness and the factor structure of a self-completion questionnaire]. *Tydskrif vir Bedryfsielkunde,* 25(1), pp. 33–43.

Swenson, L.E. (1997). *Psychology and law* (2nd edition). Pacific Grove, CA: Brooks/Cole.

Swenson, W.M., Rome, H., Pearson, J., and Brannick, T. (1965). A totally automated psychological test: Experience in a Medical Center. *Journal of the American Medical Association,* 191, pp. 925–927.

Tanzer, N.K. (2005) Developing tests for use in multiple cultures and languages: A plea for simultaneous

development. In Hambleton, R.K., Merenda, P.F., & Spielberger, C.D. (Eds.) (2005). *Adapting Educational and Psychological Tests for Cross-Cultural Assessment* (Chapter 10, pp. 235–244). Mahwah, NJ: Lawrence Erlbaum Associates, Inc.

Taylor, I.A. (2000). The construct comparability of the NEO PI-R Questionnaire for black and white employees. Unpublished doctoral thesis, University of the Free State.

Taylor, T.R. (1987). *Test bias: The roles and responsibilities of test users and test publishers.* NIPR Special Report Pers – 424. Pretoria: Human Sciences Research Council.

Taylor, T.R. (1994). A review of three approaches to cognitive assesssment, and a proposed integrated approach based on a unifying theoretical framework. *South African Journal of Psychology,* 24(4), pp. 184–193.

Taylor, T.R. & Boeyens, J.C.A. (1991). The comparability of the scores of blacks and whites on the South African Personality Questionnaire: an exploratory study. *South African Journal of Psychology,* 21(2), pp. 1–10.

Taylor, C., Jamieson, J., Eignor, D. & Kirsch, I. (1998). *The relationship between computer familiarity and performance on computer-based TOEFL test tasks.* TOEFL Research, 61. Princeton, NJ: Educational Testing Service.

Taylor, J.M., & Radford, E. J. (1986). Psychometric testing as an unfair labour practice. *South African Journal of Psychology,* 16, pp. 79–96.

Taylor, N. (2004). *The construction of a South African five-factor personality questionnaire.* Unpublished master's dissertation, Rand Afrikaans University, South Africa.

Taylor, N. & de Bruin, G.P. (2003). *Development of the South African Five Factor Personality Inventory: Preliminary findings.* Paper presented at the Ninth Congress of the Psychological Society of South Africa (PsySSA), Johannesburg.

Taylor, N., & De Bruin, G.P. (2006). *Basic Traits Inventory.* Johannesburg: Jopie van Rooyen.

Tchanturia, K., Anderluh, M., Morris, R., Rabe-Hesketh, S., Collier, D., Sanchez, P., & Treasure, J. (2004). Cognitive flexibility in anorexia nervosa and bulimia nervosa. *Journal of the International Neuropsychological Society,* 10(4), pp. 513–520.

Terre'Blanche, M. & Durrheim, K. (1999). *Research in practice.* Cape Town: UCT Press.

Theron, D. & Roodt, G. (1999). Variability in multi-rater competency assessment. *Journal of Industrial Psychology,* 25(2), pp. 21–27.

Theron, D. & Roodt, G. (2000). Mental models as

moderating variable in competency assessments. *Journal of Industrial Psychology*, 26 (2).

Thissen, D. & Steinberg, L. (1988). Data analysis using item response theory. *Psychological Bulletin*, 104, pp. 385–395

Thornton, G. III & Rupp, D.E. (2006). Assessment Centers in Human Resource Management: Strategies for prediction, diagnosis, and development. Mahwah, New Jersey: Lawrence Erlbaum.

Tollman, S.G. & Msengana, N.B. (1990) Neuropsychological assessment: Problems in evaluating the higher mental functioning of Zulu-speaking people using traditional western techniques. *South African Journal of Psychology*, 20, pp. 20–24.

Torgerson, W.S. (1958). *Theory and methods of scaling*. New York: John Wiley.

Vaas, V. (2002). Standardisation of Raven's Standard Progressive Matrices for secondary school African pupils in the Grahamstown region. Unpublished master's thesis, Rhodes University, Grahamstown.

Van den Berg, A.R. (1996). Intelligence tests. In K. Owen & J.J. Taljaard (Eds). *Handbook for the use of psychological and scholastic tests of the HSRC*, pp. 157–190. Pretoria: Human Sciences Research Council.

Van der Post, W.Z., de Coning, T.J. & v.d. M. Smit, E. (1997). An instrument to measure organisational culture. *South African Journal for Business Management*, 4, pp. 147–165.

Van de Vijver, F.J.R. (2002). Cross-Cultural Assessment: Value for Money? *Applied Psychology: An International Review*, 51(4), pp. 545–566.

Van de Vijver, F.J.R. & Leung, K. (1997) *Methods and data analysis for cross-cultural research*. Sage: New York

Van Eeden, R. (1991). Manual for the Senior South African Individual Scale – Revised (SSAIS–R). Part I: Background and standardization. Pretoria: Human Sciences Research Council.

Van Eeden, R. (1993). The validity of the Senior South African Individual Scale – Revised (SSAIS–R) for children whose mother tongue is an African language: Private schools. Pretoria: Human Sciences Research Council.

Van Eeden, R. & Prinsloo, C.H. (1997). Using the South African version of the 16PF in a multicultural context. *South African Journal of Psychology*, 27, pp. 151–159.

Van Eeden, R. & Mantsh, T.R. (2007). Theoretical and methodological considerations in the translation of the 16PF5 into an African language. *South African Journal of Psychology*, 37(1), pp. 62-81.

Van Eeden, R. & Van Tonder, M. (1995). The validity of the Senior South African Individual Scale – Revised (SSAIS–R) for children whose mother tongue is an African language: Model C schools. Pretoria: Human Sciences Research Council.

Van Eeden, R. & Visser, D. (1992). The validity of the Senior South African Individual Scale – Revised (SSAIS–R) for different population groups. *South African Journal of Psychology*, 22, pp. 163–171.

Van Heerden, R. (2007). Exploring Normal South African and British Children: A Comparative Study utilizing the Griffiths Mental Development Scales – Extended Revised. Unpublished masters treatise. Nelson Mandela Metropolitan University.

Van Ommen, C. (2005). Putting the PC in IQ: Images in the Wechsler-Adult Intelligence Scale – third edition (WAIS III). *South African Journal of Psychology*, 35(3), pp. 532-554.

Van Rooyen, K. (2005). The Performance of South African and British Children on the Griffiths Mental Development Scales – Extended Revised: A Comparative Study. Unpublished master's treatise. Nelson Mandela Metropolitan University.

Van Rooyen, S.W. (2000). The psychosocial adjustment and stress levels of shift workers in the South African Police Service, Flying Squad. Unpublished master's treatise, University of Port Elizabeth.

Van Tonder, C. & Roodt, G. (2008). *Organisation Development: Theory and Practice.* Pretoria: Van Schaik.

Van Tonder, M. (1992). *Die Gerekenariseerde Passingstoets van die Algemene Skolastiese Aanlegtoets (ASAT) Senior* (The Computerized Adaptive Test of the General Scholastic Aptitude Test (GSAT) Senior). Pretoria: Human Sciences Research Council.

Van Zyl, E. & Visser, D. (1988). Differential item functioning in the Figure Classification test. *South African Journal of Industrial Psychology*, 24(2), pp. 25–33.

Van Zyl, E.S. & Van der Walt, H.S. (1991). *Manual for the Experience of Work and Life Circumstances Questionaire*. Pretoria: Human Sciences Research Council.

Veenhoven, R. (1991). Is happiness relative? *Social Indicators Research*, 24(1), 1–34.

Vernon, P.A. (1990). An overview of chronometric measures of intelligence. *School Psychology Review*, 19 (4), pp. 399–410.

Vernon, P.A. & Jensen, A.R. (1984). Individual and group differences in intelligence and speed of information processing. *Personality and Individual Differences*, 5(4), pp. 411–423.

Veroff, J. (1982). Assertive motivation: Achievement versus power. In A.J. Stewart (Ed.), *Motivation and society*, pp. 99–132. San Francisco, CA: Jossey-Bass.

Veroff, J. & Feld, S.C. (1970). *Marriage and work in America*. New York, NY: Van Nostrand Reinhold.

Viljoen, G., Levett, A., & Tredoux, C. (1994). Using the Bender Gestalt in South Africa: some normative data for Zulu-speaking children. *South African Journal of Psychology*, **22**, pp. 163–171.

Vincent, K.R. (1991). Black/White IQ differences: Does age make the difference? *Journal of Clinical Psychology*, 47(2), pp. 266–270.

Vygotsky, L.S. (1978). Mind in society: The development of higher-order psychological processes. Cambridge, MA: Harvard University Press.

Wang, P.S., Beck, A.L., Berglund, P., McKenas, D.K., Pronk, P.N., Simon, G.E. & Kessler, R.S. (2004). Effects of major depression on moment-in-time work performance. *The American Journal of Psychiatry*, 161(10), pp. 1885–1892.

Watkins, C.E., Jr., Campbell, V.L., Nieberding, R., & Hallmark, R. (1995). Contemporary practice of psychological assessment by clinical psychologists. *Professional Psychology: Research and Practice*, **26**, pp. 54–60.

Watson, A., Davies, C., & Foxcroft, C.D. (2006). *The assessment of English Second Language test-takers: Issues and implications*. Paper presented at a symposium on Monolingual and Multilingual Testing at the 5th Conference of the International Test Commission on Psychological and Educational Test Adaptation across Languages and Cultures, Brussels, Belgium, 6–8 July 2006.

Wechsler, D. (1958). *The measurement and appraisal of adult intelligence* (4th edition). Baltimore: Williams and Wilkins.

Weiss, L. (2003). *WISC-IV: Clinical reality and the future of the four-factor structure*. Paper presented at the 8th European Congress of Psychology, Vienna, Austria, 6–11 July 2003.

Weiss, D.J., Dawis, R.V., Engand, G.W. & Lofquist, L.H. (1967). *Manual for the Minnesota Satisfaction Questionnaire*. Minneapolis: University of Minnesota.

Westaway, M. S., & Maluka, C. S. (2005). Are life satisfaction and self-esteem distinct constructs? Black South African perspectives. *Psychological Reports*, **97**, pp. 567–575.

WHO Global Status Report on Alcohol (2004). Retrieved September 27. 2008, from http://www.who.int/substance_abuse/publications/en/south_africa.pdf

WHO Online Question and Answer: What is Mental Health? (2008). Retrieved September 27, 2008, from http://www.who.int/features/qa/62/en/index.html

Wicken, A.W. (2000). Wellness in industry. *Work,* 15, pp. 95–99.

Wilcocks, R.W. (1931). *The South African Group Test of Intelligence*. Stellenbosch: University of Stellenbosch.

Williamson, D.M., Bauer, M., Steinberg, L.S., Mislevy, R.J., Behrens, J.T. and DeMark, S.F. (2004). Design rationale for complex performance assessment. *International Journal of Testing*, 4(4), pp. 303–332.

Willig, A.C. (1988). A case of blaming the victim: The Dunn monograph on bilingual Hispanic children on the U.S. mainland. *Hispanic Journal of Behavioral Sciences*, **10**, pp. 219–236.

Wilson, M (2004). *Developing measures: An item response modeling approach*. Mahwah, NJ: Lawrence Erlbaum Associates.

Winter, D.G. (1973). *The power motive*. New York, NY: The Free Press.

Winter, D.G., & Stewart, A.J. (1977). Power motive reliability as a function of retest instructions. *Journal of Consulting and Clinical Psychology*, 45, pp. 436–440.

Winter, D.G., Stewart, A.J., John, O.P., Klohnen, E.C., & Duncan, L.E. (1998). Traits and motives: Toward an integration of two traditions in personality research. *Psychological Review*, 105, pp. 230–250.

Wise, S.L., Barnes, L.B., Harvey, A.L., & Plake, B.S. (1989). Effects of computer anxiety and computer experience on computer-based achievement test performance of college students. *Applied Measurement in Education*, 2, pp. 235–242.

Worley, J. A., Vassar, M. Wheeler, D.L. & Barnes, L.B. (2008). Factor structure of scores from the Maslach Burnout Inventory: A review and meta-analysis of 45 exploratory and confirmatory factor-analytic studies. *Educational & Psychological Measurement*, **68**, pp. 797–823.

Zenisky, A.L. & Sireci, S.G. (2002). Technological innovations in large-scale assessment. *Applied Measurement in Education,* 15, pp. 337–362.

Zhu, J. & Tulsky, D.S. (2000). Co-norming the WAIS-III and WMS-III: Is there a test-order effect on IQ and memory scores? *Clinical Neuropsychology,* 14(4), pp. 461–467.

Zikmund, W.G. (2003). *Business Research Methods*. Mason, OH: Thomson Publishing.

Zunker, V.G. (2006). Career counselling. A holistic approach. Belmont, CA: Thomson Brooks/Cole.

INDEX